More Praise for *Practical Speculation*

"*Practical Speculation* distills an unusual breadth of hard-won (and costly) experience and insight into an immensely readable and instructive b⌐⌐¹ and Bears are drawn and quartered alike by the ⌐⌐⌐¹ quantitative scalpel."

> Stephen M. Stigler
> Professor of Statistics
> University of Chicago

"In my judgment, Victor Niederhoffer is the single most insightful speculator in the world. This new book displays Victor's unique gift for recognizing the subtle confluence of seemingly disparate events. Although this book is partially a guide on investment strategy, it is principally a remarkable explanation of market function."

> Herbert London
> John M. Olin Professor of Humanities, New York University
> President, Hudson Institute

"Whatever Victor Niederhoffer writes is worth reading—not once but at least twice. His analysis of markets is as brilliant as it is unorthodox. Readers will discover a host of nuggets in *Practical Speculation* that will stretch their minds and tease their imaginations."

> Lawrence S. Ritter
> John M. Schiff Professor of Finance Emeritus
> New York University

"Victor Niederhoffer outdoes himself beginning with the first paragraph of the introduction. Victor and Laurel uniquely see the interrelationships and dependencies among the complex factors that are daily life and are able to interpret observations in terms of how people will react to the sequences of events. *Practical Speculation* is an extraordinary insight into the thinking of probably the most original thinker of our time."

> Kenneth W. Rendell
> Founder, Kenneth W. Rendell, Inc.

"Vic and Laurel are breathtakingly insightful. They paint on a global investment canvas stretching across space and time. This is their dazzling journey through the art, science, sport, and literature of investing. Don't risk a penny on stocks until you have read *Practical Speculation*."

> Professor Elroy Dimson, London Business School
> Co-author, *Triumph of the Optimists*

Practical
Speculation

VICTOR NIEDERHOFFER
LAUREL KENNER

 John Wiley & Sons, Inc.

Published by John Wiley & Sons, Inc., Hoboken, New Jersey.
Published simultaneously in Canada.

For general information on our other products and services, or technical support, please contact our Customer Care Department within the United States at 800-762-2974, outside the United States at 317-572-3993 or fax 317-572-4002.

Wiley also publishes its books in a variety of electronic formats. Some content that appears in print may not be available in electronic books. For more information about Wiley products, visit our web site at www.wiley.com.

Library of Congress Cataloging-in-Publication Data:

Niederhoffer, Victor, 1943–
    Practical speculation / Victor Niederhoffer, Laurel Kenner.
        p.   cm.
    Includes index.
    ISBN 0-471-44306-9 (alk. paper)
    ISBN 0-471-67774-4 (paper)
    1. Speculation.   2. Stocks.   3. Investment analysis.   I. Kenner, Laurel.   II. Title.
    HG6041.N52   2003
    332.63′2—dc21

                                                            2002190747

Printed in the United States of America.

10 9 8 7 6 5 4 3 2 1

A fragment of a wartime speech moved through my mind: 'We shall fight them in the fields, and in the streets, we shall fight in the hills; we shall never surrender.' True then for one people, it was true always for the whole human race.

—*Invasion of the Body Snatchers*

From *My New York* by Kathy Jakobsen. Copyright © 1993, 2003 by Kathy Jakobsen. By permission of Little, Brown and Company, (Inc.).

ACKNOWLEDGMENTS

This book was written from the firing line. Most of the ideas were subjected not only to the pitiless judgment of the market itself but also to the critiques, often withering, by readers of our columns for CNBC Money, worldlyinvestor.com, and thestreet.com.

The list of those who helped us accomplish our writing task amid the daily fray is long. Almost everything in this book benefited from the insights of our editor at CNBC Money, Jon Markman. Pamela van Giessen, our editor at John Wiley & Sons, inspired this book and shepherded it through many iterations.

Our thinking was sharpened and augmented by the daily discussions on our Speculators' List, a group of extraordinary individuals who read and responded to our columns and then accepted our invitation to join a philosophical e-mail forum in the spirit of Ben Franklin's junto. We are deeply grateful to James Goldcamp, who put the list together for us. From an original membership of fewer than 10 people, the Speculators' List now encompasses more than 150 experts on diverse subjects, united by a common interest in markets, statistical analysis, and mutually beneficial discussion. Dr. Brett Steenbarger, whose contributions appear throughout this book, was among the early readers who became dear friends. Our thinking and our lives have been enriched by Gitanshu Buch, Henry Carstens, Duncan Coker, Nigel Davis, "Mr. E," Bill Egan, Glenn Escovedo, Ed Gross, Bill Haynes, David Hillman, James Lackey, John Lamberg, Paul Lewis, Alix Martin, Mark McNabb, Shui Mitsuda, Bipin Pathak, Tom Ryan, Ken Sadofsky, Dick Sears, Russell Sears, Saurabh Singal, Don Staricka, Gary Tate, Jack Tierney, and Steve Wisdom, to name only a few. There are many other eagles too numerous to mention.

Market Warriors (Artist: Susan Slyman, 2000).

The traders in Vic's office contributed research and analysis in addition to their daily duties. Shi Zhang and David Ciocca produced many of the studies and scatter diagrams. Patrick Boyle researched the chapters on physics and Benjamin Graham. Rob Wincapaw located books, letters, and articles with unfailing patience. Gitanshu Buch kept track of a multitude of projects while simultaneously running the trading operation.

Bill Egan, John Lamberg, Gaylen Larson, and Adam Robinson reviewed drafts and made many helpful suggestions.

Rip MacKenzie contributed much of the material for the hubris chapter.

James Cramer at TheStreet.com and Jeremy Pink at worldlyinvestor.com encouraged our early writing endeavors.

We are grateful to Steve Stigler and Jim Lorie of the University of Chicago, and to Lee Henkel, Vic's long-time mentors, and friends. Also to Dan Grossman, Vic's partner of 30 years, for valued insights and steadfast friendship.

Laurel thanks her music teachers, Aube Tzerko, Bruce Sutherland, and Robert Winter, for teaching an approach to music she has found valuable in all areas of life.

We thank our families for sharing the pain and the pleasure.

VICTOR NIEDERHOFFER
LAUREL KENNER

CONTENTS

INTRODUCTION

The Hope Snatchers

Look! You fools! You're in danger! Can't you see? They're after you! They're after all of us! Our wives . . . our children . . . they're here already! You're next!

—Dr. Miles Bennell, *Invasion of the Body Snatchers* (1956 film version)

The nightmare is always the same. I am lying in bed, staring at headlines flashing across a huge monitor installed on my ceiling:

Stocks Fall on Earnings Pessimism

Stocks May Fall for Fifth Consecutive Week on Fears Economy Is Sputtering

Money Market Yields Fall to 1 Percent as Stock Market Woes Deepen

Stocks Fail to Top Y2K High for 450th Consecutive Day

Study Shows More Than 60 percent of All Issues Below 52-Week High

Markets Plummet as January Barometer Signals Decline for Rest of Year

Oracle of Omaha Says Investor Expectations Are "Too High"

Market Plunges on Fears Before Fed Meeting

Break of Revered Gann Pivot Triggers Massive Selling

Dividend Yields Now 25 Percent Below 1996 "Irrational Exuberance" Speech

In my dream, I am long IBM, or priceline.com, or, worst of all, Krung Thai Bank, the state-owned bank in Thailand that fell from $200 to pennies while I held it in 1997. The rest of the dream is always the same. My stock plunges. Massive margin calls are being issued. Related stocks jump off cliffs in sympathy. Delta hedgers are selling more stocks short to rebalance their positions. The naked options I am short are going through the roof. Millions of investors are blindly following the headlines. Listless as zombies, they are liquidating their stocks at any price and piling into money-market funds with an after-tax yield of –1 percent.

"Stop, you fools!" I scream. "There's no danger! Can't you see? The head-lines are inducing you to lean the wrong way! Unless you get your balance, you'll lose everything—your wealth, your home!"

The perfect allegory for this state of affairs is found in *Invasion of the Body Snatchers*, a 1954 sci-fi classic book by Jack Finney.[1] Aliens secretly invade the fictional small town of Santa Mira, California, one by one taking over the bod-ies of unsuspecting residents as they sleep. In the morning, the victims look just the same as they did before, but they no longer have the human emotions of joy, fear, ambition, sorrow, excitement, and hope.

The hero, Dr. Miles Bennell, arriving home after an absence in the midst of the alien takeover, at first dismisses the victims' strange demeanor. How-ever, he soon realizes that something terrible is happening. Using forensic medicine and nitty-gritty detective work, he and his plucky love interest, Becky Driscoll, figure out that the aliens are parasitic seedpods that replicate themselves in greenhouses so they can take over yet more human victims. Their only aim is to survive by parasitism; they cannot make love or have chil-dren, and their gray existence ends after five years.

After a harrowing escape from the town, Miles and Becky set fire to the vanguard of an army of advancing pod people. The rest of the pods conclude that Earth is an inhospitable place, and drift back into space to find new victims.

Often interpreted as a warning against blind obedience to authority, *Inva-sion's* depiction of the victims serves as an extraordinarily apt description of average investors' vacant, resigned demeanor after the fallacies and propa-ganda embedded in headlines like the ones in my recurring nightmare have once more led them in the wrong direction.

The overriding problem is that these headlines induce hysteria and then paralysis. They can blind investors to the 1,500,000 percent-a-century re-turn that an investment in the stocks of the United States and most European nations yielded in the twentieth century. On average, the backdrop then seemed every bit as bleak as it does now. As science and enterprise help us live increasingly healthier, more prosperous lives, a century is a highly relevant time frame to contemplate for the children of this book's readers.

Let's take another look at the first three headlines:

Stocks Fall on Earnings Pessimism

Stocks May Fall for Fifth Consecutive Week on Fears Economy Is Sputtering

Money Market Yields Fall to 1 Percent as Stock Market Woes Deepen

These headlines share a common defect: They label conditions that are *bullish* as *bearish*. We explain in detail later in this book:

Stocks Fail to Top Y2K High for 450th Consecutive Day

Study Shows More Than 60 percent of All Issues Below 52-Week High

Markets Plummet as January Barometer Signals Decline for Rest of Year

The phenomena reported in these three headlines are true of any time series with a large random component—such as stock returns. These observations are meaningless to the investor.

Oracle of Omaha Says Investor Expectations Are "Too High"

Market Plunges on Fears Before Fed Meeting

Break of Revered Gann Pivot Triggers Massive Selling

Dividend Yields Now 25 Percent Below 1996 "Irrational Exuberance" Speech

These headlines tell stories about misremembered facts that sustain fallacious beliefs harmful to those who trust such pronouncements.

Headlines that induce fearfulness are often based on myths, not reason. Propaganda techniques, not the verifiable propositions of science, convey these ideas. Just as the high priests of prescientific societies used myths to maintain the social order and extract offerings from the masses, today's market professionals use bold, simple myths to extract contributions from credulous investors. This phenomenon explains why the public contributes so much to the commissions, spreads, research expenditures, communications costs, skyscraper rents, sales outlays, marketing expenses, and phantasmagoric bonuses for traders and executives that make up the massive infrastructure of Wall Street.

The headlines listed here are by no means isolated examples that we have culled to make our case. They are typical of the backdrop of myth, misinformation, and propaganda bombarding investors daily

through every media channel. Uncritical acceptance of the fallacies embodied in such headlines—whether wildly bullish or terrifyingly bearish—leads investors straight to the slaughter.

Although propaganda is ubiquitous in the market and in other aspects of our lives, a simple antidote can protect us from manipulation: the scientific method. If theories about the market are framed in a testable fashion, they can be verified by counting. Not only will embracing the scientific method preclude debates about the meaning of words such as "irrational" and "exuberant," but also it will relate market theories to the real world. A side benefit will be that those theories that are verified can actually lead to practical profits (which is, after all, why you are reading this book).

Don't get us wrong. It is not that skepticism toward bullish propaganda is inappropriate. We take a backseat to no one in loathing the bullish flummery invariably fed to investors after the market has displayed a sharp rise. Many companies store earnings in a silo and release them at opportune times to lure investors into buying stocks, enabling executives to cash in their options. We are strident critics of the conflicts of interest that can cause brokerage house analysts never to recommend selling shares in a company that is a client of the investment banking side of the firm. We abhor the hubris that leads executives like Enron's Jeffrey Skilling to curse analysts who question the bona fides of the corporate balance sheet, and the egomania that encourages other executives to authorize golf courses as a necessary management perquisite.

That said, if you are going to err on one side or the other, it pays to err on the side of optimism. After all, until 2000–2002 the last time the U.S. stock market went down three years in a row was 1939–1941. The situation is much the same in other countries. It is hard to overcome a 1,500,000 percent-a-century upward drift in common stocks worldwide, even with clever market timing.

Erroneous, untested suppositions dominate the market today. Despite the advances that have come about in the four decades since efficient markets theory was developed, finance is still largely in the Dark Ages. The public is barraged with commentary from journalists who offer nothing but superstitions, descriptions, backward-looking observations, and interviews with fund managers struggling to keep up with the market averages.

Most of these reports purport to find a relation between the day's market performance and reports of a certain company's earnings feats or woes, attributing an "up" day to earnings optimism in a few stocks, or a "down" day to earnings pessimism in some other stocks. But the market landscape is so enormous and varied that on any given day some companies inevitably will report conditions are better (or worse) than an arbitrary standard. If investors place any credence in such reports, they become victims of market vagaries. They search for anecdotal evidence that is always available to justify something in retrospect, but that offers nothing whatsoever of predictive value. Worse, unscientific investors lose the ability to differentiate the helpful from the unhelpful, or to build a foundation for making informed, rational decisions in the future. Since none of the commentators ever presumes, for example, to determine the precise magnitude of the relation—if any—between earnings and market performance, investors are led to accept nebulous untestable assertions about the market without applying the normal skepticism that they have learned is essential in other areas of their lives.

Faced with market moves that seem to bear no relation to what they believe to be true, investors quickly become disenchanted and disgusted when the market declines, and hyperactive and wildly exuberant when the market rises. In either case, they are being primed to overtrade and to make more than their fair share of contributions to the market infrastructure. The end result is an army of disgruntled investors, ironically ever more ready to be batted around by the next pronouncement from a market guru, each ready to leave the market at the drop of a hat for money-market funds with negative real returns at precisely the juncture when conditions for equities are best. Ultimately, the market is the richer, and customers and investors are left without any yachts—or pensions.

Worse yet, the market's victims become like the pod people of Santa Mira, cynical about all new ideas, bereft of optimism and hope. They are ready to fall into step with those who do not believe in technology, do not believe in growth, and, after many disclosures of corporate fraud, do not believe in the enterprise system itself. Dr. Bennell could very well have been talking about investors when he said:

> I've seen how people have allowed their humanity to drain away. Only it happens slowly instead of all at once. They didn't seem to mind . . . All of us—a little bit—we harden our hearts, grow callous.

But life, like the markets, offers the greatest rewards to those willing to assume risk. Assuming risk brings uncertainty, anxiety, and occasional loss, but it also brings out the best in us. In becoming a speculator in life, each person embarks on a heroic quest, becoming more than he or she already is. Heroism is a potent antidote to the cynicism and alienation so many of us accept.

If you're familiar with my story and you've read this far, you may be asking: "Where does Victor Niederhoffer come off writing another book about speculation and investing? Didn't his hedge fund go defunct in 1997?"

Until 1997, my record was the best in the investment world. Barclay's, the hedge fund industry scorekeeper, named me the top hedge fund manager in 1996. I collected "best-performing hedge fund manager" awards and toured the world giving lectures in elegant settings about markets and music, accompanied by concert pianist Robert Schrade. I employed a large staff of traders and analysts from top schools, many of whom had been with me for a decade or more. I was a partner with George Soros in numerous investment ventures, and we were inseparable throughout the business and recreational day. My book, *The Education of a Speculator,* had just been published and was a bestseller.[2] My funds under management and personal wealth were growing exponentially, yet at a measured pace.

Then the roof caved in. I lost everything. In popular Wall Street parlance, I "blew up."

The story has been extensively chronicled. On December 13, 1998, an article in the *New York Times,* "Trappings of Faded Richness: Sold!" by Geraldine Fabrikant, captured my decline with the inimitable schadenfreude of the *Times:*

> A five-foot horn of plenty made of silver and podollan ox horn, once the property of King Charles XV of Sweden, is Victor Niederhoffer's favorite in his collection of silver trophy pieces. But Mr. Niederhoffer can no longer afford his horn of plenty. The money manager lost all his capital in October 1997, when the Global Systems funds he managed for himself, his family, and investors were hurt first by his leveraged and unhedged speculations in the Thai stock market, and then by his bet that the United States market would not decline dramatically. The two catastrophes wiped out the funds. And so Mr. Niederhoffer is struggling to pay his debts, support the four of his six children who are still at home, maintain the family's lifestyle, and tiptoe back into the only business he knows: trading.
>
> A comeback—both financially and psychologically—from the devastation of his funds' collapse has been far harder than even Mr. Niederhoffer had imagined. "It is hard to be resilient when you're 55," he said during an interview in the library of his home. "When you have bad fortune, your suppliers and customers are afraid. I'm on a very short leash."
>
> After 20 years of success, many investors had become friends. But many of his friendships unraveled. "My phone stopped ringing a lot," he said. He feels it's important that he suffered with his investors. "I'm saddened and chastened," he said. "My wisdom is quite suspect." He compares his downfall with the bailout of Long-Term Capital Management, the much bigger hedge fund recently rescued by Wall Street. "I could have used Long-Term's breathing time," Mr. Niederhoffer said. Instead, he is selling his silver.[3]

In an instant, I plunged from the top of my profession to the depths. My employees quit *en masse*. My customers, many of whom had been my best friends for years, deserted me.

To boost my returns and stay number one, I had invested in the stock market in Thailand, a country I knew too little about. In the United States, it is a good bet that a 90 percent decline in bank stocks precedes a rebound. In Southeast Asia, that is apparently not the case. My biggest holding—the largest bank in Thailand—lost a whopping 99 percent. My losses abroad depleted my reserves. The rest of the tale is still too sad and raw to retell. Suffice it to say that the decline in Asian stocks spilled over into an unprecedented one-day, 550-point decline in the Dow Jones Industrial Average. This was enough to trigger a stock exchange rule that closed the market before 2 P.M. that day. Confronted with a demand to come up with many millions to meet margins the next day, I was forced to close my fund.

In addition to losing my investment business, I had to sell my holdings in my other financial activities. I took out a large mortgage on my house, with rates starting at 15 percent a year. The final indignity was selling my extensive collection of antique silver. A representative quote from my introductory note in an auction house brochure captures the flavor:

> From a reading of business history, I had learned that many Wall Street speculators at various times in their tumultuous sagas had placed their silver up for sale in time of malaise. . . . One of my most enjoyable purchases in this regard was a trophy presented to Jay Gould for winning a professional tennis championship. Little did I figure on those occasions of Schadenfreude that I would one day be joining such immortals.

I was devastated in every way. My sister, Diane, is a psychiatrist. She noted that patients with severe (a euphemism for suicidal) depression normally have 10 symptoms of clinical depression, ranging from weight loss to loss of sexual abilities. I had all 10 of them. At a meeting with outside lawyers, I mentioned this as a joke and perhaps an appeal for pity. My own lawyer took me aside afterward and admonished me never to do that again: "The only reaction the other side will have is anger that you didn't pull the trigger."

Friends and family did their best to see me through. I received 55 copies of *Tuesdays with Morrie*.[4] The senders all emphasized to me that Morrie was able to deal with his impending death with dignity, and they advised me to take a similar stance.

I also received 10 copies of the Rudyard Kipling poem "If," which remains an inspiration. Some of the senders underlined the following words:

If you can make one heap of all your winnings
And risk it all on one turn of pitch-and-toss,
And lose, and start again at your beginnings
And never breathe a word about your loss;

. . .

If you can fill the unforgiving minute
With sixty seconds' worth of distance run,
Yours is the Earth and everything that's in it,
And—which is more—you'll be a Man, my son!

Suffused with *Tuesdays with Morrie,* thoughts of my own deathlike experience, and other melancholy contemplations and nightmares, I paid frequent visits to the grave of my father, Arthur. He was a scholar and a cop of infinite strength and support whose good spirit has uplifted his family at times of trouble and all other times since his untimely death in 1981 at the age of 62. I later asked my uncle, Howie Eisenberg, who served as a model for my loss by snatching defeat from victory in the finals of 43 separate national handball championships (he also won 18 of them) what he thought Artie might have said about my fall. Together, we came up with the following:

> So what of it? It's not the end of the world. You and your family are in good health; you're still able to live the life that you wish. That's what's important. All of your strategy, practice, and experience led to taking that shot at that point. You went for the overhead to get further ahead in the match and missed. It was still the right shot for you then. It was the same strategy that got you the substantial lead that you had.
>
> Suppose, which I don't believe for a moment, you don't come back. It's not so terrible. You can still teach, and I'll help you with the bills. Here. I've taken a mortgage from the co-op.
>
> The consequences of missing the shot were a revelation for you. You now realize that while you had every reason to believe your advantage would be increased, you exposed yourself and those who were playing with you to possibly losing the whole match. You now have a different perspective. You can see that although the potential to maximize your advantage may seem to be the correct course of action, it should be tempered by a strategy that limits, if not precludes, the possibility of not only losing the match but all of your racquets. You don't want to be in the position of not having the wherewithal to continue playing the way you want, or causing those who bet on you to lose their pants. The crucial thing is that you are still in the game, once again racking up points.
>
> Whatever you do, be more careful in the future. Be good to your family and friends. You have a beautiful life and everything in the world to look forward to. Take it easy.

I did not have the luxury of wallowing in my misery for too long. I had six kids, six private-school tuitions, a former and current wife, extensive recurring household expenses from the previous good days, and the usual legal expenses for events of this nature. We pick a basket of berries, the basket falls, and we fill the basket again. I had to fill the basket once more. But I did not have any capital of consequence to meet these expenses. More important, none of the usual suspects for my kind of trading had any interest in establishing a normal working relationship with me.

I was well experienced in losing from my career in sports. But this comeback was much more difficult. Not only had I lost my standing in the tournaments, I had lost my equipment, my coaches, my entourage, and my fans. I could not even get into the qualifying tournaments, because the officials there were afraid of adverse consequences.

Under the circumstances, an alternate pursuit seemed appropriate. That alternative was to combine with Laurel Kenner in writing a column that would communicate the remedial lessons I had learned from my fall and perhaps prevent others from succumbing. I figured that by trying to teach others, I might learn something myself.

When I met Laurel in 1999, she was the chief editor for North American stock markets at Bloomberg, one of the two biggest financial news wire services. Ironically, she was one of the very people responsible for perpetuating the misinformation and disinformation about the market described in this book. Life being short and time constantly ticking away, she decided to write a column herself. Readership soon topped that of other columnists. The kind of pieces she wrote, filled with lessons for investors from baseball, *Moby Dick*, and Beethoven symphonies, did not endear her to her traditionally minded bosses; and she was being eased out the door. Finally, she quit without any source of income in sight. It might have been a tragedy except for the fact that she now had the freedom to collaborate with me in writing columns she considered worthwhile.

We both were sick of seeing investors leaning on the wrong foot so often. The mumbo jumbo constantly fed to investors was painful to us, and we both had a reason and the knowledge to do something about it.

To Overwhelming Applause

"Get out of here!" was a typical reaction when we started writing. Reader after reader wrote in to say that this was the most ridiculous thing in the world: a guy who had lost everything writing columns to tell other people what to do.

One of the first letters we received suggested that instead of writing a column, I should be working as a dishwasher to pay my investors back.

Here are representative responses that came in early 2002, after we warned investors against blindly following those who believe "the trend is your friend":

> Let me conclude by encouraging you to continue writing your column on MSN Money and sharing your thoughts with us. A good way to trade profitably seems to be to take the opposite side of your trades.

> This is probably one of the worst articles I have ever read. Keep sending the same message to the sheep, leading them to the slaughterhouse. Vic used to be one of the best money managers in the world . . . guess that's why he is peddling stock advice on MSNBC. Give me a break.

> It's very clear why you blew out your account.

> I find it interesting that a man who lost $125 million in one day and skipped out on the bill has a job giving out advice to investors.

> My thinking is that you guys are some comedy act. Show me your actual trade figures over the past five years. I hear you went belly up. I don't think many trend traders did.

> All I can say is, how many times has Niederhoffer gone belly up and had to beg his friends to pony up some cash for him to start trading again? (from the Turtle-Trader Web site).

> Last time I checked, Niederhoffer was not the lead investor in the Boston Red Sox ownership group. John Henry is.

> Your articles are uncivilized, but I will forgive you if you change your life.

Some readers simply send us viruses:

> Subject: Fwd: Possible Virus Found in E-Mail

> A message from: vze24cgd@verizon.net may contain a virus. This message will be quarantined under the name vm.02285185015.10682 in the quarantine area on host mh2dmz4.bloomberg.net.

We usually reply to the nonviral letters, and find that a soft answer turns away wrath. One reader, James Taylor, asked in an October 4, 2002, e-mail:

> Why/how are you an authority on investing? After all, you blew up your fund.

I replied:

> I am not an authority. I am trying to learn. I guess they figure that people trying to learn might have an audience. Perhaps it was my education and my need of a job?

The reader quickly wrote back:

> Sorry about my prior e-mail. It was rude and not fair. I was just venting because I
> see so many "analysts" and so-called experts on CNBC daily, who don't have sense
> to come in out of the rain.
>
> Your insight and experience can only be a great addition to the column. I do
> have your book, *The Education of a Speculator,* and thought it was a good read.
> Trading is a difficult business and can test us, especially if we are aggressive.

One of the reprehensible traits of market commentators is to pretend that
they are lonely voices in the wilderness, bereft of support and praise. The
truth is, we are hardly bereft in that respect. Hundreds of thousands of people
read our columns on CNBC Money each month. For every barb, we receive
many hundreds of letters of thanks. No matter what we say, some critics will
inevitably say, "Forget about anything these two advise, because Vic couldn't
make a dollar if his life depended on it." We encourage such beliefs; they let
us go about our affairs in peace. We sometimes reply to such correspondence
by saying:

> Yes, you're right. Vic has been reduced to writing a column to cover the ex-
> penses of his large extended family, starting with the tuitions of his six daugh-
> ters. He couldn't get a job as an assistant squash coach because the hardball
> game he used to play is extinct, so he took a job as a night watchman. The col-
> umn is a good second job because he can write during the day. With any luck
> and continued hard work, he will be able to climb up the first stair of the invest-
> ment ladder once again so that eventually he will not need to supplement his in-
> come by writing.

We do not always feel patient. A Texas economics student, responding to
a column on dividends, wrote us that the 100 years of data on dividends we
used wasn't enough, and that he intended to do some real econometric work
that wasn't so simplistic. Vic, as usual, had a mild reply: "Hopefully, you will
find a data series of relevance for more than 100 years and be able to teach
us." When the reader responded by calling Victor a name too obscene to put
in print and wished us both great financial misery, Laurel became indignant
and wanted to go beat him over the head with her three-inch heels.

Although we may be hurt by such correspondence, we understand that
people have lost a great deal of money and are angry with everyone—from
CNBC to analysts to pundits and columnists.

In fact, neither of us has to write for a living. The income derived from
writing columns and books does not go far to defray our living expenses, or
to pay for the databases we need to debunk the fallacies that enthrall the investing public. But for the sake of the open-minded who are interested in

participating with us in mutual education, we are offering a serious response to the critics.

Since Laurel and I began writing together in 2000, we have heard countless heartbreaking tales from readers in shock from seeing their wealth and retirement accounts cut in half or worse. People wrote to us for advice on how to rebuild, on how to live with themselves. They specifically wanted to know how I handled my own bout with disaster.

The answer we give these distressed readers is not to avoid risk. Risk is part of all heroic endeavors, whether in trading, business, philanthropy, construction, exploration, art, music, sports, sailing, or romance. Not only is risk necessary for gain; it is the inescapable lot of human beings. As Paul Heyne wrote in *The Economic Way of Thinking*, "Everyone who makes a decision in the absence of complete information about the future consequences of all available opportunities is a speculator. So everyone is a speculator."[5]

When my fund closed in 1997, the returns to that point had been such that most of the investors who had been with me for any length of time ended up with net profits. Since 1997, I have climbed back up the stairs. Along the way, I have made and lost millions, with the former providentially much greater than the latter.

Avoiding risk can lead to the cynicism often produced by failure. One philosopher clearly saw the dangers:

> Cynicism may be a by-product of anomie in the social structure; at the same time it may also prepare the way for personal anomie. . . . Anxious over a personal failure, the individual . . . often disguises his feelings with a cynical attitude, and thus negates the prize he did not attain. Frequently he includes in his cynicism all persons who still seek that prize or have succeeded in winning it, and, occasionally, deprecates the entire social system within which the failure occurred. As the cynic becomes increasingly pessimistic and misanthropic, he finds it easier to reduce his commitment to the social system and its values.[6]

The author was my father. He was a cop, and he was writing about law enforcement officers. But his words apply equally well to the forlorn state that investors often fall into, especially after years of market losses.

Anyone who ventures out into the thick propaganda of Wall Street risks ruin. A rudder is necessary. To discover what people should understand if they want to improve their financial situations by trading in the market, we read hundreds of books on trading, investment, statistics, risk, and behavioral finance. Alas, almost everything disseminated about buying stocks is promotional, and most of the advice is completely untested. Indeed, these authors are careful not to frame their assertions in terms that can be tested.

Irrational faith in untested propositions is a throwback to feudal times, when people lived in utter squalor and poverty and had no possibility of improving themselves, no opportunity to retire early and do creative things, no chance to find cures for disease and extend their lives. Academic studies might seem to promise a better approach, but they often suffer from Monday-morning-quarterbacking biases and are almost always outdated by the time they are published.

Just like the victims in *Invasion of the Body Snatchers,* the victims of investment fallacies seem perfectly normal and rational. Yet their collective behavior can lead to evil and terrifying consequences. Professional market parasites who make their living off investors can only thrive when people give in and become unthinking pods. Only in an environment that is without skepticism and the scientific method can investors' losses mount wildly.

It all makes want us want to say, along with Dr. Bennell, "Help! Halt! Stop. Stop and listen to me! Don't you see? They want us to be like the pod people so that we'll pay our dues to the market system!"

In this book, Laurel and I play the roles of Becky Driscoll and Dr. Bennell, to help readers escape becoming pod creatures and succumbing to the market fallacies replicated daily, if not hourly, by those who would take away their wallets. Laurel draws on a vast knowledge of deceptive alien techniques gained from her work as U.S. stock market editor at Bloomberg News, a financial news wire service. Unlike Dr. Bennell, who cured patients and prevented alien invasions, I am merely a doctor of statistics. The main help such a doctor can provide is assistance in understanding the regularities and uncertainties of numbers. Like Dr. Bennell, however, I am in the habit of clipping odd articles from newspapers for items that might add up into grand insights somewhere down the line. For the past quarter-century, I have searched my favorite newspaper, the *National Enquirer,* for tales about the heroics of common people, their survival skills, and their unquenchable common sense and good nature, to fit myself for an optimistic approach to investments that roots out the pods before they can grow in the bearish greenhouses. We hope that readers will find this approach profitable.

Practical Speculation extends the themes that Laurel and I have been developing in our columns over the past three years. Together, we have fought off mysticism, hubris, and market propaganda in some 500 hard-hitting columns for four different Web sites. (It is true we were fired from most of these jobs, starting with a seven-week run of Laurel's column at Bloomberg and a two-month stand at thestreet.com, where we debuted our first joint column, "The Speculators' Corner." We put in a year and a month—quite a long spell for us—writing a daily column at worldlyinvestor.com, where we were eased out by new editors who wanted us to educate financial planners instead of concentrating on our clarion calls to the public to beware of ballyhoo. The odds are better than even money that by the time this book is published, we will have been fired by our current employer, CNBC Money.

We are not unmindful that we have burned many sacred cows in this book. None of them, or others in the barnyard and factories where they come from, are likely to react over kindly to the conflagration or what they are more likely to call a mere smokescreen.

One thing we should make clear, however, is that there is a wealth of original material appearing in this book that has never seen the light of day. It required much percolation, for example, for us to disclose here for the first time the results of a content analysis of 10 years of weekly financial writing. Same for our analysis and reformulation of the use of scatter charts, the discussions of conservation of energy, and the Value Line periodic table of elements. Furthermore, all the thoughts are fresh thoughts representing our best thinking several years into the new millennium. They have evolved from our experiences on the battlefield of actual trades as well as scholarly and practical criticism from a network of dispersed experts with knowledge and insights that could only have been assembled in modern Internet times.

Through it all, our readers' comments have augmented our work in immeasurable ways, leading to new areas of inquiry and new friendships. Above all, we have enjoyed the profit and pleasure of finding and testing ideas drawn from patterns observed in the real world, rather than passing along the received wisdom of gurus. Laurel and I hope that the lessons we have learned over the past three years from counting, deflating propaganda, avoiding unwarranted negative thinking, and developing a proper investing foundation will help readers of *Practical Speculation* prosper.

The Framework for This Book

The first part of this book—Mumbo Jumbo and Moonshine—dissects the common errors, myths, fallacies, and propaganda that induce investors to lean the wrong way and make a maximum contribution to the market's infrastructure.

Chapter 1: The Meme

Everyone knew that the mere mention from a Federal Reserve chairman of fears about stock prices would lead to an explosive and completely unpredictable reaction in the market. Alan Greenspan's December 5, 1996, "irrational exuberance" speech set off such a dire chain of events that we have devoted our Chapter 1 (with apologies to Guy de Maupassant's classic horror tale, "The Horla") to detailing all its consequences, including the reaction against technology, optimism, and growth.

Chapter 2: Earnings Propaganda

As Kuhn noted in *The Structure of Scientific Revolution*,[7] science often finds itself in a state in which a growing number of facts conflict with prevailing theory. Such was the state of Newtonian mechanics in the late nineteenth century as experimental evidence concerning the spontaneous decay of particles from the nucleus of atoms began to accumulate. Such is the state of today's prevailing wisdom that stock market prices are determined by earnings or price/earnings ratios. We subject the most widely accepted beliefs about the earnings-market relation to counting, and offer ways to spot earnings propaganda in media coverage, analyst reports, and company pronouncements to help readers reject the market's numerous invitations to trade the wrong way.

Chapter 3: The Hydra Heads of Technical Analysis

Violent declines in the market promote fear and dread. Being able to predict up moves in the market would guarantee immeasurable wealth and power. It is not surprising, then, that there is a mythology of momentum, replete with stories of great heroes and heroines who have conquered the mighty forces, to ease investors' anxieties, to fuel their hopes—and to keep them making wrong moves with no chance for improvement. We apply some science to the cult of technical analysis and its central mystery: "The trend is your friend." As we demonstrate, the trend is regrettably not your friend.

Chapter 4: The Cult of the Bear

How can a writer be wrong for practically his entire working life and still be the most influential figure in financial journalism? We interviewed Alan Abelson to find out why, after searching in vain for a hint of optimism in the hundreds of weekly columns he wrote for *Barron's* during the great 1990s bull market.

Chapter 5: "We Are Number One" Usually Means "Not Much Longer"

To the ancient Greeks, the most grievous sin was hubris, the arrogance of power. Vic's father, Artie Niederhoffer, who inspired and is memorialized in

Vic's first book, *The Education of a Speculator,* wrote with great insight on how this flaw impaired the judicial system. We attempt to carry forward his analysis by studying the effects of hubris in the marketplace.

Chapter 6: Benjamin Graham: Mythical Market Hero

The ancients had their gods and demigods, and we moderns have ours. In the Golden Age of Greece, as scientific thinking took hold for the first time, some thinkers began to question the reverence and sacrifices demanded by the gods. It is always a good idea to ask questions. A figure high in today's pantheon—Benjamin Graham—is the subject of this chapter.

Chapter 7: News Flash: Computer Writes Stock Market Story!

The brilliant mathematician Alan Turing once proposed that a computer might be said to be intelligent if it could fool a human into mistaking it for another human. The converse must also be true: If we can program a computer to replicate a human's speech, we can say the human is not acting intelligently. Most contemporary financial news reports could be done by computers working from a limited database of erroneous ideas and quotes from mediocre money managers. We explain why, and present our patented program for stock market reporting.

Looking at Part Two—Practical Speculation

Part Two offers a foundation for making rational decisions about the market. Survival comes first, and we start with a strategy that will keep readers from being wiped out before they can enjoy the fruits of their efforts. It is based on the thinking of one of the greatest geniuses ever in a pursuit that has demanded the best strategic thinking of sharp minds for more than a thousand years: chess.

Chapter 8: How to Avoid Spurious Correlations

The main tool for succeeding in the investment battle is so simple that a child can comprehend it: the scatter plot. By plotting the joint values of two things, the investor can determine whether and how much the things are related. The technique provides a way to understand almost all information about the stock market. We explain it step by step and show how to use it to analyze the effect of interest-rate moves on the market.

Chapter 9: The Future of Returns

In the twentieth century, stock markets in all major industrialized countries recorded returns on the order of 1,500,000 percent. That is the remarkable conclusion of three London Business School researchers who assembled a magnificent 102-year worldwide database on stock prices and wrote what we consider the best investment book available today, *Triumph of the Optimists*.[8] We describe some systems we have developed from their database to improve on a long-term buy-and-hold strategy.

Chapter 10: The Periodic Table of Investing

We tell the story of Value Line's beginnings from the perspectives of Sam Eisenstadt, the firm's research chairman and Henry Hill, the Florida investor who made millions by religiously following Value Line's systems. The tale includes Value Line's conclusive demonstration of growth's superiority over value.

Chapter 11: When They Swing for the Fences, We Run for the Exits

A remarkable predictive relation exists between baseball and long-term trends in the market, and it all begins with Babe Ruth.

Chapter 12: Boom or Bust?

Real estate, fixed and immovable, might seem to be an ideal alternative to a roller-coaster stock market. Yet real estate investment trusts (REITs)—the main way in which small investors can invest in large-scale income properties—have failed to measure up to stocks as long-term investments. We demonstrate that great profits may come from studying the patterns linking real estate and business cycles.

Chapter 13: Market Thermodynamics

The fundamental laws of conservation and entropy are amazingly helpful in making predictions in a world of seemingly constant change. We demonstrate with experiments and a day in the life of Vic's youngest daughter, Kira.

Chapter 14: Practical Market Lessons from the Tennis Court

Vic has won numerous championship titles in racket sports of all kinds, and in 2001 was among the first players to be named to the newly founded Squash

Hall of Fame. He shares strategies that have proved useful both on the court and in the market, before, during, and after the game.

Chapter 15: The Fine Art of Bargaining for an Edge

Everyone has a right to state the price he or she is willing to pay. Investors should not hesitate to use bargaining methods to gain an edge in the market.

Chapter 16: An Amiable Idiot in the Biotechnology Revolution

The main criticism of Vic's first book was that it had a lot of principles, but nothing to help people make money. When we began writing columns, we found ourselves on the firing line every day to come up with specific recommendations. Readership of our column went up by a factor of 10 when we began mentioning individual stock purchases and sales. Happily, although our dedication to readers goes beyond the dollar and the clock, our stock-picking efforts on their behalf have not been without benefit to us. We put drug stocks on trial for money-making efficacy.

Chapter 17: Earnings Imposters

Constantly evolving techniques of "earnings management" have made net income—once known as "the bottom line"—a chimera. We show how to mine information in balance sheets and cash flow statements to arrive at a truer picture of a company's financial health. Stock buybacks, dividends, inventory, accounts receivable, and tax payments all are helpful in differentiating between reality and artful distortions.

Chapter 18: Finale

We hear four questions more than any others. We explain whether we use any technical indicators in our trading, what book we recommend for speculators, and why we say such awful things about Alan Greenspan. We also divulge the secret weapon that keeps us on our toes and eager to learn: a group of investors and sages we met through our columns. We communicate with them daily by e-mail to discuss market philosophy and strategy. We include a few of the tens of thousands of extraordinary posts these eagles have generously shared over the years.

Explanation of Icons

In this book, we return again and again to five broad themes, in highly varied forms. To help readers recognize them more easily, we highlight these themes with icons:

Propaganda: In politics, the systematic dissemination of false beliefs is called propaganda. Schoolchildren nowadays are taught how to recognize the seven main techniques of propaganda—name-calling, glittering generalities, transfer, testimonial, plain folks, card-stacking, and bandwagon. Regrettably, nobody tells investors how to recognize these techniques in the financial field. That is going to change right now. Propaganda methods crop up over and over again as we discuss the widespread acceptance of false information. When we encounter these techniques, we highlight them with the old Soviet Union's favorite villain: the capitalist **Mr. Moneybags.**

Untested propositions: Much of what passes for market analysis today is done in a manner related more to Dark Ages mysticism than scientific reasoning. When we discuss untested propositions and leaps of faith, we include our mumbo-jumbo icon, a **wizard's hat.**

Count, count, count: The antidote to propaganda and untested propositions is a skeptical frame of mind that asks for proof when a market-related idea is put forward. The kind of mind that queries: "Should I swallow this, or not?" As Steve Stigler writes in his magisterial *Statistics on the Table:*[9]

> If a serious question has been raised, whether it be in science or society, then it is not enough merely to assert an answer. Evidence must be provided, and that evidence should be accompanied by an assessment of its own reliability. The evidence need not be quantitative, although it will often find its clearest expression in quantitative form or through attempts to interpret it in quantitative form. If the question is important and one position has been advanced with well-considered supporting evidence, then it is incumbent on a critic to put "statistics on the table." Clearly this test requires more than simple number collection. It involves a careful analysis of the forces that would affect any data, methods for measuring and expressing the uncertainty of the conclusions, and conventions for settling issues such as how much uncertainty is too much, or when an assertion should be rejected and when not.

We find it appropriate to put statistics on the table often as we try to provide an approach and a framework that will get investors off on the right foot. We use a **pencil and envelope** icon as a reminder of the importance of counting.

Spurious correlations: A great part of this book is devoted to examining random relations that are assumed to be predictive. When we uncover a spurious correlation, we highlight it with a **pair of storks,** a reference to a complex but fictitious relation between population growth, bad wurst, double vision, misinterpretations of Kant's work (*unkantverstehenlassenhummels*), and a jump in stork sightings in Oldenburg, Germany.

Ever-changing cycles: Our job as market commentators, which has involved writing more than one million words over almost four years, has been to discover useful knowledge, test it, and make it general and practical. The ironic thing about knowledge is that it is constantly changing, in line with the shifting kaleidoscope of market price moves. Our **racehorse** icon highlights the law of ever-changing cycles that Robert L. Bacon first put forward in *Secrets of Professional Turf Betting:* "The principle of ever-changing trends works to force quick and drastic changes of results sequences when the public happens to get wise to a winning idea."[10]

Part One
Mumbo Jumbo and Moonshine

1   THE MEME

A curious piece of news comes to us from Rio de Janeiro. Madness, an epidemic of madness, which may be compared to that contagious madness which attacked the people of Europe in the Middle Ages, is at this moment raging in the Province of Sao Paulo. The frightened inhabitants are leaving their houses, deserting their villages, abandoning their land, saying that they are pursued, possessed, governed like human cattle by invisible, though tangible, beings, a species of vampire, which feed on their life while they are asleep.

—Guy de Maupassant, "The Horla"[1]

July 18, 1996: What a beautiful century! As the beginning of the third millennium nears, America is looking forward to continued peace and growing prosperity. Communism has been discredited, and the Cold War is over. World trade is opening up. We're starting to spend money on goods and ideas, rather than multibillion-dollar schemes of mutually assured destruction. The federal budget has a surplus for the first time in decades. Interest rates are at half the level of 15 years ago. Productivity and earnings are rising, and unemployment and inflation are negligible, something thought impossible just a few years ago. The computer is transforming work and home life. Revolutions in biotechnology and high-speed communications are under way. Parents can reasonably expect their newborns to live to age 100 and beyond. Almost 50 million people are using the Internet. Many investors are becoming rich from investing in technology, and entrepreneurs are finding it easy to raise money for new ventures. Millions of people are more comfortable financially than they have ever been before. The standard of living is better than ever. People are optimistic about improving their lot in life. The future seems promising indeed.

I turn on CNBC to hear the financial news. One of my technology stocks is up 15 points! I call my broker to sell half my shares. Now I can pay my kids' tuition bills. Federal Reserve Chairman Alan Greenspan comes on the air. He says that remarkable technological breakthroughs in microchips and software are boosting productivity. He doesn't see any reason that the economy's growth should not continue for the foreseeable future. The Dow is up 120. I salute his image on the TV screen, I hardly know why, except his words give me great pleasure.

The TV anchor then begins an interview with one of the bearish money managers who has been short the market since 1987. The manager launches into a familiar speech: "Market valuations are ridiculously high . . . dividend yields aren't what they were in the 1950s and early 1960s . . . the Dow has already risen almost 9 percent so far this year, enough for an average year, after rising 33 percent in 1995." Indeed, with dividends reinvested, it has returned 1,200 percent since the end of 1979. But he sounds a little desperate, as well he might, given that so many who had bet against the market beginning in 1987 have gone belly up. He makes no mention of the decline in interest rates, or the doubling of earnings retention rates, or the fact that buybacks are now running equivalent to dividend payouts. Nor did he provide evidence that stocks must go down after going up at more than the average rate. If only he would take out a pencil and envelope, he could see that after a rise, the chances of another rise the next year are 53 percent versus 52 percent after a decline and that the average move after a rise is slightly greater than after a decline.

December 6, 1996: I turn on the 6 A.M. business news when I wake up. Catastrophe has struck. Last night, after the U.S. markets closed, Greenspan suggested that investors are "irrationally exuberant." Markets are diving in Asia and Europe.

A sudden shiver of agony runs through me. The chairman is like the father of the market. If the market were to heed his words, if it were to start worrying that he might punish it by requiring more margin, it might fall beneath his big heels.

His words, taken alone, do not seem too foreboding. He was not even ad-dressing Congress. It was just an after-dinner speech at the American Enter-prise Institute on the history of monetary policy. I pull up the quote on the Internet:

> Where do we draw the line on what prices matter? Certainly prices of goods and services now being produced—our basic measure of inflation—matter. But what about future prices or more importantly, prices of claims on future goods and ser-vices, like equities, real estate or other earning assets? Is stability of these prices essential to the stability of the economy?
>
> Clearly, sustained low inflation implies less uncertainty about the future, and lower risk premiums imply higher prices of stocks and other earning assets. We can see that in the inverse relationship exhibited by price/earnings ratios and the rate of inflation on the past. *But how do we know when irrational exuberance has un-duly escalated asset values, when they become subject to unexpected and prolonged con-tractions as they have in Japan over the past decade? And how do we factor that assessment into monetary policy?* [Emphasis added.]
>
> ... Evaluating shifts in balance sheets generally, and in asset prices particu-larly, must be an integral part of the development of monetary policy.[2]

"But how do we know . . . ?" It sounds like such an innocent question. By the time the market closed, everything seemed pretty much back to normal. The Dow ended 55 points lower at 6382, a drop of less than 1 percent, after falling as much as 144. But why did our self-confidence change so quickly into timidity? How strange it is that a simple feeling of discomfort—perhaps the irritation of a nervous center, a small disturbance in the imperfect and deli-cate functions of our mental machinery—can turn the most lighthearted of men into a melancholy one, and make a coward of the bravest.

I walk down to the river near my house to watch the tugboats and barges go by. After walking a short distance in the sun, I suddenly, inexplicably, feel anxious and wretched. I return home immediately to check the stock prices on my monitor. Why am I worried? Is it a phrase that, passing through my memory, has upset my nerves and given me a fit of low spirits? Is it the frown of CNBC's Money Honey as she passes along word of an analyst's downgrade, or is it her new short hairstyle? Everything that surrounds us, everything that we hear without listening, every idea that we meet without clearly distin-guishing it, has a rapid, surprising, and inexplicable effect on us and on our organs, and through them on our ideas and on our being.

February 25, 1997: President Bill Clinton has been letting big campaign con-tributors stay in the Lincoln bedroom! The White House released a list of more than 800 people who stayed overnight in the room where President Lincoln signed the proclamation freeing America's slaves. The guests—including Hollywood moguls and stars—came through with at least $5.4 million in contributions to the Democratic National Committee in 1995 and 1996 alone, according to a computerized study commissioned by CNN. Producer Steven Spielberg donated $336,023, and MCA Chairman Lew Wasserman gave $225,000. The tawdriness is troubling.

March 3, 1997: A crisis is unfolding far away. It seems that cheap Chinese labor is taking away Thailand's share of the electronics export market. The country's fabulous growth has slowed so much that the banks are neck-deep in bad loans to real estate speculators, and a devaluation of the currency—the baht—is probable. The stock exchange temporarily halted trading in bank stocks today. An incomprehensible feeling of disquietude seizes me, as if this news concealed some terrible menace. I walk up and down my hallway, oppressed by a feeling of confusion and irresistible fear.

July 8, 1997: NASA uses the Internet to broadcast images taken by the Pathfinder spacecraft on Mars. An Internet traffic record is set: 46 million hits in one day. These stunning displays of twentieth-century science make my spirit soar.

August 21, 1997: Southeast Asian markets are collapsing before our eyes. Thailand admitted today it had borrowed $23 billion in an unsuccessful attempt to avoid devaluing its currency. Thailand owes a total of $89 billion to foreigners, $40 billion of which comes due within the next year. Indonesia, Malaysia, and the Philippines are in trouble, too. Stocks are toppling, interest rates are soaring, and outside money is fleeing. Malaysian leader Mahathir Mohamed says it's all because Jews are trying to keep Muslims poor.

I have just come from consulting my medical man, for I can no longer sleep. He said my pulse is high and my nerves are highly strung, but that otherwise I exhibited to him no alarming symptoms. He prescribed a regimen of vigorous exercise.

That night, I manage two or three hours of sleep. A nightmare lays hold of me. I feel that I am in bed and asleep . . . and I feel also that somebody is coming close to me, looking at me, touching me, getting onto my bed, kneeling on my chest, taking my neck between his hands and squeezing it with all his might to strangle me. I struggle, bound by that terrible powerlessness that paralyzes us in our dreams. Then suddenly, I wake up, shaken and bathed in perspiration.

October 15, 1997: I have made a complete recovery. The Microsoft shares I purchased the day after the "irrational exuberance" speech are up 73 percent.

October 20, 1997: I turn on the news and learn that the Justice Department is accusing Microsoft of violating a court antitrust order. How strange. Microsoft has done more than any company to bring the computer revolution to consumers. Is success now suspect?

About 10 o'clock that evening I go up to my room. As soon as I have entered, I lock and bolt the door. I am frightened—of what?

October 27, 1997: A rolling panic that began in Hong Kong last week has engulfed every stock market in the world. In the United States, exchanges halted trading today after the Dow plunged 550 points. The value investor David Dreman said, "Investors finally realize the market is overpriced."[3]

October 28, 1997: I look up from my desk in the New York City offices of Bloomberg News. Ken Kohn, the New York bureau chief, sitting opposite me, is cackling. "Victor Niederhoffer went under!" he says.

April 30, 1998: The shadow has passed. Jeremy Siegel, the Wharton finance professor, just introduced an expanded edition of his *Stocks for the Long Run*, showing that stocks have averaged an annual return of 7 percent after inflation for the past two centuries, twice the return on bonds.[4] The Dow has risen 28 percent since that terrible Monday last October, and my Microsoft shares are up 40 percent. I feel cured.

August 31, 1998: In one month, the world has fallen into chaos. More than 250 people were killed when terrorists simultaneously bombed our embassies in Kenya and Tanzania. The Saudi terrorist Osama bin Laden said strikes against the United States would continue "from everywhere." The next day, President Clinton ordered a retaliatory strike against bin Laden in Afghanistan and a nerve gas factory in Sudan—but the strike missed bin Laden, and Sudan insists the factory did not make nerve gas at all, just drugs. People are calling our counterattacks a terrible instance of life imitating art. Just three days earlier, Clinton admitted on television that he had had an "inappropriate relationship" with Monica Lewinsky, a White House intern. A grand jury is investigating whether he lied about it under oath. A new Hollywood hit, *Wag the Dog*, released just before the attacks, features a U.S. president who declares war to divert attention from a brewing sex scandal.

On top of everything else, Russia devalued its currency last week and defaulted on its debt. In an attempt to clear my mind with fresh air, I went for a walk in Central Park. I turned into a shady path in a little-visited area. A sudden shiver of agony ran through me, and I hastened my steps, frightened without reason. Suddenly it seemed as if I were being followed, that somebody was walking at my heels, close, quite close to me, near enough to touch me. I turned round suddenly, but I was alone. I returned home to find the Dow average had closed down 512 points. In four days, it has lost 12 percent. All the major indexes are down for the year.

September 28, 1998: Some very big hedge funds have lost billions in August and September. One fund, Long-Term Capital Management, had to be bailed out for $3.6 billion by 14 banks after losing all but $400 million of what had been $4.8 billion in net assets. Fear was rampant that the financial system might collapse under the strain if Long-Term failed to meet its obligations. Quantum, Omega, and Tiger suffered stiff losses. The public is scared and is dumping bank stocks. Goldman Sachs, the king of Wall Street, had to cancel its scheduled initial public offering today. Congress is howling to regulate hedge funds. I feel the frightening presence of my nightmares lurking outside my window almost every evening now. It seems to be laughing wickedly.

I went to a dinner at New York University tonight to hear a speech by Arthur Levitt, chairman of the Securities and Exchange Commission (SEC). Levitt said managers are putting out hocus-pocus financial statements with the complicity of their auditors to pump up market capitalization and increase the value of their options. He warned executives to put their houses in order. No more inflated write-offs for restructuring charges, future operating expenses, and "in-process research" to make future earnings look better. No more stashing profits in the cookie jar for a rainy day. No more booking sales before delivery takes place. No more quibbling over how big a lie has to be before it is "material" under Generally Accepted Accounting Principles.[5]

The lawyers and accountants in the room put down their forks and started taking notes.

I suddenly felt a chill in the room. An unearthly voice seemed to be laughing, and I could not escape the feeling that he was mocking Levitt.

May 5, 1999: Was it really a case of *Wag the Dog?* The U.S. government said it wouldn't contest a lawsuit for damages filed by the Saudi owner of the drug factory we bombed in Sudan last August. I sense the shadow is laughing.

August 2, 1999: Huge accounting frauds are coming to light every week. Bankers Trust has paid $63 million in fines for stealing dormant client funds to cover general expenses. Cendant, Livent, McKesson, Rite Aid, and Sunbeam are embroiled in scandals. Carol J. Loomis, writing in *Fortune* about the SEC crackdown, said the cascade of cases suggests "great expanses of accounting rot, just waiting to be revealed." She noted that when the *Wall Street Journal* published a front-page story in 1994 about how Jack Welch "smoothed" earnings at General Electric with the "creative use of restructuring charges and reserves," the company got calls from other corporations saying, "Well, this is what companies do. Why is this a front-page story?"

Eventually, "Someone may go to jail,"[6] she wrote. I shivered. The nightmare presence seemed to smile and grow larger as though he somehow gained strength from these scandals, as bacteria thrive in dirt and darkness.

November 22, 1999: My copy of *Fortune* arrived in the mail today. I start idly reading a transcript of speeches that Warren Buffett made in July and September at small but influential private gatherings of technology entrepreneurs and venture capitalists. A shadow seems to fill the room, and I shiver. The great investor said that had he been at Kitty Hawk in 1903, he would have shot down Orville Wright as a service to capitalists. "There were about 300 aircraft manufacturers in 1919–1939. Only a handful are breathing today," Buffett said.[7] Is he mad? Or am I mad? Has not air transport vastly improved travel and commerce? Is not aerospace the largest U.S. export industry? Yet here was the most admired capitalist in the world, telling people that investing in innovative industries does not pay off.

Buffett did not say if he had considered the impact of dividends, mergers, acquisitions, or name changes. He did not say whether the early aircraft makers had gone bankrupt. Nor did he provide numbers on returns or variabilities to support his assertion that the aerospace industry was a bad investment. He had selected an industry that may very well have yielded poor returns. Any student of market history knows that instances of success and failure can be found in accord with any untested assertion. But many other industries looked just as promising in 1903—pharmaceuticals, tabulating machines, and packaged foods, to name a few—that have matured to yield the 1,500,000 percent-a-century returns that the typical investment has averaged since then.

I am amazed to read that Buffett's remarks drew tremendous applause and admiration. Jeffrey Bezos, founder of amazon.com, is insisting that all his executives study the speech. Lenin is supposed to have once said, "We will all live to see the day that capitalists swing by our ropes from high trees." A member of the audience, doubtless with lips closed, shouted out, "Who will sell us the rope?" Lenin promptly answered, "The capitalists will sell it to us."

Who but Lenin himself could have predicted that such a baseless claim, so at odds with the dynamic and creative nature of the enterprise system, could have been greeted with such acclaim at conferences on the marvels of technology?

Mary Buffett's book, *Buffettology*, says Buffett views stocks as groceries, or perhaps a glorified type of annuity, to be bought only when available at discount.[8] He refuses to invest in growth stocks such as technology issues because he does not understand them. Instead of taking the time to learn and be able to discern what is worthwhile about the new, Buffett rejects innovation. He is like those people who live in the hills hoarding goods necessary for survival, precious metals for barter, and guns to fight off any desperate survivors of the apocalypse they are convinced is inevitable.

The antidote to this negativism is a belief in the creative power of individuals to improve their situations through mutually beneficial exchange. This belief, combined with a belief in the continuing wonders of technology and innovation, leads to viewing stocks as an excellent investment.

Preparations for millennial celebrations are beginning all over, yet I cannot get Buffett's odd anecdotes and the puzzling hatred of the dynamic nature of the enterprise system out of my mind.

I went to bed and fell asleep, only to be roused two hours later by a terrible shock. Imagine a sleeping man who wakes up with a knife in his chest, gurgling in his throat, covered with blood, no longer able to breathe, a man who realizes he is going to die and does not understand why it is happening— there you have it. Oh! Who can understand my horrible agony? I must escape these fatalist obsessions.

December 31, 1999: It's bonus time on Wall Street, and the rewards are worthy of maharajahs. Morgan Stanley's Internet analyst, Mary Meeker, will make $15 million, Bloomberg News reported. Jack Grubman, a Salomon Smith Barney telecommunications analyst, will probably receive $10 million. At least 5,000 bankers, analysts, and traders will take home $1 million.[9]

The value of Bill Gates' Microsoft shares topped $100 billion this year; more, as Bloomberg's Brian Rooney noted, than the gross domestic product of Greece. If Microsoft stock continues to rise 59 percent a year, as it has for the last decade, Rooney said, Bill's fortune will surpass U.S GDP by 2010.[10]

Every business related to stocks is thriving this year. Assets in Fidelity Investment's mutual funds have reached a record $1 trillion, and investment banks have raised almost $24 billion for Internet companies. The Nasdaq has risen 51 percent from October 19 through today.

It's all fine, very fine. Yet I keep thinking of Albert Jay Nock's description in *Memoirs of a Superfluous Man* of the turn of the nineteenth century. Nock quoted a passage from Turgenev's *Clara Militch* to describe the spirit of the time:

> He dreamed that he was in a rich manor-house, of which he was the owner. He had lately bought both the house and the estate attached to it. And he kept thinking,

"It's nice, very nice now, but evil is coming!" Beside him moved to and fro a little tiny man, his steward; he kept laughing, bowing, and trying to show Aratov how admirably everything was arranged in his house and his estate. "This way, pray, this way, pray," he kept repeating, chuckling at every word; "kindly look how prosperous everything is with you! Look at the horses, what splendid horses!" And Aratov saw a row of immense horses. They were standing in their stalls with their backs to him. Their manes and tails were magnificent, but as soon as Aratov went near, the horses' heads turned toward him, and they showed their teeth viciously. "It's very nice," Aratov thought, "but evil is coming!" "This way, pray, this way," the steward repeated again, "pray come into the garden; look, what fine apples you have." The apples certainly were fine, red and round, but as soon as Arratov looked at them they withered and fell. "Evil is coming!" he thought. "And here is the lake," lisped the steward. "Isn't it blue and smooth? And here's a little boat of gold—will you get into it?—it floats of itself." "I won't get into it," thought Aratov; "evil is coming!" but for all that he got into the boat. At the bottom lay huddled up a little creature like a monkey; it was holding in its paws a glass full of a dark liquid. "Pray don't be uneasy," the steward shouted from the bank. "It's of no consequence. It's death. Good luck to you!"

"For the great majority, the last decade of the century seemed to offer every encouragement to complacent hopefulness," Nock wrote. "All the institutional voices of society were blended to form the sycophantic reassurances of Aratov's steward."[11]

January 5, 1999: I've been reading a deeply unsettling theory proposed by the evolutionist Richard Dawkins. He thinks that a new replicating entity has recently emerged on earth. This entity is still in its infancy, but has already achieved an evolutionary rate far ahead of traditional genes. He calls this new entity a *meme:*

> Examples of memes are tunes, ideas, catch-phrases, clothes fashions, ways of making pots, or of building arches. Just as genes propagate themselves in the gene pool by leaping from body to body via sperms or eggs, so memes propagate themselves by leaping from brain to brain in a process which, in the broad sense, can be called imitation. If a scientist hears, or reads about, a good idea, he passes it on to his colleagues and students. If the idea catches on, it can be said to propagate itself.[12]

A fertile meme acts like a parasite in the brain, turning it into a vehicle for the meme's propagation just as a virus takes control of the genetic mechanism of its host cell. A meme, although Dawkins says it rhymes with "dream," is no mere ethereal concept. A meme that takes hold actually manifests itself physically, as it modifies the nervous systems of millions of individuals.

For more than three billion years, DNA was the only self-replicating mechanism. Now, the new replicators, memes, are taking over and initiating their own kind of evolution. As was the case with genes, selection will favor the memes that exploit the environment to their own advantage.

I can scarce believe that a mere thought can yield such awesome power. The meme concept has me altogether perturbed.

Seeking to escape my troubled reflections, I started leafing through "The Horla," a short story by de Maupassant. Suddenly I came across a passage relating the narrator's conversation with a monk:

> Do we see the hundred-thousandth part of what exists? Look here; there is the wind, which is the strongest force in nature. It knocks down men, and blows down buildings, uproots trees, raises the sea into mountains of water, destroys cliffs and casts great ships on to the breakers; it kills, it whistles, it sighs, it roars. But have you ever seen it, and can you see it? Yet it exists for all that.

January 6, 2000: I am not mad. I have seen . . . I have seen . . . I have seen it! After closing the millennium at a record high, the Nasdaq 100 has dropped 12 percent in the past three days. That fiber-optics stock everyone has been making so much money on, JDS Uniphase, fell 20 percent. Rumors have it that George Soros' hedge funds are dumping huge holdings of Nasdaq stocks.

February 17, 2000: The meme is coming at me from all sides. I hear it, I see it everywhere. It came out of the mouth of Greenspan while I was watching his twice-yearly speech on the state of the economy to the House Banking Committee. First he said the economy was better than he had seen in half a century. But then he proceeded to float an incredible theory that overturned an axiom as fundamental to economics as gravity is to physics. He claimed that demand created by market wealth threatened to outstrip the supply of goods because stocks are too high:

> Without doubt, the synergies of the microprocessor, laser, fiber-optic glass, and satellite technologies have brought quantum advances in information availability. These advances, in turn, have dramatically decreased business operational uncertainties and risk premiums and, thereby, have engendered major cost reductions and productivity advances. There seems little question that further major advances lie ahead.
>
> · · ·
>
> *The problem is that the pickup in productivity tends to create even greater increases in aggregate demand than in potential aggregate supply* [Emphasis added]. This occurs principally because a rise in structural productivity growth has its counterpart in higher expectations for long-term corporate earnings. This, in turn, not

only spurs business investment but also increases stock prices and the market value of assets held by households, creating additional purchasing power for which no additional goods or services have yet been produced. . . . [S]o long as the levels of consumption and investment are sensitive to asset values, equity values increasing at a pace faster than income, other things equal, will induce a rise in overall demand in excess of potential supply. But that situation cannot persist without limit because the supply safety valves are themselves limited.

. . . [T]he necessary alignment of the growth of aggregate demand with the growth of potential aggregate supply may well depend on restraint on domestic demand, which continues to be buoyed by the lagged effects of increases in stock market valuations.

Shaken and in need of an independent opinion, I e-mailed Richard Zeckhauser, professor of political economy at Harvard's John F. Kennedy School of Government. Zeckhauser's work examines possibilities for the democratic, decentralized allocation of resources in accordance with the preferences of the citizenry. He wrote back:

Neither supply nor demand can be out of line for long. Shortages are always a short-term phenomenon unless the government interferes and fixes prices. The reason, of course, is that price adjusts to equate supply and demand.

I think that Greenspan would be worried about a supply shortage because he does not like the consequence of a temporary shortage; namely he does not like it when prices rise to bring about an equilibrium. But, of course, this is a healthy response, because this is the only way to bring out the resources that will produce additional supply. But if you hate inflation above all else, you will not like this response.

This could be a little like hating the swollen, red state of an infection. But of course, the infection is really just our white blood cells fighting off some foreign agent. We are better off with these fighters, despite their side effects, than we would be without them. So, I would say that the price system does a good job of dealing with supply inadequacies, but not without some dislocation in prices.

One of the elementary, inviolate principles of economics is that if supply is scarce, prices for that good or service will rise until demand for it falls. This natural equilibrium is based on rational expectations, and requires no interference from government. In the eighteenth century, Adam Smith wrote of an invisible hand. In our day, Heyne observed in his classic text, *The Economic Way of Thinking*, "People want more or less of a good as the cost those people must pay decreases or increases."

Now I know. I can divine. The reign of rational thought is over. Woe to us! It has come. I have heard . . . the Meme . . . it is here . . . the Meme!

March 1, 2000: Now the Meme is replicating and mutating. I saw it today in Berkshire Hathaway's annual report. Buffett again! "Equity investors currently seem wildly optimistic in their expectations about future returns."

Greenspan again! Today, the Fed released verbatim transcript of its 1994 meetings. Never before had meeting transcripts been released to the public. The Fed had decided in 1994 to release them with a five-year lag.

The transcripts show that Greenspan and his cohorts had been patting themselves on the back for arresting a possible stock market bubble. "I think we partially broke the back of an emerging speculation in equities," Greenspan told members of the Fed's policy-making body, the Federal Open Market Committee, in a February 1994 conference call. "As we look back on this, I suspect that there was a significant overshoot in the market. We pricked that bubble."

The horror! When did the stock market become the Fed's business? Greenspan repeated his comment the following month, according to the transcript of the March 22, 1994, FOMC meeting. "When we moved on February 4th, [1994], I think our expectation was that we would prick the bubble in the equity markets," Greenspan told the committee members. (In the previous year, the Dow Jones Industrial Average had risen 18 percent—to 3967.)

Ah, I can imagine the scene. The Fed governors, seated at the long polished table in grand chairs, served on china by obsequious waiters, laughing genially at the chairman's jokes, grinning at their victory over the market. It makes me think of the old men who used to sit in armchairs at the windows of Manhattan's grand clubs, murmuring with disapproval at the sight of a stray Jew walking along Fifth Avenue.

The federal funds rate increases over the past eight months with no inflation in sight—all is clear now! The old men at the Fed do not like to see ordinary people making money in the stock market. They do not like the young entrepreneurs making money in new technology ventures. They especially do not like the day traders, who are said to make hundreds of thousands in a day without even knowing the business of the stocks they trade. The old men want investors to have graduated from the schools that they did and to look like them. An elitist meme has taken over a country where everyone should have equal opportunity to profit from an investment in capitalism. Alexander Pope once said: "Most old men are like old trees. Past bearing themselves, they will suffer no young plants to flourish beneath them."

Despite the grotesque servility with which the media treat the old men, they are only reincarnations of the *senex amans,* that comic character who appears throughout the centuries in literature and opera, the old man who tries to win the young girl for himself. In *The Canterbury Tales,* he is the 60-year-old bachelor January who insists on marrying a girl who is not more than 20, only to be cuckolded by a lusty young rival. In Rossini's *Barber of Seville,* Dr. Bartolo pants after his young ward, Rosina. In Mozart's *The Marriage of Figaro,* old Marcellina tries to snare young, handsome Figaro by lending him money. Victorians appreciated the *senex amans* theme so much that Gilbert and Sullivan used it in *Iolanthe, The Mikado, H.M.S. Pinafore,* and *The Pirates of Penzance.*

I went to bed and had a terrible nightmare. I felt somebody sucking my life out—sucking it out of my neck as a leech would suck blood. Then he got up, satiated, and I woke up, so beaten, crushed, and annihilated that I could not move. Have I lost my reason? What has happened? What I saw is so strange that my mind wanders when I think of it!

March 14, 2000: The Meme, moving with incredible speed now, has reached the White House and London. President Bill Clinton and Prime Minister Tony Blair called for immediate public access to raw genetic data collected by private companies. "Our genome belongs to every member of the human race," Clinton said. "We must ensure that the profits of human genetic research are measured not in dollars but in the betterment of human life." Craig Venter, whose company, Celera, was on the verge of beating a government team in a race to map the human genome, commented, "Being a business seems to be an awful thing today." The Amex Biotech Index plunged 13 percent today.

March 21, 2000: I can only wait, paralyzed, powerless. I feel the Meme's presence nearby, looming over me, looking at me, dominating me. The Fed raised interest rates today to 6 percent from 5.75 percent, claiming it "remains concerned that increases in demand will continue to exceed the growth in potential supply, which could foster inflationary imbalances that would undermine the economy's record expansion."

April 4, 2000: Judge Thomas Penfield Jackson ruled last night that Microsoft violated antitrust law. The Nasdaq, synonymous with technology, lost 349 points yesterday in advance of the decision, and dived 575 points this morning before miraculously wafting up to close at 4148, down 75.

A new blockbuster has hit bookstore shelves: *Irrational Exuberance,* by Robert Shiller, the Yale professor who invented the contagious phrase and passed it to the Fed chairman back in 1996.[13]

April 28, 2000: Nobody thinks there will be any more miraculous levitations in the Nasdaq. Stanley Druckenmiller resigned from the Soros organization today, saying he lost billions on technology stocks. "I never thought the Nasdaq would drop 35 percent in 15 days," he said. Yet, in the three terrible weeks leading up to the April 15 tax deadline, that is exactly what happened.

May 16, 2000: The Fed raised interest rates yet again today, to 6.5 percent. Does the Meme want to destroy all?

August 31, 2000: The first year of the new era so happily welcomed is not even over, but everything has changed to fear and viciousness. Rising interest rates have choked off capital spending. Hundreds of thousands of entrepreneurs and workers are out of work.

An enveloping torpor has set in everywhere from corporate boardroom planning sessions to ordinary investors' kitchen-table discussions.

The Meme is ubiquitous now. Reporters are reaching into their Rolodexes to find "experts" whose chronic pessimism had discredited them in the 1990s. The leader of the claque is Alan Abelson, the star columnist at America's most influential financial weekly, *Barron's.* Two new stars were elevated to the pantheon: David Tice of the short-selling Prudent Bear Fund and Robert Shiller, whose thoughts on "irrational exuberance," high price/earnings ratios, and general bearishness are in much demand on the TV networks.

December 6, 2000: The Meme is spreading like a viral pandemic. More and more are being infected. The big shoes of the Fed chairman are higher off the ground than the Nasdaq, already down 50 percent from its Y2K high. The only thing lower than the Nasdaq is the record of the New York Knicks, whose center fights with his own teammates when he does not get the ball. Alan Greenspan and Patrick Ewing have too much hubris for their positions. They could switch roles, and everyone would benefit.

December 7, 2000: We send Size 12 basketball shoes to Greenspan and suggest that he trade places with the big center of the Knicks. We send him *The Education of a Speculator* as a further gesture of goodwill.

January 2, 2001: We receive an e-mail: "I've been reading your stock market column on the Internet, and I liked the one where you said you were going to buy a googol of Internet stocks on margin. I called my broker from my cell phone. I tried to say, 'Buy me such-and-such stocks.' But instead of this I shouted—I did not say, but I shouted—in such a loud voice that all the passers-by turned around: 'JUST . . . SELL . . . EVERYTHING!' "

January 3, 2001: The Nasdaq rises 324 points. The reader who sold everything is lost! Like a pestilence, the Meme relentlessly pursues both those in its path and those who flee from it. No one is safe.

February 7, 2001: A box and a letter arrive from the Fed. "Thank you very much for sending the sneakers to Chairman Greenspan. However, it is against our ethics policy to accept gifts, and we are accordingly returning them herewith along with your book."

We wonder whether the chairman scrupled to return the book by the professor of irrational exuberance, Robert Shiller, who told us he sent a copy to him.

April 4, 2001: When a plague overwhelms a city, people trying to escape only carry the disease to new places. So, too, the market has resumed its slide. The value of the U.S. stock market has fallen by $5 trillion—31 percent—in just over a year since its March 24, 2000, peak. It makes us feel so weak, so ignorant, so small. But that is what the Meme wants!

August 31, 2001: I awoke from a restless sleep last night and heard a chilling voice chanting in the corner of my room: "You can't trust yourself, can't trust the Street, can't trust the CEO, can't trust your broker, can't trust the market." I turned on the light. The voice fell silent. No one was there.

September 15, 2001: Unspeakable horror. On September 11, a group of Islamic fanatics destroyed the World Trade Center and one side of the Pentagon, the very heart of America's military power. Everyone is in a state of shock, practically immobilized by fear. The attack destroyed communications links in lower Manhattan, the location of the New York Stock Exchange, and the market has shut down indefinitely. All airliners and crop dusters have been grounded. Nobody wants to leave home anyway. In Manhattan, the few open hotels, restaurants, and theaters are deserted. The terrorists are the very ones President Clinton failed to deal with after the attacks on our embassies.

September 16, 2001: A strange trio appeared on television today. Robert Rubin, Jack Welch, and even Warren Buffett are on the side of the bulls. Rubin "sees long-term strength," and Welch says the United States is "the best place in the world to invest." With reluctant optimism, the Nebraska icon himself opined that it would be "crazy" to sell stocks now. If only he had not added: "If prices would fall significantly, there are some things I might buy," he might have helped stanch the market's hemorrhage. Then again, there are rumors that if the market declines, Buffett will make $500 million. I am not relieved, but frightened and haunted, by what this trio has said.

Then there are the eerie charts. Loews Corporation reportedly lost hundreds of millions of dollars in the last half of the 1990s by betting on market declines. Loews Co-Chairman Lawrence Tisch often perused a chart showing the Dow at the time of the 1929 crash and Japan's Nikkei when it began its tumble from 40,000 to 10,000. The chart now finally bears a macabre resemblance to the Dow and Nasdaq.

September 21, 2001, Morning: Last night, President Bush gave what many called the finest American presidential address ever. He said that our grief had turned to anger, and our anger to resolution; that we would bring our enemies to justice, or bring justice to our enemies. The market shot up on his speech. But then the Meme called on one of its brothers in France to explode a chemicals factory. With the terror that had already spread, the explosion was more than enough to cause the greatest decline in market history.

I was short the naked put, and there was a special open that might have killed me. My brokers seem to be cousins with the Meme, and ordered me to cover up my nakedness.

September 21, 2001, Evening: Ah! The Meme would make of us what we have made of the horse and of the ox: its chattels, its slaves, its food. Woe to us! But nevertheless, the animal sometimes revolts against the one who has subjugated it. . . .

The little nail can topple an empire. But the empire, when it knows that it needs to protect itself, can fight back and accomplish marvels. Scientists first split the atom to beat the Nazis. The countries of the world have finally awakened to the fact that if they do not defend the technology and the trade that are the Western way, then freedom itself will vanish. The market gained back almost everything it lost during the day. The brainwashing of the West by the Meme has ended. I predict that there will be a gigantic rally in the market from the Dow 8235 level reached today, and that the Meme, like Frankenstein and many other monsters, will die in the fire that looked to be its greatest victory.

January 8, 2002: The Dow is now at 10,150, in an abundance of delight. The puts that were selling at 100 to 200 have gone down to pennies. It is the same as with the Thai banks that I owned during 1997. But this time, I am short, not long, and the profit is mine, and the loss is the Meme's. The Meme has blown itself up. It is dead.

March 9, 2002: I look at the morning newspaper. A headline catches my eye: "Buffett: 'No feasting on this market.' " I read on. " 'Our restrained enthusiasm for these securities is matched by decidedly lukewarm feelings about the prospects for stocks in general over the next decade or so,' Buffett wrote in his annual letter to shareholders. 'Charlie [Munger] and I believe that American business will do fine over time, but think that today's equity prices presage only moderate returns for investors.' "[14]

No . . . no . . . no! Without a doubt, the Meme is not dead! When will it die? Only when people realize they must think for themselves: To count for themselves. To believe in their abilities to create. To live longer and better. To lend money to the men and women with the good ideas.

March 31, 2002: The market is up almost 20 percent from the low it set after the World Trade Center attack last year. Perhaps the Meme and his darkness are finally gone.

July 23, 2002: I am so sad I can hardly get out of bed. I sleep to escape the Meme, who now seems to rule my waking hours. I bought stocks after the panic last September, and neglected to sell them before going abroad. Upon my return several months later, I find that my accounts have dwindled to pathetic shadows of what they were. I am afraid, deeply afraid.

September 10, 2002: Tomorrow is the anniversary of the World Trade Center attack, and everyone is in dread that something even more terrible will happen. A dirty bomb, perhaps, spewing radiation? S&P futures rise 10 points and close at 911. Today's New York Lottery numbers are 9-1-1. Any rational person would call them coincidences. But maybe we have gone beyond rationality. Maybe the Meme has signed his name.

September 17, 2002: A thousand unspeakably horrible stories of evil hidden in the lights and flash of the 1990s boom are crawling out, pulled out of the darkness by prosecutors and the media. Dennis Kozlowski, the CEO of Tyco and a golden boy of corporate America, has been indicted with his chief financial officer for bilking the company of $600 million. According to the company's own SEC filing, Kozlowski billed Tyco for his wife's $1 million birthday party on the island of Sardinia. The details included a welcoming line of gladiators and a waiter pouring Stolichnaya vodka into an ice sculpture of a boy with the liquid dispensed through the penis. The Kozlowskis did invite a few Tyco executives, and regarded it as a business expense.

The Meme loves it. I can hear its sarcastic laugh.

October 2, 2002: Hardly a week has gone by this year without a fresh disclosure of secret deals, false earnings statements, or frauds committed in broad daylight under the noses of corporate directors. The U.S. Justice Department has opened more than 400 investigations into possible corporate fraud since the beginning of 2000, and has charged more than 500 people with corporate crimes. Enron's chief financial officer has made a court appearance in handcuffs, as have Tyco's CEO and CFO. The former controller of WorldCom pleaded guilty to cooking the books to come up with $5 billion in fraudulent profits, and is facing a five-year prison term. More analysts are under investigation nowadays than are writing research reports—not that anyone believes the reports any more.

Global Crossing, WorldCom, Enron—all golden 1990s stocks, all bankrupt now. The Meme feeds on the news. I sense him growing stronger and bolder. He has made the stock market his food. Just looking at the numbers make my head ache. Nasdaq: down 3,908 points from the high of early 2000 to the low on October 4, 2002. The Dow: down to 7,528 from 11,700.

Time Line of a Meme

Date	Action
December 5, 1996	Federal Reserve Chairman Alan Greenspan opens Pandora's box with "irrational exuberance" speech; makes case for targeting the market's "wealth effect."
October 20, 1997	U.S. Justice Department sues Microsoft for requiring computer makers to install the company's Internet Explorer browser if they want to license Windows 95.
May 18, 1998	United States, 20 states file antitrust case against Microsoft.
August 7, 1998	Bombings of U.S. embassies in Nairobi, Kenya, and Dar Es Salaam, Tanzania.
August 20, 1998	President orders retaliatory bombing of Osama bin Laden base in Afghanistan; bin Laden leaves one hour before attack.
July and September 1999	Warren Buffett, in private speeches reported in November by *Fortune,* says he would have shot down Orville Wright's plane as a service to capitalists, predicts years of poor performance for U.S. stocks.
November 5, 1999	Judge Thomas Penfield Jackson rules Microsoft used monopoly power to stifle innovation.
February 17, 2000	Greenspan signals further increases in interest rates; says stock market gains may create more demand for goods than can be supplied.
February 18, 2000	*Boiler Room,* a film about a shady brokerage that cheats naïve investors, released. "A thoroughly enjoyable movie which does an excellent job showing us how the lust for money can corrupt us all," wrote critic John Beachem.
March 1, 2000	Warren Buffett writes in annual report to Berkshire Hathaway shareholders that "Equity investors currently seem wildly optimistic in their expectations about future returns."
March 8, 2000	Al Gore wins Democratic presidential nomination, inveighs against big business.
March 10, 2000	Nasdaq peaks at 5048.
March 14, 2000	President Clinton and U.K. Prime Minister Blair call for immediate public access to raw genetic data collected by private companies. "Our genome belongs to every member of the human race," Clinton said. "We must ensure that the profits of human genetic research are measured not in dollars but in the betterment of human life." Nasdaq falls 200 to 4706. "Being a business seems to be an awful thing today," says Craig Venter, founder and president of Celera, a genomics

Date	Action
	firm. "Instead of celebrating that a public company is doing this and releasing it for free, they are complaining because a company is doing it faster than they are and for less money."
April 2000	Robert Shiller, an economist who briefed Greenspan two days before the "irrational exuberance" speech, publishes book of that name, becomes instant media star.
April 3, 2000	Judge Thomas Penfield Jackson rules Microsoft violated antitrust law. Nasdaq drops 349. Next day, Nasdaq falls 575 to 3649; rebounds to close at 4148.
October 12, 2000	Suicide bombers attack the *USS Cole* in the Yemeni port of Aden.
November 7–December 13, 2000	United States gripped with uncertainty as Florida presidential election ballots are counted and recounted. Gore concedes election to Bush on December 13. Nasdaq loses 17% in the intervening five weeks, S&P drops 5%.
September 11, 2001	Islamic terrorists destroy the World Trade Center, World Financial Center, and much of lower Manhattan; Pentagon attacked.
September 21, 2001	U.S. stocks conclude their worst week in 70 years.
December 2001	Enron files for bankruptcy protection.
January 2002	Global Crossing files for bankruptcy protection.
June 2002	Adelphia files for bankruptcy protection. CEO arrested on fraud charges.
June 2002	Arthur Anderson convicted of obstructing justice in Enron fraud case, can no longer audit public companies.
July 2002	WorldCom files for bankruptcy protection. CFO and controller arrested on fraud charges.
September 2002	Tyco's former CEO and CFO charged with looting the company of $600 million.

Ah, I understand it all now. The Meme knew all along that the contagious optimism of the 1990s had left no one able to withstand a decline. It didn't want any short-sellers still solvent when the market finally went down. Now, the market and business are subjects of public contempt.

The passing of the 1990s' ebullience has left a vacuum. Viktor Frankl said, "Unlike an animal, man is not told by drives and instincts what he must do. And in contrast to man in former times, he is no longer told by traditions and values what he should do. Now, knowing neither what he must do nor what he should do, he sometimes does not even know what he basically wishes to do. Instead, he wishes to do what other people do—which is conformism—or he does what other people wish him to do—which is totalitarianism." I fear this will not end well.

2

EARNINGS PROPAGANDA

The poor bastard didn't even know that 10 percent of the net was 10 percent of nothing.

—Mario Puzo, *The Last Don*[1]

Let's start at the very beginning. The one thing that everyone, from the most uninformed layperson to the most erudite professor, knows about the stock market is that earnings determine returns. Chapter 1 of every finance textbook, Lecture 1 of every Investment 101 class, and every news dispatch all agree:

- Earnings and the market move up and down together.
- The greater the earnings increases, the higher the market's return.
- When earnings are up, it is time to buy stocks, and when earnings are down, it is time to sell.
- When the market's price/earnings (P/E) ratio is high, it is time to sell.

Each of these axioms is false. As you'll see, each is completely opposite to the actual empirical relations. Almost everything investors are taught about the relation between earnings and stock market returns, whether in business schools or on the stock market pages of newspapers, is wrong.

Why do people so readily embrace these fallacies? Like all propaganda, they have an appealing, superficial plausibility. The interests of those who promote propaganda are always diametrically opposed to those of the propaganda's targets. What better way to maintain the propagandist's power and profits than to encourage investors to buy and sell stocks in ways that further shift the wealth to the propagandists?

It is true that professionals value stocks based on a discounted stream of earnings, cash flows, and dividends. But that is one of those maxims, such as "Never be disrespectful to authority," that contains enough misinformation to cause abundant harm if the investor follows it to the letter without considering the rest of the picture.

Stock moves from one day to the next are primarily related to transient factors and random changes. In short-term periods, the market tends to go down after several days of excessive optimism, and it tends to go up after a similar run of excessive pessimism. Attributing these swings in optimism and pessimism to earnings would be incorrect. It would also be dysfunctional, because no matter whether news reports say stocks are going up on earnings optimism or down on earnings pessimism, these assertions amount to nothing more than an invitation to trade—and to trade the wrong way. If the public were to realize this, however, it might also figure out that its interests would be better served by less frequent trading—and that would mean less power and fewer perks for the more successful and powerful players.

In addition to maintaining Wall Street in its accustomed comfort, the earnings-returns fallacy gives an opening to other classes of players with different incentives: those who have no truck with American enterprise and markets. A poor earnings report always brings out the chronic pessimists, who seem to relish the idea that business stinks and that stocks will fall. It gives them one more off-the-wall reason that the American economy has been, is, or will be much worse than it appears on the surface. A whole herd of stale financial academicians with their own money safe, though stagnant, in T-bills are always ready with flawed studies showing that when P/Es are above the levels of the 1930s, the market is likely to fall dramatically. When P/Es get high and stocks by chance go down in some subsequent period, how these scholars swell with pride.

These studies, in turn, energize the value boys, who still revere Benjamin Graham even though his methods enabled him to go broke at least twice and kept most of his followers out of the bull market of the 1980s and 1990s, when the Dow rose 14-fold. The Rea-Graham mutual fund actually put Graham's methods into practice in 1976. Investors who put money in the fund at inception would have had two-thirds less 10 years later than if they had put the same amount in the S&P 500, with dividends reinvested.

If only stocks would be down when past, current, and future earnings look great, the sponsors and champions of these fallacies would be in ecstasy. Unfortunately for them, things never work out that way. As they wait for that sweet spot in time, they find they miss all the great accretions in wealth, much to their seething resentment. There is no hatred more virulent than that of old guard members who have stood idly by watching more vigorous minds replace them in the firmament.

Fuzzy Measures

The truth is, there is just too much uncertainty, latitude, and fuzziness in the level, timing, and volatility of earnings comparisons and expectations to place undue reliance on them. Consider this scene from Mario Puzo's *The Last Don*. The studio big is talking to Ernest Vail, the gifted but naïve best-selling author: "I smell a big hit. And remember—you have 10 percent of the net. You have a natural flair. You can get rich on this picture, especially if it wins the Academy." (Previously the big had told Claudia, the heroine, that the script was "a piece of _____.")

Claudia, like a select few investors, and now the readers of this book, knew better. She "could see Vail swallow the hook. The poor bastard didn't even know that 10 percent of the net was 10 percent of nothing."

The catch to getting a percentage of net was highlighted by a 1989 article in *Los Angeles Lawyer*.[2] The authors, Steven Sills and Ivan Alexrod, wrote that fewer than 5 percent of films showed a profit for "net participation purposes." In just one example, the 1994 film *Forrest Gump* was one of the most successful movies of all time, grossing some $650 million. Winston Groom, the author, had a contract to receive 3 percent of net profits. But like Ernest Vail and the many investors who have watched with amazement as the value of their shares vanishes along with corporate earnings, Groom was astonished to find Paramount reporting a $60 million loss on the movie. Paramount had charged a 32 percent commission on *Forrest Gump* "to cover costs of future films that might fail." (The film's star, Tom Hanks, more experienced in the ways of Hollywood and perhaps benefiting from better legal advice, negotiated a share of the gross. As for Groom, he settled his lawsuit against Paramount for a promise of a share of the gross in a *Gump* sequel that never materialized.)

Vail and Groom both learned the hard way about the all-too-ephemeral nature of earnings. Unfortunately, financial life and death often hang in the balance.

Testing the Beliefs

Shrewd articles know that they will not get far in life by relying on conventional explanations of market moves. But the great majority of investors are deceived on both the big and the small aspects of this relation. To ensure that our readers do not fall prey to the deceptions, we tested each one of the commonly held beliefs enumerated earlier.

First, it is necessary to examine the actual relations between earnings and market returns. There are many different leads, lags, and ratios to be tested. The best way to reveal these relationships is with a scatter diagram, as discussed in Chapter 8. If these data tend to lie close to the line of best fit, then there is a strong relation. If the data appear to lie in a shapeless mass around the line, there is little or no relation. Each of the charts uses earnings data from the Standard & Poor's Securities Price Index Record for 2001, updated with current figures, and returns data from the London Business School's comprehensive database of global markets, discussed in detail in Chapter 9.

We start with the relations in the same year. Stocks are supposed to go down when earnings are down and go up with earnings are up. But they don't. In fact, the opposite relation holds:

1. If reported S&P 500 earnings rise in a year, the S&P 500 is likely to perform *worse* than average that year.
2. If reported earnings *fall* in a year, the S&P 500 is likely to perform *better* than average that year.

The inverse relation is shown in Figure 2.1. Notice how the line of best fit slopes gently from the northwest quadrant to the southeast. This is the hallmark of what statisticians call a *negative correlation*. When earnings are down, there are many more occasions when stocks are up than when stocks are down. (Unless otherwise noted, both the *y* variable and the *x* variable—the dependent and independent, respectively—will be measured as percentage changes throughout this book.)

Earnings declined in 22 of the 65 years studied. The average return for the S&P 500 during each of those down years was up 14.2 percent. This compares

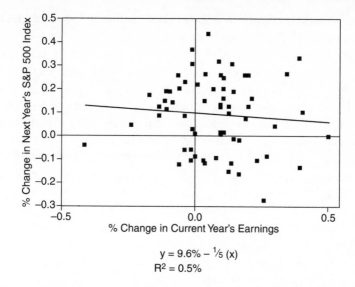

$$y = 9.6\% - \tfrac{1}{5}(x)$$
$$R^2 = 0.5\%$$

Figure 2.1   Change in Current Year's Earnings as Predictor of Change in Next Year's SPX, 1937–2001. *Source:* **Standard & Poor's Security Price Index Record.**

with an average annual return of 4.9 percent in the other 43 years, when earnings increased.

We used regression analysis to calculate an equation that expresses this slightly inverse relation between earnings and the next year's market return as a line of best fit: S&P 500 return = 9.6 percent minus one-fifth of the annual percentage change in S&P earnings.

$$9.6\% - 1/5\ (\text{S\&P 500}\ \Delta)$$

For example, say S&P 500 earnings rose 22 percent in a year. Plugging that number into our formula gives 9.6 percent − 1/5 (22 percent), or a predicted rise of 5.2 percent for the S&P 500. (Bear in mind that the upward drift in the market averages 9.6 percent a year, so a 5.2 percent gain would be subpar.) If S&P earnings *fell* 22 percent in a year, we would expect the S&P to return 9.6 percent − 1/5 (−22 percent), or 14 percent.

The equation explains some 5 percent of the total variation in stock prices from normal. Another way of saying this is that if a person knew nothing about earnings change in a year, the best forecast of S&P 500 returns in 2002 would be 9.6 percent—the average drift per year. That forecast would have a wide margin of error, which would be reduced by 0.5 percent by using the earnings formula. A reduction at least as large as that would occur a mere 7 in 100 times through chance variations alone.

Given that earnings and S&P 500 returns are inversely related during a year, then, the question arises whether relations based on quarterly numbers are predictive. No. The same inverse relation holds. The scatter diagram of quarterly percentage changes in earnings versus the next quarter's S&P 500 return shows this. Again, the dots cluster in the northwest and southeast parts of the graph, indicating a negative correlation.

If earnings rise in a quarter, the S&P 500 is likely to perform below average in the next quarter. If earnings fall in a quarter, the S&P 500 is likely to outperform in the next quarter, as shown in Figure 2.2.

Using the data for the 65-year period, during which time the trend of quarterly S&P 500 returns was 2.5 percent a quarter, we worked out a regression formula that roughly predicts S&P 500 returns based on earnings changes. The best formula for predicting the expected change in the S&P index from one quarter to the next is:

Expected S&P return in next quarter = 2.5% less 1/16 of the year-over-year percent change in S&P quarterly earnings

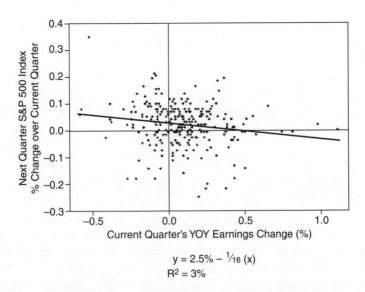

$$y = 2.5\% - \tfrac{1}{16}(x)$$
$$R^2 = 3\%$$

Figure 2.2   Change in Current Quarter's Earnings as Predictor of Change in Next Year's SPX, 1937–2001. *Source:* **Standard & Poor's Security Price Index Record.**

This predictive relation explains 1 percent of the total variation in S&P 500 Index prices. Because this calculation is based on 258 quarters, compared with the 40 observations that went into the yearly relation reported previously, the chances that this one is due to chance alone are less than 1 in 200.

While we were examining earnings and returns data up, down, and upside in search of relations, we discovered an unexpected predictive link (see Figure 2.3). It is an old saw in the market that stocks have predicted nine of the last five recessions. But as we analyzed all the possible relations between earnings and market returns, we discovered that S&P returns in one quarter anticipate profit changes in the next. The relation here is:

Next quarter's earnings change = 2% plus 1/3 of the previous
quarter's stock return

The preceding formula explains 3 percent of the variations in earnings changes, and this is a highly statistically significant result for the 258 quarters considered. The relation, of course, is good for predicting earnings, not returns.

We ran our conclusions by one of our readers, Bill Egan, a PhD whose specialty is a rare combination of analytical chemistry and applied statistics. Not only that, he is married to a psychometrician, so statistical acumen runs in the family. The Egans ran some calculations of their own on independent

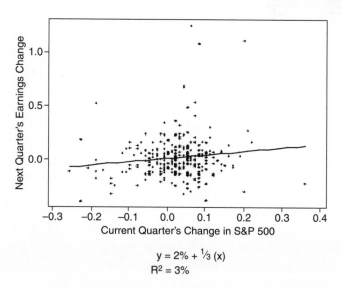

$$y = 2\% + \tfrac{1}{3}(x)$$
$$R^2 = 3\%$$

Figure 2.3   S&P 500 Predicts Earnings: Current Quarter's Change in S&P 500 as Predictor of Change in Next Year's Earnings. *Source:* **Niederhoffer Investments.**

data sets that verified our conclusions. Using weekly data from 1962 to 1994, the Egans also found that the return in the S&P 500 is good at predicting future earnings but that earnings moves themselves are inversely related to future S&P 500 changes.

These regression equations do not explain past variations in stock returns; they merely account for a portion. But this knowledge, scant as it is, is better than being buffeted by the financial media like a tumbleweed in the wind, and far better indeed than to end up like the unprofitable scriptwriter Ernest Vail because you have tied your fortunes directly to "net."

Irrational Ratios

The P/E-return relation follows like a carriage behind a horse from the earnings-return relation. Low P/Es, in the popular mind, tend to be associated with good returns and high P/Es with bad returns. That idea figured prominently in the famous "irrational exuberance" speech of Fed Chairman Alan Greenspan on December 5, 1996. Yale University Professor Robert Shiller had used the phrase irrational exuberance when he presented a P/E study to Greenspan at the Fed the day before. Shiller, in his 2000 book *Irrational Exuberance,* makes the case that high P/Es are associated with inferior performance over the next 10 years and low P/Es are associated with good performance over the next 10 years. He uses 10-year averages of P/Es and 10-year forward returns to derive his conclusions. Because of the high degree of overlap, one might reason that there are not enough observations in a statistical or practical sense to come to any conclusions with a reasonable degree of confidence. After all, in 100 years, there are only 10 independent 10-year periods, and certainly the last 30 years (in which there are three independent nonoverlapping 10-year periods) might be assumed to be more important than the previous 70.

Professor Shiller told us at a luncheon interview that what actually prompted the chairman to cross the long-standing line that had prevented the Fed from fighting stock market battles was a calculated query that he had posed to Greenspan at lunch: "When was the last time a Fed chairman actually commented that he thought the level of stock prices might be too high?"

Counting out the actual relation between broad-market P/E and subsequent stock performance is not as easy a task as it might seem. In March 2002, the price-earnings ratio of the S&P 500 was 29, according to Standard & Poor's; or 40, according to Barron's; or 62, according to Bloomberg. Take your pick. Compare those levels with the 16.1 average over the past 50 years—

or, again, some other number of your choice. You might well ask how it is possible to conclude anything about so mercurial a financial ratio.

There is no easy solution to the problem of such discrepancies in P/E data. Many companies on a calendar year don't report results until mid-April. As a result, it is often difficult to determine whether a particular P/E number reflects the past 12 months of reported earnings or calendar-year earnings. Moreover, it is uncertain whether companies that lost money (and hence have "negative earnings") are included in the overall market's P/E calculation. Yet another problem is that the earnings may be revised subsequently, so that data originally reported are quite different from what eventually appears in summaries, price records, and data sources many years thereafter.

Looking back in time, the P/E-returns link is nebulous. The P/Es of 30 that prevailed in 1929 and the poor returns in subsequent years are always cited as evidence of a predictive relation. But at the beginning of 1970, the S&P 500 P/E was 16 and the subsequent five-year annualized return was –6 percent per year. At the beginning of 1994, the P/E was 21.3 and the subsequent five-year annualized return was 21 percent.

How can we determine, in a systematic, scientific fashion, the actual relation of P/Es and returns, instead of just relying on anecdotes and vague impressions? The first step in discovering what relations exist, if any, is to use the information that would have been available to an investor when making the decision to buy or sell. We use the printed past copies of the Standard & Poor's Price Index Record for this purpose.[3] The data considered were from 1974 to 2001.

Next, it is necessary to examine scatter diagrams. Figures 2.4, 2.5, and 2.6 show the relation between P/E levels at the opening of a year to S&P 500 returns in subsequent years one, five, and nine.

The charts show the shakiness and time-sensitivity of the P/E-returns relation. In Figures 2.4 and 2.6, which illustrate one-year and nine-year returns, the line slopes down from left to right, showing a slight inverse relationship. In other words, high P/Es have a slightly negative, but statistically insignificant, and almost certainly random, impact on the market in the next one- and nine-year time frames.

In Figure 2.5, the five-year returns chart, the line is horizontal, showing no association between P/Es and returns for the next five years. For that time period, P/Es had no predictive value.

In his 2000 book, *Irrational Exuberance*, Robert Shiller omitted to show the five-year chart or those of any other time frames that showed a positive relationship. Those charts would not have shown irrational exuberance. A

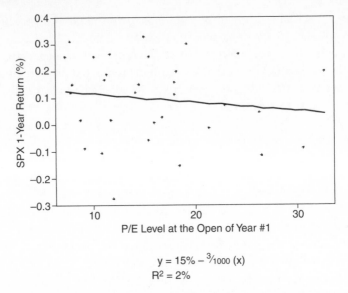

$$y = 15\% - {}^3\!/_{1000}\,(x)$$
$$R^2 = 2\%$$

Figure 2.4   P/E Level at Open of Year One as Predictor of One-Year SPX Return. *Source:* **Standard & Poor's Security Price Index Record.**

further problem with his work is that in a century, you only get 10 nonoverlapping 10-year periods (years 1–10, 11–20, etc.), and thus, statistically there are only 10 data points even though a century of returns is included. As any statistician will tell you, fewer than 30 points is too few to reach a judgment given the variability involved.

In sum, our studies show the relation between P/Es and returns from 1950 to 2001 is completely consistent with randomness.

We are not alone in our conclusion about the lack of a strong relation between P/Es and market returns. Kenneth L. Fisher and Meir Statman, in a definitive study covering the years 1872 through 1999, also concluded that P/Es provide unreliable forecasts of future returns. "There is no statistically significant relation between P/E ratios at the beginning of the year and returns during the following year, or during the following two years," they wrote.[4]

In an e-mail to us, Fisher alluded to the "weird assumptions" underlying Shiller's conclusions. "The Shiller stuff is largely a data mine," he wrote. "It makes no real difference how you redefine high and low P/E, regardless. P/E has no significant predictive power for markets so far into the future that it is enough to drive most folks crazy, that is, longer than five years."

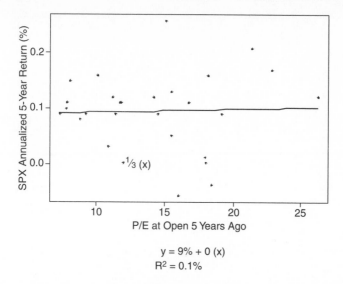

$$y = 9\% + 0 \, (x)$$
$$R^2 = 0.1\%$$

Figure 2.5   P/E Level at Open of Year One as Predictor of Annualized Five-Year SPX Return, 1974–2001. *Source:* **Standard & Poor's Security Price Index Record.**

Because of the way P/Es are calculated, there is a strong bias for the data to show a positive relation. The bias hinges on the little-noted fact that earnings of calendar-year-reporting companies are not released as of year-end. They're released from a month to three months later. If there is a nice positive surprise in these earnings, then the return that year will get a head start. That introduces a bias in favor of the negative correlation that Shiller wished to show.

For example, assume that the P/E for the market is always 10. Thus, on December 31 of each year, the price of a particular stock is 100 and prospective earnings are 10. Assume that in March, surprisingly good earnings of $12 are reported. The price will move to 120 once the earnings are reported. But the P/E in the data files, retrospectively calculated with year-end prices and the earnings announced in March, would be 100 / 12, or 8.5. The stock's "return" that year would already be 20 percent at the time of the earnings report. Thus, low P/Es are associated with high returns. Similarly, high P/Es will tend to be associated with low returns.

We have brought this bias up in meetings with many academics who have studied these relations, including Professor Shiller. Invariably, the professors respond that they adjust for this bias when they can by using price

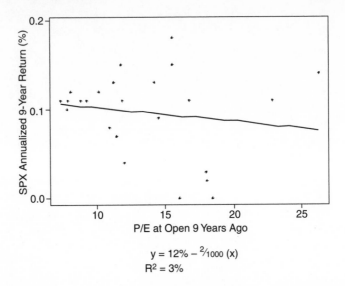

$$y = 12\% - {}^{2}\!/_{1000}\,(x)$$
$$R^2 = 3\%$$

Figure 2.6 P/E Level at Open of Year One as Predictor of Annualized Nine-Year SPX Return, 1978–2001. *Source:* **Standard & Poor's Security Price Index Record.**

data on announcement dates to as great an extent as possible. But adjustments are only possible in recent years. The professors always add something to the effect that the whole thing is nebulous because the only companies that are included in their data are those that reported positive earnings in the years under consideration.

There are so many things wrong with using data such as these that no meeting of the minds is possible between the academics and skeptics like us. As mentioned, there are other biases, such as the look-back bias, that make conclusions based on historic files even more tenuous. No wonder that almost all the practical applications of low P/E/high return funds have shown such dismal performance. Even with all the biases that would tend erroneously to support the P/E-return relation posited by Shiller, the actual data show a correlation close to zero.

The only way that academics have had of supporting such relations is to use numerous overlapping data points in their studies and, in the case of certain academics, to leave out recent data that shows a completely opposite relation from the one that started the war.

Considering that the relation is so weak, why do so many people believe it? Fisher and Statman believe that the answer lies in a psychological phenomenon

SPOTTING CORPORATE EARNINGS PROPAGANDA

To an economist, earnings represent the recurring cash flows that can be paid out to stockholders without reducing the value of the firm. But the earnings reported to stockholders are accounting earnings, subject to numerous conventions and assumptions that permit wide latitude. Furthermore, accounting practices are always evolving. The best minds among accountants, consultants, and managers unfortunately have strong incentives to use their knowledge and talents to develop more dynamic, sophisticated, and opaque accounting techniques. As Darwin and Wallace pointed out with numerous examples, the end result of an adaptation is far removed from its original expression. As a result, explanations of earnings quality contained in books tend to be dated and incongruous.

For example, Haim Levy's excellent text, *Introduction to Investments*, first published in 1980, advises the reader that high-quality earnings are conservative, distributable, stable, ongoing, domestic, understandable, operating, and normal. Low-quality earnings are said to be volatile, liberal, unpredicted, nonrecurring, unrealistic, overstated, complex, offshore, and related to financial transactions. While all these examples are sensible, they lack the compelling sharpness of a firing-line study of current accounting practices such as the *Wall Street Journal* and the better financial publications are always documenting. It is as though a current book on manufacturing were to rely on a study of mid-19th century division-of-labor practices.

Levy's list of "red flags," including long audit reports, reductions in discretionary costs, and changes in accounting practices, seems more appropriate for the new millennium. All the specific examples of overstated assets and understated liabilities, however, can be subsumed under the rubric of excessive accruals relative to cash earnings, as described in this chapter.

To keep the stock price ball in the air, companies must strive to constantly meet analysts' expectations. Accountants often seem to act as promoters of the desired earnings picture rather than as watchdogs or independent checkers. To guard against naïve digestion of earnings reports, good analysts maintain checklists to sort out the good from the bad. We compiled our own list of some currently popular accounting techniques that obscure the picture of a company's financial health.

(continued)

1. **Front-end income loading.** Reporting income from a job immediately although the work will take an extended period of time.
2. **Borrowing.** Using leverage to give the appearance of growth.
3. **Capitalizing costs.** Some companies capitalize costs as assets, then amortize the deferred expenses over future periods. America Online, for example, capitalized the expense of sending out its software to potential future customers rather than expensing the costs as incurred. Firms have substantial discretion as to software development costs, start-up costs, and so forth. Investors should look out for sudden increases in capitalized costs.
4. **Timing costs.** Manipulating discretionary costs such as advertising and R&D to smooth earnings.
5. **Timing sales.** Accelerating or decelerating sales activities to smooth earnings.
6. **Acquisitions Accounting I: Writing off R&D.** When one company buys another company, any excess paid above the acquired company's assets is allocated between specifically designated intangible assets and goodwill. Some firms allocate a large portion of the excess purchase price to an intangible asset called R&D in progress. After the purchase, they write it off and incur a one-time loss. From then on, any benefits derived from such research are not offset against any R&D costs. To get a better overall picture of the company, a good analyst will ignore the write-off, keep R&D as an asset on the balance sheet, and amortize it.
7. **Acquisitions Accounting II: Fuzz.** Combining big acquisitions with cloudy disclosures that make it difficult to compare earnings with previous periods.
8. **Acquisitions Accounting III: Goodwill.** Amortizing goodwill over a long period of time will not affect earnings as much as amortizing it over a short period. Thus companies that can write off goodwill over a longer period have an advantage.
9. **Restructuring charges.** The costs involved in a restructuring are usually expensed immediately. In a "big bath" strategy, companies can "accidentally" overestimate the size of the restructuring reserve, then gradually reverse this error over time, generating a nice stream of noncash income for the future.

10. **Consolidating results.** The widely used "equity" method lets a company report its entire share of a subsidiary's income as part of its own income, without having to report the subsidiary's assets or liabilities on the parent's balance sheet.

11. **Asset impairment charges.** The Financial Accounting Standards Board's Rule 121 requires firms to write down the value of assets on their balance sheets whenever the present value of the projected cash flows to be generated by those assets is less than their book value. This gives management a lot of leeway, because it is management that estimates future cash flows. Managers may write down assets during years when earnings are poor anyway, hoping investors will ignore this as a one-off event. With future depreciation expenses thus reduced, future earnings will look much better.

12. **Accounting for stock options.** Companies have much leeway in deciding whether and how to report executive and employee stock options as an expense. FASB gives a choice of three methods to companies that voluntarily choose to expense options.

13. **Inventories and receivables.** Manipulating reported earnings by playing around with current assets such as accounts receivables and inventory, with apt estimates of the salability of the former and the collectability of the latter.

14. **The storehouse.** Relying on reserves, one-time gains in marketable securities, or sales of assets to smooth earnings.

15. **Timing an accounting method switch.** Adopting new accounting standards early or late to maintain the earnings trend.

16. **Changing auditors.** This can mean that the management wants to use accounting trickery to maintain the earnings trend. The market generally punishes companies that change auditors, as it can give the appearance of impropriety. In the wake of the Enron/Andersen scandal, many firms had the chance to switch from Andersen and be rewarded for it by the market.

S&P's New Standard

The Standard & Poor's securities rating firm has introduced a method of calculating earnings that is designed to reduce earnings distortions. The new measure, called "core earnings," adjusts net income to include:

(continued)

- Expenses from stock-option grants.
- Restructuring changes from ongoing operations.
- Write-downs of depreciable or amortizable operating assets.
- Pension costs.
- R&D expense assumed through acquisitions.

The measure excludes:

- Gains or losses from asset sales.
- Pension gains.
- Unrealized gains or losses from hedging securities.

In some cases, the change would be quite material. GE, for example, reported net income of $1.42 a share in 2001. If the company had excluded gains from pension investments, however, earnings would have been $1.11, according to S&P. Cisco Systems reported net income of 14 cents a share in fiscal 2001, but if the company had included stock-option expenses, that would have been a 35 cent-a-share loss, S&P said.

Between the list of modern techniques of manipulation highlighted here and S&P's core earnings concept, the reader should have a good heads-up on the usual suspects in the early naughties. These might be supplemented with a foundation provided by the excellent books *Quality of Earnings* by Thornton L. O'glove,[5] *Financial Shenanigans* by Howard Schilit,[6] or *The Dark Side of Valuation* by Aswath Damodaran.[7]

known as the "illusion of validity." People are prone to believe and rely on the accuracy of their judgments much more than the facts warrant. Fisher also speculates that people believe in the P/E fantasy because our ancestors found great survival value in being afraid of heights, and they passed along their genes to us. "Anything in a heights framework generates fear," Fisher wrote. Even high P/Es.

Our friend Dr. Brett Steenbarger, professor of psychiatry and behavioral sciences at the SUNY Upstate Medical University in Syracuse, New York, whose primary research interest is multivariate behavioral modeling of the stock market, suggested in a May 2002 e-mail to us that a second type of illusion might be at work:

A group of researchers at the London Business School recently completed a study in which they showed that traders who display a high degree of "illusion of control" also achieve subpar results in their trading.

The way "illusion of control" was measured was by giving the traders a computer game that involved guessing numbers in a sequence and then assessing their confidence re: future success. The traders didn't know that the numbers represented a random walk. So the confident traders were a bit like chart readers who express confidence in reading patterns derived from coin flips.

I would argue that traders and investors focus on earnings numbers for the same reason that dying people focus on the afterlife. It's also the reason why the No. 1 search engine topic immediately after 9/11 was "Nostradamus." In the face of uncertainty, people have a need for understanding and control. They will latch onto any explanation rather than go without one. An illusion of control is better than no perceived control.

This is why panic attack sufferers will construct elaborate hypotheses about their illness. If their attack happens in a mall, they avoid malls; if the attack occurs while thinking about a particular topic, they try to banish that topic from consciousness. The example I use in my book is the patient who had her first attack on the ramp of an interstate highway and who, thereupon, refused to drive on ramps, including those of indoor garages and the like.

Such avoidance caused practical problems for the patient (who stopped driving altogether), but also reinforced the illusion that she could control her anxiety.

Seen from this perspective, when the media goes into a frenzy about the relation between earnings and future stock prices, this can be seen as a response to threat and uncertainty. It provides information about the psychological state of market participants. And that might even be tradable information, though not in the way that the media pundits intend.

Note how the financial news viewer ratings skyrocket in bull markets and during market plunges. Those are the times viewers most feel a need to figure out what to do with their money. They are either missing opportunities or losing money. Latching onto technical and fundamental analysis is their way of searching for answers and gaining control.

Ironically, one could probably use those viewer ratings as a fairly accurate market timing tool!

Student Questioner

When we held our luncheon interview with Dr. Shiller, we expected the sparks to fly. Strangely, Shiller was tentative about the robustness and resilience of his results. He pointed out that one of his students, Bjorn Tuypens, had prepared a paper that questioned the accuracy of his conclusions. "Perhaps the relation has changed or is no longer valid," he told us.

Tuypens' paper, "Stock Market Predictability: A Myth Unveiled," provided further support for our conclusions:

> The use of overlapping data for long-term stock returns, combined with the nonstationary behavior of the dividend yield, gives rise to spurious regression problems when regressing long-term stock returns on dividend yields. . . . This regression (dividend yield versus subsequent one-year and two-year returns) provides additional evidence for the argument that the strong long-run forecasting power of the Campbell-Shiller regressions is a myth, due to the use of overlapping data in too small a data set.[8]

On the other hand, Shiller told us that he remains confident that the market is in for a period of abnormally low returns. He also expressed confidence that "econometric studies will verify the significance of the negative P/E relationships" that he and his colleagues have found. He appeals here to an *ito* process, a highly complicated, almost impossible-to-test relation involving what is called *stochastic calculus*. Since the essence of such results is that current P/Es influence returns in distant years much more than they influence current years, the relation seems to us to be completely implausible. Furthermore, such topsy-turvy relations relative to time are completely opposite to any that we have found in real-life applications involving the calculation and testing of tens of thousands of such relations.

It seems more likely, for example, that the P/E of the market as of year-end 2002 will have a much stronger influence on 2003 returns than the P/E that prevailed in 1993. Only a professor could argue against this.

Shiller emphasized to us that his current interests are in other fields.

How Earnings Propaganda Works

 The adherence of investors and academics to causal relations that are completely opposite from the empirical facts raises some deep why and how questions.

Our explanation draws on lessons learned from the study of propaganda. The propagandists of the market, who specialize in fear and greed to the same degree as advertising pros and political propagandists do, make efficient use of these spurious relations. When we first reported in 2002 in our column for CNBC Money that the relation between P/Es and returns was almost entirely random—contrary to the standard paradigm that guarantees that the public will always be leaning the wrong way—our ideas generated considerable skepticism. Incredulous readers of our columns checked our credentials and wrote in to say that Laurel, who earned a bachelor's degree in fine arts, should go back to playing the piano and that Vic should stick to racquet sports, as his economics analysis was as bad as his hedge fund management. We were told that we had completely misconstrued what the academics say about earnings: that it is expectation that matters, not realization. The kindest thing said about our theory was that we had simply rediscovered and put in convoluted, abstract prose the simple maxim that you should buy when there is blood in the streets and sell when the trumpets are sounding.

Still other readers objected that stock prices are determined by expectations of earnings rather than the actual earnings themselves. As earnings come in, they might provide little information about future expectations and thus would not be expected to have an impact.

We do not buy that for a minute. Revisions in expectations must be highly correlated with the actual reported comparisons of the earnings themselves. Furthermore, numerous academic studies of the impact of earnings revisions on the S&P 500 have been made, and none of these have found any relationship between revisions in earnings and future returns. (One curious result that has been found is that the variability of the revisions in earnings expectations has a weak positive relation to returns several years later.)

The article also brought a deluge of invective from the bearish camp. The following was typical:

> I think you guys are liers [sic] or just bad reporters. If you are a lier, you are a bad reporter. So you must be both a bad reporter and a bad lier. Get a conscience. You sound like you are long on your investments. . . . One can only conclude your extreme irrational almost military-like bias can only mean that you are long, you lost lots of money, and are holding on till death do you and your money part.

The irony is that on April 1, the day we received this letter, we had a massive short position in the market, which we memorialized in a CNBC Money dispatch that day.

The kind of name-calling employed in that message is a typical propaganda technique. Propaganda induces individuals to take actions that benefit the messenger more than the listener. *The Fine Art of Propaganda,* a 1939 classic on the topic published by the Institute of Propaganda Analysis, outlined seven basic techniques to disseminate false information.[9] To simplify the ideas enough for young students in public schools, the book gave each technique a catchy name: "name-calling," "glittering generality," "transfer," "testimonial," "plain folks," "card stacking," and "bandwagon."

Here is our take on how each technique is used to disseminate the fallacies involving the relation of earnings and P/E to returns:

Name-calling: "Only a blindfolded bull would buy stocks at these levels."

Glittering generality: "There's no value in the market with these stratospheric P/Es."

Transfer (invokes a name or symbol): "Until P/Es fall to Graham & Dodd levels, we're forecasting a Dow of 100."

Testimonial: "The oldest and canniest investor I know is waiting for P/Es to fall by another 50 percent before he considers buying."

Plain folks: "I don't know much, but the last time P/Es were this high and dividend yields were this low was year-end 1928."

Card stacking: "P/Es were above 20 at the beginning of 1929 and stocks fell 40 percent in the next two years." (Forget that P/Es were the exact same level at the beginning of 1950, when prices rose 40 percent over the next two years.)

Bandwagon: "None of the hedge fund managers at the conference in Bar Harbor will touch these high P/Es with a 10-foot pole."

How frequently is misinformation on the relation of earnings to market returns transmitted? Millions of articles contain variants of the misleading belief that the better the market earnings, the better the market return. Our own search, using the Internet search engine www.google.com, found 2.7 million articles containing the words "U.S. stocks," with about 1.3 million also containing the word "earnings" or "profit." Of those, 323,000 contained "optimism" or synonyms thereof. Some 75,000 articles contained a combination of the words "earnings" or "profit" and "pessimism" or a synonym. No doubt, some of these word conjunctions had nothing to do with our topic. But we can make a rough estimate that the lie appears in half of all stories that mention earnings and the market.

Why Do the Beliefs Persist?

Regardless of the propaganda techniques, rational people usually have a mechanism to overturn false beliefs that hinges on the prospering of those who can differentiate truth from falsehood. In this particular field, however, it is hard to make such a distinction because the things that people observe most clearly are P/Es and returns of individual stocks. They know that when earnings are bad for companies they own stock in, that they suffer losses, and conversely, when earnings are good, they enjoy gains. This is true. The problem comes when they try to generalize this to the broad market.

Such generalizations suffer from logical errors: the fallacy of composition, the fallacy of aggregation, and the ecological fallacy.

The following trains of thought show the fallacy of composition:

- "Since I can see the concert better by standing on my seat, it follows that if everybody stood on their seats, we would all have a better view."
- "Phil and Mary are excellent singers. They will form an excellent duo."
- "The person who gets a gold medal is happy. If everyone got gold medals they would all be happy."

This error crops up in investors' thinking as a confusion between what people know about individual stocks and what they know about the market: "If good earnings are good for my stock, and bad earnings are bad, then when earnings for companies that make up the broad market are generally good, that's bullish and when earnings are generally woeful, that's bearish."

The fallacy of aggregation is the assumption that what holds true on a small scale is also true on a large scale. The fallacy is usually illustrated by pointing out the error of the statement that a six-foot man cannot drown in a pond with an average depth of one foot. For our purposes, a better example is that of the isolated miner who picks away at a mountain trying to find gold. It is true that the more he picks away, the less the size of that mountain. However, without taking into account soil erosion, weather patterns, landslides, and sloughing, as well as the feedback that occurs between the mountain and efforts of hundreds of similar miners, we cannot make any assumptions about the relation of one miner's activity to the size of the mountain.

Similarly, everyone knows that individual stock prices are related in some direct way to the favorability of earnings. But to generalize from that to the system of the stock market and total profits in the economy requires hundreds of leaps that ignore effects just as great as landslides down a mountain; for example, the landslides of interest-rate rises and declines, tax policy changes, and Federal Reserve actions.

A related error is the ecological fallacy—the assumption that what is true on the large scale is true on the small scale. This mistake is common to most studies of diet in a given population. A typical study will conclude, for example, that the amount of fiber intake is positively related to longevity. The finding, however, cannot be particularized to the recommendation that an individual in a particular country should eat more fiber to live a longer life.

Time to Get Out (Artist: Susan Slyman, 2001).

Our finding that earnings changes and stock prices are inversely related brings disbelief because of the ecological fallacy. Those who hear it particularize the finding. They say that, if true, this inverse relationship would mean that individual stock returns are also inversely related to earnings changes, just as the health studies fail to note differences between the activities and eating habits of individuals within the individual countries. Victims of the ecological fallacy fail to take into account industry differences and time differences within the stock market. Thus, because they cannot accept that our inverse relation could possibly be true, they reject it out of hand as antithetical to what they know is true.

Another reason for the longevity of these mistaken notions undoubtedly is that earnings are defined so vaguely as to defy scrutiny of any supposed relation to market returns. Should the investor look at year-over-year comparisons or reported earnings relative to expectations? Current expectations, or initial expectations? Official expectations or whisper numbers? Earnings relative to the stage in the business cycle, or relative to industry peers? And which earnings are key? Operating? Pro forma? GAAP? Cyclically adjusted? Net?

The vagueness about precisely which earnings are being discussed barely hints at the problem. Our friend Larry Leeds provided some insight into the complexities involved. Larry has been running a hedge fund specializing in stocks of retailers and has managed to garner a seven-year annual return of 42 percent as of year-end 2002. He likes to buy stocks of companies that report poor first-quarter numbers. Often, their Christmas season was so good that they have nothing in stock to sell, and so they miss their comparisons. Retailers that report good first quarters still had plenty of good winter merchandise to sell because their Christmas was terrible.

Furthermore, companies have developed multiple ways to paint the rosiest possible picture of their finances. Chief executives who guide research analysts' earnings estimates down so that their firms can beat them later are practicing a nice form of card stacking. Such "positive surprises" have the virtue of triggering the systems and recommendations of quants who have found, based on stale studies, that such earnings surprises have predictive significance.

The Escalation of Hide-and-Seek

Corporate earnings propaganda has long been part of Wall Street routine, and reporters love to catch companies at the game. As a wire service editor, Laurel observed firsthand the corporate art of timing an earnings announcement. If GAAP earnings are up, the company releases its statement just before or after the close, and schedules a telephone conference an hour later so executives can issue "guidance" on the next quarter to reporters and analysts. But if even pro forma earnings are poor, then the time to announce is late at night, after most news organizations have closed up shop or have only one reporter on duty. The best time of all for discreet announcements of bad news is late on a Friday, after newspaper editors have put the weekend business sections to bed and left the office.

Any junior reporter is expected to find the obvious red herrings in earnings reports. In the first week on the job, the reporter learns that a glowing account of record sales in the first paragraph is often followed by understated references to a decline in profits or margins. No self-respecting beginner would ever miss the announcement buried in the seventeenth paragraph that the auditors quit rather than sign off on the latest financials, or that Chief Executive Smith, 49, is retiring immediately to pursue other interests and spend more time with the family.

But an arms race of sorts developed. The more sophisticated financial reporters became, the better the weapons the companies used to fool them. Companies developed an amazing capacity to report earnings that top those of the corresponding quarter of the previous year. General Electric, for example, reported 38 consecutive increases in quarterly earnings beginning in the third quarter of 1993. From the first quarter of 1995 through the third quarter of 2000, all of the increases were between 11 percent and 16 percent, except for gains of 18 percent, 21 percent, and 20 percent, respectively, in the first three quarters of 2000. One theory is that General Electric puts its profits in silos and takes them out as needed. But General Electric's practice of "managing earnings" was just the beginning. As the twentieth century drew to a close, a rage developed among corporate finance officers for pro forma statements, off-balance sheet debt, and off-income statement losses.

Enron was the acknowledged leader in the new way of accounting. "General Electric's next chairman may want to borrow a lesson or two from Enron, which has been voted America's most innovative company five years running and displaced General Electric as the 'best managed company' in *Fortune* magazine's last 'most admired' survey," wrote management consultant Gary Hamel admiringly in the September 18, 2000, *Wall Street Journal.* Investors who probed too deeply risked being publicly called an "ass_____," as then-Enron Chairman Jeff Skilling called Richard Grubman, a Boston hedge fund manager who dared ask for a balance sheet at an April 17, 2001, earnings news conference. (We received similar treatment when we requested a no-holds-barred interview with a General Electric executive in 2002. Not only were we informed that all their executives were too busy to meet with us; we were told never to call General Electric again.)

Within the weeks after Enron's dramatic plunge from stock market star to bankruptcy in November 2001, however, all earnings reports came under suspicion, even those of General Electric and other companies that for years had been above reproach. Newly skeptical investors beat one company after another to within an inch of its life. General Electric, the world's most highly valued company, fell 39 percent in the first nine months of 2002. Criticism of General Electric's accounting was so widespread that the company developed a new mantra: "We manage companies, not earnings." IBM dropped 6 percent on February 15, 2002, when the *New York Times* reported that the computer maker didn't disclose that fourth-quarter earnings had been increased by the sale of a subsidiary product line.[10] Tyco International Ltd., Computer Associates, and Sprint Corporation were caught up in the chill.

The truth is that many companies try to prettify their earnings one way or another. In the sidebar (pp. 55–58), we enumerate some considerations to take into account when evaluating reported earnings.

Wall Street's Cheery Analysts

Investors once counted on analysts to provide objective evaluations of corporate self-portraits. But in the late 1990s, analysts had been drafted into becoming rainmakers for their firms' underwriting departments. Gloomy reports were banished to avoid the possibility of lost public offering fees. Statistics on the number of buy, hold, and sell recommendations for the years 1997–2002 put this in perspective (see Table 2.1).

Until the market's devastating plunge in 2000–2002, the media largely ignored the co-opting of the analysts. Analysts had become celebrities, and celebrities are valued commodities in the news business. Journalists were under pressure to beat rival news organizations in snagging interviews with bulls like Henry Blodget and Abby Joseph Cohen. During the waning days of the twentieth century, hot news was having a sexy reporter speak "direct from the NYSE floor" to an analyst who just upgraded a Nasdaq-listed company recently taken public by his firm. The public's appetite for such material was limitless; as recently as the year 2000, the Silicon Investor Web site hosted 26 chat boards devoted to the leading business network, CNBC.

Wall Street's brokerages have always distributed analyst reports as lagniappes, to make the inflated commissions they charge to retail customers and money management firms more palatable. Before the Securities and Exchange Commission took steps in 1999 to eliminate the practice, analysts treated favored customers to not-yet-public information gleaned from private conversations with corporate executives.

Analysts ended up taking the fall for the Internet crash. On May 21, 2002, Merrill Lynch paid $100 million to settle charges that its Internet group had maintained misleading ratings on stocks underwritten by the

Table 2.1   Analyst Recommendations, January 1997–March 2002

Year	Number of Recommendations	Buy (%)	Hold (%)	Sell (%)
1997	425,087	74.0	23.7	2.3
1998	748,450	67.8	30.4	1.8
1999	1,010,235	67.1	30.9	2.0
2000	1,373,107	73.3	25.0	1.7
2001	1,482,100	65.3	32.0	2.7
Jan–Mar 2002	359,881	62.6	34.2	3.2

Source: Bloomberg L.P.

firm. The settlement came after New York Attorney General Eliot Spitzer released excerpts of e-mails showing that analysts privately disparaged companies they publicly recommended.

At the time in question, Merrill's rating system had five categories:

1. Buy
2. Accumulate
3. Neutral
4. Reduce
5. Sell

Ratings could be shaded, with 1–1 being higher than 1–3 and so forth. Spitzer put together e-mail comments with published ratings in Table 2.2.

In sworn testimony, Merrill's senior Internet analyst, Henry Blodget, and his subordinate, Kirsten Campbell, both confirmed that the group never rated a stock 4 or 5, according to an affidavit filed by Spitzer. "In lieu of assigning reduce or sell recommendations to stocks they no longer favored, the Internet group instead merely quietly stopped covering the stock, without any announcement or meaningful explanation to the retail public."

Table 2.2   E-Mail Comments

Published Company	Date	Analyst Comments	Rating
Aether System (AETH)	3/15/01	"fundamentals horrible"	3-1
Excite@home (ATHM)	12/27/99	"we are neutral on the stock"	2-1
	12/29/99	Six-month outlook is "flat" without any "real catalysts" for improvement seen.	
Excite@home (ATHM)	6/3/00	"such a piece of crap"	2-1
GoTo.com	1/11/01	Nothing interesting about company "except banking fees"	3-1
InfoSpace (INSP)	7/13/00	"This stock is a powder keg, given how aggressive we were on it earlier this year and given the 'bad smell' comments that so many institutions are bringing up"	1-1
InfoSpace (INSP)	10/20/00	"piece of junk"	1-1
Lifeminders (LFMN)	12/04/00	"POS" (piece of shit)	2-1
24/7 Media (TFSM)	10/10/00	"piece of shit"	2-2

Source: Affidavit filed April 8, 2002, by Eliot Spitzer, Attorney General of the State of New York, in New York State Supreme Court.

While sophisticated investors knew that Merrill's "3" rating meant "sell," Spitzer said, the general public did not.

In one notable case, Merrill's Internet analysts initiated coverage on Internet Capital Group, a client of the firm, with a 2–1 rating on August 30, 1999. The stock reached $212 on December 22, 1999, then began a long descent. On October 5, 2000, with the stock at $12.38, Blodget predicted in an e-mail to another senior analyst that the ICGE "was going to $5." The next day, he wrote: "There really is no floor to the stock." Even so, the rating remained 2–1. Despite Blodget's pessimism, ICGE was on Merrill's top 10 technology stocks list as late as September 12, 2002, Spitzer's affidavit said.

Laurel had questioned Blodget's ratings in an August 6, 1999, column for Bloomberg that turned out to be her last for the company. The decision to end the column was doubtless based solely on the news judgment of her bosses and had nothing to do with Merrill's 20 percent passive ownership in Bloomberg.

Final Note

The objection may be raised that we have failed to consider the question of earnings disappointments, or changes in analysts' earnings projections, or to compare the top-down predictions of the strategists with the bottom-up estimates of the spoon-fed analysts. Some might complain that we have no black box to which we feed data from the last business cycle. Some sophisticated readers may even darkly hint that we have failed to consider the tens of thousands of academic articles that have tried to wrestle with these questions.

Truth to tell, even the Spec Duo would find it taxing to review the bulk of all this admirable knowledge. We reckon that it would take us two lifetimes to 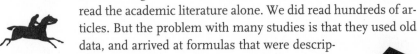 read the academic literature alone. We did read hundreds of articles. But the problem with many studies is that they used old data, and arrived at formulas that were descriptive instead of predictive. For a theory to be testable, it must offer predictions. And it has not yet occurred to any financial academic to investigate the effect of ever-changing cycles.

Exhausted by our battles, fearing that we will still be receiving variations on the queries we have addressed here if we live to be 100, and eager to be about our business, we can only retreat for a few happy hours to reread one of our favorite Greek myths, the labors of Hercules, in preparation for our chapter on the legendary value investor Benjamin Graham.

When Vic played racquet sports, he would first break down the opponent's backhand. Then he would break down the opponent's forehand. Next, he would hit some short shots that the opponent was not fast enough to reach. Finally, when the only way that the opponent could possibly compete was by leaning forward at all times, he would hit them deep. He prospered by getting his opponent to lean the wrong way at all times during his matches.

If investors were to figure out that the market, by deluging them with spurious correlations about earnings and stock returns, is playing that kind of game against them, the broad flow of revenue to the market would be reduced by 95 percent. The people who always buy at the high and sell at the low, who jump in and out of mutual funds at precisely the wrong time, would sit out the game. Of course, they might hold too long or sell too quickly, and there might be some transfer of wealth—but they would not overtrade, and they would be far better off. As it is, they call up their brokers and sell on earnings pessimism.

But guess what? Tomorrow there will be earnings optimism, and they will have to do just the opposite.

3 THE HYDRA HEADS OF TECHNICAL ANALYSIS

The Hydra haunted the unfathomable Lernaean swamp, the grave of many an incautious traveler.

—Robert Graves, *Greek Myths*[1]

In Greek mythology, the second task that the King of Mycenae demanded of Hercules was to kill the Hydra, a nine-headed monster whose poisonous breath killed everything nearby. Hercules went after the beast with his club, but as soon as he knocked off one head, two grew to replace it.

Hercules had it easy. When we accidentally call up the menu of technical indicators on our Bloomberg monitor, we find not just nine, but dozens of colorful charts that we have concluded are poisonous to the investor: adjustable moving-average charts, regression lines, money flows, parabolic stops, Bollinger bands, various oscillators, pivots, relative strength, trading envelopes, stochastics (both bar and candle), point-and-figure charts, exponentially smoothed lines, advance-decline lines, TICK, TRIN, Fibonacci retracement levels, and a software function that lets you draw straight lines between whichever peaks or troughs strike your fancy. This cornucopia of indicators does not begin to include all that are available. The Market Technicians Association—the "official spokes-organization for technical analysts in the United States," according to the group's president, Ralph Acampora—lists 177 on its Web site.

In 45 years of trading, Vic and his staff members have tested every indicator to which value is ascribed. So far, not one has passed the test. However, any important question deserves to be settled by putting "statistics on the table." Haphazard anecdotes, confident assertions, and appeals to authority—even, or especially, our own authority—will not do. We are always open to quantification and testing of any rule.

The problem with technical analysis is that practitioners and advocates fail to follow standard scientific procedure in presenting and evaluating its techniques. Scientific procedure in this case would include an exact definition of an event, a test of the accuracy and uncertainty of the predictions based on the event, a method for entering and exiting trades based on the event, and a method for communicating and repeating the experiment so that it can be verified and improved on. Practitioners of technical analysis often object that it is an art, not a science, and cannot possibly be refuted. We agree. The propositions of technical analysis are simply not testable, as visual interpretations are not susceptible of precise definition. Technical analysis is so rife with subjective interpretations that it must be regarded as more of a religion than a method, complete with priests who bewilder the unwashed at high-priced seminars. Because subjective interpretation does not permit the formulation of precise hypothesis or testable predictions, knowledge cannot advance.

Take Martin "Buzzy" Schwartz's explanation of the secret of markets: "When you look at the letter T, there's an equal distance on the left side and the right side of the T, hence the Magic T formula." The investor is advised to "totally embrace" the Magic T by "drawing trend lines and charts, recalculating averages, figuring inflection points, setting entry and exit prices." Schwartz offers this account of his success with the method: "The Magic T and I became as one. Data ebbed and flowed in the most primal way, and I rose and fell with it instinctively, viscerally, like a mollusk in the sands of high finance."[2] Would that we were all happy as clams. While Schwartz truly seems desirous of helping investors, we wish for more cerebral ways to separate the market's ebbs and the flows.

Or, consider this majestically broad statement of Joseph Granville: "The market follows all the laws of physics, easily explained in terms of momentum, gravity, attraction, acceleration, harmonics, time, space, energy, magnetism, and even color as we deal with the entire spectrum of technical analysis weaving a tapestry of infinite beauty."[3] Sounds beautiful. But somehow, we doubt that Granville's "on-balance volume contributor," which the guru claims to have taken "to a new level of excellence," or even the "climax indicator" or the "net field trend theory indicator" could justify his belief that any of them would continue to be as accurate as they were when he took "investors and traders completely out of the market" before the 1987 crash.

Turning to the 775-page collection of interviews with all the great knights and damsels in the technical analysis brotherhood, compiled by Jack Schwager, who can help being heartened by Schwager's promise that charts reflect market behavior that is subject to certain repetitive patterns and that, with sufficient experience, some traders will uncover an innate ability to use charts successfully as a method of anticipating price moves?

As Schwager sums it up in his Trading Rule No. 4: "Find a chart pattern that says the timing is right—now. Don't initiate a trade without such a confirming pattern."[4] (Occasionally, he says, you might consider a trade without such a pattern if there is a convergence of any measured moves, and support/resistance points at a given price area and there is a well-defined stop point that does not imply much risk.)

It is enough to keep anybody awake at night wondering how to find such patterns, and how to measure the moves, and where those well-defined stop points might converge.

But whenever we do formulate a technical pattern in a quantifiable way, test it, and discuss our findings, we find ourselves at the center of a great uproar, as followers of these and other indicators accuse us of failing to evaluate the virtues of their chosen chart properly. So convinced are these critics of their indicator's value that settling the question by putting any of their propositions to the test seems futile. The hydra is always ready with another head—a new technique, a new practitioner, a new market, a new source of past data—to replace discredited technical indicators.

In the end, Hercules realized that the Hydra's heads would stop growing only if he sealed off the source with fire. That is what we're going to do here. We are going to take the key theme common to the hundreds of technical analysis techniques and test it with fire. The theme in question is, "The trend is your friend."

Is the Trend Really Your Friend?

For a representative sampling of the many variations of "The trend is your friend," we turned to *The Global-Investor Book of Investing Rules: Invaluable Advice from 150 Master Investors,* edited by Philip Jenks and Stephen Eckett.[5] We found that more than two dozen of the traders proffered "The trend is your friend" in various permutations. A few examples:

- The trend is your friend in the last hour. (Alan Farley)
- Never short-sell stocks when they are going up. (Simon Cawkwell)
- Draw trend lines. (John Murphy)
- Frequently, what is low will go even lower, and what is high will continue to rise. (Marc Faber)

And our favorite:

- The trend is your friend unless it is about to end. (Thomas DeMark)

None of the writers of these trend rules backed them up with even a simple test. In fact, no test of "The trend is your friend" is possible, because the rule is never put forward in the form of a testable hypothesis. Something is always slippery, subjective, or even mystical about the rule's interpretation and execution.

Prescientific societies, needing a feeling of control over storms, natural disasters, predators, food sources, and other unpredictable vagaries of life, relied on myths and rituals for explanation and guidance. They sacrificed the best part of their food to the gods, made costly pilgrimages to holy places, and showered gifts on priests, all to propitiate the gods who ruled their fortunes. By and large, these practices have died out as the efficacy of the scientific method became obvious. Yet, myth survives in the modern age, partly as a reaction against the rapid change that science has brought about. Even in the market alongside the most sophisticated mathematical strategies and cold-eyed calculations of veteran traders, myths can be found thriving.

But perhaps this is not so surprising. Modern investors, after all, find themselves at the mercies of mysterious forces just as the cave dwellers did. The market is changeable, complex, and seemingly fathomless. Sharp rises can create great wealth and power. Sharp declines can lead to disaster and death. The market is sometimes as giving as a mother, sometimes as hostile as an angry ocean. It is no wonder that traders, faced always with the question "What should I do now?" long for a simple indicator to navigate the market's mysteries.

Reviewing many of the 378,000 references to "trend following" on our favorite search engine, Google, we found an abundance of sites featuring testimonials from satisfied students of such systems, as well as stories about trend followers who have achieved incredible riches. No wonder that a record 830 aspiring chart-readers, the most ever, took the Market Technician Association's annual competency exams on April 26, 2002, in Jupiter Beach, Florida. Who could resist the allure of a trend-following indicator that makes it "virtually impossible to miss a major market move," as the *Cabot Market Letter* put it so tantalizingly in a spring 2002 edition?

The advertisements of technical trading indicators available to the seeker for a price are indeed enticing. *Active Trader* magazine's Internet store, for example, offers a "groundbreaking primer," *Trading Classic Chart Patterns:*

> This comprehensive guide includes easy-to-use performance tables supported by statistical research. By using a simple scoring system, you'll learn how to predict the performance of a chart pattern almost by looking at it. The "Trading Classic Chart Patterns" section will serve as a handy reference guide for your favorite chart patterns, including broadening tops, head-and-shoulders, rectangles, triangles, and triple tops and bottoms. You'll quickly learn about the Adam-and-Eve combinations of double tops and bottoms, and how to select the best performers while avoiding the losers. You'll discover:
>
> - How to use the price trend leading to a chart pattern as a gauge of future performance.
> - How tall formations perform substantially better than short ones.
> - What a partial decline is and how to buy in early for a larger profit.
>
> This book is an invaluable resource that provides the obvious answer—Yes!— for every investor who has wondered if trading chart patterns can be profitable.[6]

Granted that some trend followers have achieved success. Doubtless their intelligence and insights are superior to our own. But it is worthwhile to step back and consider two fundamental questions:

1. Is their central rule, "The trend is your friend," valid?
2. Might their reported results, good or bad, be best explained as due to chance?

Our initial observation is that common sense argues against trend following. Take two points on a price chart, draw a straight line between them and extend that line. If the point later in time is above the first, the line slopes up. If the later point is below the first, the line slopes down. What does that show, except that a stock has been up or down?

What strikes us as common sense, however, is not enough to settle the question. We tested the trend proposition as best we could by running numerous tests of our own devising. We also surveyed the extensive academic literature on technical analysis, and updated and tested others' work. We report the results in this chapter.

Numerous obstacles beset anyone who tries to test momentum-trading theories. The patterns themselves, as well as the studies purporting to show their efficacy, all suffer from a basic problem: Patterns are based on prospective events that had not taken place when the fish was supposedly caught. The fish, in other words, is counted while still in the water.

Two professors at Southern Methodist University, Venkat Eleswarapu and Marc Reinganum, illustrated some of the difficulties in studying momentum in a recent paper, "The Predictability of Aggregate Stock Market Returns: Evidence Based on Glamour Stocks."[7] The study concludes that the returns of the market are negatively correlated with the returns of glamour stocks in the previous 36 months. They find no evidence that value stocks predict future returns. The study uses data from 1951 to 1997 and therefore does not take into account the regime shift that has taken place in glamour stocks since 1997. The Nasdaq doubled from the end of 1997 to March 24, 2000, and tumbled 72 percent thereafter through July 2002. Such dragons require new powers of divination in those who would confront them. Moreover, the professors' selective use of a group of companies for which continuous earnings data were available on Compustat may well have resulted in the omission of some beasts and stocks pertinent to the results.

Testing for Trends

We began our own tests by looking for trends from year to year. Using data provided by the authors of *Triumph of the Optimists*, which we consider the best investment book ever written, we found that trends in annual returns have been absent for the last 102 years. For consecutive years, the correlation is minus 0.02. (The correlation between the return in one year and the return two years *later* is minus 0.25—much better.) In recent years, the correlations have been even more negative; three consecutive negative annual returns in the S&P 500 were last seen in 1939–1941. (As we write, near the end of 2002, it looks like the market may complete a third down year, finally throwing the trend followers a bone after their long privation.)

Table 3.1   Up/Down Combinations

Year 1	Year 2	Year 3 Gain (%)
−	−	16
−	+	16
+	−	13
+	+	9

As authors Elroy Dimson, Paul Marsh, and Mike Staunton point out in *Triumph of the Optimists,* there have been only six occasions in the past 102 years when the market has declined for two years in a row; too few observations for reliable statistical conclusions. But the average return in the following year was 16 percent, a tie with the down-up combination (see Table 3.1). We have calculated the market's return the next year after all four combinations of the previous four years' returns.

Furthermore, the correlation of market returns between past and future years for all relevant periods is negative, as shown in Table 3.2.

Perhaps short-term trends in the averages support the trend-following view? No, not there, either. Correlations between consecutive nonoverlapping periods of various durations of less than one year in the most widely traded stock futures are negative, showing what is called "mean reversion." In other words, declines in the averages tend to be followed by rises and rises tend to be followed by declines.

The scatter plot in Figure 3.1 shows the correlation of consecutive 20-day moves in the S&P 500 Index from July 1994 to May 2001 to be −0.053. The dots cluster around the horizontal axis with little or no pattern, and a slight down slope from top left to bottom right. The correlation for longer periods is even more negative. After declines in the market over a 20-day period, the

Table 3.2   Annual Market Return Correlations

Number of Years Back	Correlation with Current Year (%)
1	−2
2	−25
3	−4
4	−2
5	−17
6	−5

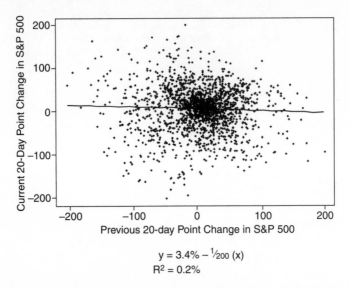

$$y = 3.4\% - \tfrac{1}{200}(x)$$
$$R^2 = 0.2\%$$

Figure 3.1 Correlation of Consecutive Price Changes in S&P 500 Futures for Periods of 20 Days, July 1994–May 2001

total gain in the market over the next 20 days is some three S&P 500 points, corresponding to a change of approximately 0.3 percent. After a rise, the total corresponding move is a bit below 0.

In general, a good ballpark estimate for short-term correlations of various durations is −0.15.

We next asked if monthly changes in the Nasdaq tend to continue or to reverse, and whether they lead to changes in the S&P 500 Index. To find out, we ran many correlations between leads and lags in the price histories of the two indexes, such as correlating the preceding two months' return, skipping a month, and checking S&P 500 for various monthly leads and lags. We performed the same exercise with Nasdaq versus S&P 500 leads and lags.

We looked at the scatter diagrams, we computed statistical tables, and we assembled tables of comovements and countermovements. All these tests tend to answer the question of whether large moves in one series are accompanied by large moves in the same or opposite direction of the other series.

After computing hundreds of correlations, we concluded that the only relation with statistical significance is that Nasdaq returns in one month tend to have a moderate positive correlation of 10 percent with the returns in the next month. This means that if the Nasdaq goes down 15 percent in one month, the best estimate is that it will fall 10 percent of 15 percent, or 1.5 percent, in

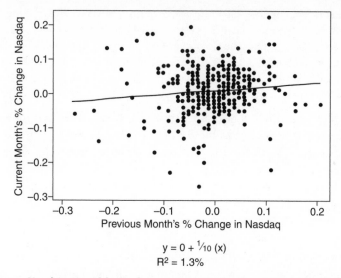

$$y = 0 + \tfrac{1}{10}(x)$$
$$R^2 = 1.3\%$$

Figure 3.2 Nasdaq Monthly Performance as Indicator of Next-Month Returns. (Data are from year-end 1971, year of Nasdaq's inception, through April 2002, a total of 370 monthly observations.)

the next month. If it goes up 20 percent in one month, the best estimate is that it will go up 10 percent of 20 percent, or 2 percent, in the next month. This can be seen in the scatter plot in Figure 3.2 as a slight uplifting of the line of best fit from the bottom left to the top right.

That does not reduce the uncertainty by much. In fact, the predictions reduce the squared error of forecasts by a mere 1 percent. Thus, while there is some evidence of momentum in the Nasdaq, it isn't very useful. All the other correlations are random and consistent with chance. Considering the many correlations that we ran, there is a reasonable likelihood that the one significant correlation that we did come up with is the kind of chance result that would occur if we picked the winner of a heads-and-tails coin-tossing contest.

Streaks in Sports

Taking a break from our scrutiny of indexes, we looked for insights on momentum in a completely different field: sports.

In sports, casinos, and stocks, there is nothing like a winning streak to thrill players and onlookers. The excitement is conveyed by the common expressions "hot hand" and "in the zone." In *Fools Die,* the late Mario Puzo described the magic of a gambler's $400,000 lucky night:

He bet two hundred on the line, backed up his numbers and then bought all the numbers for five hundred dollars each. He held the dice for almost an hour. After the first fifteen minutes the electricity of his hot hand ran through the casino and the table jammed full.... [When] the dice passed from his hands to the next player, the gamblers at the table gave him a cheer. The pit boss gave him metal racks to carry his chips to the casino cage.[8]

Plenty of examples of winning streaks in sports come to mind, particularly in basketball. There was the 8,829-game run of the Harlem Globetrotters from the 1960s to the 1990s. Before Michigan State's basketball team beat them in November 2000, they had not lost a college game since 1962. The Los Angeles Lakers won 33 games in a row from November 5, 1971, to January 7, 1972.

North Carolina's NCAA Women's soccer team had a 103-game unbeaten streak from September 30, 1986, to September 17, 1990. From 1987 to 1997, the Cuban National baseball team won 150 consecutive games.

Sometimes the hot hand shows up in an individual player during a single game. In Game 3 of the NBA playoffs between the New Jersey Nets and Boston Celtics on May 22, 2002, the Nets were ahead by 21 points at the end of the third quarter, 74–53. That's when Paul Pierce of the Celtics, perhaps inspired by rousing comments from teammate Antoine Walker, entered "the zone." Until then, he had scored just 9 points, but he piled up 19 in the final quarter. The Celtics won the game 94–90. (In this case, Walker's individual streak won out over a statistical streak in NBA history that had favored the Nets. Until that day, 171 teams had headed into the fourth quarter with leads of 18 points or more, and none had ever lost.)

The critical question is whether streaks are consistent with chance. If athletes or teams are good, they are likely to win more than half the time. Is their chance of winning better after they win a few times than when they lose? Are hot hands real, or do they just seem that way because of the vagaries of memory?

Most researchers who have studied hot hands conclude the concept is a myth. The expert in the field is Cornell University psychology professor Thomas Gilovich. In a series of studies, he looked at records of shots from the floor by players in the Philadelphia 76ers, foul shots by the Boston Celtics, three-point shots in the All-Star contest, and a shooting experiment with the Cornell college team. In each case, he concluded, "detailed analyzes provided no evidence for a positive correlation between the outcomes of successive shots."

After sinking a few in a row, a player may think he is in the zone. But the numbers show that the chance of hitting the next shot tends to decrease slightly from the average level of some 50 percent.

One of the criticisms of these basketball studies is that they attempt to measure individual hot hands in team sports where there is significant interaction. However, Jim Albert and Jay Bennett examined streaks of baseball batters and teams during the 1998 season in their 2001 book *Curve Ball: Baseball, Statistics, and the Role of Chance in the Game,* and found that only six of 30 teams showed streakiness, a result consistent with chance.[9]

Some studies have found evidence of streaks in other sports. A study of hot hands in the Professional Bowling Association tour found some short-term persistence in individual scores. In a noteworthy study of horseshoe pitchers' hot hands, Pomona College economics professor Gary Smith found that the number of double ringers pitched showed strong persistence. After two doubles in a row, the players in world championships pitch doubles 60 percent of the time. After two nondoubles in a row, they pitch double ringers only 47 percent of the time. Smith disagreed with the basketball data of Cornell's Gilovich, and concluded that horseshoe players do have modest hot and cold spells. Barry Nalebuff and Avinash Dixit, game theory experts and coauthors of *The Competitive Edge in Business, Politics, and Everyday Life,* have this to say about the apparent difference between individual and team streaks:

> While the statistical evidence denies the presence of streak shooting, it doesn't refute the possibility that a hot player might warm up the game in some other way. The difference between streak shooting and a hot hand arises because of the interaction between the offensive and the defensive strategies. Suppose Andrew Toney does have a truly hot hand. Surely the other side would start to crowd him. This could easily lower his shooting percentage. That is not all. When the defense focuses on Toney, one of his teammates is left unguarded and is more likely to shoot successfully. In other words, Toney's hot hand leads to an improvement in the 76ers team performance, although there may be a deterioration in Toney's individual performance.[10]

 "Which," observed Hany Saad, the equities and derivatives trader at the Royal Bank of Canada who called our attention to the Dixit-Nalebuff study, "takes us back to Robert Bacon's handicapping principles and ever-changing cycles."

The Market's Momentum Pendulum

The belief in streaks is as common in the market—where it goes by the names "trend" and "momentum"—as it is in gambling and sports. Just as a card player feels "in the zone" after filling in a few flushes, everyone's bullish when stocks go up three weeks in a row and bearish after three down weeks. While players have memories, most people would agree that cards don't have memory. But do stocks have memory?

The evidence on individual stocks favors the antitrend school. Jonathan Lewellen, an instructor at the Massachusetts Institute of Technology, concluded in a series of seminal studies that the evidence for mean reversion is strong. He used 66 years of data, from 1932 to 1998, going through millions of careful calculations and correcting for all the usual biases in studies of this nature. Calculating the mean average price of a stock in a single year, he found that stocks returned 41 percent toward the mean, on average, over the next six quarters. From 1968 through 2000, Lewellen found the correlation was a negative 24 percent. Thus, if the return on a stock was 50 percentage points below the mean in one year, the best prediction for the next six quarters would be a rise of 24 percent times 50 percent, or 12 percent above the mean.

Normally, after showing that all the evidence is against a theory, we would be content to end with a snappy conclusion to the effect of "The trend is not your friend." Yet no fixed rule can be expected to last forever. Too many smart people are around to anticipate and dissipate the effect. The cycles, as we often remind ourselves, are always changing.

Have Things Changed?

Given that the evidence over the past 60 or 70 years is antithetical to the trend followers on individual stocks, and that recent evidence on trends in the averages is equally unfavorable, we nevertheless had to ask ourselves, how is trend-following doing right now, at the start of the new century, compared with mean-reversion investing?

After all, academic findings too often come down the pike at exactly the wrong time for investors. Take the groundbreaking 1981 study published in the *Journal of Financial Economics* which concluded that small stocks consistently registered higher returns than larger ones. The study's release was followed by 18 years in which small stocks lagged larger stocks. Regrettably, the bad stretch began in 1983, after a honeymoon period gave the numerous new small-cap investment vehicles inspired by the study enough time to attract a lot of money. Dimson, Marsh, and Staunton called attention to this reversal of fortune in a 1999 article entitled "Murphy's Law and Market Anomalies."[11] Ironically, in 1999, the year the article was published, small caps recorded one of their best years ever. In 2000 and 2001, they continued to do well enough to outperform the S&P 500.

The truth is that the market panorama is rich enough to find anecdotes that seem to support any kind of market relation. To find out whether the cycle might be changing once again, whom are you going to call? The Speculators.

We took the 20 best and worst performers in the S&P 500 during the year 2000. (The current S&P 500 contains a few companies that were not around at the beginning of 2000, so it was necessary to eliminate all such new additions from our tally.) We found that the 20 best stocks of 2000 returned an average of –11 percent over the subsequent 16 months (through April 29, 2002). Calpine, down 76 percent, PerkinElmer Inc., down 76 percent, and Allergan, down 32 percent, were among the bests that stumbled badly. (The situation would have been even worse if such stocks as Enron, a stalwart member and top performer of the S&P in 2000, had been included. Enron was delisted in November 2001, and we had to drop its bad results, which would have taken another 5 percentage points from the 20 best.)

The 20 worst stocks of 2000 were unchanged in the next 16 months, on average. That list included some standout winners such as American Greetings, up 91 percent from December 29, 2000, through April 29, 2002; Apple Computer, up 55 percent; Cendant, up 91 percent; Circuit City, up 86 percent; and Dell, up 48 percent. The S&P 500 Index itself declined 19 percent in the 16-month period (see Table 3.3).

Of course, buying the worst is by no means the road to guaranteed riches. Yahoo!, down 86 percent in year 2000, went on to lose 53 percent more in the next 16 months. Novell, Lucent, and Gateway suffered similar fates. World-Com collapsed from $13.15 to $2.35, and proceeded to fall to 6 cents a share on July 1, 2002.

We next tested large stocks to see if they are subject to trending. We had noticed that large pharmaceutical companies often show three consecutive weeks of rises or declines. For example, Johnson & Johnson fell three weeks in a row starting the last week of April 2002. Would you have predicted that the stock would rise the next week? Or would you have bet that it would fall further into the cellar? A "yes" answer to the first question would indicate a

Table 3.3   Rankings and Returns

S&P 500 Stocks 2000 Rank	Return Next 16 Months (%)
20 best	–11
20 worst	0
S&P 500 index	–19

"gambler's bias" and a vulnerability to the law of small numbers. The second question would show a "representation," or hot hands bias. (In fact, Johnson & Johnson fell for 10 straight weeks.) But this seeming piece of evidence for the trend followers is anecdotal, nothing more. As Daniel Kahneman, Paul Slovic, and Amos Tversky point out in their classic *Judgment under Uncertainty: Heuristics and Biases,* the common habit of assessing the probability of an event by the ease in which instances can be brought to mind leads to an assortment of predictable biases.[12] An example would be assessing the risk of heart attack among middle-aged people by recalling such occurrences among one's acquaintances. No one would take such an estimate seriously, but people do its equivalent in the market all the time.

There are not enough Big Pharma companies to run a proper test of these perceptions. Therefore, we chose as proxies the current 10 largest Nasdaq stocks and the 10 largest S&P 500 stocks by market capitalization. Since Intel and Microsoft were common to both lists, we were left with 18 companies. We studied weekly prices from May 1997 to May 2002. To simplify our tests and maintain a reasonable homogeneity in the results, we calculated the signs of the moves in each of the first three weeks for each stock. There were eight possibilities in all. Then we looked at the results that occurred in the remaining week of the month for each stock. The averages and numbers of observations appear in Table 3.4.

We conclude that stocks in the lead triumph and prosper in the last week, whereas those that are near the bottom meet disaster in the final week. When a stock is up three weeks in a row, it adds an average 1.6 percent in the final week. When a stock is down three weeks in a row, it falls an average 0.8 percent. If stocks fall the first two weeks and then rise, they drop 1.4 percent by

Table 3.4   Streaking Stocks—Moves in the Last Week of the Month Compared with Previous Weeks, 1997–2002

Week 1	Week 2	Week 3	Number of Observations	Average Move Week 4 (%)
Up	Up	Up	156	+1.6
Up	Up	Down	165	+0.6
Up	Down	Up	188	+0.6
Up	Down	Down	125	+1.3
Down	Up	Up	108	−1.3
Down	Up	Down	91	+2.8
Down	Down	Up	114	−1.4
Down	Down	Down	100	−0.8

the end of the month. Most striking of all was the group that reversed like a pendulum during the first three weeks. Stocks that were down the first week, up the second week, and down the third week tend to go up 2.8 percent in the final week.

We can classify eight different groups of stocks based on their persistence and reversibility in the first three weeks. Within each group and within the sample of 1,047 company-weeks, there is much variation in performance. The average variation in the performance of an individual company during the final week is 10 percent. Chance doubtless contributes in large measure to the results.

Yet putting it all together, after some simulation and calculations, we conclude that the superior performance of 2.8 percent in the final week for the group of companies that zigzagged down up down during the first three weeks is unlikely to have occurred by chance. Let's call it a 1-in-20 shot.

By contrast, the tendency for momentum to continue in the final week for the companies that registered three consecutive rises or three consecutive declines is suggestive but not conclusive. It is about a 1-in-10 shot.

Putting one consideration with another, we found no evidence of a regime shift in market dynamics that would favor trend following. The weight of academic findings and practical results showed the tendency to mean reversion to be intact, for all periods, all individual stocks, all averages, and all new indexes that we might reasonably think of.

We conclude that the pendulum, rather than the streak, is the superior model for U.S. stocks.

A Venerable Indicator of Great Ambiguity

Some countries have developed forms of technical analysis that are ideally suited to their own cultural traits. In Japan, where ambiguity in negotiation is a way of life, traders have developed and refined over many centuries the technique of candlestick analysis. As Steve Nison notes in his popular reference book, *Japanese Candlestick Charting Techniques,* "As with all charting methods, candle chart patterns are subject to the interpretation of the user."[13] This should come as no surprise. All who have done business with the Japanese know of their polite reluctance to give a simple "yes" or "no." It would have been amazing indeed if a country that prizes indirection had come up with a precisely defined method susceptible of confirmation by experimentation.

Candlesticks show open, high, low, and close points. A rectangular bar— "the body"—encompasses the close and the open, while "whiskers" extend from the top and bottom to mark the high and low, if necessary. The body is empty when the close is higher than the open, and colored in when the close is lower than the open. A candlestick's features and its relationships to the candlesticks on adjacent days constitute the raw material of candlestick analysis. A typical chart for the S&P for the last six months of 1999 appears in Figure 3.3.

With no intended disrespect to Japanese politesse, we undertook a test of the validity of Japanese candlestick patterns. We began by selecting five of the most prominently mentioned patterns found in two sources: the Nison book and a standard Internet source for candlestick analysis, LitWick.com.

The test consisted of defining each of the occurrences of these patterns, using daily high-low-open-close for the six-year period 1995–2001. One of the patterns did not show up in the data at all. (An Abandoned Baby has not been found in the S&P 500 since 1995.) We made predictions for three separate intervals for each of the remaining four patterns. The intervals were to the next close, to the next open, and to the close two days after the occurrence of the pattern. Each trade was initiated at the open of the day after the appearance of the candlestick pattern (see Table 3.5).

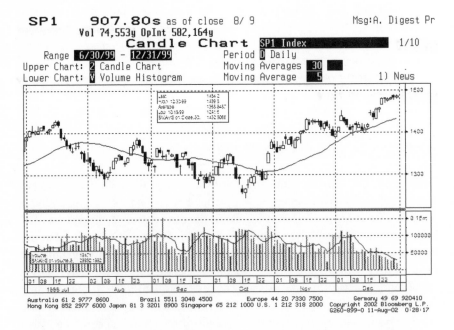

Figure 3.3   S&P 500 Candlestick Chart, July–December 1999. *Source:* Bloomberg L.P.

Table 3.5   Japanese Candlestick Pattern Trades

Pattern	Bearish/ Bullish	Period	Number of Observations	S&P Point Change	Up %	Z
Three black crows	Bearish	Open to close	21	3.7	57	119
		Open to open	21	4.9	67	156
		Open to next day's close	21	5.7	57	156
Engulfing	Bearish	Open to close	22	2.3	36	−79
		Open to open	22	3.2	41	−92
		Open to next day's close	22	2.2	50	−47
Doji in an uptrend	Bearish	Open to close	10	−0.6	50	−21
		Open to open	10	−3.0	50	−69
		Open to next day's close	10	−2.5	40	−69
Abandoned baby	Bearish	Open to close	0			
		Open to open	0			
		Open to next day's close	0			
Tweezers top	Bearish	Open to close	57	0.9	51	
		Open to open	57	0.8	56	
		Open to next day's close	57	−0.5	60	

Of 15 tests, 4 came up with results in the direction of traditional candlestick interpretations. None of the patterns was statistically significant at the usual 1-in-20 levels typically used by researchers as the minimum cutoff for determining whether the phenomenon was consistent with mere chance variations. Our tests thus failed to verify the validity of Japanese candlestick analysis.

But perhaps we have been too scientific. Perhaps an unusual ability to interpret these patterns might yield better results. "Technical analysis is an art as well as a science" is an oft-repeated refrain we hear from technical analysts. Doubtless many practitioners are more gifted with visual modes of decision making than with numerical methods. Chess players, for example, often see visual relations that they find difficult to quantify when explaining how they came up with that one perfect move that won the game. Similarly, architects, engineers, and artists frequently can look at a depiction of a scene and fathom many relations that would be difficult even to define, let alone quantify.

The great problem with that line of reasoning is that people are prone to the "validity bias"—they believe that they are much more accurate in coming to valid conclusions than they actually are. Humans are much too adroit at believing that relations exist when they don't, and this illusion is responsible for many errors in judgment and decision making in the markets and in life. In particular, people tend to place unwarranted confidence in predictions that match stereotypes, "with little or no regard for the factors that limit predictive accuracy," as Kahneman, Slovic, and Tversky wrote in *Judgment under Uncertainty*. And they persist in this misplaced confidence even if they know the input information is scanty, unreliable, or outdated.

Even if a psychological bias were not involved in interpreting candlestick charts and the like, it would not seem overly useful to tell the average investor that certain people are gifted in visualization but find it impossible to put their finger on how they arrive at their interpretations. The investor would have no clear path to learn such techniques. And by merely following the guidance of the superior visualizer, the investor could never know with assurance that the person's gifts would continue to yield superior forecasts under different conditions.

Technical analysis is silent on such crucial questions as what time frame to use when searching for patterns. As our friend Shui Mitsuda, a great market philosopher who works for a Japanese brokerage, observed: "By changing the range of variables in a chart (duration, price range), the graph often shows completely different faces. In the one-year range, Sony is a strong buy. In the 10-year range, I get too scared. In the one-month range, I have no idea."

 The greatest problems with using candlestick patterns to trade, however, lie in the principle of ever-changing cycles and the role of deception in the market.

Our friend Glenn Escovedo, a chess expert who trades for a white-shoe Wall Street firm, sent us one of the most popular books in China, *The Book of Stratagems* by Harro von Senger, to give us some insight into Japanese technical analysis.[14] The book contains deceptive techniques of great antiquity, two of which we summarize here:

1. **Fool the emperor and cross the sea:** The Emperor Taizong, arriving at the shore of the Yellow Sea with an army of 300,000 on the way to a battle in Kogouryo, loses heart. Turning to his military advisors, he asks for advice. Fearing the emperor will abort the campaign, the advisors build a boat camouflaged as the home of a wealthy merchant. They lure him aboard, then take to sea. When the candelabra starts swaying, the emperor orders the curtains to be pulled back. "Where are we?" he roars. Faced with a fait accompli, he regains his decisiveness and bravely sails on.

2. **Openly repair the walkway, secretly march to Chencang:** In 206 B.C., the military leader Liu Bang retreats to Hanzhong to escape a murderous rival. To protect himself from attack, he burns the wooden walkways and bridges in the mountain gorges along the way. Later that year, he prepares for a new campaign in Chencang. To distract his enemies, he orders a few troops to begin repair work on the walkways. The military commander in Chencang laughs, thinking it will take such a modest number of workers many years to restore the walkways. But Liu Bang's forces secretly march on a different route to Chencang, taking the city by surprise.

"The Chinese have lived and died by deception for thousands of years," observed Escovedo. "Hard to believe they or the Japanese would take charts at face value."

What is even harder to fathom is the Western craze for Japanese candlestick analysis. In *Japanese Candlestick Charting Techniques,* Nison talks about the technique's gratifying popularity:

> Online traders, day traders, institutional proprietary traders, and market makers are just some of the candle charting enthusiasts. Web sites, real-time trading systems, and technical analysis software packages include candle charts. This attests to the popularity and universal appeal candles have to trading today's volatile markets. Candles are hotter than ever.

Even so, Nison's book includes many Western-style elaborations on pure candlestick patterns for "the seasoned technician," including candlesticks with trend lines, candlesticks with retracement levels, candlesticks with moving averages, candlesticks with oscillators, candlesticks with volume and open interest, candlesticks with Elliot Wave, and candlesticks with market profile.

Acquaintances familiar with our thinking take care to discuss candlestick patterns only behind our backs. Sometimes, however, a stray reference will slip through, as when an e-mail extolling Nison's book, meant for a more receptive target, mistakenly was sent to us. "Candlestick charting dates from

Tokugawa times—late 16th, early 17th century," the writer gushed. "The book has pages and pages on the psychology underlying patterns like head and shoulders, which the Japanese rice traders called 'Three Buddha Top.' The one I like is 'High Waves'—makes me seasick just to think about it." After confiding his yen to explore such formations as "Doji Star," "Three White Soldiers Advance on the Dark Shadow," and "Candles Exhaust Themselves to Give Light to Men," the writer concluded:

> Much as I admire Vic and Laurel, for me it is going to take [a lot] to overturn 400 years of profitable tradition.

Others among our correspondents tell us they have found creative uses for their books on candlestick analysis. John Lamberg of Minnetonka, Minnesota, one of our most sagacious correspondents—engineer, Monty Python aficionado, *Father Knows Best* family man, and reformed technical analysis practitioner—uses his book on candlestick patterns to steady the shaky leg of his coffee table.

The Hydra's Arms

We next studied another prominent Hydra head–the well-known TRIN, short for the New York Stock Exchange Short-Term Trade Index. Its inventor, Richard Arms, who charges $8,000 a year for his advisories, prefers the eponymous "Arms Index." CNBC, the most widely watched financial TV network, uses the latter name when it flashes the current index reading every 20 minutes past the eyes of viewers.

The Arms Index represents the ratio of New York Stock Exchange up volume scaled down by number of rises, divided by the ratio of down volume, scaled down by the number of declines. Some traders use a five-day average for short-term forecasts.

 Some favorable press came in early 2001, when pundit Don Hays told *Barron's* that he used the Arms Index to call the exact bottom of the Dow Jones Industrial Average on March 22.[15] (The Dow peaked 60 days later on May 21 after rallying 21 percent, then resumed its decline.)

So TRIN works, right?

It sounded intriguing. We decided to check. Working with Dr. Brett Steenbarger, who has used TRIN in his own trading, we ran hundreds of regressions with many lags and leads for many different back periods. We studied correlations of one-day, two-day, five-day, and 10-day TRIN with S&P 500

Index moves over the next 1, 5, and 10 days. Briefly, we found the results to be consistent with randomness, with correlations close to or right at zero over the last three and a half years. In other words, the Arms Index does not predict the future.

We were not the only ones to find difficulties with TRIN. In a study cited by *The Encyclopedia of Technical Market Indicators*, Robert Colby and Thomas Meyers tested TRIN from January 1928 to March 1987.[16] Using daily data, they performed many different tests to come up with predictions for one to twelve months. Their finding: "We can only conclude that it has relatively limited forecasting value for stock prices."

Some may feel that the above conclusion is premature since it is based on only 59 years of data. But in *The New Technical Trader*, Tushar Chande and Stanley Kroll note three difficulties with using TRIN:

1. The ratios used in TRIN often obscure, rather than clarify, market action. This is particularly true when market action is "mixed."
2. The very process of smoothing TRIN with moving averages distorts the picture of relative volume flows.
3. TRIN has a bounded scale for upside activity, but an unbounded scale for downside activity.[17]

We spoke with Richard Arms in May 2001 to find out what he thought of our conclusions, and to learn how he uses the index. In his words:

Laurel: Do you trade much?

Arms: I trade some money for myself, but my primary work is talking with my clients. I put out an advisory for dozens of institutions. I don't trade much any more, because I'm occupied with other things.

Laurel: Millionaire? Centimillionaire?

Arms: Somewhere in the middle.

Laurel: From trading?

Arms: From trading, and from the fees I charge my clients.

Laurel: How would you advise people to use the index?

Arms: If you're a trader, watch the five-day moving average. When it's in the 0.75 sort of area, you become a seller, and when it's over 1.25 you become a buyer. It's a judgment thing. . . . The 10-day moving average allowed us to call the bottom perfectly on March 22, 2001.

Laurel: Can you elaborate on how to use judgment?

Arms: After working with it for so many years, it becomes a little . . . instinctive. I'm not sure I can explain it, really. I explain it to my . . . institutional clients. I look at a lot of things. I'm not just looking blindly at this index and saying buy or sell. It's not just a simplistic sort of thing.

Laurel: How many times have you used the Arms Index as a primary signal in the past five years?

Arms: It has given only two of those big major signals in the last five years, this one and in October 1997. Then we have to go back to 1987 to get a similar signal.

If There Is Proof, We Cannot Find It

The problem is that "buy" levels for the 10-day average do not happen enough to scientifically evaluate the Arms Index. You cannot estimate uncertainty based on something that happens twice every five years.

Also, the signals happen to occur at times when the market is most down, so basically what you are taking advantage of is the old adage to buy in panics.

Statistically, it is exceedingly difficult to evaluate a ratio of two ratios. In statistical terms, the distribution of the ratio of two normal variables has an infinite mean and an infinite variance. Larger samples do not help you reduce uncertainty about the mean or variability of the indicator.

Numerically, the ratio is also highly problematic. Its variations are dominated by changes in volume, which are themselves highly correlated with price changes. The ratio itself varies from zero to infinity. A more stable measure might be based on the differences between volume and advances versus declines, perhaps with a logarithmic operator thrown in for stability.

All things considered, working with the Arms Index is about as easy and useful as holding a moonbeam in your hand.

We told Arms that we had found no correlation between TRIN's moving averages and subsequent S&P 500 moves, and he said it bothered him to hear us say that. "All of Wall Street uses the index," he said, "because it works."

A Disagreement That Speaks Volumes

Many technical analysis (TA) practitioners, after reviewing one study or another showing that their favorite technique doesn't work, object that we failed to consider volume. We merely point out that technical analysts themselves cannot agree on how volume might work. Hany Saad, our trader friend at the Royal Bank of Canada, took all three levels of the CMT exams before becoming convinced that technical analysis does not work. He pointed out in a July 2002 e-mail to us:

> Any technical analyst would argue that volume is 50 percent of the puzzle. Classical technical analysis suggests that a price move in certain direction should not be trusted unless volume is flowing in the same direction of the move. In a bull market, for example (whatever that is), volume should be higher on up days than on reactions. That's in a nutshell how Magee's theory goes. In fact, this is even mentioned in Charles Dow's letters as described by Hamilton in "The Stock Market Barometer."
>
> Here is where it gets real funny. Your favorite technician, Richard Arms, developed an indicator called Ease of Movement. Here is a description of the indicator from "Technical Analysis from A to Z":
>
> The Ease of Movement indicator shows the relationship between volume and price change. As with Equivolume charting, this indicator shows how much volume is required to move prices.
>
> High Ease of Movement values occur when prices are moving upward on light volume. Low Ease of Movement values occur when prices are moving downward on light volume. If prices are not moving, or if heavy volume is required to move prices, then the indicator will also be near zero.
>
> The Ease of Movement indicator produces a buy signal when it crosses above zero, indicating that prices are moving upward more easily; a sell signal is given when the indicator crosses below zero, indicating that prices are moving downward more easily.
>
> So while Charles Dow states that volume should be there on up days of uptrends to generate a buy signal, Richard Arms suggests the exact opposite. Who should you trust? Neither. Studies conducted on volume as an independent variable prove that it has no predictive value whatsoever.
>
> Finally, you probably should know that if not for Vic, I would probably be using the same TA tools I am ridiculing today.

Shouldering Ahead

Midway through the great crash of July 2002, a post came across our monitors from a publicity-shy hedge fund manager whom we call Mr. E. "The technical action in the S&P since the big-cap rally last week is being threatened by a massive head and shoulders going back to January 1998," he wrote.

Since his July 10 message, the S&P broke through its January 1998 lows and headed straight down to April 1997 levels. On Tuesday, July 23, 2002, it fell below 800. By the usual methods of reckoning, the next stop for S&P futures was 540. As for the Nasdaq 100, it looked to be headed for negative 2,690.

We asked John Lambert, who estimated the next stop as 540, if he was joking. He replied:

> No, it was actually a mistake. I graphically made a quick measurement from the top of the head to the neckline and used the length of that line segment to "predict" the low. Alas, I was on a semi-log scale so I did not measure the "correct" number of points. Don Van made the measurement per Edwards and Magee and came up with 300, close to what I get.
>
> Your query prompted me to remove Edwards and Magee from under the coffee table: "If the up move preceding the formation of the reversal area has been small, the down move following it may, in fact, probably will, be equally small. In brief, a reversal pattern has to have something to reverse. So, we really have two minimums, one being the extent of the advance preceding the formation of the Heads-and-Shoulders and the other derived by our measuring formula; whichever is the smaller shall apply."
>
> Well now, this gives me some leeway. What is large and small? When does the move preceding the formation of the reversal pattern start? Let's define the start of the move as a breakout in 1995. With a bit of engineering judgment, I come up with 407 points preceding the formation of the Head & Shoulders pattern. Subtracting 407 from 540 produces 543. Let's round this down, as TA is not, shall we say, a completely precise science. I get a target of 540. It appears my initial calculation was not a mistake after all. That is a very good thing as I divided all of my money and bet half on 540 and the other half, using Rick's famous advice, on 22.

Did the apparent predictive success of Mr. E's gigantic pattern mean that trading head-and-shoulders patterns works? And with the financial world's very foundations seemingly about to crumble, did it matter?

It always helps to know what works and what does not, particularly during panics. As the nineteenth-century author and journalist Daniel Defoe documented in his account of London's 1685 plague, worthless nostrums sell well to desperate people.[18] It is important to keep a clear head and take the long view. As to whether head-and-shoulders patterns work well enough in the stock market to be profitable—they don't, as we can show.

Traders have used head-and-shoulders patterns since at least 1930. The pattern consists of three peaks, the highest being in the middle. A horizontal line—the "neckline" is drawn to connect the troughs between the shoulders and the heads. The crossing of the neckline is supposed to signal that prices will continue down away from the head.

An inverted pattern is read as bullish. Figure 3.4 shows a hypothetical head-and-shoulders pattern.

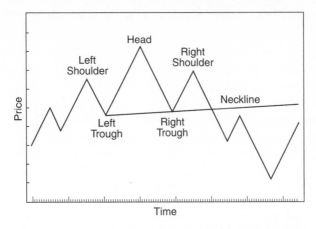

Figure 3.4 Hypothetical Head-and-Shoulders Pattern

Hypothetical Head-and-Shoulders Pattern

We believe that any wealth that accrued to Mr. E as a result of trading this pattern—and we congratulate him for it—was due to luck and not a sure indica-

tor of future success. Any important question deserves to be tested, however, and the results should be made public. Haphazard anecdotes, confident assertions and appeals to authority—even, or especially, our own authority—will not do.

As it happened, shortly before receiving Mr. E's missive, we came across a remarkable study, "Identifying Noise Traders: The Head-and-Shoulders Patterns in U.S. Equities," by Carol Osler of the New York Federal Reserve.[19] After rigorous tests, she concluded that trading in individual equities based on head-and-shoulders patterns is, on balance, unprofitable.

Osler wrote a computer program to identify head-and-shoulders patterns based on the descriptions in eight technical analysis manuals. She applied it to 100 firms with price data spanning July 2, 1962, to December 31, 1993, selected at random from the Center for Research on Securities Prices at the University of Chicago. All the technical analysis manuals were ambiguous about the criteria for exit, but they agreed that a head-and-shoulders pattern signified a major change of trend. Osler therefore wrote her program to require that a position be held until the price stops moving in the predicted direction, with a stop loss of 1 percent.

Amazingly, given the lack of profitability associated with head-and-shoulders patterns, volume around the time of the neckline crossing, the signal to put on a trade, increased by as much as one-quarter of an average day's volume.

How to account for the popularity of an unprofitable trading strategy? According to Osler, certain peculiarities of the human mind may account for its acceptance. People are prone to see nonexistent connections between groups of things. They tend to be overconfident in their own judgment. And they remember pleasant or successful experiences (e.g., profitable head-and-shoulders trades) with far greater clarity than they do unpleasant experiences.

A few successes may bring the head-and-shoulders trader fame and funds, encouraging new entrants. As Osler notes, cognitive psychologists have shown through experiments that unrewarding beliefs and behaviors can survive a long time when they are randomly reinforced.

Many market players say they do not believe in trading head-and-shoulders patterns or any other visual chart patterns, but they like to know what such traders are doing so they can eat their lunch. Lots of luck, says Osler. Even before transactions costs, trading against head-and-shoulders traders is just not profitable in individual stocks. Another objection is that technical traders are simply profiting from the psychology of uninformed individuals. The point still holds—selling after such formations is unprofitable, whether the trader is familiar with chart arcane or not.

When Laurel interviewed her, Osler had accepted a professorship in the international economics and finance department at Brandeis, where she plans to research the role of stop-loss and take-profit orders in the currency market. One area of interest is the possible clustering of orders at round numbers. She did not plan to extend her head-and-shoulders work to S&P futures. "Technical analysis is just not a hot topic," she explained.

Osler grew up in the Boston suburbs and attended graduate school at Princeton after graduating from Swarthmore. An afficionado of both squash and ballet, she has avoided the risks of the trading floor, but enjoys taking academic risks. Ever since she went to the trading floor at Citibank to see how order flow affected the currency market, she has been outraging the academic establishment. "Order flow was an extremely unprofessional thing to care about," she said. Osler also fell astray of the norms by talking to traders, whom academics widely view as too deceptive to yield valuable information. She recalls sending a colleague an e-mail outlining empirical evidence she had collected on a certain subject, and asked him what he thought. He wrote back: "First I'd have to see a careful worked-out model to see if it worked in theory."

"My primary goal is to understand reality," she said. "That is not universally accepted."

Table 3.6   Zhang's Five Incidences

Left Shoulder	Neckline Crossing
11/21/97	12/18/97
6/9/98	8/27/98
10/23/00	11/20/00
5/4/01	6/13/01
12/5/97	1/11/02

Always ready to jump into the breach, we tested the head-and-shoulders strategy on S&P futures prices beginning in 1996. Shi Zhang, one of Vic's staff members, wrote a computer program based on Osler's description of her head-and-shoulders algorithm.

Zhang's program specified that the time between the six points on a bearish head-and-shoulders pattern—the right shoulder, the right trough, the head, the left trough, the left shoulder, and neckline crossing—had to be at least five days and no longer than 180 days. Various price change magnitudes were used to make sure that no patterns were missed.

After running his computer nonstop for 10 hours, Zhang came up with five incidences of the pattern, which he then evaluated for profitability 1, 2, 3, 4, 5, 10, 20, 30, and 60 days out. The start and end dates of each point for each incidence are shown in Table 3.6.

Assuming that the trader took a short position at the neckline crossing, the returns for different holding periods would have been as shown in Table 3.7.

We conclude that head-and-shoulders trading does not work either as a signal of a trend change or as a profitable strategy.

Table 3.7   Returns for Different Holding Periods

	Number of Days after Neckline Crossing								
	1	2	3	4	5	10	20	30	60
Average profit/loss	0.5%	1.6%	1.3%	1.4%	1.4%	−0.5%	0.5%	−0.2%	−3.5%
Standard deviation	0.01	0.03	0.01	0.02	0.02	0.03	0.03	0.05	0.11

Did You Really Expect a Straight Line to Point the Way?

It is not surprising that simple techniques like extrapolating trends do not lead to consistent profits. All of us know from our childhood up that a key aspect of winning in games and other competitive situations is deception. The first game a child plays is peekaboo, and that may be our first step toward understanding that indirection is a better way to achieve goals than to lay all one's cards on the table. Animals practice deception, from the lowliest insect to the highest primates. Adult humans are at least as knowledgeable as insects, and they have the benefit of reading thousands of years of history going back to the Trojan horse. Certainly the shrewd traders in the market should be more capable of raising the level of trickery above that of extending a straight line.

As the great New York Giants pitcher Christy Mathewson observed more than a half-century ago: "Anybody's best pitch is the one the batters ain't hitting that day. If they start hitting my fastball, they don't see it anymore that afternoon. If they start getting a hold of my curve ball, I just put it away for the day."[20]

Siege of Troy, 1184 B.C. (Artist: Milton Bond, 2001).

On the battlefield, the best generals are the greatest masters of deception. Our favorite in this regard is Stonewall Jackson, acknowledged as the greatest leader in the Confederacy:

> A favorite device with him was to institute inquiries in the presence of the crowd around him as to roads and watercourses in a direction which he did not intend to take; even to order maps to be prepared, and roads laid down, as though for instant use. Having thus set every gossip talking and predicting his intentions, he would calmly march directly in the opposite direction.[21]

Vic was fortunate enough to have been raised on board games from the age of 3. His father was an avid checkers player, and as an adult, Vic took lessons for more than 15 years each in checkers and chess from two U.S. champions—Tom Wiswell and Art Bisguier, respectively. All board game players know that deception is one of the keys, if not *the* key, to success. Wiswell wrote some 15,000 maxims on checkers, a few of which Vic included in his first book; we here present 10 from Vic's unpublished collection that are particularly pertinent to deception:

1. **Minefield**—On the other hand, there are many tricks, traps, and swindles on board, and you must keep a sharp lookout for them, or be ambushed and defeated. There is no safety guarantee; strategy, after all, is the name of the game. Eternal vigilance is your best hope for survival . . . in checkers or chess.
2. **Black Magic**—The best trick of all is concealing your tricks.
3. **The Confidence Game**—It's when you are most confident that you walk, wide-eyed, into the hidden trap. It happens to patzers and world champions: it goes with the territory.
4. **Close to the Vest**—Don't telegraph your punches. Old-timers had a saying: "Play your moves close to the vest." It's a good maxim to follow even if you don't wear a vest.
5. **The Switcher**—You play hard against strong lines of play, but you may be off guard when you are up against a weak opening. Before you know it, your wily opponent has a winning game.
6. **Action or Inaction**—Some positions call for an aggressive attack or a spectacular sacrifice, while others call for a quiet waiting move or an innocent-appearing move that is really a "Lorelei," tempting your opponent to go astray.
7. **Confusing the Issue**—Beware of the opponent who intently studies the left side of the board, then quietly moves a key piece on the right side. You have to look at the whole board to get the whole picture.
8. **The Unexpected**—Unless you are prepared to expect the unexpected, be prepared to expect unexpected defeat.

9. **Houdini**—Successful chess and checkers players have to be master magicians. They must escape unscathed from hopeless positions.

10. **Hidden Trap**—Sometimes you see a brilliant move, but fail to note a fatal flaw at the very end. Try to see your combinations in their entirety.

Deception is as constant in the market as it is among the great masters of board games. In response to a fellow trader's query on the value of bid-asked and trade size data, James Lackey described in a 2002 post to the Spec List some deceptions that take place on a typical day:

> What does it mean when Mr. Big touches his left ear after lighting a cigar and bets his usual line in poker? What does it mean when Goldman goes high bid on Nvidia and pushes the stock up by repeating his high bid up a dollar right before lunchtime? What does it mean when the specialist for 3M spreads out the stock a dollar after a decline of 50 cents then prints 50,000 shares?
>
> Each stock has a personality. The personality is from the traders and the market makers trading the stock. The key to intraday moves is to find the Ax. The Ax is the market maker or makers who have the orders on a big day. The big pushes of a dollar or more, when it is obvious who the buyer is, usually indicate the end of the order. The best is Fidelity; they blast stocks. The worst is Janus; they drip orders through many different firms.
>
> One must realize the different motivations of traders, specialists and now the ECNs [Electronic Communications Networks]. A great example is Goldman Sachs. Not only are they GSCO on your Level 2 machine, they can be SILK, which is Spear Leeds, which they own. Also they can be Spear's ECN, REDI or be any other ECN, INCA, Instinet, or they take or hit ISLD to fake out day traders. We have a machine that tells us who bought or sold on ISLD. So if I offer 100 shares at 50 and Goldman takes the stock, I know. Which is probably somewhere close to the end of the order. He has shown his cards, especially if he is high bid for a time.
>
> They key to using time and sales and bid ask size is to know the players in the stock. Much deception is used when printing those so-called blocks of stock. Also bid ask size and spread is used to deceive traders into thinking stocks are either strong or weak. It is much more difficult to judge NYSE because the market makers can't be seen. The market makers actually stand in front of the specialist on the floor. Therefore, you must judge the specialist's moves. Usually if he is not playing his usual games, he has big orders and no time to play. That is where you want to be in, with a good hand, with a big pot.

 Despite all the evidence that results relating to technical analysis are consistent with randomness or the efficient markets hypothesis, the field's multifarious techniques continue to exert a certain fascination even on highly educated people. We found ourselves with a front-row view of this phenomenon when Lamberg, the aforementioned

Monty Python fan, wrote a spoof of Martin Pring's Know Sure Thing (KST) indicator, to use in one of our columns debunking technical analysis:

> I have spent over 10 years developing a technical indicator that allows me to predict the future movement of stocks with uncanny accuracy. My indicator, known as the Guaranteed Known Thing (GKT), is based on number sequences that occur throughout nature. It has made me a fortune. The GKT is based on the work of two famous mathematicians: Johann Heinrich Lambert (1728–1777) and Leonardo Pisano Fibonacci (1170–1259).
>
> Lambert is renowned among physicists as the founder of the theory of light measurement, and his *Cosmological Letters* are famous among astronomers. Lambert attempted to explain the structure of the universe in these writings. In the course of his work, he became aware of a color-triangle developed by Tobias Mayer in Gottingen in 1758 to systematically construct many of the possible colors. Building on Mayer's work, Lambert created a triangle-based pyramid. King's yellow, cinnabar, and azurite occupy the three corners, and each side combines the two corner colors to form seven hues. On the inside, all three basic colors contribute to the color of each respective surface. The 45 hues of the lowest triangle give way to increasingly higher and brighter triangles of 28, 15, 10, 6, and 3 hues. The pyramid's tip is white, for a total of 108 hues.
>
> What does this have to do with making my fortune? I check the entire universe of stocks for action around the 45- and 108-day moving averages, then look for golden-hued crosses at a sequence of 28-, 15-, 10-, 6-, and 3-day moving averages. The stocks that survive this incredibly powerful screen are then checked for Fibonacci Fan and Arc intersections.
>
> So powerful is this analysis that I caught the start, top, and bottom of the entire Internet move. But I am not greedy and have decided to divulge the stocks picked by the GKT indicator on my new hotline, the King's Ransom. You can be my first subscriber.

Lamberg's mention of real mathematicians lent a certain believability to the fabrication.

In fact, the GKT indicator sounded so good that one of our editors, one of the sharpest minds in financial journalism, assumed it was real. When we innocently referred after the column's publication to the brilliance of Lamberg's fabrication, we were within a cat's whisker of being fired once again.

Propaganda Aspects of Technical Analysis

Momentum indicators, straight-line extrapolations, reliance on subjective interpretation by the specially gifted—where have we seen this kind of reliance on authority and glittering generality before? In the techniques of propaganda. In Chapter 2, we examined propaganda and advertising techniques in an attempt to explain the persistence of popular misconceptions about the relation of earnings and stock market returns. These same techniques may be discerned in the successful persuasion of the public to buy technical analysis software, books, and seminars. Each of the seven basic propaganda techniques enumerated in the Institute for Propaganda Analysis' classic text, *The Fine Art of Propaganda,* has an application in the field of technical analysis:

Name calling: Those who do not subscribe to technical analysis are denigrated and ridiculed. Vic found himself the subject of this in 2001 after he gave an interview to the magazine *Technical Analysis of Stocks and Commodities.*[22] The TurtleTrader, a leading trend-following technical analysis Web site, ran a post emphasizing Vic's massive trading losses in 1997 (trading short-term strategies against the trend). "Here's a guy who blew up his own trading account in a spectacular fashion, and he's knocking systematic trend-following?"

Testimonial: The TurtleTrader also remarked: "To accept any of what Niederhoffer says is to ignore the existence of Bill Dunn, Jerry Parker, Richard Dennis, John W. Henry, and all of the many Turtles." (It might be fair to note here that Richard Dennis, founder of the Turtles, has authored his own share of losses and has closed funds amid massive drawdowns and liquidations.)

Glittering generality: The need for technical analysis is presented in a formulation so general that it cannot be pinned down. The pioneering technical analyst Charles Dow, originator of the Dow Theory and the Dow Jones Industrial Average, gave a beautiful example of this technique: "The market reduces to a bloodless verdict all knowledge bearing on finance, both domestic and foreign. . . . Price movements, therefore, represent everything everybody knows, hopes, believes and anticipates. Hence, there is no need to supplement the price movements." With untestable statements like that, it would be very hard for a man from Mars to distinguish the level of knowledge in the field of technical analysis as we begin the twenty-first century from that existing at the beginning of the twentieth.

It is hardly surprising that Dow's quote is featured on the home page of the main selling document of perhaps the most respected technical analyst in the world. This analyst's system of reading money flows was featured exclusively on the financial information service where Laurel was an editor. Her bosses mandated daily coverage of its readings. In 1999, however, at Vic's suggestion, Laurel asked her reporters to obtain the technician's actual results. A moment of truth occurred when an office researcher at the firm called back after a few days and said there were no data to support the validity or predictability of the technique espoused. The researcher pointed out that the analyst had bought winning stocks over the previous several years of the bull market, and said that the record spoke for itself.

Transfer: In the nonfinancial world, individuals and groups often use religious or patriotic symbols, such as the cross or the flag, to cloak themselves with an air of virtue. Technical analysts have put this to good use. The very name "technical analysis" carries an aura of science. Perhaps because interpretation is so subjective, the field also carries a whiff of magic; one of the most well-known books on technical analysis is called *Market Wizards*. All financial Web sites, magazines, and television programs like to have a technical analyst in their stable of pundits to achieve "balance," thereby conferring an air of authority to the analysts. Many technical analysts invoke the names of George Soros and Warren Buffett, contending that the success of these legends is the result of a trend-following strategy related to technical analysis rather than the fruit of leveraged tax-sheltered buy-and-hold investments in a wide range of growing American businesses during a bull market.

One of the best uses of transfer we have seen appears in *Trading Chaos: Applying Expert Techniques to Maximize Your Profits*.[23] Author Bill Williams references Einstein when discussing his Market Facilitation Index: "Comparing this to Einstein's formula $E = mc^2$, we can solve for the constant c^2 by transposing the m (mass) $c^2 = E/m = $ Range / Volume."

Card stacking: In technical analysis, examples to prove a point are chosen retrospectively and selectively. The market is rich enough to provide examples to both prove and disprove the validity of any chart pattern.

Bandwagon: One of the more prominent Web sites selling instruction in technical analysis ("Just $999") lists traders who supposedly use methods similar to the ones of the course.

Plain folks: "Hey, I'm just a regular Jane or Joe, but I got rich by learning how to connect the dots and draw a trend line. You, too, can make big money in the market."

Some of the earmarks of pseudoscience apply here as well. Robert L. Park, a physics professor at the University of Maryland, compiled this list in a book called *Voodoo Science: From Foolishness to Fraud:*

1. A discovery is pitched directly to the media.
2. A powerful "establishment" is said to be suppressing the discovery.
3. An effect is always at the very limit of detection.
4. Evidence for a discovery is anecdotal.
5. A belief is said to be credible because it has endured for centuries.
6. An important discovery is made in isolation.
7. New laws of nature are proposed to explain an incredible observation.[24]

Investors who are susceptible to the lure of propaganda and pseudoscience may be disinclined to ask for scientific proof. Indeed, whenever we have tried in our columns to provide a fair test of whether trend following works, we have been greeted with vitriol. That is guaranteed to happen when members of a cult are exposed to views that threaten their belief system. We often publish examples of this hate mail in our column, to indicate the resistance toward questioning the roots of the beliefs. A couple of samples:

> I think it is horrible you are telling people to not use a system that could help them save or make money just because you do not know how to use it (and probably are too lazy to take the time to really learn how to use it).

> I'm so glad there are shortsighted, uneducated people like yourselves that write such nonsense. Keep up the bad work . . . it just makes it easier for me to make money from all of the "fundamentalists" who will never make a dime in the market. No reply required.

> That's why you went broke. You belong in jail.

At least we are with distinguished company in being vilified for our views on momentum. Amos Tversky, the father of research in cognitive biases, collaborated on many studies with Gilovich, the Cornell professor who concluded that hot streaks in basketball are a myth. Tversky said that he lost more friends from his studies than he could count. At least Tversky's collaborator, Kahneman, was compensated for losing all these friends. He won the Nobel Prize for economics in 2002 for his demonstration that these streaks are mere random variations.

We are consoled every now and then when we get a positive letter:

I've been following your contrarian methods and recently formed a hedge fund to implement them. Suffice it to say my results and the anti-trend-following systems that you led me to are making me, my family, and my investors very happy.

We are not alone in concluding that the virtue ascribed to technical analysis is a chimera. Those who have studied the subject with a reasonable degree of objectivity are fairly unanimous in concluding that many of the conventional techniques of technical prediction are not of great merit. Here is what Zvi Bodie has to say in the classic textbook, *Essentials of Investments:* "It should be abundantly clear from our presentations that most of technical analysis is based on ideas totally at odds with the efficient market hypothesis."[25] While markets are not completely efficient, they're pretty close, so any method that purports to find inefficiencies had better be good.

Why Does the Myth Persist?

Beyond the psychological biases and propaganda, the persistence of belief in technical analysis techniques is unsurprising, given the size of the industry that has sprung up around it. If the premises of technical analysis were subjected to testing, what would be the prognosis for all the seminars, courses, trade fairs, software, analysts, hardware, societies, news programs, support services, and staff that provide trend-following systems, not to mention those involved in marketing and evaluating the systems? Technical analysis practitioners are not anxious for a new paradigm that threatens their livelihood, even if their own paradigm does not jibe with the facts.

We are reminded of the centuries-long success of the Delphic oracle. The priesthood no doubt benefited to no small degree from a vast network of spies who gathered intelligence on fleet building, military preparations, and the potential for new colonies. But the most important reason for Delphi's long success was surely that the predictions were just ambiguous enough to keep people coming back for more.

A Technical Approach That Can Be Tested

The question arises: Don't you do anything but knock things down? Is there an indicator that you do have hope for? If there is some predictive value to a chart, then the numbers that create the charts will contain that information. Science has always proceeded by trying to quantify rather than by relying on visual impressions and anecdotes. We do believe that prices contain predictive significance. But we prefer to work with the highs, lows, opens, and closes of the daily prices that go into the charts.

The approach we take is based on a test-taking method pioneered by our friend Adam Robinson, cofounder of the *Princeton Review*. It involves putting yourself in the mind of the people who write questions for the Educational Testing Service's college entrance exams. The tests always begin with easy questions where the obvious answers are correct and proceed to tricky ones, where the obvious answers are wrong (but close to the right answer).

The way to handle those tricky questions is to avoid the obvious response. The way to make money in stocks is to do the opposite of what seems obvious—and recently profitable. (For example, if selling the rallies works three days in a row, then it probably won't work the fourth day. And if a tested system fails to work one day, it probably will the next day.)

It is at least as hard to make money in the markets as it is to score high on the SAT or the GMAT. But instead of throwing you hard questions toward the end of an exam, the market likes to throw you tricky moves when you are off guard, in hopes that you will give the wrong answer and thereby contribute toward your broker's Porsches, profit-sharing plans, and well-appointed dining rooms.

On a long-term basis, the market loves to throw in a nice 10 percent rally when the gloom is greatest. That a rally was coming always seems obvious after the fact.

On a day-to-day basis, the market likes to throw out trick questions that will make monkeys out of people who rely on visual impressions of charts. Take, for example, the 80 times during the six-year period ending December 31, 2000, that S&P 500 futures have gone up 20 or more points, or about a 2 percent rise. (We use futures in all our calculations because they represent prices that you can actually trade at and make or lose money, while the slow-moving index often lags behind the real price moves.)

On days after big rallies, wise-guy traders like to set up for a decline because the market has a slight tendency to retreat on those days. What the market likes to do on such occasions is to give those traders an easy profit the first time. Next time, they will go short and the market will stick it to them.

The *Princeton Review* technique that we use in our own trading involves the quantification of some 1,700 separate answers to questions posed by the market. Before making a trade, we like to measure the accuracy or profitability of each of these 1,700 answers to the questions that are most similar to what the market is asking today. We take account of the uncertainty of the results in each case and the ideal position relative to today's range to place entry and exit orders.

This approach uses standard technical data only. Thus, in essence, we have devoured the Hydra.

Doubtless many other practitioners of technical analysis are using similar methods. We hope that others will modify their visual and nonquantitative techniques, to come into line with scientific procedure.

Testing the VIX Indicator

Now that we have described an approach to technical analysis in line with the scientific method that has been so effective in advancing knowledge in every other field, we can apply it to our own favorite indicator, the Chicago Board Options Exchange's Volatility Index, commonly referred to as the VIX.

People forget that the market can go up when it has been declining for a while, just as they forget it can fall after a prolonged rise. These swings in optimism are among the most notable regularities in the market. Sentiment indicators—the degree of bullishness and risk in options, the percentage of bullish advisors, the percentage of advancing stocks, and the percentage of cash held by mutual funds—swing back and forth from high to low like pendulums. The big question is whether these changes in sentiment have any predictive power vis-à-vis future moves in the general market.

As everyone knows, it is always darkest before the dawn. There is no measure for "darkest," but the signals provided by the VIX are among the best we have found. The index provides a measure of the expected level of volatility in the market.

The normal level for the VIX is about 25. A good working hypothesis is that when volatility is high—above 30 percent or so—investors tend to be frightened, and it is a good time to buy. When volatility is low—below 25 percent or so—investors tend to be complacent, and it is a good time to sell. "When fortune means to men most good, she looks upon them with a threatening eye," as William Shakespeare wrote in *King John*, Act 3, Scene 4.

The VIX is calculated based on the coming month. As a practical matter, however, expected volatility for periods up to a year correlates almost 100 percent with the changes in one-month VIX.

We tested the VIX hypothesis by calculating the return on buying S&P 500 futures the first time the VIX closed above 30 and selling them the first time the VIX closed below 25. Similar results could be obtained by buying an index-tracking mutual fund such as the Vanguard 500 Trust, or by purchasing SPDRs Trust shares (spiders).

Figure 3.5 shows that using a 25–30 VIX system to swing from buy to sell yields an average profit of 3.4 percent on 12 trades since October 1997. There were two small losses.

David Simon and Roy A. Wiggins III came to similar conclusions separately in a rigorous study, "S&P Futures Returns and Contrary Sentiment Indicators."[26]

The professors looked at the effect on S&P 500 futures of each percentage point change in the VIX. They concluded that for each point increase above the norm, the S&P goes up an extra 0.1 percent in the next 10 trading days. Thus, given a normal VIX reading of 25, if VIX goes up to 35—10 percentage points above the norm—the S&P can be expected to rise 1 percent extra in the next 10 days. Conversely, when the VIX falls to 15 percent, the S&P can be expected to perform 1 percent worse than its normal move.

Simon and Wiggins also show what happens when the VIX is at high levels and at low levels. Most impressive of all, they run what is called an "out-of-sample test." They demonstrate that with information available at the beginning of each year, a forecaster could make a useful prediction. For example, based on VIX levels, they came up with 39 forecasts that S&P futures would go up in the next 10 days. In actuality, 22 of them went up and the average change was exactly as predicted: up 1 percent. Similar results occurred for the occasions when the market was predicted to go up by 3 percent.

Professors Simon and Wiggins are not the usual run of academics who obscure their results with impenetrable mathematics and statistics so that the results are meaningful only to a handful of finance PhDs. Perhaps the reason is that Simon, who teaches at Bentley College in Waltham, Massachusetts, has an unusual background for a professor. He actually worked for a hedge fund before going to academia, rather than the much more common reverse situation. The professor is not averse to a bit of trading of his own, and he is active in individual stock options. Furthermore, Bentley College has a trading floor equipped with dozens of workstations and live feeds from all the major data providers that most traders would envy. The students use these machines to answer realistic trading questions that they are assigned in class.

An indicator like VIX might have validity because expected volatilities are related to the returns that investors demand. When VIX registers high anxiety and uncertainty in the market, investors naturally demand a higher rate of return to compensate them for the extra risk they perceive. Put another way, they will only buy if the price is low enough.

Date	VIX	Buy S&P 500	Sell S&P 500	Chg.	Duration of Trade (Days)
Oct. 27, 1997	39.96	876.99			
Dec. 1, 1997	24.88		974.77	11.10%	35
Dec. 24, 1997	30.47	932.7			
Dec. 30, 1997	24.93		970.84	4.10%	6
Jan. 9, 1998	34.46	927.69			
Jan. 14, 1998	24.21		927.94	0.00%	5
Aug. 4, 1998	33.1	1,072.12			
Nov. 5, 1998	24.8		1,133.85	5.80%	93
Dec. 14, 1998	32.47	1,141.20			
Dec. 18, 1998	24.66		1,188.03	4.10%	4
Jan. 13, 1999	31.26	1,234.40			
Mar. 8, 1999	24.98		1,282.73	3.90%	54
Sept. 23, 1999	30.28	1,280.41			
Oct. 6, 1999	23.53		1,325.40	3.50%	13
Oct. 15, 1999	31.48	1,247.41			
Oct. 21, 1999	24.77		1,283.61	2.90%	6
April 5, 2000	30.59	1,487.37			
June 1, 2000	24.74		1,448.81	-2.60%	57
Oct. 11, 2000	30.95	1,364.59			
Jan. 23, 2001	23.86		1,360.00	-0.30%	104
Feb. 28, 2001	31	1239			
May 18, 2001	24.26		1,291.96	4.30%	79
Sept. 6, 2001	32.48	1,103.50			
Nov. 23, 2001	24.78		1,153.00	4.50%	78
June 20, 2002	32.5	1,007.10	N/A*	N/A*	N/A*

*At time of writing, VIX was still above 25.

Swing System Results		
10 wins in 12 trades		
Average Return/Trade		3.40%
Standard Deviation		3.40%
Average Duration of Trade (Days)		44.5

Figure 3.5   Swing System

This link between risk and expected return is central to the modern theory of finance. The lower the expected risk, the lower the return required by investors; and the higher the expected risk, the higher the required return. All portfolio analysis, all Nobel Prizes given in the field, all students in business school, all analysts taking exams, are taught and understand and accept this relation. Corporations use it to determine which investments to accept, and regulators use it to determine how much to let regulated companies charge. Underwriters use it to determine the pricing of new and secondary securities.

It is therefore not surprising that when market risk is perceived to be high, subsequent returns are indeed high. That is exactly what a high level of VIX indicates: a higher-than-average expected volatility for stocks during coming months. Similarly, it is not surprising that when the level of VIX is low—that is, the expected future risk of the market is perceived to be low—subsequent returns from holding the stock market would turn out to be low.

While a 3.4 percent-per-trade return may not seem much, bear in mind that it's a multiple of the money market rates currently being paid for an entire year.

Conclusion

We are under no illusion that our suggested recasting of technical analysis to bring it into conformity with the scientific method will convince many technical analysts to change their ways. Nor do we think our workout showing the theoretical and empirical utility of our own favorite indicator, the VIX, has much chance of setting the world of technical analysts on fire. That is fine with us. Not only does it make the game more interesting, but it will lengthen the time that it takes for our approach and favorite indicator to become worthless.

No doubt certain technical indicators, under certain vague interpretations, work for certain selective periods. That is, in fact, guaranteed to happen. But overall, the outcome has not been fruitful to the technical analysts. For 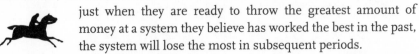 just when they are ready to throw the greatest amount of money at a system they believe has worked the best in the past, the system will lose the most in subsequent periods.

A good indirect indicator of the ever-changing cycles in technical analysis is the marketing of technical trading systems. Such tools and techniques typically are marketed as being the very ones used by the greatest technical traders of all time. Such systems start off being offered to a handful of specially picked wealthy investors for tens of thousands of dollars. Next, they are offered to those wealthy enough to spend their time attending a seminar, where the developer or a disciple explains the method. In the final stage of the life cycle, these systems are offered in the back pages of technical analysis magazines and books at prices ranging from $2 to $200. Only in America do firms exist that specialize in wholesaling beaten-down trading systems.

All of which tends to support another rule included in that massive compendium, *Investing Rules:*

- See what the trend followers are doing, and do the opposite.

Need we add that this one was from us?

Epilogue: Ode to the Hydra of Trin

Dr. Brett Steenbarger, the behavioral finance expert we introduced in Chapter 2, was an ardent devotee of many of the techniques of technical analysis before he met us. The mutual experimenting and reporting that he and Vic have each undertaken since then have increased Steenbarger's skepticism about technical analysis to a large extent. He has memorialized the conversion process and his current thinking with particular reference to material in this chapter as follows:

Of Heroes and Hydras

Gather 'round, ye Speculators, and I shall tell you a tale of heroes and hydras, and that fiercest Hydra of all: the Hydra of TRIN. She was said to possess nine heads of poison, the middle one immortal. A single bite from a single head was enough to fell any hero.

I was but a young lad, filled with the enthusiasm of battle, when I set forth to vanquish the monsters. Many complex strategies had I devised to party with the likes of Cerberus, Medusa and, of course, the Hydra of TRIN. Indeed, my strategies were so complex that I believed myself to be beyond defeat.

On my sojourn, however, I came across a teacher who questioned my ways. He was a wise but strange man, speaking portentously of music and games of skill. He warned me that my intricate battle plans would come to naught against these fierce monsters. "Always take the direct approach," he counseled. "Indirection is the quickest path to ruin."

I would have none of it. "Is it not written," I asked, "that Medusa cannot be approached directly, lest the hero be turned to stone?"

"Ah, yes," the teacher smiled. "It is so. But did not Theseus take a direct path nonetheless? He could not go after a different monster to conquer Medusa. He had to go to her lair and seek her out with no intermediary."

The teacher's words made sense to me, and I vowed to make direct warfare upon the Hydra of TRIN.

She was gruesome in appearance, filling me with fright and awe. Her heads bobbed and weaved, dropping poison on the ground around her. Nothing could grow in that ground. I found myself in a true wasteland. Around her serpentine body lay the skeletons of heroes before me, who had proven inadequate to their task. I prayed that I not meet their ignominious fate.

With my heart steeled, I approached the Hydra of TRIN with my mighty club and gave a ferocious swing. So vicious was my blow that one of the heads—the five-day TRIN—was severed from the body. Before I could rejoice, however, another head sprang in its place: the 55-day TRIN. Furiously, I struck another blow. This head, too, fell from the neck only to be replaced by the Open TRIN.

In the interim, the other heads swooped closer and closer to my body, snapping their jaws and dripping their venom. I realized that I had to act fast or face a painful death.

With a wide arc, I swung my club and severed two heads. But, alas, the Eliades TRIN and the Bretz new TRIN replaced these.

The venomous heads swung lower, nipping the edge of my robes. I realized in that moment that Death was upon me.

In anguish, I called out to the spirit of my teacher. To my amazement, his words filled my ears, as surely as if he were standing barefoot beside me. "Take the direct approach," he intoned. "There is power in simplicity."

"But what will vanquish the Hydra of TRIN?" I cried in desperation.

"Remember, my pupil," the words came to me. "Volume is a proxy for volatility. The TRIN measures volatility as a function of price rises and declines. There is nothing in the ratio that cannot be derived from a direct investigation of price change and volatility."

With that, a brilliant torch appeared in my hands. My confidence renewed and my resolve strengthened, I held the eight heads at bay with the torch, searing them before they could grow back. The center head thus exposed, I chopped it at the root with my sword, burying it forever in the ground where it could menace heroes no more.

I am an old man now, and have fought many a battle. But no lesson shines so brightly as the one I learned from my teacher that day. I say to you now, valiant speculators and heroes: "Listen to the words of my teacher. In the midst of darkness, always take the straight, illumined path. The torch of wisdom is mightier than any warrior's club."

All in all, our battle with the market momentum Hydra shows her to be a myth. We hope that this chapter will help illuminate the murky caverns of the mind where the Hydra dwells. Furthermore, we hope our approach will allow readers to reflect on and build beliefs about market momentum that are closer to science than superstition. There is an infinite poetry and beauty to market moves, with inexhaustible wealth awaiting those who can unravel the future course of movement.

4

THE CULT OF
THE BEAR

This will all end badly, we've not the slightest doubt, and the only question is when. Probably not tomorrow, as we say. But that's as far out as we'll go.

—Alan Abelson, "Up and Down Wall Street," *Barron's,* May 24, 1993
(Dow Jones Industrial Average at 3492)

When we see a man who persists in wearing galoshes on his feet, mittens on his hands, a heavy wool jacket on his back, and a ski cap on his head on a warm summer day, we know that we are witnessing someone who has succumbed to false beliefs. The man must have believed that it was going to be very cold and wet outside, and he was wrong. If we were trained psychologists, we might attribute the behavior to a dysfunction in separating reality from belief. Very young children have a similar problem in differentiating between the two. By the age of 10 or 11, they usually can identify fantasy, and except for autistic children, they behave in a manner consistent with reality.

It is amazing to see an adult who has not only maintained a false belief for his entire working life, but has also consistently ridiculed others who do not share his beliefs. Such an adult still sits in the catbird seat at one of the world's most prestigious financial publications—a news magazine that, according to its marketing materials, circulates among hundreds of thousands of the world's wealthiest and most influential decision makers.

The man is Alan Abelson, author of the weekly *Barron's* column, "Up and Down Wall Street," for the past 36 years. Abelson's irreverence toward the most powerful figures in politics and finance, his facility with words, and his puns have earned him a reputation as the wittiest writer about Wall Street. No one, be he the chairman of the Federal Reserve or a U.S. president of either party, is safe from his sardonic pen. Circulation doubled in his first year of writing the column, and kept growing. Today, the paid circulation of *Barron's* is 300,000, and the average household net worth of its readers is $1.2 million.

From the start, Abelson played a dual role as editor-columnist at the publication that gave him far more than the usual power for a columnist. In 1998, he received a Lifetime Achievement Award from the Loeb Foundation, arguably the most important organization in financial journalism. While he no longer serves as editor, he commands speaking fees of $10,000.

Skepticism, Science, and Self-Esteem: A Multitrillion-Dollar Case Study

Though he is a clever and talented writer, by any objective standard Abelson has the distinction of being one of the worst market forecasters in history. He has been skeptical, if not outright bearish, on the stock market for his entire tenure as a *Barron's* columnist. Yet during this period, the Dow Jones Industrial Average and S&P 500 gained some 3600 percent, with reinvested dividends, perhaps the greatest accumulation of wealth in history. On January 21, 1966, the Friday before Abelson's first column appeared, the Dow closed at 988.14. Thirty-four years later, on January 14, 2000, the average reached a high of 11,722.98.

The key to a happy, successful life is to be humble about one's knowledge and open enough to admit the possibility of change and to adjust our thinking when facts contradict our beliefs. In the market, it means a determination to keep up with new ideas and academic theories that influence the practitioners and to have a procedure for judging and testing the work of others before touting it to us.

We all know people who do not rely on logic, who cling defiantly to biases and errors in thinking in the face of incontrovertible evidence to the contrary. The tendency to hold onto manifestly illogical beliefs is the subject of an entire line of study in psychology. One of the great contributions of the psychologist Leon Festinger was the theory of cognitive dissonance. Festinger cataloged rationalization techniques that people use to preserve their self-esteem when facts run afoul of their beliefs. The theory was developed as a result of Festinger's famous study of a doomsday cult, recounted in his 1956 book, *When Prophecy Fails.*[1]

With two colleagues, Festinger infiltrated a small group of believers led by Marian Keech, a Midwest woman who claimed to be hearing messages from outer space. Keech believed that a flood would destroy the world, but that flying saucers would take her and her followers safely to the planet Clarion before the devastation began.

Keech's adherents quit their jobs and shed their money, houses, possessions, and, in some cases, their spouses to await the day of rescue. One evening, Keech heard from Clarion that the saucers would come at the stroke of midnight on December 21. On the evening of December 20, her followers gathered in Keech's living room. The moment passed in utter silence. No one knew what to do. At last, at 4:45 A.M., Keech's face lit up. She said she had just heard from Clarion that the world had been saved by the faith of the little band of believers.

Until then, the group had shunned publicity and not sought new recruits. Now, they called up the media and handed out leaflets on street corners that described how they had saved the world through their purity, prayers, and steadfast faith.

When facts and belief come into obvious dissonance, the logical response is to adjust the beliefs. Whether the dissonance occurs in a doomsday cult or in a corporate boardroom or a trading room, self-esteem often gets in the way, and the adjustment does not always occur. For Marian Keech and her followers, the unresolved inner conflict was so great that mere rationalization could not ease the discomfort; affirmation from others was required to allay the shame of having acted foolishly.

Undercover research is frowned on today, and since Festinger's study, research into cognitive dissonance, groupthink, and similar irrational phenomena has consisted mainly of Monday-morning quarterbacking of past events and contrived experiments involving college students. The remarkable thing about Abelson's columns is that they provide a real-world case study of cognitive dissonance involving trillions of dollars of lost wealth and the reputations of powerful securities firms.

As Festinger noted, the attempt to maintain consistency in one's beliefs and self-esteem gives rise to maladaptive behavior. When you have gone far out on a limb and so many people have followed you, and there is much "sunk cost," as economists would say, it is difficult to admit you have been wrong. That is exactly why the scientific method was developed: so that people, be they scientists, traders, doomsday cult leaders, or leading financial columnists, could adjust their beliefs based on constant feedback between hypotheses and evidence.

 The scientific method involves experiment and observation. Its essence is a humble attitude toward one's state of knowledge. There are as many ways of doing science as there are scientists, but everybody agrees that it involves four elements:

Induction: Forming a hypothesis—a testable statement.
Deduction: Making specific predictions based on the hypothesis.
Observation: Gathering data.
Verification: Testing the predictions against the data.

Throughout the 1990s, while the Dow and S&P 500 quintupled and the Nasdaq enjoyed a ninefold gain, Abelson predicted an imminent crash based on one or more of the following: overextended prices; high price/earnings ratios; weak pessimism; weak bullishness; strong bullishness; high interest rates; inflation resulting from low interest rates; a weak dollar; fiscal extravagance; low dividend yields; the weakness of the Fed; Clinton's fiscal extravagance; the narrowness of the market's advance; the percentage of stocks below their 52-week highs; market capitalization as a percentage of GDP; the growing number of chartered financial analysts; the oversupply of new equity; a shortage of stocks to meet the demand of mutual funds; the presence of the "little guy" in the market; the generous salaries paid to nannies in Greenwich, Connecticut; an indoor skating rink in a Hamptons home; similarities to conditions prevailing before past crashes; trouble overseas; the imminence of recession; the imminence of recovery; debt reduction; the inability of companies to raise prices; and Abelson's favorite, speculative excess.

The adjustment of beliefs afforded by the scientific method surely was not taking place.

The market's major decline in the new century made Abelson's ideas finally appear relevant. This does not chasten us in the least. Investors who followed the columnist's advice during the many years he was wrong would have long ago lost all their chips.

The Critic's Story

In a July 25, 2001, interview, Abelson told Laurel that he approached the market as a skeptic. "That's the contribution I think I've made to financial journalism," he said. "You're supposed to bring a critical presence to the field." Without in any way minimizing the importance of skepticism to the field of financial journalism, or Abelson's own laudable contributions to the field, we would draw a line between skepticism and unrelenting gloom in the sunshine.

Laurel interviewed Abelson at *Barron's* offices in the World Financial Center in lower Manhattan. Barely two months later, terrorist attacks destroyed the neighboring World Trade Center, forcing *Barron's* and its parent company, Dow Jones & Company, to abandon 200 Liberty Street for New Jersey. On the day of the interview, lower Manhattan really did look like the center of the financial world. The harbor was full of private yachts, and the mirrored buildings reflected the July sun.

Abelson was waiting at the elevator doors to lead the way to his office. A short, trim man, he wore tan slacks and a blue-and-white shirt with a bright plaid tie. His office was not particularly large, but it was private and it had a river view. A four-shelf bookcase lined one wall. Two computer terminals sat on the desk. A few cactus plants provided the only greenery. Laurel and Abelson sat at a small table.

Abelson had not contemplated a career as a financial journalist, he said. Born October 12, 1925, in New York City, he graduated from Townsend Harris High School, then earned a dual degree in English and chemistry from New York City College. He earned a master's degree in creative writing at the renowned University of Iowa Writers' Workshop.

Back in New York, he took a job as copy boy at Hearst's *New York Journal American,* one of the city's several now-extinct afternoon papers. He became a reporter in the business section, and in 1956 went to work as a jack-of-all-trades at *Barron's.*

His first job at *Barron's* was editing investment stories, "which was interesting because I didn't know anything about investing." To learn, he read a manual on markets from cover to cover. The rest of his market knowledge came through interviewing sources and from perusing Securities and Exchange Commission filings in the fray of reporting.

He began developing a style of reporting—tough-minded, skeptical—modeled on nonfinancial journalism. "Until the 1960s, nobody ever wrote anything critical of the stock market," he recalled. Press releases and the speeches of corporate chairman were summarized unquestioningly. The best writing—Ida Tarbell's exposé of John D. Rockefeller's Standard Oil Trust, for example—had been done by generalists, not financial journalists.

"There's so much bullishness in Wall Street," he said. "Brokerage houses turn out tons of material, companies issue press releases—that's all bullish. I don't think sounding a skeptical note is threatening the life of the republic; I think that's what journalists are supposed to do."

In 1966, then-editor Robert Bleiberg asked Abelson to write a column. Speculation was rampant. The market was filled with colorful characters. It seemed to Abelson that the period had been created especially for him to write about.

Nevertheless, he said he took the job reluctantly. "The column was always a sideline," he said. "I was assistant managing editor, I was running several departments. Those were my priorities. We always had a very thin staff."

Laurel noticed two copies of Peter Bernstein's *Against the Gods: The Remarkable Story of Risk,* one of the finest histories of statistics available, on Abelson's shelf.[2] She remarked on them to Abelson, and asked if he had studied statistics. The answer was no. "Statistics can really be the undoing of a journalist," he said. "They're too fascinating, like crossword puzzles. People are always making statistical comparisons—in the end, they don't add up to anything." He does not, he added, read financial books.

Neither does he own stocks, to avoid conflict-of-interest accusations in lawsuits, an occupational hazard for business journalists. Fortunately, Dow Jones had a generous profit-sharing plan for the greater part of his tenure.

Laurel asked him if he had indeed been bearish all through the bull market. "Some people think I've been bearish all my life," he replied.

Had he ever had doubts about what he had written or felt embarrassed by his calls?

"How can you be right all the time?" he said, with the magnanimous humility of someone who had been wrong almost all the time. "I've never been in doubt, or I wouldn't have written it. I can't say I've ever been embarrassed by anything at all."

It is worth noting that a number of writers besides Abelson have been bearish for decades. But most of them have been relegated to the world of newsletters of the hard-money persuasion, the kind sold on late-night television and by direct mail. They require unusual promotion because they have been so wrong, and most sensible people ignore them. Howard Ruff, with his 1970s-era forecast for $1,000-an-ounce gold, comes to mind. (As we write, gold is at $350, down from $850 in January 1980.)

The unusual thing about Abelson's columns is that they appear at the front of arguably the most credible financial publication of all. It is as though the American Medical Association or the *New England Journal of Medicine* told us to not to go outside because the air pollutants would cause suffocation. As Carl Hovland and Herbert Kelman have shown, people change their responses much more in response to high-credibility sources than low-credibility sources.[3] As we tried to understand Abelson's enduring influence, our research on cognitive dissonance led us to other insights from social psychology, and to the literature on cults.

Comfort and Fear

One similarity is that both cults and financial writing like Abelson's play to the human need for certainty, control, and simplicity in a complicated world. The price/earnings ratios and naïve measures of length and breadth cited as reasons for bearishness by Abelson and his sources over a decade are readily available to the technologically unsophisticated investor, and thus provide illusory comfort. Statistical testing, by contrast, requires knowledge and effort, and occasionally—if not usually—rejecting hypotheses that are disproven by the facts.

A further parallel is the reliance on fear. Cults rely on a mix of positive and negative controls, but to keep followers in line, negative emotions dominate. David Koresh, leader of the Branch Davidians, "was always putting things in the negative, always threatening," one cult member told Flo Conway and Jim Siegelman, authors of the 1995 book *Snapping*.[4] "He would describe hell and start screaming in the most horrible way to show people what it was like to burn in hell."

A recurring theme in Abelson's columns is the appeal to fear. Over and over, without regard to changing conditions, he conjures up the horrible catastrophe of 1929, when people jumped out windows and ruination came to those who speculated. After rallies followed the severe declines of 1973–1974, 1987, 1997, and 1998, you would think that common sense would indicate a suspension of calamitous predictions, but no.

Psychologists have shown that an emphasis on fear provides a powerful incentive for change. Driver education films are more effective when they show the blood and broken bones of accident victims than when they display a controlled crash with plastic dummies, according to a well-known study by Ronald W. Rogers and C. Ronald Mewborn.[5] One has to admire the vividness Abelson brings to the feared prospect of a market disaster.

Vic learned early in his career that people pay a lot more for a negative forecast than a positive forecast, and they will pay more attention to it. Why? Most people tend to be optimistic, and it is usually justified in the market. If someone predicts disaster, it's unusual and noteworthy. A more important question is whether the forecaster's reasoning is logical. In Abelson's case, we must ask: What pursuit could have been more pointless than to write a bearish column week in, week out, during the entire run of the greatest bull market in history? We like to visit university bookstores to keep abreast of the latest books. Often we come across titles so specialized and arcane that we throw up our hands in disbelief that anyone could devote the necessary time to such a topic. Vic, for example, spotted a tome in the Williams College bookstore on the influence of Oriental coin collectors in nineteenth-century Mexico. The late Senator William Proxmire entertained America by awarding similarly point-less taxpayer-funded studies the Golden Fleece Award. (One memorable award went to the Environmental Protection Agency for spending $1.2 million in 1980 to preserve a Trenton, New Jersey, sewer as a historical monument.)

As we perused hundreds of Abelson's columns, we could not help being reminded of the coin collectors and the Golden Fleece Awards. Abelson's ir-relevance, however, was potentially harmful to any of the hundreds of thou-sands of *Barron's* readers who might actually have traded on his advice—or who had become so accustomed to seeing him wrong that when the crash did come, they held tight to their stocks in the belief that Abelson was crying wolf once more.

Taxonomy of the Oeuvre

In Chapters 2 and 3, we noted how investors are manipulated into leaning the wrong way by what amounts to promotional propa-ganda about earnings fallacies and untested folklore about trading patterns. Tables 4.1 and 4.2 show how the characteristics of propa-ganda and pseudo-science show up in Abelson's columns.

One of the beauties of the marketplace is that traders who are wrong in their views tend to be replaced by those who are right. The wrong traders lose their money. The accurate traders tend to gain more money and support. A similar feedback mechanism works in the scientific field. Those who report correct results find that other scientists extend and confirm them. Those who report flawed results tend to be discredited. They lose students and funding, and their articles are not accepted for publication.

Feedback, in fact, is a fundamental law of nature. Standard biology texts contain many pages devoted to the feedback mechanisms that keep the body's systems from getting too far out of order. Feedback is used in almost every electronic device. It is, for example, the basis of the modern amplifier.

Table 4.1   Propaganda Devices and Abelson's Rhetoric

Propaganda Device	Example
Name calling	Calls evidence of stocks offering superior returns "blah blah."
Glittering generality	"How can you be right all the time?"
Testimonial, bandwagon	Describes his distinguished, invariably bearish sources as the most perceptive on Wall Street, "the smart money."
Testimonial	Quotes analysts with bearish forecasts.
Plain folks	Does not read any financial books.
	Has no interest in statistics.
Card-stacking	Relies on indicators as diverse as the strength of the dollar to the salaries of nannies in Greenwich, as long as they offer a bearish forecast.

No such self-correcting mechanism exists in the field of writing. It is possible to be wrong for a long time and still maintain one's cachet and power. Indeed, the lone wolf, the chronic iconoclast tends to be even more rare and more newsworthy as others stampede to the other side. Such has apparently been the case with our hero. His views became very rare, and his sources tended to retire or wither. Yet he survived and thrived, helped, of course, by his brilliance, his creativity, his wide swath of nonfinancial knowledge, his flair, and his rapier wit. When his employees at *Barron's* moved on to other careers, they created similar bastions of bearish thought in major brokerages and newsletters, where they, too, benefited by standing against the tide.

In short, Abelson was not subject to the normal self-correcting process that exists in other fields. That is probably the answer to why beliefs that are not in accord with profitability or survival often are prevalent in nontrading, non-self-correcting fields.

When we started writing our column together, we decided that we would try a different tack. Trading is hard. We knew that our forte was not specific trading suggestions for individual stocks, but rather principles and forces that affect markets, and predictions of broad market moves based on a scientific historical approach.

To overcome our limitations, we decided to trade based on our own research. Rather than recommending what readers should do, we gravitated to a level where we reported what our own research was and how we would trade

Table 4.2   Why People Believe Alan Abelson

Reason	Percent of Time Used to Justify Bearish Forecast
Problem-solving inadequacies: seeking only examples that confirm a hypothesis, slowness to change the hypothesis even when obviously wrong; finding causality in coincident relationships.	100
Appeal to authority.	95
Representativeness (ignoring larger context in which a seemingly unusual event occurs).	90
Hasty generalization; a handful of members (facts) used to judge the entire group (situation).	85
Post hoc, ergo propter hoc: Correlation mistaken for causation.	85
Use of scientific language but not method.	80
Unprovable assertions.	60
Anecdotes used as evidence.	55
Emotive words and false analogies.	50
Reductio ad absurdem: the slippery slope fallacy (eating ice cream will lead you to put on weight; soon you will weigh 350 pounds and die of heart disease; therefore ice cream leads to death).	35
Bold but unsupported statements.	30
Ad hominem: redirecting focus from thinking about the idea to thinking about the person holding the idea.	30
Rationalization of failures.	25
Circular reasoning.	5

based on that. This practice gave us the benefit of a self-correcting process in that if our trades were good we would prosper, and continue, and if our trades were bad, we would lose and tend to pull in our horns.

In retrospect, we wish we had given ourselves the luxury of staying in the ivory tower. On the other hand, the information and knowledge we communicated would have been less focused, less practical, and less falsifiable had we not been eating our own cooking.

It seems on the surface that Abelson shares some of the characteristics that people talk about when they're describing unscientific and untested thought. Probably the reason is that he's not subject to the feedback process. On the other hand, he's been quite correct in the past few years. While we've had our share of good trades and bad trades, certainly the reader who followed Abelson's advice since early 2000 would have done much better than if they had followed ours. We tip our hats to him.

That said, we found some insight in Michael Shermer's *Why People Believe Weird Things: Pseudoscience, Superstition and Other Confusions of Our Time* as to how Abelson, his sources, and his followers were able to maintain erroneous beliefs for so long despite so much evidence to the contrary.[6]

Using the *Weird Things* classification as a guide, we systematically analyzed the 525 "Up and Down Wall Street" columns that appeared in *Barron's* during the decade of the 1990s. Table 4.2 provides an estimated breakdown of the use of illogical reasoning.

Table 4.3 lists highlights of Abelson's columns during the 1990s, with notes on how the forecasts turned out. We chose each quote to give a flavor of the anecdotally inspired predictions, the reliance on discredited authorities, and the endless repetition of simplistic, untested indicators. Some quotes are included merely to illustrate Abelson's general opinion of his subject.

We will not continue with 1998 and 1999, as the Dow rose 50 percent and the Nasdaq 100 more than tripled, except to mildly observe that Abelson disapproved of the rise.

But we cannot forgo reprinting at length the wildest hodgepodge of indicators ever to be found in one column. On September 30, 1996, Abelson, citing Robert Farrell, "Merrill Lynch's master sage and our good buddy," wrote:

[T]he dividend yield on the Standard & Poor's 500 of 2.1 percent is the lowest of this century. The value of stocks relative to GDP is the highest ever. The Tobin Q Ratio (financial assets/corporate balance-sheet assets) is the highest ever. And so is the ratio of the S&P 500 to book value. Ditto, the SP 500 price-to-sales ratio of 4.45.

The value of stocks relative to house prices is at peak levels. The number of hours a working stiff must labor to buy the S&P 500 has risen to a record 53.75.

Trading volume on the New York Stock Exchange is the most ever. The ratio of Nasdaq to Big Board volume is also at a peak. IPOs, mergers, and stock buybacks are all record highs. There are an unprecedented number of mutual funds, and the volume of money pouring into them is twice last year's peak annual rate. As never before, investors are snapping up the shares of aggressive growth funds.

The number of people registered to sell stocks and bonds is 527,000, the most in history and 30 percent more than in 1987. There are a record number—32,000—of candidates to become Chartered Financial Analysts. Seat prices on the NYSE have

Table 4.3 Selections from Alan Abelson's "Up and Down Wall Street" (1990–1999)

Date	Quote	Reality Check
12/31/90	We're convinced that the bear market will awake from its snooze and come roaring back to life, red in tooth and claw. Serious bear markets, like this one, don't quit until they've totaled the investment landscape (for confirmation, see 1973–1974).	The Dow, then at 2629, rose 20% in the following year.
1/6/92	We're also fascinated by the two ominous below-the-line black bars of 1973 and 1974, a melancholy span that followed another stock market era in which multiples didn't count and the only thing that did was growth.	The Dow, then at 3201, rose 3% in 1992. In 1973–1974, the market lost two-thirds of its value, after inflation.
9/28/92	This market's headed for a full-fledged fall. The uncertainty of the election, the sorry condition of the economy, the weakness in the dollar, the inability of lower rates to furnish their customary lift, the woeful spirits of the consumer and the blighted job market, add all of these to stock prices that are still way overvalued by any reasonable standard—and how can you be anything but bearish?	The Dow was then at 3250. Thereafter, its lowest point in the 1990s was 3136 on October 19, 1992.
10/12/92	Dick Russell, "the true disciple of Charles Dow, the latter-day incarnation of William Peter Hamilton, the tireless keeper, defender and explicator of the Dow Theory," says a bear market began October 5, when the Dow closed below a magic level, confirming similar behavior by the Transports months earlier. "This is the really big one," he told Abelson—the end of the bull move that began in 1974.	The Dow, then at 3136, rose 14% over the next year.
5/24/93	That we contemplate the possibility of a further rally, however, doesn't mean we've undergone a midnight conversion. The market is still horribly overvalued in all the ways that count. Froth is everywhere. And the false god of momentum has in his thrall legions of lobotomized followers who have kited scores of stocks to lunar levels. This will all end badly, we've not the slightest doubt, and the only question is when. Probably not tomorrow, as we say. But that's as far out as we'll go.	The Dow, then at 3492, had more than six years and 8200 points to go before peaking at 11722 on January 14, 2000.

Table 4.3 *Continued*

Date	Quote	Reality Check
10/4/93	You know the sort of blah-blah-blah we mean: those earnest sermons whose text describes the kind of wonderful returns common stocks have delivered going back to when Noah finally beached the ark and whose message to the flock is simple: the devil is in the deposits, so hurry to your bank, gather up what pittance remains in those musty vaults, proceed immediately to put it to work in a mutual fund and you'll be rewarded way beyond dreams of avarice.	A dollar invested in the Vanguard 500 Index fund at the end of September 1993 would have become $1.72 by April 30, 2002. A dollar invested in a CD at 5% would have become $1.43.
11/1/93	Turmoil in Russia, atrocities in Bosnia, murders in Haiti, strife in Somalia, fires in Southern California, weakness in the bond market, higher taxes, you name it—this market responds with admirable consistency: Everything's for the best. And maybe it is. But for some unfathomable reason—the relative handful of stocks that are able to follow the averages to new high ground or the steady decline in cash in the hands of mutual-fund managers (which is the real gauge of investor sentiment these days) or the swell of over-the-counter trading or the soggy action in utilities or the rich price-to-book-value multiple, nearly 3.5 times, at which the Industrials are selling or the poor excuse, less than 2.8%, that passes for a yield on the Dow or the flood of equity offerings or the slight itch behind our left ear—we don't believe it. Just ornery, we guess.	The Dow rose 7.5% over the next year.
6/27/94	It isn't that we're congenitally predisposed toward a negative view of equities. It's merely that we date this bull market to the end of 1974, which suggests it's way past its natural span.	The bull market had more than five years to go. The Dow was then at 3636.
11/20/95	Barton Biggs, "in one of his wonderfully literate weekly commentaries" for Morgan Stanley, likens buying technology stocks today to sitting in on the "last poker games on the *Titanic*."	It was a very long poker game. The Morgan Stanley High Tech Index, then at 171, peaked at 1162 on March 27, 2000.

(continued)

Table 4.3 *Continued*

Date	Quote	Reality Check
2/5/96	Felix Zulauf, "our friend and Swiss sage," says gold is "the buy of a lifetime."	Gold peaked three days previous at $415.50, a level not topped for six years and counting. The price slid as low as $253 on August 25, 1999.
3/18/96	Joe Rosenberg, "investment consigliere of Loews Corp." and "a virtual portfolio paragon," shows a chart of the Dow as proof that the bull market is in a final climactic stage. "When pressed for how far a decline will carry, he turns a bit demure and hazards at least 25%. But he obviously anticipates something nastier."	Five years later, from January 2000–September 2001, the Dow fell 28%.
3/25/96	Barton Biggs, "a firm believer in regression to the mean," thinks the pendulum is bound to swing away from financial assets. He envisions returns on stocks, for example, averaging a 4%-a-year improvement through the rest of the decade, a steep drop from '95's astounding 37.5% jump and the hefty 16.7% annual average gain over the past five years. He thinks the big returns will come from Asian equities, emerging markets and nonresidential real estate."	The average annual gain for S&P 500 futures was 24% for the rest of the decade.
5/27/96	Andrew Smithers, "a world-class investment professional" bearish on U.S. stocks since year-end 1993, presents "for the first time . . . a coherent reasoned case for a secular bear market." Smithers, following the indication of the Q ratio, put his own money in cash, in safe banks, and advised everyone to do likewise.	From year-end 1993 through year-end 2002, a period that included one of the worst bear markets in U.S. history, S&P futures rose 88%, an average annual gain of 7%.
8/18/97	(After a 247-point drop in the Dow) Commiserate as we do with the victims—we haven't seen so many wailing widows and screaming orphans since way back in '87—we felt the same rush we get from viewing an eclipse of the sun.	After the October crashes in both 1987 and 1997, the Dow rose 11% through the end of the year.

Table 4.3   *Continued*

Date	Quote	Reality Check
10//21/97	Even the most casual observer of the investment scene knows that intelligence is more of a handicap than a help in achieving success on Wall Street. Name any successful Wall Streeter. We rest our case.	Too bizarre to rebut.
11/3/97	[After the worst point drop in the Dow ever prompted the closing of financial markets]: What do you call a 550-point drop in a single day? A start. And what do you call a 337-point rise on over a billion shares the very next day? A mistake.	Ditto.

reached an all-time pinnacle of $1.45 million. There are more investment clubs active—22,000—than ever before. And there are 4,700 hedge funds, or comfortably more than one for every stock listed on the Big Board (3,419).

Farrell comments that he remembers drawing up similar lists back in 1968, time of the last secular market peak. Trouble developed in the second half when the only thing that stopped making record highs was prices.

"Similarly," Bob observes, "we have posted many activity and participation records in 1996, and prices have shown limited response. This failure to respond to record demand suggests informed selling and, when combined with record valuation levels, raises doubts about the longevity of the bull market." As that last phrase suggests, Bob is a true pundit. A true pundit always says the end is near, but he never says the end is here.

It was not until January 2000—more than three years later—that the Dow reached a peak. The average was then at almost exactly double its level of 5882 on the day the article on Farrell was published.

Abelson has, on rare occasions, quoted sources who do not subscribe to his views. In the "Up and Down Wall Street" column of June 22, 1998, John Hussman, a hedge fund manager and University of Michigan professor, explained why price-to-book, dividend yield, and price/earnings multiples had been "worse than useless" as investment guides. Hussman said the P/E ratio has not been of much help in determining whether the market is too high because of "the hazards inherent in the ratio, notably the volatile nature of earnings" and because "the ratio is often highest when profits are most depressed." Stocks have at times been extravagantly overvalued and still have performed well, he noted, "if earnings have been good, inflation benign, interest rates subdued, and the technical trends, especially breadth, favorable." Which had been the case in recent years.

But the following week, on June 29, 1998, Abelson was back to citing a Bob Farrell statistic du jour: The percentage of the average family's assets invested in equities had climbed to an unprecedented 38.3 percent. The previous peak was in 1968, when 37.9 percent of financial assets were made up of stocks. "What ensued, it greatly grieves us to report, was the vicious market plunge of 1969."

Time after time, Abelson provided forums to market gurus whose forecasts had gone badly awry, often for years. If the seer provided a chart purporting to show how the market's latest fever graph ascent resembled that before 1929, 1973, 1987, or Japan in 1990, a dozen paragraphs were not out of the question.

At the dawn of the twenty-first century, the market's Cassandra finally had his day. The Dow Industrials peaked on January 14 and began a long descent. The technology stocks of the Nasdaq followed soon after in a calamitous, drawn-out crash that was indeed reminiscent of the terrible times of 1973–1974. Yet we cannot help but recall the account of the stock market panic of April 1864, as told by William Worthington Fowler in his 1870 book, *Ten Years in Wall Street:*

> Signs and portents of coming disaster multiplied. . . . When [Anthony W. Morse] entered the regular board that morning, he found nearly every broker eager to sell at heavy concessions, before the call of stocks opened, and the feeling in the street was still worse. At half-past eleven o'clock, a broker rose in his seat, and announced the failure of Morse & Co. An appalling stillness, like that which precedes a tornado, followed the words, then the storm burst. . . . The palace of enchantment, built by a strong and cunning magician of so many golden hopes, passed away like a cloud-pageant. . . .
>
> We started to go home early in the afternoon. At the corner of William Street and Exchange Place, we met S_____. He was a harmless but very disagreeable lunatic, a Cassandra, who predicted nothing but evil. He had for six weeks been uttering his doleful prophecies. When he caught sight of us, he began to throw up his hands and give vent to hollow laughs, which grated very disagreeably on our keyed-up nerves. "I told you so! I told you so! Ha, ha, ha!" We tried to shake him off, but he stuck to us like a leech, hovered about us like an owl, and chuckled when he had wrenched out of us the reluctant acknowledgment that we had not yet sold our stocks.[7]

A sweet triumph, indeed. How we wish Abelson had written novels instead. As Shermer pointed out in *Weird Science,* heresy does not equal correctness.

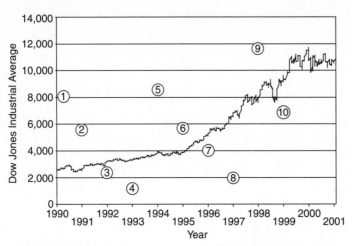

1. (Dow 2629)
   The bear market will awake
   from its snooze and come
   roaring back to life, red in
   tooth and claw. (12/31/90)

2. (Dow 3101)
   We don't see the economy
   recovering with sufficient vigor and
   speed to bail out the current awesome
   valuation levels of share prices. (12/30/91)

3. (Dow 3250)
   The market's headed
   for a full-fledged fall. (09/28/92)

4. (Dow 3442)
   We kind of doubt this bull market
   still has six months, let alone two years,
   of life left. (02/08/93)

5. (Dow 3636)
   We date this bull market to
   the end of 1974, which suggests
   it's way past its natural span. (06/27/94)

6. (Dow tops 5000)
   Balloons have been
   known to burst. (11/27/95)

7. (Dow 5705)
   The decline and fall of the
   techs is a preview in living
   color of the decline and fall
   of the market as a whole. (06/24/96)

8. (Dow 7442)
   What do you call a 500-point drop
   in a single day? A start. And what
   do you call a 337-point rise on over
   a billion shares the very next day?
   A mistake. (11/03/97)

9. (Dow 7539, bottom that still stands)
   With the market still selling at a
   fabulously elevated P/E, the effect
   on multiples—and the stock market—
   of a rate cut this time around will be
   pallid, putrid, or pathetic. (08/31/98)

10. (Dow tops 10000)
    Even while the markets were
    legging it to new highs, the
    advance/decline lines were
    sinking to new lows. The last time
    it happened was in 1929. (03/29/99)

Figure 4.1   Abelson and the Dow, 1989–2001

Abelson should be given due credit for criticizing Wall Street's cheerleading machine. Moreover, no one would argue that he has upheld the prevailing ethical standard of financial journalism by holding no interest in any of the securities he writes about. We have a different approach that we believe is equally ethical, or more so: We tell our readers what we are going to buy, and after our columns are published, we do what we said we would do. That way, we play on the same field as our readers do. We suffer with them—or profit with them—as the case may be. The prospect of putting one's chips on the table tends to concentrate the mind wonderfully and to bring sobriety to the act of writing.

It has become an adage to many on Wall Street that the time to become bearish on stocks will occur when Alan Abelson finally turns bullish. We doubt that this apostasy will occur in our time. Nor can we expect any of his followers to abandon their hero. At this point, they have too much invested in their beliefs, emotionally and financially—and may have lost too much money—to be swayed by reason.

Psychologists, looking back on our age, may wish to use the 36-year panoply of irrational, dysfunctional belief as a case study to replace the rather limited and specialized post-World-War-II religious example of the Keech cult used in today's social psychology classes. They doubtless will explain the reasons for the destructive behavior in terms of the tremendous blow to self-esteem that would occur from admitting the falsity of one's leitmotiv, both social and financial, during this period.

But we prefer a simpler assessment. The columnist has been so wrong for so long on his one-sided prediction that if he were ever to close the trade out, he would lock in a terrible loss by maintaining the unrealized loss in perpetuity. No closure is possible, either in Abelson's mind or in his readers' minds. As long as the prediction is open, the nuclear catastrophe that stops civilization and brings the Dow down to the triple-digit level of his beginnings might occur and provide vindication (see Figure 4.1).

Like many others, we will be saddened when, in the words of the physicist Max Planck, the financial columnist is "dragged kicking and screaming from his aerie perch." However, this chapter in history should serve in the minds of all investors as an example of the folly of failing to adjust one's beliefs to the constantly shifting weight of evidence and structural changes in our economy.

5 "WE ARE NUMBER ONE" USUALLY MEANS "NOT MUCH LONGER"

Pride goeth before destruction, a haughty spirit before a fall.
—Proverbs 16:18

We can be the one company that can change the world. It's maybe the first time there's ever been such a company. Cisco is in the position. This is the Internet revolution. . . . We can be perhaps the most successful company in history.
—John Chambers, Chief Executive Officer, Cisco Systems[1]

Most people would agree that powerful corporate leadership is important in considering which stock to buy. The star CEO whose words put wings to a grand vision attracts capital. But as the Greek historian Herodotus observed in the fifth century B.C., power can bring outrageous arrogance, or *hubris*, characterized by moral blindness and temptation to abuse the weak. This tragedy is occurring in our time as one company after another collapses under charismatic but flawed leadership, destroying the wealth of its shareholders.

Much has been written about the comeuppance of the dot-coms. But far more wide-reaching in impact on America's pocketbooks and the economy was the crash of three big New Economy blue chips: Enron, Cisco, and Lucent. Enron went from $90 a share on August 17, 2000, to the largest corporate bankruptcy in history on December 2, 2001. (It was soon eclipsed by the demise of WorldCom.) Cisco fell from $80 a share in March 2000 to $8.60 as of October 2002, and Lucent declined from $77.77 in December 1999 to 58 cents in the same period. An investment of $100,000 at the height of these stocks would have been reduced to less than $5,000.

Yet all three had been 1990s wonder stocks, featured on countless brokerage "recommend" lists right through the catastrophic denouements. So firm a grip did these stocks have on the nation's imagination that the January-February 2002 issue of AARP's magazine, *Modern Maturity* (which claims the largest circulation in the United States), cited unnamed "experts" who were recommending Lucent and the already-bankrupt Enron as good safe investments in the post-September 11 downturn.[2]

We do not insist that a comeback is out of the question for any of these companies; we are great believers in the second chance. But we would all like to spot the next Enron before it blows up. We began studying in earnest how to go about this in January 2002, after a reader sent us the following letter (Enron's shares were by then trading in pennies):

> I am a retired person who invested all my savings in Enron since it was considered a blue-chip company and paid dividends. What do you suggest I should do? Do you think they could successfully restructure the company? Will the stock come back to $20, if not to the high? I would be very grateful if you would kindly reply to my e-mail. I am extremely depressed and very anxious to know your thoughts on Enron's future. Thanks.

In studying how to spot a company destined to plunge from the heights to the depths, we studied CEOs who made outrageous boasts, and we searched for executives known for humility. We delved into the Wall Street superstition which says a jinx often afflicts companies that build flashy headquarters buildings, talk their way onto magazine covers, name stadiums after themselves, or make headlines with big acquisitions. Our tests showed that there is something helpful in all of these, and we report the results in this chapter. Our first insights came from an ancient Greek tale that involved, curiously enough, technological genius.

The Tale of Icarus

Daedalus, a brilliant engineer, earned much honor from Crete's King Minos by building a splendid palace with a running-water system. Daedalus also built a labyrinth to hide the Minotaur, the monstrous issue of the king's wife's passion for the white bull of Poseidon. When King Minos learned that Daedalus had assisted the queen in consummating the union, he imprisoned Daedalus. Daedalus secretly fashioned wings from wax and feathers for himself and his son, Icarus, to escape to Sicily. When the time came, Daedalus counseled his son:

> Icarus, I advise you to take a middle course.
> If you fly too low, the sea will soak the wings;
> If you fly too high, the sun's heat will burn them.
> Fly between sea and sun!
> Take the course along which I shall lead you.

But Icarus could not resist the temptation to soar high into the sky. His wings disintegrated as the sun softened the wax, and he plunged into the sea.

Hubris is the sin to which the great and gifted are most susceptible, and it provided Greek tragedians and historians with a rich source of material. Recounting the punishments of heroes who aspired to godly heights provided catharsis, scholars say, allowing Greek audiences to cleanse themselves of fear and pity without becoming paralyzed by those emotions. Some writers presented the hero as wholly blameless. Aeschylus, for example, believed that the gods begrudged human greatness and inflicted hubris on men at the height of their success.

Twenty-five centuries later, hubris is still a potent force in our lives, from the moment we reach out as toddlers and challenge the gods with our invincibility by touching the stove's red-hot burner. We all have our own examples of hubris. Vic's personal favorite is of Old Man Hemingway. He heard the tale from the owner of a pipe company he visited in Houston during his days in the mergers-and-acquisition business. Hemingway was in the habit of ending meetings with lower-level executives by picking up a copy of the *New York Times* and holding it in front of his face. One day he was found dead, with 15 bullet holes in his paper. Apparently, a lower-level employee, enraged by his boss' hubris, knew the newspaper gesture only too well and took the opportunity to do him in.

Our favorite newspaper, the *National Enquirer*, is adept in recounting stories about hubris. Jennifer Lopez is apparently a frequent culprit. According to the *Enquirer*, J-Lo's handlers warn you never to look her directly in the eye, and never to call her by her name.[3] This custom has historical roots in the royal French court under Louis XIV. Courtiers were under orders to always avert their eyes in the Sun King's presence, and they were expected to proffer their wives as a token of their esteem.

In Wall Street's tragedies, hubris often turns out to have been the culprit. The late historian Robert Sobel, surveying the past century of business downfalls in his 1999 book *When Giants Stumble: Classic Business Blunders and How to Avoid Them,* prominently featured hubris in his list of 15 deadly sins that destroyed such leading companies as Osborne Computer, LTV, Schwinn, and Packard Motor Car.[4] (Sobel's list also included nepotism, nonstrategic expansion, cutting corners, isolation, and dependency.)

The sense of being above the world is basic to hubris. The revered British negotiator Sir Harold Nicolson pinpointed the attitude in his 1939 classic, *Diplomacy:* "The dangers of vanity in a negotiator can scarcely be exaggerated. . . . It may bring in its train vices of imprecision, excitability, impatience, emotionalism, and even untruthfulness."[5]

The "above it all" element of hubris may have been present when Cisco president John Chambers accused Silicon Valley executives in February 2000 of undermining the value of their companies by awarding "hired gun" options that allowed executives and employees to cash out after only three years. Chambers made his admonition just 17 days after he cleared $142.9 million by exercising 1.15 million Cisco options at what turned out to be near-peak prices, according to *Infoworld,* an online news site.[6]

Both Cisco and Enron employed ingenious mechanisms to banish debt from the corporate books. In 2002, the *Wall Street Journal* caused a sensation by reporting that Enron traders had secretly forced up consumer energy prices in California by using trading strategies with such nicknames as Fat Boy, Ricochet, Load Shift, Get Shorty, and Death Star.[7]

The Corporate Story Board

Beyond the arrogance of power, a common theme in corporate stories of hubris and downfall is that executives tell—explicitly or implicitly—stories that analysts want to hear. In an e-mail to us, Flavia Cymbalista, a Brazilian-born PhD who studies the effects of uncertainty on behavior, observed, "Analysts love a 'savior.'" Sometimes, she said, analysts like a story enough to help make it come true, by encouraging their firms to provide cheap capital to the company. "Other times the story is unsustainable and sooner or later this becomes apparent." Some successful traders gain an edge by exploiting their backgrounds in the arts and humanities to practice "script analysis," she noted. "They listen to the stories companies are telling and to the stories that the market is hearing and make their bets according to their judgment of how good the story is as such and how it's likely to unfold."

With such a willing audience, it is only natural for a CEO to boast a bit. But woes follow when executives start to believe their own fish stories.

The leaders of Lucent, Enron, and Cisco were nothing if not storytellers. At Lucent, Carly Fiorina ran a $90-million brand-building campaign that, as *BusinessWeek* said in an August 2, 1999, cover story, "helped transform the company from a humdrum maker of phone equipment to an Internet player supplying the gear for the New Economy." The ads asked: "Who's at the Center of the Communications Revolution?"[8] In the next three years, Lucent high-flying stock lost 97 percent of its value, leaving its investors wishing they had put their money into something a bit more humdrum.

In 1999, Enron Chairman Kenneth Lay boasted of his company's ninefold growth in value to $40 billion during the 1990s. "We will do it again this coming decade," he predicted to a group of awed oil and gas executives. Two years later, Enron was ruined, its leaders under federal investigation for massive fraud. On August 14, 2001, shortly before Enron's downfall, Lay wrote in an e-mail to employees: "Our performance has never been stronger, our business model has never been more robust. We have the finest organization in American business today." The e-mail surfaced in congressional hearings five months later.

Fiorina and Lay were treading a well-worn path. Cisco Systems Chairman John Chambers' 1999 prediction of continued 30 percent-to-50 percent annual profit growth was promptly followed by four straight quarters of 50 percent-plus profit declines. Cisco is a true modern tragedy and Chambers an exemplary storyteller.

Cisco's Storyteller

As a child, Chambers suffered from dyslexia. He went on to earn law and business degrees, but never overcame a dislike for reading. Like many successful dyslexics, he compensated by relying on a prodigious memory. He often gave speeches without notes.

His first job was as a salesman at IBM. The *Washington Post*'s Mark Leibovich reported in an April 6, 2001, profile that Chambers still remembered what the recruiter told him: "You're not selling technology; you're selling a dream." He became a great salesman for IBM and then for Cisco, tirelessly promoting a vision of a New World Network with Cisco at its center. "Chambers' sales pitches included the implicit message of invincibility," Leibovich wrote. In August 1996, the year after becoming CEO, Chambers told *USA Today,* "There's only one company in this industry that controls its destiny, and it is Cisco."[9] Chambers hobnobbed with President Clinton and other world leaders, spreading his network vision. In 1998, *Forbes ASAP* named Cisco the country's most dynamic company. A September 13, 1999, *Business Week* cover story dubbed Chambers "the Internet's No. 1 salesman."[10]

By September 1999, stock options had made millionaires of 2,000 of Cisco's 17,000 employees. Chambers used his sales talent to keep turnover among his workers low, personally distributing ice cream and sweets. Behind the talk and the ice cream, though, Cisco was not winning much business in the $225-billion market crucial to his vision of growth: selling equipment to the big local phone companies. In 1999, Cisco accounted for less than 1 percent of telephone equipment sales. The Bells preferred to buy from Cisco's far bigger rivals: Lucent, which Chambers loved to mock as an "Old World" company, and Canada's Nortel.

On August 26, 1999, desperate to catch up, Cisco agreed to buy Cerent, a two-year-old maker of fiber-optic networking equipment, with just 285 employees, for a whopping $6.9 billion in stock. On September 15, 1999, he told *Sixty Minutes* anchor Diane Sawyer: "We're going to change everything in this industry."

In early 2000, after the big corporate push to buy computer and networking equipment for the new century was over, doubts about future growth began to surface. Chambers would have none of it. His executives were still predicting sales growth in the 30 percent to 50 percent range in companies where the economy was strong, according to a February 9, 2000, article in the *Los Angeles Times.*[11]

In March 2000, the huge gains in Internet stocks began to unravel. Cisco shares traded at a high of $80.06 on March 27, 2000. In the next 18 days, the stock slumped 29 percent. Chambers remained optimistic, likening Cisco to a weapons broker in wartime. "We're the experts in everything," Chambers told *BusinessWeek* for a May 15, 2000, cover story. "We sell arms to everyone."[12] More and more companies cut back on their growth forecasts, but Chambers would have none of it. Well into 2001, he stuck with his projections of 30 percent to 50 percent long-term revenue growth, relying on what *CIO Magazine,* in an August 1, 2000, article,[13] called Cisco's "godlike ability to peer into every nook and cranny of the business, 24/7" with its "virtual close" tracking software. Unfortunately, customers, fearful of shortages, had inflated their orders. By year-end 2000, demand had fallen off a cliff. The alternative telecommunications companies and dot-coms—Cisco's primary customers— began disappearing. Cisco switches sold for 15 cents on the dollar.

Undaunted, Chambers continued to sell the story. Speaking in New Delhi to the Confederation of Indian Industry on January 17, 2001, Chambers told his audience that "voice transmission and then data transmission over the Internet would become free of cost. . . . that education would change forever with the advent of education over the World Wide Web . . . and that E-business over the next five years would grow by over five times. . . . Mr. Chambers stated that Cisco learned from every company in the world and became No. 1 or No. 2 in four years in each market it entered."[14]

On February 6, 2001, Cisco fell short of Wall Street earnings estimates. Its "godlike ability" to forecast had failed. In March, Cisco announced plans to cut 16 percent of its workforce, or 8,000 jobs, and Chambers acknowledged that Cisco's growth rate went from 70 percent in November to negative in January and February. "No one has ever decelerated at that speed," he told the *Washington Post*. It goes with the territory "of being the most profitable, fastest-growing company in history."

Four quarters of declining earnings followed, breaking a steak of 40 quarters of growth. The stock market had valued Cisco at $532 billion at its peak, making it briefly the most valuable company in America. By October 2002, its market value had declined to $62 billion.

The Executive Boast

Our friend Ed Gross, whose adept card-counting on the blackjack tables led to his banishment from Las Vegas casinos (and a new career as an options trader and market maker), says gamblers, even skillful ones, who entered the casino bragging how easily they expected to win invariably ended up losers.

The tendency for stocks to go down in like manner after executive boasting is part of a general character flaw that might be called, "Did You Summit?" *Outside* magazine's February 2002 issue has an illuminating article on mountaineering search-and-rescue missions observing that whenever a climber descends from the heights, the onlookers who rush over do not ask, "Did you enjoy?" or "Did you learn?" but "Did you summit?" The insistence on reaching the peak, regardless of weather conditions and the abilities of the climbers, is what leads to disaster. Many famous mountaineering deaths, including Mallory's fatal attempt of Everest in 1924, can be traced to it.[15]

Once on the summit, CEOs naturally want to stay there. But competition at the top is always the most intense. Rivals are bent on coming up with alternate ways to make or market every product, and the consumer is fickle. When CEOs believe that they are the best at something, it breeds an atmosphere of invincibility that opens the door for disaster. The CEOs who show lack of humility by boasting could be demonstrating unwillingness to face up to the harsh and ever-changing realities of the marketplace. Perhaps they find boasting easier than putting in the energy necessary for the humdrum pursuit of profits. In the worst case, boasting could be a cover-up for a serious problem.

The scientist Albert Einstein put it nicely in a 1936 speech on education in Albany, New York, that was reported in *Great Ideas in Physics:* "Desire for approval and recognition is a healthy motive; but the desire to be acknowledged as better, stronger, and more intelligent than a fellow being or fellow scholar easily leads to an excessively egoistic psychological adjustment, which may become injurious for the individual and for the community."[16]

The desire to be on top is not limited to CEOs. Money managers, too, suffer from the tendency. In response to one of the columns we did on hubris for MSN MoneyCentral, a reader wrote: "Niederhoffer is the best example of pride signaling the fall. Right after he was the No. 1 hedge fund manager, in 1996, he wrote a book, gave the keynote speech at many conferences, and promptly fell into oblivion."

We cannot deny the truth of what our correspondent wrote, but we can guarantee that in the future Vic will never again strive to be first in the hedge fund world. He has learned that "sure and steady" wins the race. The power of compounding is such that a slight but consistent edge over the 10 percent return from a buy-and-hold strategy is sufficient to achieve anyone's financial goals. To strive for a much greater return requires taking more risk. That extra risk can be ruinous, especially when the adversary's bankroll is much bigger than yours.

Hubris and Chutzpa

We want to draw a clear line between visionary ideas and delusions of grandeur. Self-confidence is prerequisite to success. Hubris, however, is an exaggerated self-confidence that is difficult to sustain in light of the facts. Alas, none of us is perfect. The trap is sprung when people afflicted by hubris try to maintain a constant sense of being on top. They can replicate the emotional feeling of confidence "either by altering their standards, rules and goals, or by reevaluating what constitutes success," Michael Lewis wrote in "Self-Conscious Emotions," in the *Gale Encyclopedia of Childhood and Adolescence.*[17]

Vic's father, Arthur Niederhoffer, unfailingly humble about his own numerous achievements as cop, lawyer, and scholar, masterfully drew the distinction between confidence and hubris in an article for the *Connecticut Law Review* of Winter 1970–1971. Artie's subject was the arrogance of power displayed by the judge in the trial of the Chicago 7. The American Bar Association's canon of judicial ethics calls for judges to be "temperate, attentive, patient, impartial." When defendant Bobby Seale's lawyer had to go to the hospital, Judge Julius J. Hoffman denied Seale's request for an adjournment. He also ordered two attorneys jailed without bond for contempt of court, repeatedly interrupted the defense lawyers, and denied virtually all their motions. Artie wrote:

> How is it possible for a Federal judge to have become so rabid toward the defense that "he upheld prosecutors' objections even when he had not properly heard or understood them," and turned the proceedings into a judicial disaster? We think the best explanation for these excesses is the classic one of *Hubris*.
>
> Implicit in the classic Greek philosophy of justice was the concept of a divinely decreed social order in which every human being had his particular place and role. *Hubris* was the fatal flaw of character that impelled a man to violate the most cherished mores. Inexorably Nemesis punished the violator who, as Aristotle puts it, "moved from happiness to misery." It was the most compelling theme of Greek tragedy, but there is no hint of this shattering experience in *Webster's Third International,* that defines hubris rather prosaically as "overweening pride, self confidence, or arrogance."
>
> In Jewish folklore we find a similar concept—*chutzpa,* which also connotes insolence, audacity, or arrogance.
>
> If both *hubris* and *chutzpa* are forms of arrogance, what is the distinction between them? Hubris is a reflection of a civilization at the peak of its power, on the verge of assuming mastery of the known world. Its heroes hurled challenges to the gods on Mount Olympus. We think immediately of Prometheus, Sisyphus, Agamemnon and Oedipus. By comparison, *chutzpa* is a relatively modern term rooted in the ghetto existence of a weak, dispersed and alienated Jewish minority. *Hubris* grows from a sense of power; *chutzpa* is a compensation for the lack of power.
>
> *Hubris* may be disguised for a long time. It is often interpreted as evidence of high standards and integrity that marks a man for honor until the fatal flaw causes him to overreach. *Hubris* carries with it an almost religious aura, but *chutzpa* rarely exceeds the limits of the profane.[18]

It Ain't Boasting If You Can Do It

How can we separate the Enrons, the Ciscos, and the Lucents—not to mention the Long-Term Capital Managements, Scott Papers, and Winstars—from
winners like Genentech, once ridiculed for saying it would use biotechnology
to develop a profitable drug? Genentech did just what it said it would; it became the first company to receive FDA approval for a biotech drug. It was
later acquired by Roche in a series of stock purchases at up to seven times the
original 1986 offering price. Even after the long tech collapse, the Nasdaq 100
as of the end of July 2002 included 23 stocks that had more than tripled over
the previous five years. Qlogic, Echostar, Idec Pharmaceuticals, Medimmune,
and Amazon.com were up more than sixfold.

Is there a way to distinguish companies with grand ambitions that will go
on to reach the stars from those destined to suffer the end deemed necessary
by the Greek tragedians?

As scientists, we need to quantify the effects of hubris. We began with a
search of boastful phrases on the google.com search engine. "We're the
best," "best company," and "We're No. 1" yielded over 100,000 entries. We
found 11 companies that used these magic phrases. We threw in a couple of
beautiful examples from Martha Stewart and Priceline.com
for good measure, although they didn't contain the exact
wording. We then calculated performance of the stocks
against the S&P 500, from the date of the remark through
year-end 2001.

The sample size is too small for any degree of statistical confidence, but
the results are shockingly bad. The average relative performance was an as-
tonishing 24 percentage points below the S&P 500. Five companies—Enron,
Gateway, Human Genome Sciences, Priceline.com. and Sprint-PCS—fell
more than 50 percent. The date, the quote that triggered it, and the subsequent performance are shown in Table 5.1.

While we may have missed some boastful remarks, we made an effort to
include the performance of all companies that satisfied the criteria, regardless
of subsequent performance.

After publishing our Boastful 13 study on CNBC Money, we received the
following extraordinary letter from a person whose insights deserve a complete quote:

> I retired from Lucent Technologies as an engineer after 30 years with the com-
> pany. My career went back to Western Electric Company. Lucent excelled at leading-
> edge manufacturing. Not very glamorous, but consistently profitable; that was
> what it inherited from Western Electric, one of the best manufacturers. During

Table 5.1   The Boastful 13

Stock	Quote Date	Quote	Percent Change to 1/14/02	Difference from S&P 500 (% points)
Continental Airlines (CAL)	1/18/00	"We're the best positioned airline for the future."	−27	−5
Dell Computer (DELL)	9/28/00	"We're No. 1 in the UK, Sweden, Ireland, and France in the business market."	−16	6
Delta Air Lines (DAL)	6/14/01	"We are the best in the business." (VP describing why Internet-in-the-sky venture will work)	−31	−25
Enron (ENE)	12/31/99	"From the world's leading energy company . . . to the world's leading company!" (banner hanging in corporate headquarters in late 1999)	−98	−76
Fidelity Nat'l (FNF)	6/14/00	"We're No. 1 in all leading financial indicators versus the competition."	45	68
Gateway (GTW)	3/26/99	"Gateway's goal is to become No. 1 on the Web, not because we are the biggest, but because we are the best."	−80	−69
Human Genome Sciences (HGSI)	5/7/01	"We are No. 1 by at least an order of magnitude, possibly two."	−52	−42
KPMG Consulting (KCIN)	6/7/01	"We are the best in the industry."	−6	5
LaSalle Hotel Prop (LHO)	7/2/01	"We were the best-performing REIT in 1999."	−33	−25
Martha Stewart (MSO)	8/21/01	"I can almost bend steel with my mind. I can bend anything if I try hard enough."	−15	−14

(continued)

Table 5.1   *Continued*

Stock	Quote Date	Quote	Percent Change to 1/14/02	Difference from S&P 500 (% points)
Priceline.com (PCLN)	8/17/99	"Priceline will reinvent the environmental DNA of global business," and produce "a totally different form of energy."	−92	−77
Rational Software (RATL)	4/20/00	"We are the best-kept secret on Wall Street."	−38	−17
Sprint-PCS (PCS)	7/21/00	"We're the best wireless phone service available."	−71	−48
		Average	**−39**	**−24**

the intervening AT&T years, exciting marketing and personnel types gradually replaced the stodgy old engineering management. Eventually, the entire management down to first-level supervisor was saturated with people who didn't know, understand or like manufacturing, nor did they like those who did.

An example: During my last days at Lucent, our vice president sent his assistant down for a number of days to our plant in order to explain—to all 1,200 people—our new, world-class manufacturing strategy that was to finally take us unquestionably past Nortel and make us "No. 1." Reportedly, this young lady's prior experience was that of a kindergarten teacher—a very good one. She sat us in groups of seven, each group composed of persons who didn't know each other very well and who had different diversity and work backgrounds—in order to promote open communication. She then handed out a coloring sheet with four crayons to each of us. We then were instructed during the next four hours to fill in picture parts corresponding to the part of the strategy that she was explaining at the time with, of course, the appropriate company-approved color. Very little had to do with manufacturing; most of it had to do with image and how we were going to enter, and by the way dominate, new markets by buying new hi-tech companies. (We ended up that year by buying and trying—unsuccessfully for the most part—to integrate 31 new companies, many of which were duplicating our own developing products. Meanwhile, we gradually dismantled our own capabilities that we could have, and should have, easily upgraded.)

Now, most of these people had 20 or so years of experience. Many had college degrees, and/or intense technical training. I'm no dummy, myself. I graduated with a BSME during Viet Nam when they only let one out of five finish in engineering, and passed my engineering licensing test on the first try. I earned an MBA in mid-career, while pursuing graduate engineering work simultaneously. I had also the experience of surviving a decade of downsizing along with most of the others present, so I knew enough to keep my mouth shut.

But one of the employees who was buying into all the "mutual trust" rhetoric kept his hand up insistently long enough that he was finally recognized. He questioned one of the more obvious flaws, and it was publicly explained to him that the company needed "team players" who were "open to change and new ideas"—that perhaps some of the people in his group with "different" cultural backgrounds could explain it to him.

In the fable, the little boy who observed that the emperor had no clothes on was not chastised. When honest, trusting, and knowledgeable employees play out the little boy's role, the effect is disastrous for the employees; when the market takes on that role, it is disastrous for the whole company.

But how does a company go overnight from aggressively executing a century-long tradition of adding real value of society, to being introspectively and passively fascinated by its own self-valued fantasy-image? The only answer that I can come up with is that it takes two components at the top: a determined ignorance and a pervasive, self-justified willingness to intimidate.

I believe pride and its twin, arrogance, inevitably produces the ignorance. After all, there's no sense wasting time learning if you're already the expert, right? But I have not yet figured out exactly how we come to so easily intimidate others who have a history of competence and who share our own self-interests. Perhaps success reinforces our confidence in our abilities to the point that we believe we are discounting the opinions of subordinates for their own good. Possibly pride and arrogance play roles also. Or perhaps, way deep down, do we suspect that our pride-produced ignorance has trapped us? At any rate, we seem to adopt the survival instincts of gladiators when we least need them. People are the strangest creation in the universe.

There is always tension between the ambition to excel that leads to corporate greatness and the excessive boastfulness that led Icarus to fly too close to the sun. Perhaps no company illustrates this better than Continental Airlines, which we mentioned in a January 17, 2002, column titled "'We're No. 1' Usually Means 'Not Much Longer'" as an example of a boastful company. (We faulted Continental for saying "We're the best-positioned airline for the future.") The airline's director of public relations immediately fired off a letter to us. "What can we do? We were voted the best on time, the most satisfactory to all passengers, the best managed. Does that really make us a candidate for shorting, as you suggest?" Actually, we specifically said we were not recommending that any of the boastful companies be shorted. We rarely recommend shorting, given the market's upward drift. Nevertheless, Continental stock did tumble 61 percent in the subsequent six months.

Hunting for Humility

To balance our investigation into hubris, we looked for humble executives. We wanted to find the corporate counterparts to Pete Sampras in tennis, Sparky Anderson in baseball, Walter Payton in football, Mike Krzyzewski in basketball, and Wayne Gretzky in hockey. Companies with executives who could say, as Anderson did: "My daddy told me, 'Son, be nice to everyone you meet—be nice and treat that person like he's someone.'" Companies with executives who, instead of doing the equivalent of the funky chicken after scoring a point, bow their heads after a spectacular putaway, as Sampras does. "He is so concentrated on the task at hand that I barely ever notice him smile," one Sampras fan wrote.

We found just 10 of these companies after searching through hundreds of thousands of articles published over the past three years, looking for conjunctions of "CEO" with such words as "low key," "down-to-earth," "modest," and "unassuming." They are Allstate, Biomet, Costco Wholesale, Electrolux, Lockheed Martin, Wal-Mart Stores, Weyerhaeuser, and White Mountains Insurance. (The list also included AOL Time Warner and Computer Associates, which have since come under federal investigation for improper accounting practices. Whoops! But this reminds us of the great Golda Meir quote: "Don't be modest. You aren't that great.")

We compared the performance of these humble companies with that of the S&P 500. It turned out they outperformed the market by 40 percentage points from the dates of the statements containing the keywords through January 21, 2002.

Humble companies won some attention in October 2001 when James C. Collins came out with *Good to Great: Why Some Companies Make the Leap . . . and Others Don't.*[19]

Collins found 11 companies—Abbott Laboratories, Circuit City, Fannie Mae, Gillette, Kimberly-Clark, Kroger, Nucor, Philip Morris, Pitney Bowes, Walgreen, and Wells Fargo—that had the kind of down-to-earth, attention-to-detail style that turned them into great companies. He found that their returns were seven times that of the market in the 15 years after their transition to greatness. One dollar invested in the good-to-great companies in 1965 would have grown to $471 versus $56 in the overall market, or almost eight times the market return.

So Much for Celebrity

The CEOs of these companies are invariably self-effacing. "There is a direct relationship between the absence of celebrity and the presence of good-to-great results," Collins said in an interview published in the October 2001 online edition of *Fast Company* magazine. "Why? First, when you have a celebrity, the company turns into 'the one genius with 1,000 helpers.' It creates a sense that the whole thing is really about the CEO. At a deeper level, we found that for leaders to make something great, their ambition has to be for the greatness of the work and the company, rather than for themselves."[20]

Much has been made of Collins' scientific, painstaking method of research. The book was five years in the making and involved 21 researchers whom Collins affectionately calls chimps. It took six months and vast banks of computers just to come up with the companies. We would point out that since Collins selected the companies for their superior market performance

Table 5.2 "Good to Great" Stock Performance June 30, 2001, to July 30, 2002

Company	Percent Change
Abbott Laboratories	−18.2
Circuit City	−2.8
Fannie Mae	−12.2
Gillette	8.4
Kimberly-Clark	3.9
Kroger	−23.9
Nucor	12.4
Philip Morris	−4.2
Pitney Bowes	−7.0
Walgreen	3.3
Wells Fargo	5.7
Average:	−3.2
S&P 500	−27.3

in the first place, of course they displayed it. There is thus no prospective evidence, no scientific finding, indeed no reason whatsoever aside from anecdotes to believe that leaders or companies showing these characteristics would perform any differently in the future than a group of randomly selected companies.

Good to Great calculated performance through June 2001. We took pencil to paper and updated the calculation through February 2002 (see Table 5.2).

The average performance of the 10 companies over the eight-month period was −3.2 percent, outperforming the S&P 500 by 20 percentage points in one of the worst market declines ever.

We would like to believe that the performance differences found by Collins will hold up in the long run. There is something ugly and unbusinesslike about the tendency of CEOs to brag about their company's superiority, instead of focusing on their own pursuit of excellence.

Just What Is Humble?

Finding indications of humility is more difficult than finding indications of arrogance. Many different statements can indicate humility, but arrogance seems to be present when certain specific types of things are said. Then, too, as Dizzy Dean once observed, "It ain't boasting if you can do it." The English chess grandmaster Nigel Davies told us that Jose Raul Capablanca, world champion from 1921 to 1927 and probably the greatest natural chess player of all time, once said, "As one by one I mowed them down, my superiority became evident."[21]

Davies commented in a January 19, 2002, e-mail to us: "Was this hubris? Probably more a statement of fact. I am much more wary of apparent humility than apparent hubris. Those who feign humility can be both arrogant and deceitful."

The one company with by far the most mentions for humility in the search engines is Berkshire Hathaway. But it was Berkshire's CEO, Warren Buffett, who made the following remark, reported in *Fortune* on November 22, 1999:

> Sizing all this up, I like to think that if I'd been at Kitty Hawk in 1903, when Orville Wright took off, I would have been farsighted enough, and public spirited enough—I owed this to future capitalists—to shoot him down. I mean, Karl Marx couldn't have done as much damage to capitalists as Orville did. . . . There were about 300 aircraft manufacturers in 1919–1939. Only a handful are breathing today.

Evidently, the "world's greatest investor" has come to believe so thoroughly in his own press that he now presumes to assist the gods in punishing today's Icaruses for their attempts to soar.

The Skyscraper Indicator

In the twenty-first century, as in the time of Cheops, there will undoubtedly be taller and taller buildings, built at great effort and often without real economic justification, because the rich and powerful will still sometimes find satisfaction in traditional ways of demonstrating that they're on top of the heap.

—William J. Mitchell, "Do We Still Need Skyscrapers?" *Scientific American*[22]

Far too often, a company, country, or civilization builds a tall, lavish building and experiences disaster shortly thereafter. Start in Babylon, circa 2800 B.C., when the conqueror Nimrod attempted to build "a tower that reaches to the heavens, so that we may make a name for ourselves." The Lord, we are told in the "Book of Genesis," threw the builders into confusion, halting construction permanently.

Right up to modern days, the landscape is littered with disastrous examples of the tendency to build high before a fall. The soaring towers of Southeast Asia, completed before the 1997 crash, come to mind. The world's current tallest buildings, the Petronas Towers, were completed in Kuala Lumpur in 1997, the year the Malaysian stock market fell 50 percent. The December 28, 1999, christening of the world's largest video display, the Nasdaq's $37 million MarketSite Tower in Manhattan's Times Square, came just three months before a 70 percent, 18-month crash in the Nasdaq Composite Index. Enron had almost completed a lavish 40-story tower designed by celebrity architect Cesar Pelli when it filed for bankruptcy in 2002.

John Newbegin, who runs a Web site called nycskyscrapers.com, wrote us: "I was totally fooled [as to Enron's true financial condition] by the beautiful building. . . . They appeared to be by far the most prosperous of all the energy companies I saw, judging from the appearance of the edifice. I was convinced that they were huge and had all kinds of innovative assets and infrastructure all over the U.S."

On October 10, 2002, Enron's brand-new skyscraper, complete with an eight-story-high trading floor, was sold for one-third of its $300 million cost to help pay off some $50 billion owed to creditors.

As we write in 2002, the new "tallest" building, the Shanghai World Financial Center, is under construction in China. Even higher towers are proposed for India and New York. Investors should beware.

Our friend Don Siskind, one of the most respected real estate attorneys on Wall Street, singled out the Lloyds of London building, Drexel Burnham Lambert's 7 World Trade Center offices, and David Paul's savings and loan in Miami as prime examples. "All of the foregoing took more or less the shape of a phallic symbol," he noted.

A great new building can indeed put spring into the step. As an unnamed Alcoa executive put it in a 1953 interview with *Architectural Forum:*

> We used to think of ourselves as a staid, conservative sort of company. But you should look at us now! Working in the most experimental office building in the U.S. suddenly put all of us into a really daring, youthful, experimental frame of mind. I think we all started to perk up.[23]

An Architect's Opinion

For further insight into the phenomenon, we consulted William Mitchell, dean of the School of Architecture and Planning at the Massachusetts Institute of Technology, in an interview and series of e-mail exchanges. In a seminal December 1997 *Scientific American* article titled "Do We Still Need Skyscrapers?" Mitchell had argued that the computer and telecommunication revolutions have reduced the need to keep centralized paper files and assemble office workers in expensive downtown locations. After the destruction of New York's World Trade Center on September 11, 2001, his ideas seem remarkably prescient.

We found Professor Mitchell in an office stacked with skyscrapers of bookshelves twice his height. (The intensive use of capital in the form of book stacks in the very valuable and limited space available in the office provides a nice metaphor of one of the major findings in urban economics: The more valuable the land, the more economical it is to build higher buildings, so as to concentrate capital and labor.) It turned out that the professor is a man of many hats as well as provocative theories. He writes a book every year or two, serves as dean of the school, teaches a few classes, and serves as architectural advisor to the president of MIT on a massive half-billion-dollar center for computer, information, and intelligence sciences.

The World Trade Center attack, Mitchell said, highlighted yet another argument against skyscrapers: security concerns. Vulnerability to natural disasters also argues for decentralization.

Sparks flew when Vic, who named four of his six daughters after Ayn Rand heroes, asked what Mitchell thought of Howard Roark, the architect hero of *The Fountainhead*.[24] Mitchell responded by recalling the book's final scene, where Roark stands proudly atop an immense skyscraper that he has designed, gazing haughtily down at the lesser mortals, as an example of absurd megalomania. "I'm more inclined to believe that great architecture comes from listening well, being sensitive to the nuances and messy complexities of everyday life, carefully solving real problems, and showing a little humility." Roark, however, saw architecture as the pure, heroic expression of an individual's will.

We pressed Mitchell for examples that support his assertion that skyscrapers were becoming dysfunctional. Since his daughter is attending New York University's Stern School of Business Administration, we asked him to imagine what he might say to her graduating class about the lessons architecture holds for investors.

"Skyscrapers," Mitchell said, "exist essentially to exploit concentrations of infrastructure and population in urban centers." Downtown land is expensive, so there is a motivation to build as high as possible to reap the maximum return on investment. "But, the higher you build, the greater the proportion of each floor that must be devoted to structure (holding the building up and providing resistance to wind) and to vertical circulation (elevators, pipes, and ducts). No matter how valuable the site, you eventually reach a point where it makes no economic sense to add another floor. It is technologically possible to go beyond this point, but the reasons for doing so are ones of pride and prestige, or bragging rights about being "the tallest." Manhattan's World Trade Towers and Kuala Lumpur's Petronas Towers are clear examples of skyscrapers that were pushed higher than the point of rationality in order to gain attention and prestige."

Investors, he went on to say, should take a good look at organizations that seek the title of "the tallest." "I suspect you would find that going for the title of 'tallest' is a pretty good indicator of CEO and corporate hubris. I would look not only at 'tallest in the world,' but also more locally—tallest in the nation, the state, or the city. And I'd also watch out for conspicuously tall buildings in locations where the densities and land values do not justify it; skyscrapers make a lot more sense in Hong Kong than they do in Omaha."

"When it comes to buildings," he concluded, "bigger may be better, but biggest usually isn't best."

Best Use, or Boast?

Despite the appealing plausibility of Professor Mitchell's theories and the great esteem we felt for him, we agreed that a quantifiable test was in order. After all, surely there are companies that build tall office buildings not out of hubris, but in the normal course of business. The question is whether very tall downtown buildings represent uneconomic hubris that will ultimately lead to comeuppance in the stock market, or merely a rational attempt to make the most of valuable land by maximizing the number of face-to-face meetings between bankers, lawyers, accountants, and traders.

Thus, we found ourselves once again taking up our favorite tools, the pencil and the back of the envelope, to do some counting. This approach is highly recommended not only for testing theories about tall buildings but for testing any other theories or conventionally accepted views about markets.

For our test, we used skyscrapers named for publicly traded companies in a list published by the Council on Tall Buildings and Urban Habitat of the 100 tallest buildings in the world. The results show that in the cumulative one-year, two-year, and three-year periods after completion of the buildings, the stocks performed 9, 19, and 22 percentage points, respectively, worse than the Dow Jones Industrial Average (see Table 5.3).

The past decade's trend for very tall towers in Asia provides further support for Mitchell's argument. In 1990, all the 50 tallest buildings were in the United States; in 2002, after the destruction of New York's World Trade Center, six of the 10 highest are in Asia. We need not elaborate on just how miserable a decade the 1990s was for Asian stocks.

The situation is actually even more unfavorable for tallest-building companies than appears at first glance. Many skyscrapers that in their day were among the world's tallest have been torn down or destroyed. In most cases, this occurred in conjunction with the failure of the company that built them. The Singer Building, built in 1908, the Manhattan and the Central buildings, both built in 1930, and the New York World building, built in 1890, no longer exist.

One of the problems with architecture in general, and tall buildings in particular, is that the occupant's fortunes and needs are likely to change over the years from design to finish. Buildings designed to give the best and brightest lawyers, engineers, financiers, and accountants a place to exchange ideas face-to-face are strangely out of date in an age when many of these specialists prefer working out of some rural paradise with high-speed telecom links instead of taking a two-hour commute to a congested urban center. Thus, architecture is subject to the same law of ever-changing cycles as the market.

Taking one consideration with another, the results on tall buildings support the hypothesis that hubris is indicative of inferior subsequent stock performance.

Table 5.3 How Stocks Did after Completion of a "World's Tallest" Building (Cumulative 1-, 2-, and 3-Year Change versus Dow Industrials)

Company	Date of Building Completion	Year (%)		
		1	2	3
Commerzbank (CBK.GR)	1997	−21	−11	−29
Dow		16	44	36
NationsBank (Atlanta) (NB)	1993	−4	42	103
Dow		2	36	72
NationsBank (Charlotte, N.C.) (NB)	1992	−7	−10	33
Dow		13	15	54
Suntrust Banks (STI)	1992	3	9	57
Dow		13	15	54
U.S. Bank	1992	9	18	76
Dow		13	15	54
Mellon Bank (MEL)	1991	52	52	32
Dow		5	18	21
AT&T (T)	1989	−35	−14	12
Dow		−4	15	21
IBM (IBM)	1988	−23	−7	−27
Dow		27	21	46
Bank One	1987	−7	35	16
Dow		12	42	36
NationsBank Plaza, Dallas (NB)	1985	−49	−61	−40
Dow		23	25	40
NationsBank Center, Houston (NB)	1984	26	−35	−51
Dow		28	56	60
First Interstate Bank	1983	−3	26	24
Dow		−4	23	51
Transco	1983	35	42	11
Dow		−4	23	51
Citicorp	1977	−12	−8	−18
Dow		−3	1	16
John Hancock	1976	−11	−18	−28
Dow		−17	−20	−17
Sears (S)	1974	−3	13	−3
Dow		38	63	35
First Interstate Bank	1974	0	7	33
Dow		38	63	35
Amoco	1973	0	−5	5
Dow		−28	0	18
Transamerica	1972	−35	−56	−55
Dow		−17	−40	−16

(continued)

Table 5.3   *Continued*

Company	Date of Building Completion	Year (%)		
		1	2	3
USX (X)	1970	−13	−11	−9
Dow		6	22	1
Bank of America	1969	−17	−10	17
Dow		5	11	27
General Electric (GE)	1933	0	18	40
Dow		4	44	80
Chrysler	1930	−29	−43	1
Dow		−53	−64	−39
Woolworth's	1913	1	−2	5
Dow		−31	26	21

		Difference (Percentage Points)
Average 1 year company performance	−5.7	
Average 1 year Dow performance	3.3	9
Average 2 year company performance	−1.2	
Average 2 year Dow performance	18.3	19.5
Average 3 year company performance	8.2	
Average 3 year Dow performance	30.3	22.1

The Magazine Cover Indicator

As our Florida attorney friend William Harrell points out, "Hubris goes out of its way to let you know of its existence, while humility does not." As media organizations depend on loudmouths for copy, we considered the question of the performance of companies featured on business magazine covers. "Whom the gods would destroy, they first put on the cover of *Business Week*," wrote Paul Krugman of Enron's Kenneth Lay, in an August 17, 2001, article for the *New York Times*.[25] Krugman gave no data to support his conclusion, and in typical fashion, used the anecdote to argue for decreased reliance on markets and increased reliance on government intervention.

In fact, many CEOs have gone on to great heights after being featured by *BusinessWeek*. What is needed to shed light on the subject is a complete enumeration of all companies featured on magazine covers during a sufficient

period of varying market conditions so we may draw statistically reliable conclusions, as well as compare the performance
of these companies to the market during relevant subsequent
periods.

Our study of *Time*'s Person of the Year awards, which go back to 1926,
does indicate a hubristic curse. The first company to receive the honor was
Chrysler in 1928. The following year, *Time* featured Owen Young, chairman
of General Electric. Both companies declined about 70 percent over the next
two years. The most recent executive to receive the *Time* award was Jeffrey
Bezos, founder of Amazon.com, on December 27, 1999. The online book-
seller's stock declined 80 percent in the year after the award.

Only in bull markets, it seems, do companies and businesspeople make
the cover of *Time*. The only others we found were General Motors Chairman
Harlow Herbert Curtice in 1955, Cable News Network founder Ted Turner in
1991, and Intel Chairman and CEO Andy Grove in 1997. On average, the six
companies to receive the award declined an average of 10 percent in the next
two years, versus an average gain of 20 percent in the S&P 500 for the same
two-year period.

Because neither the *BusinessWeek* covers nor the *Time* awards were
numerous enough to permit statistically valid conclusions, we studied
every company featured on the cover of *Forbes* from 1997 through 2001. The
results show that companies perform about 5 percentage points worse
than the market in the month after making the cover, and in line with the
market over the subsequent five months. The one-month underperformance appears unlikely to have occurred by chance variation alone—
roughly 1 in 20.

The Stadium Indicator

The naming of stadiums comes to people's minds immediately when they
think of corporate excess. A recent and vivid illustration came February 27,
2002, when Enron, having filed for bankruptcy protection, was forced to sell
the naming rights for Enron Field for $2.1 million to the Houston Astros,
with 27 years remaining on a $100 million contract. "Enron went into bank-
ruptcy and caused a great deal of pain for their employees and people who did
business with Enron," Astros owner Drayton McLane explained during a
Houston press conference. "Their name really didn't have the connotation
that we wanted."[26]

The stadium jinx has been widely noted. The *Wall Street Journal,* inspired by the unfolding Enron debacle, published a lead article in December 2001 about the inordinate tendency of companies to suffer bankruptcy, financial difficulties, or drastic declines in market value after naming stadiums after themselves. Enron, TWA, PSINet, and Fruit of the Loom went out of business under the "stadium jinx," while CMGI Inc., Savvis Communications, 3Com, and Conseco merely showed stock price declines ranging from 85 percent to 92 percent.[27]

Chris Isidore, a sports-business columnist at CNN/Money, created a Stadium Sponsors' Stock Index after Enron's bankruptcy filing. The index tracks 50 publicly traded companies that have paid to put their names on stadiums. The index fell 34 percent in 2002, 11 percentage points worse than the S&P 500 Index.

Corporations are beset by the same harmful tendencies as investors. When they are at their peak, they reach for the sun. The stadium itself is not only an example of a wasteful expenditure unrelated to the company's primary activity; it also signals boastfulness, excessive pride, and a resulting lack of focus.

The problem is that all studies of stadiums that we have seen are anecdotal in nature. The lists of stadiums tend to be incomplete, with no source cited, and often leave out great rises in stocks after renaming deals. Qualcomm (San Diego Padres), General Motors (Vancouver Canucks), PepsiCo (Denver Nuggets), and Compaq Computer (Houston Rockets) all named stadiums after themselves, and all are still very much alive and kicking.

We performed a systematic study of the stadium jinx. The *Almanac of Architecture and Design* contains a complete list for all Major League baseball, football, hockey, and basketball stadiums, including data on cost, capacity, architecture, and completion date.[28]

We went to the Web sites of the companies and found the year the renaming took place. We then constructed Table 5.4 showing the performance of 31 companies from the year of acquisition of naming rights to three years thereafter. The results indicate that during the year of naming and in the subsequent year, the companies performed significantly worse than the S&P 500. However, in the second and third year after the naming, the results are mixed to bullish. The results were helped by Qualcomm's 2680 percent gain in the second year.

Like most transactions in life and markets, acquisitions can be very good or very bad. For an acquired company, a good acquisition lets the owner cash in and enjoy a profit—the self-interested, wholly appropriate incentive for starting a company in the first place. For the purchaser, a good acquisition provides an opportunity to save on costs, to improve marketing or to invest capital at higher returns than are available internally.

At worst, an acquisition is a desperate attempt by the seller to unload bad merchandise based on adverse private information, or an effort by the acquiring company to create a facade of enhanced profitability.

Most acquirers, we hasten to say, would never dream of succumbing to the alluring temptations that come with acquisition accounting. But some find that a steady stream of purchases much improves their ability to deliver the consistent quarterly growth so dear to analysts, and they are not averse to painting the lily for temporary advantage.

Nothing improves a corporation's ability to manipulate earnings like a series of acquisitions. With a few flourishes of the pencil, a chief financial officer can find a cornucopia of profits in an acquired company's earnings, pension plans, medical plans, and assets held on the balance sheet below market price.

In Table 5.5, we show the results from our statistical test of what numerous or infrequent acquisitions signal in a relatively homogenous sample of large buyers—the companies that make up the S&P 100 index. After reporting the results, which seem to support the virtue of abstemiousness on the part of large companies, we share some insights for acquirers and investors from a highly successful serial acquirer of privately held companies.

For more than 50 years, accountants have been trying to create rules that will make acquisition accounting fair. The Financial Accounting Standard Board's 2001 ban on "pooling of interest" accounting in mergers is a recent example. (Without pooling, companies must amortize the premium, or "goodwill," they paid for the target company over a period of years, thereby depressing earnings.) But as in all arms races, acquirers—and their consultants and experts—are vigorous in mounting new attacks and finding new ways to put the best foot forward.

With investors paying more attention these days to accounting treatments, we are fascinated by the possibility of developing statistical profiles of serial acquirers versus abstainers. Might a predilection for acquisitions be a sign of hubristic overconfidence in the company's ability to run other businesses? Are abstainers unusually confident in their ability to run their businesses without benefit of acquisitions? Because these questions are difficult to test, we started

Table 5.4 The Stadium Indicator: Naming Rights and Stock Returns

Stadium	Ticker	Naming Rights	Naming Year	1 Year After	2 Years After	3 Years After
The Target Center	TGT	1990	−3.5	−20.8	−4.2	−27.3
The Delta Center	DAL	1991	−7.7	−40.7	−43.3	−48.5
America West Arena	AWA	1992	−86.0	28.0	666.6	1502.8
The United Center	UAL	1994	−38.6	−9.8	12.4	45.4
Coors Field	RKY	1995	−2.0	−47.9	−12.8	69.3
The Fleet Center	FBF	1995	−8.2	−7.2	20.7	8.4
General Motors Place	GM	1995	−8.6	−28.9	−59.0	−88.3
Key Arena	KEY	1995	10.9	40.7	72.0	−11.6
Trans World Dome	TWA	1995				
3com Park	COMS	1995	46.7	123.3	−75.8	−93.8
Continental Airline Arena	CAL	1996	9.6	63.7	−45.6	−34.5
Ericsson Stadium	ERICY	1996	34.5	33.8	45.9	435.2
Edison International Field	EIX	1997	5.8	−25.7	−66.6	−99.6
Qualcomm Stadium	QCOM	1997	−4.4	−33.1	3414.4	1507.6
Alltel Stadium	AT	1997	−0.1	24.7	65.2	20.8
Network Associates Coliseum	NET	1998	61.3	−75.7	−124.2	−45.0
Bank One Ballpark	ONE	1998	−23.3	−86.6	−61.9	−39.2
American Airline Arena	AMR	1998	−34.3	−47.1	0.3	−40.7
Safeco Field	SAFC	1999	−61.6	−30.8	−20.9	
Conseco Fieldhouse	CNC	1999	−61.1	−64.2	−78.8	
Pepsi Center	PEP	1999	−33.3	13.8	25.7	
Staples Center	SPLS	1999	−48.3	−66.8	−29.2	
Adelphia Coliseum	ADLAC	1999	23.9	5.4	−25.2	
Fedex Field	FDX	1999	−27.7	−17.8	22.9	
Mellon Arena	MEL	1999	−20.4	35.7	16.0	
Gaylord Entertainment Center	GET	1999	−20.1	−38.1	−11.7	
Comerica Park	CMA	2000	37.3	44.6		
Enron Field	ENE	2000	97.5	−76.8		
Xcel Energy	XEL	2000	59.2	64.1		
PNC Park	PNC	2001	−10.0			
American Airline Center	AMR	2001	−30.1			
		Average	−4.75	−8.58	148.13	180.05
		Median	−7.97	−19.29	−11.74	−27.27
		Standard deviation	39.86	50.47	695.60	513.15
		% Up	33	39	44	41
		# OB	30.00	28.00	25.00	17.00

Source: www.ballparks.com.

Table 5.5 Paying the Piper for Serial Acquisitions: Purchases 1998–2001 versus Performance January 1–July 12, 2002

Company	Ticker	Purchases	Percent Change
15 most acquisitive			
General Electric	GE	66	−28.6
Tyco	TYC	32	−76.7
Clear Channel Communications	CCU	31	−33.9
Citigroup	C	28	−28
AES	AES	15	−79.6
AOL Time Warner	AOL	14	−59.1
United Technologies	UTX	14	−2
General Motors	GM	13	−4.1
American International Group	AIG	12	−20
Microsoft	MSFT	12	−21.7
Wells Fargo	WFC	12	−13.6
Cisco Systems	CSCO	11	−62.4
Ford Motor	F	11	−19.8
Intel	INTC	11	−40.2
J.P. Morgan	JPM	11	−16.9
Average % return			**−33.8**
Companies with 1 acquisition			
Bank of America	BAC	1	9
Black & Decker	BDK	1	13.9
EMC	EMC	1	−36.4
Harrah's Entertainment	HET	1	19.1
International Paper	IP	1	1.5
May Department Stores	MAY	1	−18.2
Medtronic	MDT	1	−24.5
Medimmune	MEDI	1	−47.7
3M	MMM	1	2.3
Merck	MRK	1	−22.5
Oracle	ORCL	1	−29.9
Pfizer	PFE	1	−19.2
Pharmacia	PHA	1	−23.6
RadioShack	RSH	1	−11.1
Sears	S	1	−2.4
SBC Communications	SBC	1	−24.3
The Southern Co.	SO	1	−0.2
Average % return			**−12.6**
Companies with no acquisitions			
Allegheny Technologies	ATI	0	−14.1
Ltd Brands	LTD	0	11.4
Anheuser-Busch	BUD	0	8.8

(continued)

Table 5.5 *Continued*

Company	Ticker	Purchases	Percent Change
Avon Products	AVP	0	3
Baker Hughes	BHI	0	−19.1
Burlington Northern Santa Fe	BNI	0	0.2
Cigna	CI	0	−3.7
Norfolk Southern	NSC	0	17.1
Campbell Soup	CPB	0	−19.4
Nortel Networks	NT	0	−95.5
Colgate-Palmolive	CL	0	−23.3
Philip Morris	MO	0	−6.4
Delta Air Lines	DAL	0	−65.3
Raytheon	RTN	0	7.3
FedEx	FDX	0	−3.8
Toys R Us	TOY	0	−10.4
Gillette	G	0	−13.5
Xerox	XRX	0	−38.1
Average % return			**−14.7**
S&P 100			**−21.5**

with a modest preliminary study of the relation of acquisitions to stock performance.

Taking the companies in the S&P 100 at the start of 1998, we counted the number of acquisitions each made over the next four years, through 2001. We came up with three groupings for comparison: the top 15 acquirers, companies that made no acquisitions, and companies that made one acquisition. We calculated their stock performance from January 1, 2002, through July 12, 2002. The results appear in Table 5.5.

As the table shows, serial acquirers underperformed abstainers by 19.1 percentage points, and they underperformed the S&P 100 by 12.8 percentage points. Abstainers beat the S&P 100 by 6.8 percentage points.

The urge to merge can be good or bad, and each acquisition must be judged on its merits. However, during the most recent four years, the urge has been inversely related to year-to-date 2002 performance.

From long experience on all vantage points of the acquisition arena—Vic founded and for 25 years spearheaded a very active mergers-and-acquisition brokerage—we suggest that in certain types of markets, an acquisition might offer the temptation to overstate earnings. If the truth comes out, the stock may be hammered.

Making Mischief with the Books

We have no knowledge of the accounting probity of any of the companies in the news today. But we can say that, in general, most mischief begins with assets held on the books of acquired companies at original cost. If the acquired company bought the assets many years before, or if the assets are worth much more than they cost (as must be assumed if they were bought at a premium), then there is great potential for an acquiring company to sell off these assets at the market price for a nice profit.

A second source of temptation is the potential boost to the acquiring company's earnings from the acquisition. When a company's stock is selling at 20 times earnings and it buys something at 10 times earnings, there is an immediate pickup that can be calculated based on the number of shares and earnings involved.

A third major line of misstatements is the prospect of writing certain items up or down to advantage. The common practices of writing up goodwill for tax purposes, or writing down pension obligations and medical plans of the acquired firms, are treasure chests in this regard.

We emphasize that we have no reason to believe that serial acquirers are any more prone to such temptations than those that acquire less frequently. Multiple acquisitions are merely a possible signal, an area of concern in certain kinds of markets. Others, however, have come to similar conclusions. In a classic 1986 study, "The Hubris Hypothesis of Corporate Takeovers," Richard W. Roll found that acquiring companies often perform worse than the market after a deal, and that the motivation for the purchase thus could not rationally be stock price appreciation. He posited that the main motivation would have to be . . . hubris.[29]

To assist our readers in evaluating acquisitions, we are pleased to present insights from a friend who is among the world's leading experts in the subject: Vic's partner of 35 years, Dan Grossman. Grossman has managed and bought a wide variety of businesses and, through his law practice, has been instrumental in forming and developing many companies, including the drug maker Syntex. Dan recently sold a number of his businesses profitably and is writing a book about his adventures in the M&A business.

Advice on Acquisitions from Dan Grossman

- Avoid businesses requiring exquisite management. Buy a company that regular people can run.

- When evaluating an acquisition, picture what it will be like trying to sell it. Look for the type of business that buyers, especially public companies, will want to acquire.
- Avoid mixing acquisition analysis with some other need in your life. Don't look to acquire a company because it will get you involved with golf or sailing, or because it is in a glamorous location, or because you have been laid off and need a place to work. It is hard enough to be objective analyzing an acquisition on its own merits without throwing in all kinds of personal needs and desires.
- Have a good accountant explain to you how inventory can be used to juggle earnings, and why, for some companies, it is almost impossible for a buyer to determine the accuracy of reported earnings for a given year.
- Time is the friend of a growth company and the enemy of the bargain or value company. The longer you are going to own, the more important to pay up for growth.

The results of our preliminary study on acquisitions may unduly reflect the unusual pessimism of the current stock market. Yet given the sad fates of serial acquirers over the past few decades—the conglomerates, the rollups, and all the companies that became marquee names in the market value rankings by paying princely sums of their own soaring stock for tiny, unprofitable companies—it does not seem inappropriate to conclude that both acquirer and investor should be on guard when reaching for the stars.

Lords on Boards

The hiring of celebrities as marketing tools is often associated with hubris in the executive office. RJR Nabisco put golf pros on the payroll before being bought by KKR (another act of hubris that brought on a long period of underperformance for the company). Kmart's association with Martha Stewart, Kathy Ireland, and Jaclyn Smith did it no good. Even in bankruptcy, Kmart continued the same losing strategy, announcing in April 2002 that it had hired the Creative Artists Agency to get its name and products placed in movies.

We tested this phenomenon systematically in September 2001 by studying the relation between stock returns and the number of board members with titles in the 50 largest companies by market value in Britain's FTSE 100. (We counted knights, baronesses, earls, a viscount, a lady, and a dame, along with lords and right honorable lords. We awarded an extra point if the chairman was a lord.)

We then listed the companies' five-year stock performance, eliminating three that had not been around long enough in their present form. It turns out that the more lords on board, the worse the stock performance over the previous five years.

Our observations on the relationship of lords and earnings raise the question of which way causality runs. Was it the lords who caused the lackluster performance or the lackluster performance that prompted the companies to use lords as window-dressing?

HSBC Holdings, the fourth most valuable company in the FTSE 100, had the greatest number of lords—seven titled board members and a knighted chairman, Sir John Reginald Hartnell Bond.

Eight of the 10 largest FTSE 100 companies had at least three lords. The largest, BP (formerly British Petroleum), has four lords. GlaxoSmithKline, the second largest, has six lords on board and a knighted chairman. About half the companies have between one and three lords. The largest company without lords was insurer CGNU, No. 13 on the FTSE.

We also invented the earnings/lords (E/L) ratio—a measure of attractiveness along the lines of the price/earnings (P/E) ratio.

A small or negative numerator (earnings) and a high denominator (lords) would result in a small or negative ratio. For example, HSBC made 75.5 cents a share last year and has eight lords on board. Therefore, it has an E/L ratio of 0.09, putting it in the bottom third of the companies with both lords and profits. Powergen plc, with one lord and $1 of earnings per share, has it the highest E/L ratio. Cable & Wireless lost 93 cents a share last year, and has three lords on board; thus, its ratio is negative.

We hypothesize that investors might want to stay away from companies with small or negative earnings/lords ratios. However, our observations are merely a first step toward defining the market implications of ossification versus innovation. Proper testing of this idea would require the analysis of several years of data unavailable in computer databases. In the spirit of science, we hope that our efforts will form the basis for further study.

Summing It All Up in Iambic Pentameter

After quantifying the market effects of executive boasting, flashy headquarters buildings, magazine cover stories, stadium deals, and big acquisitions, we conclude that such instances of hubris can send a company's stock plunging. We suspect that corporate golf courses (Lucent), opulent offices (RJR Nabisco), moves to Florida (Scott Paper), sex scandals (General Electric, Bendix), and executive pay exceeding $100 million a year (General Electric, Apple, Siebel Systems, Oracle, Cisco) might be profitable areas for future hubris tests.

The Greeks believed that the stately and portentous language of iambic pentameter, which corresponds to the emotional heights of human speech, enhances the impact of tragedy. (An iamb is a weak syllable followed by a strong syllable, and iambic pentameter contains five weak-strongs to a line, with many artistic liberties taken.) We will therefore close with some heroic verses by Victor's daughter, the producer and writer Galt Niederhoffer, whose coming-of-age novel *American Thighs* is written in iambic pentameter:

> Hubris is on everybody's mind of late
> Humility seems like a memory.
> It seems that only yesterday that
> Enron's chairman, Kenneth Lay
> Did boast of feats unmatched in a decade:
> "We've grown nine-fold to $40 billion
> And we'll do it again before too long."
> A messenger from the **Economist**
> Was witness to his grandiosity
> Reporting on the New Economy
> He found in Enron the epitome.
>
> So often history repeats itself
> And so was Cisco twinning over times
> Referring to its staunch predecessors
> As relics of the Old Economy
> Behold, not more than 12 months ago,
> Cisco offered its own grand prophecy
> Predicting 30 percent to 50
> Though such growth occurs mainly in tragedy
> So diminished is the growth of tech firms now
> The media now calls them shriveled men.

6 BENJAMIN GRAHAM: MYTHICAL MARKET HERO

When Benjamin Graham died at age 82, he was one of the great legends of Wall Street, brilliant, successful, ethical—the man who invented the discipline of security analysis. Now, 20 years after his death his memoirs are reaching the public at last—a hugely successful chronicle of one of the richest and most eventful lives of the century.

—*Kirkus Review,* June 9, 1996

The ancient Greeks had Hercules, the mighty hero deified by Zeus for noble deeds and worshipped by men. In the twenty-first century, Americans have Benjamin Graham.

Tales of the prowess of Hercules—and his promiscuity—passed from generation to generation in Greece. The modern hero of the investment world has similar characteristics and impact. On the Internet, we found thousands of articles eulogizing Graham and not a single one with any negatives. The most frequent epithets: "father of security analysis," "a prophet," "the legendary investor," "founder of value investing," "master of the investment game," "the Confucius of value investing," "pioneer of value investing," and "the revered mentor to the most successful investors of all time." Graham is said to have amassed a fortune by following a method of buying stocks selling below half their net cash liquidation value. The method is outlined in *Graham and Dodd's Security Analysis,* a book widely known as the bible of value investing.[1]

Graham's followers include such famous and successful investors as his former student Warren Buffett, who was active during his mentor's lifetime in leading worshipful tributes to him. "We are here for only one reason," Buffett said on a cruise with Graham that he organized for wealthy investors, "to listen to the wisdom of Benjamin."

Like most legends, many of these encomiums are half-truths at best.

Illusory Bargains

Let's start with the difficulties of buying companies at 50 percent of net current asset value. Common sense would tell you that if a business were selling at half its net liquidating cash value, the major owners or the chief executive or their friends or the company's bankers or accountants would quickly buy the stock for themselves and their families and good friends, and then liquidate immediately at a beautiful premium.

Vic operated one of the most extensive merger-and-acquisition businesses in the United States for more than 35 years. In the course of his business, he visited tens of thousands of privately held companies. He never found a single one available for such a price. Nor has anyone else he knows of.

The stock exchange in the 1930s seemed to offer such bargains. However, high commissions and wide spreads between bid and ask prices made the bargains illusory.

Modern companies that seem to have Graham-type characteristics and have not been gobbled up are mere will-o'-the-wisps, luring investors to buy them with bad news likely to follow. We, and all others we know of, have been victimized much more often than we have profited by trying to grab at such ephemera. A recent notable example came when we bought Aether Systems, a company with $50 cash value per share that was selling for only $30. Aether lost money at such a remarkable rate that the stock slid to $2 soon after we bought it. The cash value fell right along with the stock price. Vic's daughter,

Katie, bought that one on Vic's recommendations, and the resulting loss quickly sobered her on her budding career as a value stock picker and sent her back to finish up her PhD in psychology.

Buffett also felt the lure of seemingly irresistible discounts from book value. In the early days of his career, he used to like to buy such companies. Everybody in the merger business has oodles of them for sale: There are regional department stores in declining towns, distributors of American steel products doomed to be displaced by imports, producers of machinery for textile firms and other manufacturing businesses in the declining stage of their life cycles, which require huge capital investments merely to compete with more economical modern substitutes.

Certainly the tax loss provided by Berkshire Hathaway allowed Buffett to make plenty of such acquisitions and must have been helpful in accumulating wealth for himself and his stockholders. Finally, however, Buffett's attorney, Charlie Munger, the legendary "Charlie" who shares the dais with him at Berkshire Hathaway's annual meetings in Nebraska, told him in effect to stop buying dying dinosaurs. As Charlie pointed out to Buffett, such companies tied up capital endlessly, consistently lost money, and were never able to be sold at higher prices than Buffett had paid for them, because nobody else wanted them.

When Vic was in the mergers business, he found that most acquirers share Charlie's views. He was never so lucky as to find buyers who would reach for bargains regardless of future profits. Thus, when the mass marketing techniques that Vic used netted companies for sale in such fields as shoe manufacturing, retail candy stores, carpets, and so forth, he would regretfully tell the owners that he was unable to find the right potential partner for them, and that he would be happy to refer them instead to an employee stock ownership specialist. For a typical melange of companies that Vic found he could not sell, see the companies owned by Berkshire Hathaway, listed in the company's annual report.

Like Buffett, Vic found that the owners of such companies always were willing to work for the new owner at salaries much lower than they currently were receiving—if the new owner did not interfere with their "entrepreneurial drive and independence," as Buffett puts it. The only mustache on the picture was that these owners would only work for the low salary until they received the highly inflated price they had agreed to sell for, or until the company came into some incredible good fortune that enabled it to rise from the grave.

Another basic problem with Graham's approach is that, in both theory and practice, investors are paid to lend capital to businesses that are growing too quickly and earning too high a rate of return on their equity to finance their opportunities for investment from internal sources or borrowing from banks. Companies selling at discounts tend to be those that are not growing businesses. By avoiding investment in such companies, one forgoes the extra returns that are in fact available.

This is all for the good. Companies tend to prosper if they produce things for which there is unsatisfied demand by responding to constantly shifting and unfathomable consumer tastes and thereby giving us the goods we want in the quantities we desire. An invisible hand tends to create incentives for people to make money, while at the same time bettering our material well being. This idea was first memorialized in 1776, by Adam Smith in *The Wealth of Nations*, developed further in *Principles of Economics* by Alfred Marshall 100 years later, and has since been featured in the introductory chapters of most economics texts. The economics texts of the 1950s and 1960s were notable exceptions, as they presented the invisible hand and the incentives as mere capitalist rationalizations for an evil system. It is our impression that those followers of Graham who have been to college were weaned on such texts.

Performance Test

Considering the great gap between Graham's theory of value investing and the chances of putting it into practice, it is not surprising that performance of the funds he managed was not as attractive as legend would have it. The universally revered apostle of prudent investing was devastated after the crash of 1929. After finishing 1928 with a 60 percent return, he lost 20 percent in 1929. He lost 50 percent more in 1930. In 1931, he lost 16 percent. In 1932, much to the relief of his investors, he lost a mere 3 percent. Journalist Janet Lowe, in *Benjamin Graham on Value Investing: Lessons from the Dean of Wall Street*, wrote:

> Though Graham was able to stumble back and regain his footing in the market rather quickly, after Black Tuesday, Ben's high-risk days were over. Afterward, he struggled to squeeze the best possible return from his investments, while at the same time seeking that wide margin of safety. The average returns on Ben's portfolio descended from the heights of the pre-Depression years.[2]

Graham always believed that a Dow of more than 100 was too high, and when it got there, he never again felt comfortable in the market. As the Dow never fell below 100 after 1942, Graham was always leaning toward being too defensive. In the early 1950s, when the Dow was about 300, he began to pull back from his business and advised his students against going into investing:

The market was "too high." Because he believed for so long that the market was overvalued, his investment performance did not measure up to a buy-and-hold strategy or any other sensible alternate strategy. In 1956, the year the Dow topped 500 for the first time, he left the business for good and devoted himself to a life of pleasure.

One of the most curious—and murkiest—aspects of Graham's performance record is the question of how much his success was attributable to Geico, the insurance company he later sold to Buffett. Graham wrote in *The Intelligent Investor* that the one investment he made without following his own methods was the purchase of Geico.[3] It is likely that the returns he realized from Geico were much greater than the total returns he realized by applying his own methods. The insurer has also been the mainstay of Buffett's success, providing copious cash float for arbitrage transactions.

One thing we do know about the returns from following Graham's methods. In 1976, a student founded a mutual fund devoted to putting Graham's theories into practice. It was called the Rea-Graham fund. When the fund was liquidated or merged in 1998, it was worth $3.6 million in assets. In this day and age, where a fund manager with a good story can often start with $500 million in seed capital and attract billions more with just a few successful years, the ending total assets of this fund shows that its actual performance was meager at best.

Table 6.1 shows how $10,000 invested in the Rea-Graham fund at its inception in 1976 would have fared versus the S&P 500.

Thus, we can summarize the performance in practice of Graham's method as follows: His performance was disastrous in the 1930s when he liquidated. He started again in the late 1930s and got out of the market in 1956, missing the move from Dow 500 to Dow 1000 over the next 20 years. A fund that put his methods into practice from 1976 to 1996 underperformed the S&P 500 by a factor of 4 to 1.

Value's Dismal Performance

On the surface, Graham's message to buy value stocks seems perfectly reasonable. Who does not want value for his money? But there is one small problem: Contrary to widespread belief, value stocks have consistently underperformed growth stocks since at least 1965. The evidence was provided, quite by chance, by the venerable research firm Value Line.

Table 6.1   Rea-Graham Fund Performance versus S&P 500 (Dividends Reinvested)

Starting Investment = $10,000 (June 30, 1976)

Period Ending	Rea-Graham ($)	S&P 500 ($)
12/31/76	10,846	10,513
12/31/77	11,194	9,758
12/31/78	12,355	10,394
12/31/79	14,362	12,312
12/31/80	15,837	16,312
12/31/81	18,391	15,516
8/19/82	18,856	13,820
3/31/83	23,035	20,734
3/31/84	23,789	22,534
3/31/85	26,928	26,774
3/31/86	34,380	36,814
3/31/87	37,602	46,455
3/31/88	38,273	42,564
3/31/89	41,182	50,234
3/31/90	43,101	59,874
3/31/91	43,478	68,473
3/31/92	45,797	76,002
3/31/93	49,662	87,548
3/31/94	48,213	88,825
3/31/95	48,291	102,627
3/31/96	54,005	135,470
3/31/97	57,467	162,290
3/31/98	65,215	240,000
9/30/98	57,709	223,290
11/15/98	60,898	247,606

Unintentional experiments often are provided by the gods to allow mortals to see the light. John/Joan, who lost his penis in circumcision as an infant, was raised as a girl. His twin brother was raised as a boy. The outcome was that Joan acted just like a boy, and eventually reassumed the identity of a boy.[4]

The gods of investment provided a similar unintentional experiment to determine which class of stocks provides better long-run returns: value or growth. Value Line is an admirable service whose research director, Sam Eisenstadt, is a young-hearted person who always looks to improve his own knowledge and the products he provides his customers, despite the firm's great track record. In 1965, prompted by gains in value stocks and by Sam's desire to offer clients an alternate rating system, Value Line started selecting the best value stocks in their universe. The firm divided its sample of 1,500 companies into 10 groups based on value, updating the selections each month. The selection system used the same key variables that almost everyone else uses to define value stock (i.e., price to sales, price to book, and price to earnings). But there was one difference that today, almost four decades later, makes all the difference in evaluating the stocks' long-term performance. In contrast to retrospective studies of value stocks, the Value Line companies were selected contemporaneously. Thus, the Value Line value stock performance record is a real-life unintentional experiment with no back-testing, survivor bias, or armchair quarterbacking.

The procedure has remained the same since 1965. Each group is updated each month. Results are reported every six months in Value Line's *Selection and Opinion* publication. The one problem is that the firm reports price appreciation rather than return, and our studies have shown that the dividend yields of value stocks are 2 percent higher, on average, than those of growth stocks.

We report the results of the experiment in Figure 6.1 and Table 6.2. Value Line Group 1, consisting mainly of growth stocks, quickly outpaced the three value stock categories. By March 2002, the growth stocks had returned almost 28 times the return of the best-performing "value" group, "low

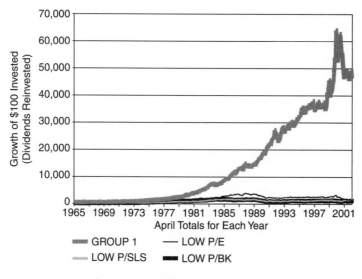

Figure 6.1   Value versus Growth

Table 6.2   Value versus Growth (Dividends Reinvested)

Starting Value	Group 1 100	Low Price/Sales 100	Low P/E 100	Low Price/Book 100
January 1970	216	191	205	188
January 1980	2,782	815	1,450	1,086
January 1990	16,540	1,326	3,034	1,296
March 2002	46,885	1,698	1,555	1,250

price/sales." (How Value Line came to be capable of such calculations is discussed in Chapter 10.)

Certain aspects of Graham's life do have a mythical quality. After the tragic suicide of Graham's son in France, Graham traveled from his home in California to collect the deceased's belongings. On arriving, he fell in love with his late son's girlfriend, Marie Louise. As Graham was already married, he suggested to his fourth wife, back home in California, that she share him with his new amour. Much to Graham's wife's distress, she thenceforth saw her husband only six months out of every year. The tale has odd echoes of Zeus' philandering and Persephone's annual six-month descent into the underworld to be with her husband, Hades, lord of the dead, during the winter months.

Belief in Zeus and the feats of Hercules eventually dwindled into insignificance. We suspect that the legendary father of value investing will be treated no better by the gods.

7 NEWS FLASH: COMPUTER WRITES STOCK MARKET STORY!

The foundation of all morality is to have done, once and for all, with lying; to give up pretending to believe that for which there is no evidence, and repeating unintelligible propositions about things beyond the possibilities of knowledge.

—Thomas Henry Huxley[1]

We are all familiar with the truth of the proverb that one lie begets another. Assertions have implications. When implications turn out to be false, obfuscation, or "further-putting-into-perspective," is necessary to extend the original lie.

Nowhere is this principle better seen than in the typical story on daily market moves in the financial media. These stories are generated with a simple formula:

Stocks (rose/fell) on (earnings/interest-rate) (optimism/pessimism)

The possible combinations are limited, but well within the capabilities of reporters without much trading experience or statistical knowledge:

Stocks rose on earnings optimism. Stocks fell on earnings pessimism.
Stocks rose on interest-rate optimism. Stocks fell on interest-rate pessimism.

A fancy report will combine the two:

Stocks fell on expectations that rising borrowing costs will cut into corporate earnings.
Stocks rose on expectations that lower borrowing costs will boost corporate earnings.

The assumption about the earnings-market return relation in this formula is, as readers know by now, completely fallacious. As shown in Chapter 2, the time to get ready to buy is exactly when earnings look worst, and the time to sell is when earnings look best. But there is another aspect to these formulaic stories: Although human beings write these reports according to the blueprint, the stories could just as well be done with a computer. In fact, we have patented a Market News-O-Matic program and debut it later in this chapter.

But back to the blueprint. Once the ball is rolling, the reporter is bound to continue down the fallacious track to fulfill the market's never-ending need for promotional material and contributions from the public. The next step, therefore, is to introduce a money manager. She just sold her position in an industry based on lowered earnings expectations. (You must know about her so that you can buy her fund, or sell that stock yourself, or possibly hire that prescient fund manager in the future.) If all the fund managers in the reporter's Rolodex are busy on TV, the statement can always be attributed to "some investors."

Next, the reporter will attempt to find a quote pertinent to the chosen theme from one of the Federal Reserve officials or government economists who are always giving a speech somewhere on any given day. If the Fed chairman himself is speaking, the story practically writes itself. "Declines deepened after Federal Reserve Chairman Alan Greenspan said consumer spending, which makes up two-thirds of demand in the U.S. economy, won't increase as much as it has following past recessions," ran one story from a major wire service. This statement "cast doubt on how much an economic recovery will fuel corporate profit growth." Bingo! The reporter has succeeded in working the chairman's words into support for the earnings fallacy embedded in his story's lead paragraph.

Next comes an enumeration of a list of companies whose stocks declined that day after analysts cut forecasts on their earnings. Propagandists call this card stacking; the reporter, apparently heedless of the worthlessness of anecdotal evidence, presents this list as confirmation of his theme.

The reporter's unconscious work on behalf of the market is now complete. He has allowed a manager to tout her fund. He has provided, based on a series of extrapolations that are possibly incorrect, an analysis of a statement by the chairman of the Federal Reserve. He has completely tied up the investor in specious conclusions. More important, he has encouraged investors to be fearful and to overtrade. For good measure, he has publicized names of brokerages available to assist investors in their overtrading.

Harm Done

Such stories are completely worthless to anybody who trades. They are purely descriptive, anecdotal, and backward-looking. They are harmful to anybody who trades on the assumptions they contain. But the damage does not end with the hapless investor. If current earnings strength is the key to market moves, by natural extension the main job of corporations is to construct and deliver a steady stream of favorable earnings comparisons. Can anyone doubt that the string of 35 positive earnings comparisons in General Electric, with the skepticism it engenders about the underlying process, as well as the massive attempt by companies like Enron to sell debt (which is good for corporate earnings per share but bad for survivability), has poisoned the atmosphere of the early Naughties?

You might think that there would be checks and balances on such propaganda because of the obvious harm. Scholars might undertake an academic study of the phenomenon, and some enterprising reporter might publicize the results to puncture the ballyhoo. But most academics have axes of their own to grind. Even to read the most basic academic journal relating to economics or finance these days requires membership in a postadvanced-calculus, postadvanced-econometrics, postcanned-computer-program-using club that only professional economists who registered for all these courses in their postdoc education could hope to unravel. Even if academics communicated their conclusions in language that laypeople could decipher, the information would not be of much use. By the time a study goes through the usual rounds of peer review and publication in an academic quarterly, a few years will have passed, and the cycle is likely to have changed.

Part of the harmfulness of a lie is that it crowds out other statements that might add to knowledge. Many investors undoubtedly know that selling stocks on bad news, earnings-related or otherwise, and buying on good news will get them in trouble. Since the main thing investors and editors are attuned to hearing is the earnings-market return myth, any commentators who might know what factors really did create the market move that day are left twisting in the wind. By focusing everyone's attention on a bogus explanation, the investor is led away from finding out the truth from some other source.

Stock moves from day to day are in the main randomly related to ephemeral factors of the day. They tend to go down after there has been excessive optimism over the previous several days, and they tend to go up after there has been excessive pessimism. These swings in optimism and pessimism have little, if anything, to do with earnings. However, it would be completely dysfunctional for reporters to attribute the swings to excesses in anything like public sentiment. Such a report might lead to the thoughtful decision that perhaps the solution would be less trading. Even worse, investors might pay less attention to what the channels of communications are transmitting. That would be bad for the ecosystem of the newspaper and TV and Internet purveyors as it would cut down on advertising revenues from brokerages and stock exchanges. Moreover, it might keep the public from making its maximum contribution to the market's vast machinery of brokers, specialists, analysts, and investment bankers.

The bottom line for investors is that no matter whether news reports say stock is going up on earnings optimism or down on earnings pessimism, these assertions amount to nothing more than an invitation to trade the wrong way. If an investor had a guardian angel, he might hear a whispered: "Listen! A lot of ephemeral things go on. The thing to know is that stocks are a claim on infinite future earnings. What happens today should not affect your view of a stock, because you are buying it for its long-term discounted value. Do not let the market take you and your loved ones away to the poorhouse."

The Market News-O-Matic

After studying the subject from a wide variety of statistical, economic, and psychological angles, after reading more than a thousand academic articles on

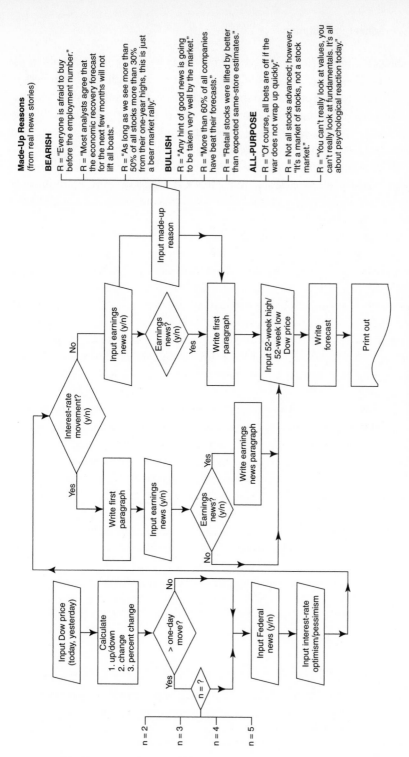

Made-Up Reasons
(from real news stories)

BEARISH

R = "Everyone is afraid to buy before the employment number."

R = "Most analysts agree that the economic recovery forecast for the next few months will not lift all boats."

R = "As long as we see more than 50% of all stocks more than 30% from their one-year highs, this is just a bear market rally."

BULLISH

R = "Any hint of good news is going to be taken very well by the market."

R = "More than 60% of all companies have beat their forecasts."

R = "Retail stocks were lifted by better than expected same-store estimates."

ALL-PURPOSE

R = "Of course, all bets are off if the war does not wrap up quickly."

R = "Not all stocks advanced; however, "It's a market of stocks, not a stock market."

R = "You can't really look at values, you can't really look at fundamentals. It's all about psychological reaction today."

Figure 7.1 Market News-O-Matic

177

the subject, after running and vetting our ideas by the greatest minds in the field, after spending thousands of our own hours calculating the numbers by hand, rechecking the original sources, and directing and supervising our multifarious talented staff in similar pursuits, we can recommend an effective antidote to financial news coverage: From time to time, investors should make up stock stories themselves for their educational amusement.

We drew our inspiration from Alan Turing, the genius British codebreaker who proposed a test for artificial intelligence. The test is, "Can a computer be programmed to produce a product that could be completely indistinguishable from a human effort?"

In the case of stock market reporting, the answer is yes (see Figure 7.1).

Our program proceeds through a simple series of steps. Say the market is up. There can be two reasons. Either it is earnings optimism or interest-rate optimism. If a major company reported good earnings and its stock went up, then attribute it to the latter. If, on the contrary, the major company reported good earnings and its stock went down, then attribute the market's up move to interest-rate optimism. Throw in some benign comments from Doc Greenspan or one of the minions dispatched daily to feather the nests of the Fed's clients at the government dealers and brokers, and you have a story.

Readers should test their understanding and creativity by trying this out at home. For practice, apply the preceding basic formula to a down day. If possible, attribute the decline to poor earnings reports from one or more companies. If you can find no plausible examples of poor earnings, go to Plan B, which is to talk instead about interest-rate pessimism. Be sure to throw in a comment or two from Alan Abelson's list of reasons to be bearish and woeful (see Chapter 4).

With the current vogue for downsizing in our economy, it is nice to know that you have within you the makings of another career, that of a newspaper reporter.

The following is a sample story generated by the Market News-O-Matic:

Today's Market: U.S. Stocks [Rise/Fall] on Earnings [Optimism/Pessimism]
By Victor Niederhoffer
Junior Staff Writer

[First Paragraph]

(New York, Niederhoffer News)—U.S. stocks [rose/fell] as unexpectedly [strong/weak] earnings from [company] fueled [optimism/pessimism] for a rebound in earnings by year-end.

[Price Paragraph]

The Dow Jones Industrial Average [rose/fell] [# points], or [percent change] to [price]. The Standard & Poor's 500 Index rose [rose/fell] [# points], or [percent change] to [price]. The technology-laden Nasdaq Composite Index rose [rose/fell] [# points], or [percent change] to [price].

[Fed Paragraph]

Stocks [pushed higher/lost ground] in the afternoon after Federal Reserve Chairman Alan Greenspan said that [technology is improving productivity and creating a virtuous circle of sustainable economic growth/too many people have made too much money from stocks, and that the resulting demand for goods threatens to unbalance the economy].

[Earnings Paragraph]

[Company] [jumped/fell] [# points], or [percent change] after beating analysts' average estimate by [# cents/dollars] per share.

[Money Manager Puff Paragraph]

"Stocks had sold off because of bad earnings, and now they are recovering," said [name of money manager], who oversees [$ amount] at [name of establishment] and recently [bought/sold] shares of [company mentioned above].

[Below Their Highs Paragraph]

A study released by [name of firm] showed that [percent] of all New York Stock Exchange issues are trading below their 52-week highs.

[Nonfalsifiable Prediction Paragraph]

"The main event is still earnings. If earnings are [good/poor], the market will respond [positively/negatively]," said [money manager name], who oversees [$ amount] at [name of firm]. "Of course, all bets are off if the war in Afghanistan against Osama bin Laden drags on."

[Up/Down, Volume Paragraph]

[#] stocks [rose/fell] for every [#] that [fell/rose] on the New York Stock Exchange. Some [#] shares changed hands, [percent change] [above/below] the three-month average.

[Made-Up Reason Paragraph]

"You can't really look at values, you can't really look at fundamentals. It's all about psychological reaction today," [money manager name], who oversees [$ amount] at [name of firm].

[Chronic Bear Paragraph]

Most observers agree that the economic recovery forecast for the next few months will not lift all boats. David Tice, manager of the Prudent Bear Fund, expects new lows in the market next year. Tice took profits recently in National Semiconductor and Intel, which have risen [percent] in the past month on optimism for an improving global economic outlook.

Part Two
Practical
Speculation

"First, Build a Palace for Your King": A Survival Lesson from a Chess Master

Part One described what is wrong with common approaches to investing. We debunked the myths and propaganda surrounding the earnings-return relation and technical analysis, presented a case study of chronic negativism, deflated the ballyhoo about value stocks, ran the media's market coverage under a whole-body scan, and quantified the effects of hubris and humility on individual stocks. But we aren't the sort of people who only tear down and never offer anything constructive.

In Part Two, we provide a series of approaches that together can serve as a foundation for investors. We begin with the one thing that comes before everything else in the quest for investment success: survival.

We are as bullish as ever on stocks. The upward sweep of research and progress will conquer the icy, old-hearted mien that descended on the market at the beginning of the century. However, the vicious declines of 2000–2002, as well as Vic's own disaster in 1997, have prompted us to rethink how we prepare for risk.

Like all simplifications, our approach is not a panacea. But it is based on a deep philosophical idea from a master of strategy in an area where the greatest minds have been at work for more than 1,000 years. What is more, it has been tested on the firing lines in millions of confrontations. It was in the chess strategy of David Bronstein, a Russian player whom some consider the greatest chess genius who has ever lived, that we found our Holy Grail for trading. In his classic work, *The Modern Chess Self-Tutor,* Bronstein set forth a combination of defense and offensive strategy that is elegant yet revolutionary:

> At the start of the game, you should not be thinking either about mate, or about rapidly gaining a big material advantage. A systematic approach consists in proceeding to one's aim in stages, and since the system is confrontational, you must all the time reckon with your opponent's ideas and counter-actions, and should be concerned not only about giving mate, but also about ensuring the safety of your own king. First you must build a shelter for your king . . . a securely defended command post."[1]

The advice may have carried a secret poignancy for Bronstein. A Soviet citizen, he tied for the 1951 world chess championship with the government's favorite, Botvinnik. Because Bronstein's father was a dissident, it has always been suspected that his family's safety would have been in grave jeopardy had he won outright.

Let's apply Bronstein's strategy to investing. At the start of the game, attend to your defenses. Reckon with the market's tendency to swing violently against you, and make sure you are not in over your head. Protect yourself and your family. Take account of the possibility that a long-term illness could keep you from working or require substantial treatment outlays for a family member. Set aside enough for college educations. Squirrel away enough to maintain the home.

We offer no hard-and-fast rules about how much to set aside. But consider Bronstein's advice:

> Players who by nature are accurate and cautious can be advised to construct not a shelter, but a virtual palace with double pawn walls and a personal guard.

Checkmate (Artist: Charles Munro, 1987).

Once your king is secure, the offense then can be mounted in three stages:

1. First, attack to weaken the adversary's pawn screen.
2. Then, attack with pawns to create a breach in the defenses.
3. Finally, mount an invasion with long-range pieces.

Applying this approach to markets, it is much more important to gain a steady, reasonable advantage than to risk a wipeout by going for a startling and enervating win. That is why people who can eke out 2 percent a year more than the averages have billions of dollars under management. It is not just chance. Therefore, when your financial defenses are in place, start out by making small, short-term "swing" trades, buying when the market is oversold and selling when it becomes overbought.

After making good profits and adding to your speculative capital with the swing method, start taking long-range buy-and-hold positions. You will thus be able to participate in the market's million percent-a-century returns without risking your survival when the inevitable storms of life and the market come.

Bronstein's advice on the dangers of being too shortsighted and too aggressive can be applied to putting together a portfolio:

> You should not bring into play only your favorite piece, but should seek a plan of action by which the pieces make moves in turn, creating a united group in attack and defense. . . . You must ask each piece what it can usefully achieve on its own, what help it requires from the other pieces, and in what it itself is prepare to help them.

Translated into trading terms, a stock that is sensitive to the market's fluctuations might balance a long-term sleeper speculation.

There it is, in all its brilliance and simplicity. Defend first. Don't give your enemy any targets. Make the opponent extend himself if he is going to attack your very formidable house.

To keep ourselves honest and to benefit from the widely dispersed knowledge outside the noisy realm of talking heads and self-promoting market gurus, we circulated our Bronstein strategy among our friends. A scholarly day trader, Bipin Pathak, objected that the approach counseled trading to avoid loss instead of trading to win.

Our answer: You can't win if you're dead. The player, as Bronstein emphasizes, should never lose sight of the main goal: to win. One great long-term winner will make up for numerous small losses, but to survive in the interim, you need a stable base.

Nigel Davies, a chess grandmaster living in London, shared an insight into tournament play that is apropos here:

> One of the peculiarities of the laws of chess is that they permit you to make an "agreed draw" at any time. You make your move, verbally offer a draw, press your clock and your opponent then thinks it over. This has led to the practice of some players making draws in very few moves, which are known as "Grandmaster draws" because of their prevalence in games between Grandmasters. They are not popular with tournament organizers, the public or anyone else for that matter. But they can be very useful weapons.
>
> When I was playing more regularly in round-robin tournaments I would immediately mark down all the games with Black against strong players as being those in which a draw is okay On those days I would play very carefully and perhaps make a draw offer around move 10–15. If my opponent wanted to fight then he'd be taking a risk, if not you get the day off and save your energy for the next game. Like any self-respecting predator I try to pick out the weaklings.
>
> In my experience, players who make a few draws in a tournament will very rarely have a really bad result. But those who go all out in every game will put much more pressure on themselves, and sometimes make a REALLY bad result.

The idea is not to seek to eliminate risk entirely by shooting only for draws or staying out of the market. The millennial market shakeup left too many people terrified of risk. They are like our grandfathers and fathers after crashes of the 1920s and 1970s, taking 2 percent profits on their stocks and selling when they have a 10 percent loss—if they dare to venture into the market at all.

Yet investors now depend more than ever on the market to meet their financial goals. Work, family life, and retirement savings are inextricably bound to the market in an ecological web of spending, confidence, and capital investment. Adapting Bronstein's survival principle has improved our own game in chess, life, and the market.

Chess players, recall, have only eight pawns and eight pieces—and yet the game is mind-bendingly complex, particularly since the opponents seek to block each other at every turn. Stock investing, by contrast, has thousands of players and practically infinite combinations. Where to start? In the following chapters, we describe how to use quantitative methods to look for cases where the market overestimates risk.

8

HOW TO
AVOID SPURIOUS
CORRELATIONS

I can only say that there is a vast field of topics that fall under the laws of correlation, which lies quite open to the research of any competent person who cares to investigate it.

—Francis Galton[1]

Most of our knowledge is based on analyzing how two things relate to one another. Folk wisdom cautions, "All that glitters is not gold." In Economics 101, we learn that prices fall when the quantity supplied rises. In the field of investments, people base their expectations on links—perceived or actual—between two things.

Here is a list of the things commonly thought to influence the movements of stocks. Some of these variables are direct: When they're high, stocks are expected to rise. Others are indirect, or inverse: When they're high, stocks are expected to fall. We culled the items on the list from several standard investment texts and hundreds of articles on the Internet.

Direct Relations

- Better-than-expected earnings.
- Change in investor sentiment toward neglected firms (in January).
- Dividend yield.
- Earnings growth.
- Earnings yield.
- Insider buying or selling.
- Level of CEO ownership.
- Liquidity.
- Debt level.
- Debt rating.
- Research and development expenditures.
- Risk.
- Sales growth.
- Short-term interest rates greater than long-term rates.
- Similarity to takeover targets in an industry.
- Stock buybacks.

Inverse Relations

- Accrued earnings minus cash earnings.
- Excluded expenses in pro forma quarterly earnings reports.
- Float.
- For mutual funds, top rating of fund or manager.
- Inventory increases.
- Membership in industry with superior recent performance.
- Price to book, sales or earnings.
- Return over previous 36 months.
- Rising interest rates.
- Size (depending on latest trend).

Research and practice related to these relations can be found in abundance on the search engine google.com. Most of the academic studies use arcane statistical analysis, retrospective data files, and old data; none takes into account the ever-changing cycles of the marketplace. The practitioners don't take account of uncertainty or luck. Few of these assumptions are ever put to the test. The sad fact is that most relations are wills-o'-the-wisp, persisting just long enough for the public to lose money.

The only way to separate ephemeral relations from the ones you can trade on is to put the assumptions to the test. Our hero, Francis Galton, the father of statistical analysis, often counseled: "Count! Count! Count!" The best method of counting, for all scientists, scholars, and investors, is to draw a scatter diagram, a plot of the values of two things on a graph.

Figure 8.1 shows the scatter diagram used in Chapter 2 to illustrate the inverse relation between earnings in one year and stock market returns in the next. The line slopes slightly downward from left to right, indicating a negative relation. Thus, contrary to popular belief:

- Rising earnings in one year lead to lower stock prices in the next.
- Falling earnings in one year lead to higher stock prices in the next.

If the line had sloped upward, it would have suggested the opposite: that rising earnings in one year lead to higher stock market prices in the next, while falling earnings lead to lower stock prices.

The importance of scatter plots is widely recognized. A host of seminars offer training in using scatter plots as a decision-making tool for businesspeople, government administrators, and researchers of all stripes. The vaunted

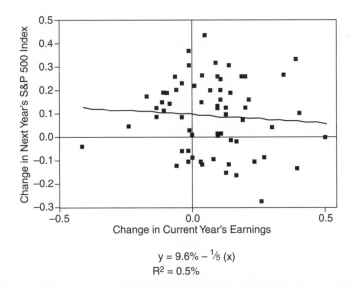

$$y = 9.6\% - \tfrac{1}{5}(x)$$
$$R^2 = 0.5\%$$

Figure 8.1   Change in Current Year's Earnings as Predictor of Change in Next Year's SPX, 1937–2001. *Source:* **Standard & Poor's Security Price Index Record.**

Six Sigma approach to management excellence, widely held to be behind the success of such companies as General Electric, the world's biggest company by market value and sales, includes the use of scatter plots, as the following Internet notice from Applied Performance Strategies Inc. describes:

Six Sigma Green Belt Training

Participants are introduced to the Six Sigma business methodology and given the opportunity to use the statistical tools required to successfully participate in a Six Sigma event. The workshop is designed around a process simulation to help learn the Define, Measure, Analyze, Improve, and Control methodology. Statistical tools include process flowcharting, SOPs, response and variables diagrams, Input-Process-Output (IPO) process, histograms, *scatter diagrams,* [emphasis added] Pareto diagrams, control charts, run charts, design of experiments, measurement systems, and FMEAs.

Some schools, realizing how critical data analysis is to their students' future careers, teach scatter plots early on. Fifth-graders at the Humboldt County School District in Nevada learn to "collect, organize, read, and interpret data using a variety of graphic representations including tables, line plots, scatter plots, [and] histograms; [and] use data to draw and explain conclusions and predictions."

Like all good things, the tools available to make scatter diagrams are constantly improving. The best by far that we have found is contained in the Number Cruncher Statistical System, a statistical analysis software package. Number Cruncher's scatter program software contains so many good features that it made Vic—who is very difficult to please—want to dance. Included are such things as trend lines, polynomial spline, lowest curve fitting, sunflower and box plots, overlays, connecting points, transformations to log or exponential scales, symbols for groups, confidence bands, three-variable plots, three-dimensional charts, and colors and font sizes of all descriptions.

How to Build a Scatter Diagram

Now, let's build a scatter diagram from scratch. Computer programs such as Excel, Minitab, or the "freeware" R will do the work, but it's all to the good if you know how it's done. Understanding the method may give you new insights and help you spot errors.

Say you decide to study the relation between changes in interest rates in one year and stock market returns in the next. The first step is to collect observations on two things. We assembled 39 years of data on each variable and

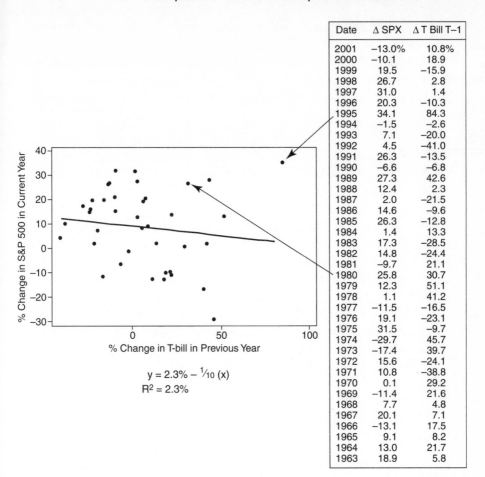

Date	Δ SPX	Δ T Bill T−1
2001	−13.0%	10.8%
2000	−10.1	18.9
1999	19.5	−15.9
1998	26.7	2.8
1997	31.0	1.4
1996	20.3	−10.3
1995	34.1	84.3
1994	−1.5	−2.6
1993	7.1	−20.0
1992	4.5	−41.0
1991	26.3	−13.5
1990	−6.6	−6.8
1989	27.3	42.6
1988	12.4	2.3
1987	2.0	−21.5
1986	14.6	−9.6
1985	26.3	−12.8
1984	1.4	13.3
1983	17.3	−28.5
1982	14.8	−24.4
1981	−9.7	21.1
1980	25.8	30.7
1979	12.3	51.1
1978	1.1	41.2
1977	−11.5	−16.5
1976	19.1	−23.1
1975	31.5	−9.7
1974	−29.7	45.7
1973	−17.4	39.7
1972	15.6	−24.1
1971	10.8	−38.8
1970	0.1	29.2
1969	−11.4	21.6
1968	7.7	4.8
1967	20.1	7.1
1966	−13.1	17.5
1965	9.1	8.2
1964	13.0	21.7
1963	18.9	5.8

$$y = 2.3\% - {}^{1}\!/_{10}\,(x)$$
$$R^2 = 2.3\%$$

Figure 8.2 Percentage Change in T-Bill Rates and S&P 500 Futures in Next Year.
Source: **Standard & Poor's Security Price Index Record.**

plotted each pair in the graph in Figure 8.2. The arrows going from the numbers in the chart to the scatter diagram show you how to plot the variables. The arrows point to the values for 1995 and 1980, when interest rates and stock returns were both exceptionally high.

It is customary to place the thing that is thought to be predicted or influenced on the vertical axis, while the predicting or influencing variable goes on the horizontal axis. The joint values are indicated by dots, X's, checkmarks, or letters.

Visually, if the swarm of points lies from lower left to upper right, then the association is positive. That would indicate:

- High values of one variable are accompanied by high values of the other.
- Middle values of one variable are accompanied by middle values of the other.
- Low values of one variable are accompanied by low values of the other.

If the swarm of points goes from upper left to bottom right, the association is negative; high values of one variable would be accompanied by low values of the other, and so on. If the points fall in a shapeless mass, then there is little or no association.

In this case, the diagram shows a negative association between interest rates in one year and stock prices in the next.

The scatter plot provides a first impression of a relation between two things. But the analysis can be taken much further. The next step is to perform a series of calculations based on the departure (or variance, or deviation) of each observation from the mean. The goal is to determine how strong the relation is.

To start, the values can be grouped in a 2 × 2 table according to whether they lie above or below the mean—in this case, 8.9 percent for stock returns and 5.2 percent for interest-rate changes (see Table 8.1).

Notice that there are 15 matches where both are above or both below, and 24 misses where one is above and the other is below. A good quick-and-dirty estimate of the degree of relation is the number of matches less the number of misses normalized by the total. In this case, that would come to:

$$\frac{(15-24)}{39} = -0.23$$

That number, −0.23, is a rough measure of correlation, +1 being the most direct relation where there are 100 percent matches, and −1 being the most inverse relation where all the observations were misses.

Table 8.1   2 × 2 Table of T-Bill Rate Changes in One Year and S&P 500 Return the Next Year

	S&P 500 Return Next Year	
	Below Mean	**Above Mean**
T-Bill rate changes		
Below mean	7	14
Above mean	10	8

The negative correlation indicates an inverse relation between interest rates and S&P changes.

To calculate the 2 × 2 table, draw a vertical line at the average of the horizontal numbers and a horizontal line at the average of the vertical numbers. The two lines divide the graph into four quadrants. Then, count the number of entries in each of the quadrants and place them in the table.

A More Accurate Measure

But much information is lost when using numbers that merely relate to their position above or below the mean. To remedy this, we can use a more accurate and sophisticated correlation coefficient that weights the matches and misses by their magnitudes. The one most often used is called the Pearson Product Moment correlation.

The correlation coefficient between two variables is calculated from the covariance between them. The correlation-covariance relationship is:

$$\Gamma yx \frac{COVyx}{SySx}$$

Where Γyx stands for the correlation coefficient and S is standard deviation.

The covariance between Y and X is defined as:

$$COVyx = \frac{\Sigma(Yi - \overline{Y})(Xi - \overline{X})}{n - 1}$$

The $\overline{Y}$ and $\overline{X}$ refers to the mean, or average, of the individual Ys and Xs. Thus, we are computing the average product of how much each pair jointly varies from their means. If one is above and the other is below, it reduces the covariance. (N is the sample size, and it is reduced by one to give the proper degrees of freedom.) In this case, the Y variable—the dependent variable—is the S&P 500 percentage change in the next year, and the X variable is the change in T-bill rates in the current year.

Here are the steps in calculating the covariance between the two variables:

1. Calculate the mean of all the values in X. Do the same for Y.
2. Subtract the mean from each individual observation.
3. Multiply each pair of differences (variances), and calculate the average.

Table 8.2 Covariance

Date	Y_i (%)	$Y_i - \bar{Y}$ (%)	X_i (%)	$X_i - \bar{X}$ (%)	$(X_i - \bar{X})(Y_i - \bar{Y})$ (%)
2001	-13.0	-13.0 - 11.8 = -24.9	10.8	10.8 - 2.8 = 8.0	-1.98
2000	-10.1	-10.0 - 11.8 = -22.0	18.95	18.9 - 2.8 = 16.1	-3.53
1999	19.5	19.5 - 11.8 = 7.7	-15.9	-15.9 - 2.8 = -18.7	-1.44
1998	26.7	26.7 - 11.8 = 14.8	2.8	2.8 - 2.8 = 0.0	-0.01
1997	31.0	31.0 - 11.8 = 19.2	1.4	1.4 - 2.8 = -1.4	-0.28
1996	20.3	20.3 - 11.8 = 8.4	-10.3	-10.3 - 2.8 = -13.1	-1.11
1995	34.1	34.1 - 11.8 = 22.3	84.3	84.3 - 2.8 = 81.5	18.14
1994	-1.5	-1.5 - 11.8 = -13.4	-2.6	-2.6 - 2.8 = 5.4	0.73
1993	7.1	7.1 - 11.8 = -4.8	-20.0	-20.0 - 2.8 = 22.8	1.09
1992	4.5	4.5 - 11.8 = -7.4	-41.0	-41.0 - 2.8 = -43.8	3.23
Mean	11.8	Mean	2.8	Covariance	14.86

Table 8.2 shows how it works with the most recent 10 years of data on interest rates and S&P 500 returns.

Thus, the covariance between Y and X is 14.86, divided by 10 years minus 1, or 9 (referred to as nine degrees of freedom):

$$COVyx \frac{14.86}{9} = 1.65\%$$

To convert this covariance into a correlation coefficient, calculate the standard deviations of Y and X. Square the differences of each observation from the mean to remove the + and − signs. Then, total them up (see Table 8.3). The variances are the totals divided by $n − 1$:

$$\frac{25.7}{9} = 2.86\%$$

$$\frac{99.6}{9} = 11.07\%$$

For the standard deviation, take the square root of these numbers. The square root of 2.86 percent is 16.9 percent. The square root of 11.07 percent is 33.3 percent.

Table 8.3   Correlation Coefficient

Yi − Ȳ (%)	(Yi − Ȳ)² (%)	Xi − X̄ (%)	(Xi − X̄)² (%)
−24.9	6.2	8.0	0.6
−22.0	4.8	16.1	2.8
7.7	0.6	−18.7	3.5
14.8	2.2	0.0	0.0
19.2	3.7	−1.4	0.0
8.4	0.7	−13.1	1.7
22.3	5.0	81.5	66.4
−13.4	1.8	−5.4	0.3
−4.8	0.2	−22.8	5.2
−7.4	0.5	−43.8	19.2
Sum	25.7		99.6

Finally, simply plug those numbers into the correlation formula:

$$\Gamma yx = \frac{COVyx}{SySx}$$

$$\Gamma yx = \frac{1.65\%}{(16.9\%)(33.3\%)} = 0.29344$$

Here is a more elegant way of expressing it:

$$\Gamma xy = \frac{\Sigma(Zx \times Zy)}{n-1}$$

where $Zx = \dfrac{Xi - \overline{X}}{Sx}$

and $Zy = \dfrac{Yi - \overline{Y}}{Sy}$

As with the rough estimate we made from the 2 × 2 table, departures from the mean were the basic elements in computing the numerator and the denominator of the preceding formula.

A Workhorse Equation

The Pearson Product Moment correlation coefficient defined previously is the workhorse for studies of relations that appear on scatter plots. It measures the linear degree of association between two things by showing how closely the observed values fit around a straight line. In simple terms, if the vertical distance of the dots from the slope line is small, then the correlation is high.

In the case of Treasury bills and S&P 500 returns, the correlation is 0.29 for the 10-year example shown in Tables 8.2 and 8.3, but it is −0.07 for the full 39-year data series displayed in Table 8.1. This shows instability all too typical of correlations between economic time series. The culprit in this particular case was just one year, 1995, when high values of interest rates and stock appreciation jumped the correlation up from a small negative to a high positive. (We thank Steve Stigler for kindly bringing this outlying data point to our attention.) In the world of stock market speculation, it would not be significant enough to trade on. In practice, we have found any number above 0.10 or below −0.10 based on 100 or more observations to be useful. The general formula we follow for usefulness is that the correlation coefficient times the number should be greater than 10. Thus, for 50 observations, a correlation of 0.20 would be useful and for 20 observations, a correlation of 0.50 would be useful.

The information provided by the correlation coefficient is useful to investors in many ways. For example, it can tell you approximately how much of the movement in the Y variable—in this case, the S&P 500—can be explained by the X variable.

Another way of putting this is that the square of the correlation coefficient is the amount by which a linear predictor of one variable by the other is not attenuated by a regression back to its mean value.

The correlation coefficient cannot be used to directly predict the amount of change in the explained variable that a change in the independent variables creates. For that, a regression equation is necessary. A regression equation consists of a straight line that fits the points on a scatter diagram. It requires a slope and a y intercept. The slope is the correlation coefficient multiplied by a factor of the standard deviation of the y variable divided by the standard deviation of the x variable.

In the case of the interest rate return data, the regression equation is:

S&P 500 return = 2.3 percent less one-tenth of a percentage change in Treasury bill rates

The most frequently used regression equation is fitted by minimizing the squared distance of the values in the graph from a straight line. The line always goes through the point corresponding to the mean of y and the mean of x. To compute the regression line by hand from a scatter diagram, calculate that point of intersection and then draw a straight line from that point to your estimate of the y intercept (i.e., the average of the y values when x is approximately 0.) If you want to gain a measure of the variability about that line for prediction or control purposes, draw two parallel lines at an equal distance from the line so that the space between them includes about 95 percent of the points.

Scatter plots have many uses in addition to revealing relations. Probably the most useful is the visual observation that leads to discovery of possible outliers caused by either an error in data collection or a changed relation. Enhancements of scatter diagrams are available and useful. Colors, symbols, or letters for various groupings can assist evaluation. The colors green and yellow and the letters H, Q, and Z are all distinctive and are often used. Circling groups of observations that share similar characteristics may highlight important relations among the points that would not be clear from the usual summaries that come out of standard computer programs. New scatter diagrams can be created by varying the tallies and shadings of the line. Detailed discussions of these and other enhancements can be found on the Internet; the search engine google.com alone has 1,580 entries on "scatter diagram enhancements."

Our favorite way to enhance a scatter diagram is to show the path of a time series. All that is required is to draw arrows between the dots in the sequence they occur.

Avoid Fallacious Conclusions

Whatever you do, never place too much reliance on scatter diagrams, correlations, or regression formulas. They are associations, not a proof of causation. Seemingly statistically significant correlations are often due to chance or hidden factors.

Graphs are particularly vulnerable to misinterpretation. A famous example of seeing patterns that indicated causal relations that were, in fact, mere random fluctuations occurred in the bombing of London during World War II. Newspapers published maps pinpointing where German aircraft dropped bombs, and people scrutinized the maps to see which areas were left untouched, in the belief that the patterns revealed the residences of German spies. Subsequent analysis showed that the bombing patterns were completely consistent with chance. A discussion of the tendency to infer causes from random data, such as the geographic incidence of cancer, is contained in *Rational Choice in an Uncertain World,* by Reed Hastie and Robin M. Dawes.[2]

The most serious problem in this regard is the drawing of conclusions on causality based on spurious or bogus correlations. Such false conclusions are usually built on one or more of the following flaws:

- Failure to account for the possibility of randomness.
- Omission of a third variable that causes the other two.
- Failure to consider mobility, or changes in the population itself.
- The fallacy of aggregation.

Sadly, most studies of market relations suffer from all these fallacies simultaneously. For a great case study, we recommend many of the academic works previously cited in this book. However, an even better introduction is provided by Purdue University's "Spurious Correlations Contest." The 1998 winner is timeless and ineffable. Ron Malzer's entry is based on the observed high correlation of the population of Oldenburg, Germany, and the number of storks sighted there: Oldenburg, Germany, has the world's highest proportion of adults who read the works of Immanuel Kant, and each year its population is increased due to the immigration of Kantonians from other places. As Kant discussions increase, there is pressure on the cooks to prepare ever-increasing quantities of wurst. As quantities increase, quality decreases. Bad wurst has been known to lead to thought disorders. This leads to serious misinterpretations of Kant's work, called *unkantverstehenlassenhummels*. Written discourse about the error leads to disorders of the eyes just from having to read such a long word. The resulting double vision leads to spurious sightings of storks, with data reported at least double the actual numbers involved.[3]

Let's examine the problem of specious correlations systematically.

The Error of Randomness

The failure to impute chance or randomness as an explanation for a supposed market relation is by far the most common problem in analyzing correlations. Almost everything you read in the financial pages about what is going on in markets is mainly attributable to chance. The most common example here is the breathless reporting of some mutual fund manager's recommendations on individual stocks or future market direction. "Mr. X could forecast the exact high. He bought at the exact low and wrote a book. He bought some ABC before the recent run-up and sets a target for the stock of $100." Yes, of course. There always are going to be managers and advisors from among the tens of thousands who called the last up wave right. But did their success come through superior insight? A much more likely explanation is chance.

A classic investment scam capitalizes on this failure to consider the role of chance. A prediction is mailed out to half the people on a list of "targets." The other half receives the opposite prediction. The ones who received whichever prediction turned out to be correct are then split into two groups, half receiving one prediction and the other half receiving the opposite. After five or so iterations, you have a small group of followers who think you are a genius. Then you ask for big bucks.

The same failure plagues discussions of correlation between technical indicators and market performance. So many technical indicators are out there, as discussed earlier in this book, that there will always be one or another indicator, one or another practitioner, one or another seminar speaker or promoter, with a hot hand.

A discussion of this in Chapter 3 of Vic's previous book, *The Education of a Speculator,* illustrates how even a very long string of consecutive price moves in the same direction is consistent with randomness. In 1995, the yen declined 16 Fridays in a row. Yet taking account of all the different commodities and days, such a run was not improbable at all. Similarly, random moves explain almost every old adage that you will hear about the market. High on the list are the Super Bowl indicator and the January barometer. This list of examples could be vastly extended.

There is a great antidote for drawing spurious relations from random phenomena. The antidote is to read a statistics book on multiple comparisons or a chapter on the subject in any of the multivariate statistics books. A good book here is *Multiple Comparison Procedures* by Yusef Hochberg and Ajit Tamhane (John Wiley & Sons, 1987). The gist of all such work is that if you search for a thousand different relations or look back on the winners of thousands, then you have to adjust the actual odds against the phenomena by a similar factor of—say—a thousand.

The Error of Omission, or the Missing Third Variable

The second most common cause of errors leading to faulty conclusions about stocks is mobility in conjunction with the omission of a third variable. Let's turn again to those messengers of fecundity, the Scandinavian storks. Data from Germany, Denmark, and Norway show that the greater the number of storks, the greater the number of births. In *The New Statistical Analysis of Data,* T. W. Anderson and Jeremy D. Finn explain the correlation in a nice way: "Districts with large populations have a large number of births and also have many buildings, in the chimneys of which storks can nest." Thus, it is population that explains both the frequency of births and sightings of storks. They illustrate with a diagram, as seen in Figure 8.3.

It would be a good idea for all students of market relations to post Figure 8.3 somewhere near their work desk as a reminder of this pitfall.

Examples of omitted third variables abound in market studies. Typical in this research are the studies of the validity of technical indicators based on sentiment. Almost all of these show that after sentiment reaches a certain optimistic level, the market becomes bearish; and after the swing to undue pessimism, the market becomes bullish. As shown in the technical indicators chapter, there is a strong negative correlation between the recent move in the market and subsequent performance. But all sentiment indicators,

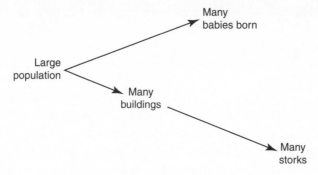

Figure 8.3   Many Storks, Many Babies. *Source: The New Statistical Analysis of Data,* **Springer-Verlag, 1996. Used with permission.**

such as the percentage of bullish advisors and the flow of money to equity funds, are highly positively correlated with the recent market move. Thus, when the market is up big over the previous two weeks, sentiment tends to be optimistic, which is bearish. Conversely, when the market has been down a lot, sentiment is negative, which is bullish. Sentiment has an indirect relation to the future market movements, but only because of its relation with the recent market move.

The Fallacy of Mobility

Correlations reported in the market literature often suffer from failing to take into account a change in the nature of one of the variables. Helen Walker, a statistics professor at Columbia University, came up with the following spurious correlation to illustrate this fallacy. Young women are taught to walk by placing one foot before the other along an imaginary line, a practice that results in pleasantly swaying hips. Older women, perhaps less preoccupied with the need to appear alluring, tend to walk with their feet on either side of that invisible line. However, age is not caused by a wide gait. A more plausible hypothesis is that age causes wide stepping, but that would fail to take into account the fact that older women grew up at a time when girls were taught to toe out, whereas today's girls are encouraged to keep their feet parallel.

Studies relating longevity to occupation are particularly vulnerable to spurious correlations. In *Statistics on the Table,* Steven Stigler discusses an 1835 Swiss study that found natural philosophers lived to 75 while the average student died at 21. A child contemplating what he wants to be when he grows up might well be advised to place more weight on the nature of the job than to any possible benefits in life expectancy, however, given mobility between occupations. After all, most students don't die students; if they can make it through those dangerous student years, they turn into natural philosophers, sculptors, or clerks.

A study on the life expectancy of conductors nicely illustrates how omission of a third variable—the achievement of living to a certain age or not—biases most studies of longevity based on occupation or lifestyle. On average, conductors live to age 74. Poets live much shorter lives. Yet, that does not mean prospective artists could improve their longevity by choosing conducting over poetry. To become a conductor, extensive training is necessary; 35 would be a reasonable expected minimum age for inclusion in the fraternity. Those who died as students and those who died in childhood have no chance of making the mark. Once this is factored in, the apparent longevity of conductors disappears. The average life expectancy of males who reach the age of 35 is about 74, the same as conductors.

This type of fallacy in correlation analysis is well known, yet this bias is often present in Wall Street studies. Using samples of stocks that were created and weighted with surviving companies, much work tends to conclude that value stocks are supreme. Careful analysis, however, often reveals that the results are skewed by the construction of the files. Small companies are included in the growth files only on attaining a certain size; as a result, many fast-growing companies are omitted. The value files, on the other hand, include many companies experiencing financial difficulties. If the company's financial difficulties worsen to the point that it goes belly up, it is not represented in the files. If it survives, it is included.

Much of the superior retrospective performance attributed to value stocks is attributable to this survivorship bias. Except for this flaw, the studies of James P. O'Shaughnessy are a model of good research. Note, however, that O'Shaughnessy decided to leave the mutual fund business after a value mutual fund based on the models in his 1998 book, What Works on Wall Street, suffered from dismal performance.[4] A subsequent venture that sold customized baskets of stocks over the Internet closed its Web site in September 2001. Almost all other mutual funds based on such correlations have had similar results. A good case in point is the Rea-Graham Fund, which was first to apply the correlations discovered by Benjamin Graham between value stocks and returns for the benefit of investors. The fund's performance since inception earned it the lowest Morningstar ranking possible in all categories. But it looked good on paper.

The Fallacy of Aggregation

If low P/Es are associated with high subsequent returns for individual stocks, then a low P/E for the market is associated with higher subsequent market returns—this is an example of what statisticians call the fallacy of aggregation.

The Curse of Specious Correlations

It has been shown that shoe size is highly correlated with reading skills, but this does not mean that buying bigger shoes would help kids read better or that reading more will make the feet grow. Instead, a third unmeasured factor is involved: age. As children get older, their reading abilities grow along with their feet.

While every student is taught to be careful about inferring causation from correlation, it is amazing how rarely this is taken into account in the numerical work of system developers and quants of all stripes. Invariably they come up with a relation, the correlation between this indicator and that, and the subsequent superior performance. If they could only remember the studies of storks, shoe size, conductors et al., and pay more attention to the scatter plots, they would waste much less time chasing after spurious systems.

In Gilbert and Sullivan's comic opera *Rudiggore*, Mad Margaret loses her sanity because the baronet she loves is doomed by a curse to commit a crime once a day. Only the enunciation of the word "Basingstoke" can bring her back temporarily to her senses.

A solution is found, the curse is finally broken, and the entire ensemble toddles off happily to settle in the bucolic Hampshire town of Basingstoke.

Back when Laurel was at the wire service editing stock market stories, Vic often cautioned her about attributing price moves to anecdotal examples of ephemera, especially those involving earnings woes or up/down volume in individual stocks. Eventually, Vic shortened his messages to the word "Basingstoke."

It is a much more serious error to attribute causal relations to two things that are attributable, as is so often the case, to purely spurious factors. In view of the seriousness of this crime, we recommend to readers that whenever they feel the tendency to succumb to such an attribution, they repeat the word *unkantverstehenlassenhummels* three times. The rewards for readers who diligently apply this technique will be early retirement to a splendid mansion and numerous wurst dinners in Oldenburg, Germany.

9

THE FUTURE
OF RETURNS

The source of all market triumphs is not bullishness or bearishness, but the investigating human mind.

—Correspondence from Brett Steenbarger, PhD, June 23, 2002

The history of science is replete with examples of monumental collections of data that sparked revolutions in knowledge. Tycho Brahe's careful and extensive astronomical calculations, based on observations made with his innovative telescopes, led to the development of Johann Kepler's laws on planetary motion. The data on plants collected by Carl Linnaeus in the early eighteenth century laid a base for Charles Darwin's discoveries and groupings. Painstakingly exact and detailed measurements by Henry Cavendish and Antoine Lavoisier on the various chemical elements led to Dmitri Mendeleyev's discovery of the periodic table.

A similar advancement in knowledge in the field of investments came during the 1960s when the University of Chicago Center for Research in Securities Prices published the first reliable and comprehensive database of daily prices of U.S. stocks, from 1926 to 1960. The science of securities analysis exploded shortly thereafter. The ensuing contributions in the fields of portfolio analysis, capital structure of corporations, option pricing, the efficient markets hypothesis, the theory of behavioral finance, and rational expectations have been well chronicled and memorialized with numerous Nobel Prizes. Accounts can be found in any standard college finance text.

It took four more decades to complete a comparable database for all countries. Elroy Dimson, Paul Marsh, and Mike Staunton of the University of London Business School undertook this immense project. The professors published their findings in a 2002 book, *Triumph of the Optimists: 101 Years of Global Investment Returns*. Within *Triumph*'s pages, an investor may find definitive information on inflation-adjusted returns for stocks versus bonds and Treasury bills, real dividends, correlation between markets worldwide, and the relative performance of value and growth stocks.

Unlike most books written by academics, *Triumph* avoids hasty generalizations and biased sampling procedures. The authors rightly fault earlier investment studies for arbitrary selection of starting and stopping points, the tendency to include the good and exclude the bad, and the exclusion of all but a small slice of the global picture. Their work epitomizes outstanding investment research.

Great works can be created in humble circumstances. Shakespeare was an actor and entrepreneur who reworked old plots so that his company could make a buck. Cervantes wrote a parody of the mania for knight errantry books to repay his debts. Rabelais wrote humor to help cure the pain of his sick patients. Dimson told us that he and his colleagues thought of *Triumph* as "a labor of love, just a small contribution that could lead to a paperback meant for light reading on planes." He added, "Our families would be less kind about our fixation." Staunton, who collected the data, prefers to gather statistics by himself from original sources at specialized libraries instead of delegating the work. He wrote his doctoral thesis on airline ticket prices.

The main conclusion of *Triumph* is that a random selection of U.S. stocks returned 1,500,000 percent in the twentieth century. Yes, big losses occurred at times, such as the back-to-back losses of −28 percent and −44 percent in 1930 and 1931, or the 10 years from 1970 to 1979 when stocks hardly budged while the dollar lost 28 percent of its purchasing power.

But overall, adjusted for inflation, the return on U.S. stocks amounted to about 6 percent a year—better than any other class of securities. Moreover, the U.S. returns were comparable to those achieved in most other industrialized nations. Sweden's and Austria's were even greater. These returns are shown in Figure 9.1.

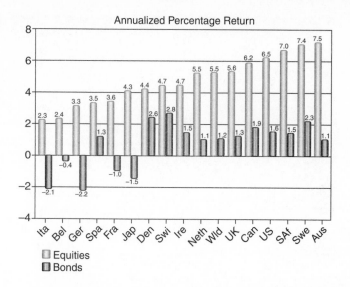

Figure 9.1 **Nominal and Real Returns, 1900–2001.** *Source:* **Elroy Dimson et al.,** *Triumph of the Optimists: 101 Years of Global Investment Returns,* **Princeton University Press, 2002. Used with permission.**

The New Forecasters

The implications for market forecasting in the twenty-first century are immense. In ancient times, people traveled to Delphi to consult the Oracle on important questions. There, among mountains of awesome height, they reverently listened to mystic pronouncements on such weighty matters as the best sites for colonies and the advisability of war. These pronouncements, muttered by a consecrated village woman of Delphi from a hidden room within the temple, may have benefited from the intelligence gathered by a priest-operated spy network that extended throughout the known world. Even more important, many of the Oracle's forecasts were ambiguous enough for Delphi's priests to claim accuracy no matter what the outcome. But we will make a bold prediction here: Future seekers of knowledge will make their way to the 14-nation database of Dimson's group at the London Business School. Indeed, imposing Greek columns give the school a certain resemblance to its ancient counterpart (see Figures 9.2 and 9.3).

The London Oracle received one such important question through us when Frederick C. Scharack, a reader, asked: "But which particular company or companies would you have chosen back in 1900 to achieve your 1,500,000 percent return? Is there an actual company that survived over this period and had

Figure 9.2   London Business School

this kind of performance, or are the returns based on indexes where new win-
ning firms regularly replace the losers until they, too, fall by the wayside?
Wouldn't this kind of substitution bias all security indexes upward?" Here is
Dimson's response:

> If we choose a company that did survive over a specific interval, it will inevitably
> have different machines and different employees. The business has changed, but
> that does not in itself matter to a stockholder. Similarly, a mutual fund that survives
> contains a changing cast of constituent securities. All one can do is "follow the
> money." That is the investment strategy underpinning our indexes. The indexes
> represent the cumulative performance of a portfolio, for a strategy to perform well
> over a long term. There is no need for any constituent company to survive.

Do Not Be Satisfied with 1,500,000 Percent Profit

We have begun to make humble attempts to stand on the shoulders of Dimson and his colleagues in our own speculations. To start, we wondered
whether one needs to be in the market all the time, or whether adroit timing,
so useful in other areas, might improve returns. We devised three variations
that may increase the effectiveness of a simple buy-and-hold long-term investment strategy. We invited a colleague, trader Alix Martin, to join in the im-
provisation, and we also report his variation.

Figure 9.3 Temple of Apollo at Delphi

Variation 1: A Stumble, a Skip, and a Jump

If Cole Porter had put the "Triumph" theme to the music of "Night and Day,"
it might have gone like this:

> Like the steady support of a lifelong friend
> Like the flow of Victoria Falls
> Like the steady state of electric flow,
> Like the steady rise of the Dow
> Like the ching, ching, ching of the cash flow
> As the ships come into dock
> So a voice within me keeps repeating, stocks, stocks, stocks.

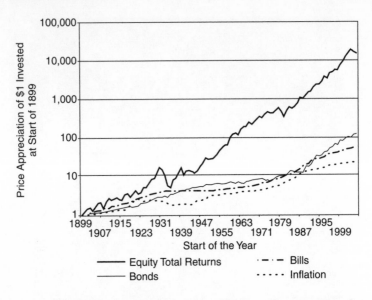

Figure 9.4   Nominal returns on U.S. Asset Classes. *Source:* **Data from 1899–2000 provided by Elroy Dimson et al.,** *Triumph of the Optimists: 101 Years of Global Investment Returns,* **Princeton University Press, 2002. Updated by Niederhoffer Investments.**

Some readers might object that, far from being steady, the stock market has ups and downs. Yet on a graph showing what a dollar invested at the start of 1899 would have come to by 2001, the declines look like little blips—even the momentous decline from 1929 to 1933. The crashes of 1987 and 2000–2002 are barely visible (see Figure 9.4).

Even so, the 1,500,000 percent return may be magnificently improved by buying in the second year after any down year (see Table 9.1). From 1899 through 2001, negative returns occurred in 26 years. The return two years

Table 9.1   Improvement of Returns

2 Years + 1		
2 Years Back	1 Year Back	Annual Return
−	−	16
−	+	16
+	−	13
+	+	9

Table 9.2 Correlation of Returns

Correlations between current year and	
1 year back	−2%
2 years back	−25
3 years back	−4
4 years back	−2
5 years back	−17
6 years back	−5

later averaged 16 percent, with 23 years up and just two years down. The standard deviation was a modest 19 percent.

Table 9.2 shows the correlation of returns between past and future years for all relevant periods. The pattern of mean reversion is amazingly consistent.

The correlation between returns in one year and the return two years later turns out to be negative 0.25. That is significant for 100 years of data, with a probability of less than 1 in 100 of occurring by chance (see Table 9.3).

As Porter might have put it:

> Up and down, that's how to trade.
> You buy after a down year, sell after a gain.
> Just make sure you skip a year
> Whether up or down when trading, dear
> We've tested this every way.

Variation 2: Lucky 5

Seasonality is always a suspect in stock returns. The authors of *Triumph* explore whether there are good months to buy and sell. They review whether January is a good month to buy and conclude that it might show a high return for U.S. small caps. They believe the market may tend to rise in the summer—the opposite of the conventional wisdom on the "summer slump." Such issues, the authors suggest, will "continue to intrigue."

They certainly intrigued us enough to inspire a study of whether certain years show higher-than-average returns. We explored whether years ending in a particular digit, such as 5, might be good times to buy, and whether years ending in other numbers, such as 0 or 7, are not so favorable.

As Table 9.4 shows, the average return for years ending in 5 is 32 percent. The average return for years ending in 0 or 7 is close to 1 percent.

To test whether these intriguing results were nonrandom, we put all 100 returns into an urn. Then we chose 10 groups of 10 returns. We repeated the process 1,000 times.

Table 9.3   Buy Stocks Second Year after a Fall

Year	Total Return (%)	Two Years Later	Total Return (%)
1903	−0.15	1905	0.22
1907	−0.29	1909	0.2
1910	−0.09	1912	0.07
1913	−0.08	1915	0.39
1914	−0.06	1916	0.06
1917	−0.19	1919	0.21
1920	−0.18	1922	0.31
1929	−0.15	1931	−0.44
1930	−0.28	1932	−0.1
1931	−0.44	1933	0.58
1932	−0.1	1934	0.04
1937	−0.35	1939	0.03
1940	−0.07	1942	0.16
1941	−0.1	1943	0.28
1946	−0.06	1948	0.02
1957	−0.1	1959	0.13
1962	−0.1	1964	0.16
1966	−0.09	1968	0.14
1969	−0.11	1971	0.18
1973	−0.19	1975	0.38
1974	−0.28	1976	0.27
1977	−0.03	1979	0.26
1981	−0.04	1983	0.23
1990	−0.06	1992	0.09
1994	0	1996	0.21
2000	−0.11		
2001	−0.11		

Number of observations	25
Average return	0.16
Medium return	0.18
Significant deviation	0.19
Percent up	92%

Next, we computed the difference between the largest and the lowest returns. This turned out to be above 30 percent just 2 percent of the time.

Thus, we conclude that years ending in 5 are great times to buy, and years ending in 0 or 7 are bad times to buy.

Studies of the best years to buy bonds, bills, and the Consumer Price Index showed completely random results.

Table 9.4   Average Return

Year Ending	Percent Return
0	1
1	6
2	10
3	10
4	12
5	32
6	11
7	0
8	25
9	13

Variation No. 3: The Limits of Leverage

Alix Martin, a Paris-based student of statistics and consultant to many European telecom companies, offered the following variation on the 1,500,000 percent theme:

> Wall Street pundits typically recommend an asset allocation split between stocks, bonds, and cash. But over the past century, an investor who had 70 percent in stocks, 20 percent in bonds, and the remaining 10 percent in T-bills would have turned $1 into "only" $5,070, one-third of what one would have made by being fully invested in stocks.
>
> Is it possible to improve on the "100 percent in stocks" strategy? It may not have been in 1899, but it is today. One can buy stocks on margin, or buy futures, to increase exposure to stock returns beyond 100 percent. If an investor had had a 200 percent exposure to stocks during the twentieth century, instead of turning $1 into $15,000, he would have made $1,723,781.

Is too much of a good thing possible? Yes: With a 300 percent exposure, our fictional investor would have lost everything in 1931. Even a winning blackjack player can go bust if his bet is too large relative to his bankroll. The same phenomenon is at work here: gambler's ruin.

Moreover, investors or funds trying to implement this strategy would face additional costs: They would have to pay margin rates to be allowed to hold more stocks than they have the cash for, and would need to buy or sell stocks at the end of each period to maintain exposure at the desired level.

To make the study more realistic, Alix subtracted T-bill returns from stock returns for the part of the exposure that goes beyond 100 percent, as an approximation of margin rates. Even with this more restrictive hypothesis, additional exposure—that is, leverage—improves the fully invested strategy. A 150 percent exposure would have more than tripled the gains over the century, turning $1 into $47,228.

With hindsight, Alex wrote, the best asset allocation would have been 164 percent stocks. This turns a dollar into $50,950, nudging up the compounded return from 10 percent to 11.3 percent. But that would have been a wild ride: from 1928 to 1932, one would have lost more than 90 percent. Anyone daring enough to muster more than 225 percent exposure would have gone bust. As he concluded, "Nobody said this was not risky."

Will the Optimists Keep on Triumphing?

While it is impossible for any rational person to dispute the returns that Dimson and his colleagues have so thoroughly documented, there is considerable controversy as to what future returns might be. From their Greek-columned London fortress, the professors have kindly given us their view on this question. In a nutshell, they believe that the twentieth century benefited from an extraordinary coalescence of factors, and that returns in the next 50 years will not be as good as those of 1900–2001.

In particular, Dimson cautions against extrapolating from America's favorable historical experience. "Should Belgians or Danes, with their much poorer historical returns, do the same and project much lower stock market returns than the United States? That would be odd. Compare a low Belgian stock market forecast with a high U.S. forecast. The investor who predicts high American returns must explain to me why she thinks America is undervalued relative to other countries. The investor who predicts low Belgian returns must explain why she thinks Belgium is overvalued relative to other countries. The only sensible position is to project returns that appear to represent a reasonable reward for risks that may occur in the future. That is what we seek to do in *Triumph of the Optimists*."

Second Opinion

For answers to truly hard questions, it was customary in the glory days of Greece to consult the Oracle of Zeus at Olympia as well as the one at Delphi. Hewing to custom, we sought a second opinion from Richard Sears, our favorite U.S. oracle. A retired managing partner of a leading actuarial firm, Richard currently presides over his investments from the Palisades Mountains in New York. He also runs a Web site, www.gtindex.com, devoted to tracking technology guru George Gilder's stock picks. Richard wrote:

> It seems to me like fatal conceit to presume to explain something as complex as free markets by reference to a few variables. With respect to the stock market, I doubt anyone can say with confidence why what happened in the past happened. Or predict the future. Any more than one can predict future weather.

The term "fatal conceit" refers to a book of that title by Austrian economist Friedrich Hayek. In it, Hayek described why the highly dispersed nature of economic information dooms all attempts at central planning.[1]

As we write in mid-2002, surrounded by pessimism, our view is that the required return for holding stocks is at levels unseen since 1990, or 1980, or 1950, when memories of depressions or crashes were still hanging in the air. If ever there were a time that investors would only buy risky investments when the anticipated returns were in the 50 percent-and-over area, this time would seem to be now. We see no reason that our expectations will be disappointed. Why shouldn't an improvement in life span or the rules of the game of business reap in the next 50 years the kind of results that greeted investors in the past 50?

As Dimson and his colleagues note, a remarkable number of positive influences converged in the twentieth century: technology, liquidity, diversification, free trade, and the victory of capitalism over socialism. But consider also that returns for U.S. stocks were about the same as those for the United States during a period in which Britain went through two world wars, lost her empire, moved through times when her very survival looked like a long shot, and then followed all that up with a variety of social policies including tax rates at the margin of more than 100 percent—all of which presumably should have been quite negative for stock performance.

Despite our differences on how much optimism is warranted for the market's next century, we and the Dimson group reach similar conclusions as to where we are going to end up in the future. "A typical real return for equities in most countries over the past century has been 4 percent to 6 percent a year," they wrote us. "Gazing into the future, a reasonable prediction to us would be to take a percentage point or two from that."

Perhaps we would add 1 percent or 2 percent to that. Taking compounding into account, the difference is that we would look for 1.5 million percent in the next century, and they might expect 1 million percent.

To put things in a homely setting, consider two travelers who start from London and head for California. One arrives in San Jose and the other in San Francisco. Whichever of us is right, the returns are superb. They are cause for great optimism. And they provide a beacon of light that should guide all investors to err on the side of optimism in planning their investments: They should buy stocks at every reasonable opportunity to gain wealth for themselves and their heirs.

10 THE PERIODIC TABLE OF INVESTING

> **It is the accumulation** of objective knowledge that brings the future in sight.
>
> —Gerard Piel, *The Age of Science: What Scientists Learned in the Twentieth Century*[1]

In any field, the pursuit of knowledge starts with the accumulation of disconnected facts and properties. The next step is to uncover the one- and two-variable effects that explain the properties. These efforts reduce the extent of uncertainty. The field then awaits a Copernicus, a Darwin, a Linnaeus, a Mendeleyev, a Watson, to come up with a classification scheme that fits the myriad properties and relations into a coherent whole.

Take chemistry circa 1870, before Dmitri Ivanovich Mendeleyev and Julius Lothar Meyer independently came up with the periodic table of elements. John Dalton had discovered the atomic structure of elements early in the century. Most of the elements had been discovered and analyzed. Methods for processing them were available, and procedures for combining them were known. Groups of elements had been observed to possess similar electrical properties.

The discovery of the periodic table simultaneously unified those disconnected facts and relations, and opened a new frontier. The ordering of the elements by atomic weight permitted the prediction not only of individual properties but relations with other elements. The elements in each column of the table show similar properties. As you proceed along the "periods," or rows, across the columns, the movements from metals to semimetals to gases are also predictable. More than a century later, the periodic table is still on the wall of most laboratories around the world, used by practitioners and students to make sense of the behavior and properties of the elements and their multifarious molecular configurations.

It is beautiful and reassuring for the chemist to know that an element's properties can be predicted based on its position in the periodic table. But where is the comparable knowledge vis-à-vis the properties, let alone the predictive qualities, of individual stocks?

Granted, stocks exhibit stochastic properties; that is, their movements may be analyzed statistically according to a random probability distribution, although not predicted precisely. Even these stochastic properties vary depending on the economy, world events, and the state of markets around the globe. The difficulty of acquiring knowledge is compounded by the peculiar readiness of markets to follow the principle of ever-changing cycles. By the time an investor has identified the payoffs, as well as the likelihood of the tendency's continuation, they are much diminished.

Moreover, in no field has such little advancement of knowledge been attained as in stock investing during the past century. Not only are most of the properties of stock prices untested; they are often described in a prescientific manner not susceptible to testing, as we have shown. On those occasions where properties are stated in a testable fashion, other deficiencies are present. Invariably, neither a measure of variability nor the uncertainty attached to the estimate is given. Often the data are analyzed in such a way that no investor could have acted in time to take advantage of the supposed relation. The influence of ever-changing cycles is everywhere neglected.

True, investments are a branch of the social sciences, not the physical sciences, and no immutable rules are to be expected. But the continual use of dubious methods and data, the avoidance of testing, the reliance on authority, the cultish reverence paid to celebrity investors, the pronouncements of selective gurus, and the attempts to mislead with propaganda, are far more widespread than in any other field. Of course, the propagation of these delusive approaches is merely a necessary and

natural part of an ecological system in which the public provides the grist for the mill that makes the market wheels turn.

But this does not excuse us from trying to rectify the situation by calling, "Statistics on the table!"

Begin with the Facts

As the current state of knowledge about investments—disconnected facts and
a few relations—is on a par with what was known in chemistry before the discovery of the periodic table, we start with the disconnected facts we know
about the market:

- Stocks tend to go up at a rate of about 10 percent or 12 percent a year
  over most long periods.
- Insiders—the officers and directors of a company—tend to buy and sell
  at propitious times.
- The higher a company's expected growth rate, the higher the current
  price relative to current earnings.
- The performance of stocks with higher or negative P/E ratios versus
  those with lower P/Es is inconsistent.
- Corporate assets available for activity are the result of and are restricted
  by various amounts of debt, original ownership equity, and retained
  earnings.

Certain relations are also known about stocks:

- The higher the risk, the higher the return.
- Risk can be reduced by diversification. This risk reduction decreases as
  the number of stocks in a portfolio increases. As much as 80 percent of
  the maximum risk reduction can be achieved with as few as 15 stocks.
- In most periods, small companies tend to perform better than big
  companies.
- Certain kinds of stocks do better at certain times of the year than at
  other times.
- Companies that innovate and spend proportionately large sums on research tend to be rewarded, prospectively and retrospectively, more
  than companies that concentrate on relatively fixed and unchanging
  businesses.
- Companies that have monopolies fixed by the government often perform
  better for extended periods than do others (e.g., large pharmaceutical

companies, with franchises essentially protected by the Federal Food and Drug Administration bureaucracy, have tended to do well).

The one characteristic that distinguished the periodic table from all previous attempts at classification was its astounding ability to predict. Mendeleyev left spaces in his table for as-yet-undiscovered elements and described their properties in advance. Scandium, gallium, and germanium were discovered shortly thereafter, with properties closely matching Mendeleyev's predictions. In the field of finance, we find a far different situation. Financial predictions are ridiculed with a contempt usually reserved for weather forecasts:

- Isn't it strange how the same people who laugh at gypsy fortunetellers take economists seriously?
- "Ask five economists and you'll get five different answers (six if one went to Harvard)."—John Kenneth Galbraith
- "An economist is an expert who will know tomorrow why things he predicted yesterday didn't happen today."—Laurence J. Peter[2]

Then there was Harry Truman, who said he wanted a one-armed economist "so the guy could never make a statement and then say, 'On the other hand, . . .'"

How helpful it would be if there existed a classification scheme for stocks as perfect as the periodic table of elements—one that would place companies into groups according to their properties regardless of their industries or balance sheets, one that had been scrutinized and tested over many years by academic and practical users, one not subject to the many ephemeral factors that affect the moves of stock groups in different bullish and bearish environments, and most important, one that would enable reliable predictions.

In addition to providing a rudder and base for further research, such an ideal scheme should provide the same sense of order that standards provide in such areas as building specifications, electrical wiring, and the diagnosis and treatment of disease.

Incredibly, a parallel to the periodic table of elements does exist in the field of stock selection. It has stood the test of time, made money for those who have used it, provided a method of predicting the performance of stocks for 37 years, and has been thoroughly vetted and reproduced by academic and industry evaluators. It is the Value Line stock ranking system.

A Classification System for Stocks

Every week since the early 1970s, Value Line has been classifying companies into groups. The group or rank is Value Line's expected price performance of the stock for the coming 6 to 12 months. Stocks ranked "1" are expected to do best, and stocks ranked "5" are expected to underperform. The classification is based mainly on the quarterly earnings comparisons of the individual companies compared with a cross-section of all companies, and the relative price performance of the companies.

The elements in the higher period, or row, of the periodic table of elements tend to be lighter and more common than those in the bottom period. Similarly, Value Line notes: "Stocks ranked '1' in timeliness are often more volatile than the overall market and tend to have smaller capitalizations." This is a key qualification that is crucial to the study of the validity and reliability of the classification scheme.

Value Line's timeliness classification system was invented by Sam Eisenstadt, who started as a proofreader at the firm in 1946, fresh out of the Army after World War II. Value Line was then a sleepy company with 15 employees in offices in the Borden Building at 350 Madison Avenue. The founder, Arnold Bernhard, had become interested in a value standard for stocks as a result of the financial difficulties his family suffered in the 1929 crash.

Bernhard felt that emotional extremes drove the market too high in the late 1920s and too low in the early 1930s. He noticed that there was a relationship between annual earnings and stock prices and plotted them on a logarithmic scale. He would plot the annual earnings of an individual company on a transparency and superimpose it over the price history, an early effort at visual regression. This fitting process would produce a multiplier on the earnings, which could then be applied to an earnings forecast to arrive at a "normal value."

This line became known as the Value Line. Stock prices fluctuated above and below the line—evidence of over- and undervaluation. "I cannot say exactly where Bernhard got the inspiration for this procedure, but I consider it a major achievement at that time, when stock selection was considered to be an art, not a science," Eisenstadt said. "This was a pioneering effort in the attempt to separate stock prices from emotional extremes."

Mendeleyev, in trying to come up with the classification that would order the elements into groups with similar properties, put each element on a playing card. On train trips, he played Solitaire with the cards as he tried to sort them into proper groups. Finally, he came up with the concept of atomic weights. It had already been observed by John A. R. Newlands—and dismissed as absurd by the English Chemical Society—that chemical groups repeated every eight elements, similar to the octave in a musical scale. (Today's periodic table sorts by number of protons, instead of by weight.)

As Eisenstadt proofread the records and got to know Value Line's operations, it gradually occurred to him that companies might be fitted into rows and columns of performance by comparing their characteristics to each other in a single time period. He came up with the idea of looking at companies in cross-sections, rather than individually. "Almost like a crossword puzzle," he recalled 55 years later in an interview.

The problem was how to order the stocks.

At City College, where Eisenstadt received his training as a statistician, the cutting-edge technique of regression was just then becoming practical to implement. As discussed in Chapter 8, regression attempts to find the best estimate of the linear effect of a group of explanatory variables on a dependent variable. The method of least squares is usually used to come up with these estimates. In simple terms, the equation minimizes the sum of squares of the deviations between predicted and actual values.

Eisenstadt reasoned that he could use least squares regression analysis to find how all the stock returns in a six-month period were fitted by their most recent quarterly earnings and price comparisons as well as by their long-term histories of prices and earnings.

In practice, regression analysis requires large-scale computer power. Such computers were just then starting to become widely available. Eisenstadt persuaded Value Line to let him rent time on an IBM 7094—a machine that computed with one-hundredth the speed of today's personal computers and cost about 10,000 times as much.

With five or more variables providing the explanation and hundreds of stocks to consider, it often took more than one week on a computer as big as a double-haul truck to come up with the results. Whenever the computer was turned on, the lights in the entire building dimmed to half their normal power. Nevertheless, the computer allowed Eisenstadt to analyze companies in relation to each other, and thereby develop the foundation for the Value Line classification system.

How Valuable Is Value Line?

How does the system stack up relative to its predictive accuracy? Does it refute in any way the proverbs about the gross errors in forecasting?

Because Value Line publishes each week a timeliness and technical ranking for each of the stocks it covers (currently about 1,700), the constant churning required for a portfolio to use all the ranking changes each week would be impractical. Many of the stocks are small and relatively illiquid, and commission costs would eat up most of the gains in a small account.

A good test of Value Line's practical value is to take the stocks classified into each group, using the information that would have been available to subscribers as of the end of each calendar quarter, to look at the performance of these companies for the next quarter without any rebalancing, and then to repeat the process for each subsequent quarter. The results of this test are shown in Figure 10.1.

The record of the timeliness rankings is stellar. There is a perfect direct relation between predicted group performance and actual. The average return of 4.3 percent a quarter for the Group 1 stocks is highly superior to the 1.0 percent average for the Group 5 stocks.

Although a difference of a few percentage points a quarter does not look like much in isolation, the power of compounding makes the differences highly significant by the end of the period. One hundred dollars invested in the Group 1 stocks at the end of the second quarter of 1983 would have grown to $1,319 at the end of the second quarter of 2001. This is 13 times as much as the hundred dollars invested in Group 5 would grow and about 2.4 times as much as Group 3. Results are reported every three months in Value Line's *Selection & Opinion*.

As for the statistical significance of the results, the average variability of the mean quarterly return for each group comes to between 1 percent and 1.5 percent. Thus, the differences between the performance of Groups 1 and 2, and the other three groups, are three variabilities away from the other, or about 1 in 500 to have occurred by chance variations alone.

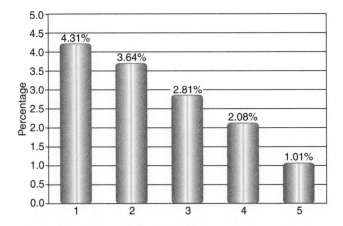

Figure 10.1   Value Line Timeliness Rankings: Quarterly Rebalance, September 30, 1983–June 30, 2002

Table 10.1 Performance of Value Line Timeliness Groups Long/Short Strategy

	(Long Group 1 with Group 5 Hedge)		
	Group 1	Group 5	Long/Short
Annual return	17.48%	3.08%	12.86%
Annual standard deviation	27.53%	23.19%	21.51%
Beta	1.323	1.225	0.097

Note, however, that the variability of the returns in Group 1 and Group 5 appears to be higher than for the three middle groups.

An interesting practical test of Value Line's timeliness system is to consider what would happen if we bought the Group 1 stocks and sold the Group 5 stocks on a quarterly basis. We found that the long-short system makes money in 75 percent of the quarters. The average performance appears in Table 10.1.

Looking at the record as a whole, the prospective record of Value Line's timeliness rankings is the greatest practical demonstration of forecasting accuracy in the history of prediction, dating back at least 4,000 years to the Oracle of Delphi. The predictions have been disseminated to millions of people, billions of dollars have been invested in following the predictions, and the methodology has not changed much over time.

Others support our analysis. Writing in 1973, the Nobel Prize winner Fischer Black reviewed Value Line's performance and concluded, "Yes, Virginia, there is hope. . . . Most investment management organizations would improve their performance if they fired all but one of their securities analysts and then provided the remaining analyst with the Value Line service."[3]

Mark Hulbert, dean of accreditation for stock-picking newsletters, put the Value Line Investment Survey record in perspective as of April 30, 2002. Value Line was among the top five performers on a risk-adjusted basis in all four of Hulbert's evaluation time frames—5 years, 10 years, 15 years, and 20 years. Hulbert's calculations are shown in Table 10.2.

Hulbert concluded that an investor need not follow all the weekly Value Line recommendations to achieve the reported returns. Rebalancing a portfolio once a year with Group 1 stocks would result in about the same performance as updating weekly because of savings on brokerage commission and spread, Hulbert reported in the January 2001 issue of the *Hulbert Financial Digest*.[4]

Table 10.2   Value Line Investment Survey Ranking

Value Line Investment Survey Annual Return (%)	Ranking among Newsletters (Risk-Adjusted)	Measured over How Many Years	Wilshire 5000 Annual Return (%)
15.8	2	20	14.4
12.3	3	15	11.4
13.5	5	10	11.8
13.7	4	5	7.7

Source: Mark Hulbert. Used with permission.

James J. Choi, in an academic review of Value Line's performance published in the September 2000 *Journal of Finance and Quantitative Analysis,* concluded:

> Value Line's raw record is impressive. Over the entire sample period, the average rank portfolio returns are ordered exactly as Value Line predicts. In addition, Ranks 1 and 2 almost double the market's annualized return, while the inverse is true for Rank 5. I find (after extensive statistical attempts to explain the anomalies away) that Value Line continues to outperform relative to current models of expected return before transaction costs, with mean abnormal portfolio returns reaching magnitudes of up to 45 basis points a month, even after controlling for market momentum and earnings surprise effects.[5]

Value Line's Other System

Not as well known as the timeliness effects, and strangely reminiscent of the periodic table's bifurcation into groups as well as periods, Value Line has developed a further classification of stocks based on their technical performance. In the spirit of pure technical analysis, these rankings are based on price moves alone, with particular reference to the changes up to the current month from each of the 11 previous months.

These rankings are developed by such elementary statistical means that it almost hurts. The technique is a cross-sectional regression of the price appreciation of each stock on the left side of the equation versus 10 measures of past short-term and long-term price appreciation on the right side. Eisenstadt likens the results of the procedure to the movements of a snake slithering up and down based on the terrain it has just passed and sees ahead but with each part of the snake's body dependent on the other. Results on a real-time basis

Table 10.3 Summary Statistics

	Timeliness Groups					VL Arithmetic
	1	2	3	4	5	
Geometric annual return	15.41%	13.13%	9.85%	6.48%	0.08%	11.37%
Excess return	4.05%	1.77%	-1.52%	-4.89%	-11.29%	
Annual standard deviation	25.90%	18.67%	16.04%	16.13%	21.63%	17.60%
Sharpe	0.60	0.70	0.61	0.40	0.00	0.65
Annual Alpha	2.55%	1.80%	-0.33%	-3.24%	-11.43%	
T (a = 0)	0.71	1.16	-0.41	-2.57	-4.76	Long-Short = 15.34%
Beta	1.23	1.00	0.89	0.87	1.10	Sigma = 19.4%
Correlation with benchmark	0.83	0.94	0.98	0.95	0.90	T = 3.394
% of times portfol > bmk	59.7%	62.5%	40.3%	27.8%	20.8%	L > S 70.8% of time
T (% outperf = .5)	1.65	2.12	-1.65	-3.77	-4.95	T(% > .5) = 3.536
T (port.ret = mkt.ret)	1.54	1.25	-1.90	-3.75	-4.43	n = 72
Wilcox RS	1.62	1.92	-2.14	-3.70	-4.73	3.40
ACF(1) for excess returns	0.03	-0.28	-0.26	0.03	0.00	0.08
ACF(2) for excess returns	-0.18	0.01	0.11	0.01	-0.02	-0.22

Technical Groups

Value Line Variability	1	2	3	4	5	VL Arithmetic
Geometric annual return	16.21%	12.08%	9.51%	6.69%	−0.90%	11.37%
Excess return	4.84%	0.72%	−1.86%	−4.68%	−12.26%	
Annual standard deviation	27.91%	18.45%	15.72%	18.00%	24.16%	17.60%
Sharpe	0.58	0.66	0.60	0.37	−0.04	0.65
Annual Alpha	2.88%	1.23%	−0.40%	−3.71%	−12.41%	
T (a = 0)	0.72	0.68	−0.43	−2.20	−3.72	Long-Short = 17.11%
Beta	1.30	0.97	0.87	0.95	1.15	Sigma = 22.6%
Correlation with benchmark	0.82	0.92	0.97	0.93	0.84	T = 3.228
% of times portfol > bmk	56.9%	56.9%	38.9%	30.6%	25.0%	L > S 69.4% of time
T (% outperf = .5)	1.18	1.18	−1.89	−3.30	−4.24	T(% > .5) = 3.3
T (port.ret = mkt.ret)	1.67	0.48	−1.99	−2.73	−3.32	n = 72
Wilcox RS	1.40	0.95	−2.26	−3.18	−3.63	3.52
ACF(1) for excess returns	0.28	−0.08	−0.16	0.18	−0.04	0.21
ACF(2) for excess returns	−0.08	−0.01	0.19	−0.21	0.01	−0.09

Source: Value Line.

are available since 1983. Amazingly, stocks in the Technical Analysis Group 1 have performed even better than the Timeliness Group 1 (see Figure 10.2).

The 1983–2002 performance difference between the top and worst ranks for the technical groups (4.7 percent versus 0.7 percent) is slightly greater than for the timeliness groups in the same period. As in the timeliness groups, the variabilities of Group 1 and Group 5 are highest, and all the results are highly unlikely to have occurred by chance variations alone (see Table 10.3).

What would happen if the timeliness and technical groups were combined? What reactions—chemical, electrical, or profitable—might arise?

The returns, when classified by both timeliness and technical analysis, seem to carry what the academics would call *incremental information* and what the average user would call *opportunities for nice extra profits*. Within each technical "period," the timeliness groups tend to further segment the returns.

For example, the Timeliness 1 and Timeliness 2 categories give an average of 6 percent a quarter when ranked with Technical 1 versus about –1 percent for the three other timeliness categories with Technical 1. Similarly, within the Timeliness 1 category, the Technical 1 and Technical 2 periods give returns of 5.5 percent versus about zero for the other three Timeliness categories within Timeliness 1.

As good as the Value Line rankings are by group and period, we can improve them by noting that they seem to work much better in the first and fourth quarters than in the second and third (see Table 10.4).

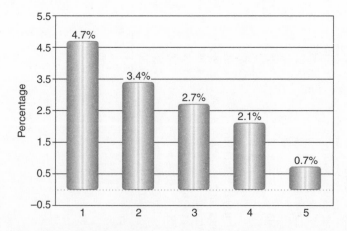

Figure 10.2   Value Line Technical Groups: Quarterly Balance, June 30, 1983–June 30, 2002

Table 10.4   Performance of Group 1 Companies Classified by Calendar Quarter

Quarter	Mean Price Appreciation	Percent Up	Standard Deviation
1	8	72	13
2	5	64	11
3	3	65	13
4	5	72	12

The Critics

The periodic table has gone through many highways and byways, critiques and improvements since it was first established. New groups of elements, such as the noble gases, have been discovered. The ordering by atomic weight has been replaced by a classification by atomic number. Similarly, the Value Line rankings have not been without problems and naysayers. The most obvious problem is that they do not work in many quarters. Timeliness Group 1 makes money in about two-thirds of the quarters. The actual return from following the Group 1 timeliness rankings in the four quarters ended September 30, 2001, would have been −30 percent, and following the Group 1 technical rankings would have led to a loss of 40 percent. Such results can try users' souls.

Even in better times, the critics had a field day negating the significance of the Value Line results. "Our findings show that the results of the Value Line enigma may reflect an association between Value Line rank and beta (i.e., risk)," wrote Robert S. Kaplan and Roman L. Weil in a 1973 study.[6] Gur Huberman and Shmuel Kandel, in a 1990 study, concluded: "The purported abnormal returns of positions based on Value Line's rankings are seen as compensation for the systematic risk associated with these positions."[7] William A. Sherden, in his 1998 book *The Fortune Sellers*, asserted: "The Value Line enigma is a myth. The investor service is not invincible, just enormously influential. This also suggests that the market is not nearly as rational as financial economists would have us believe."[8]

We will not deign to consider whether we should fault a service that nearly everyone can use in the form disseminated and explain away the results because of its wide use. Let the reader decide. A much more disturbing problem is the performance of the Value Line mutual fund. From 1987 through 2001, the fund's average quarterly performance was 0.96 percent, versus 4.6 percent for the Value Line timeliness rankings over 1983–2001 (see Figure 10.3).

"We'll always lag the Group 1's," said Alan Hoffman, the Value Line mutual fund's manager, in an interview. "The Group 1 is a theoretical number that ignores transaction costs and dividends." Moreover, he noted, the Value Line fund's assets range between $300 million and $350 million. Many of the Group 1 stocks trade only a couple of thousand shares a day. "You could never buy enough of the 1's to actually make a portfolio of them."

Mr. Hill Strikes It Rich

We would contrast these results with those of Henry Hill, a long-time Value Line subscriber from Florida. Starting in 1977, Hill religiously rebalanced his portfolio every week based on the Group 1 rankings. We spoke to Hill, who is 85, in March 2002. He told us that he turned an initial investment of "$80,000, something like that," into $48 million as of 2000, or $26 million after taxes and living expenses.

Hill began studying the stock market as a civil engineering student at Purdue University in Lafayette, Indiana, in the 1930s. "My math professor and I were both interested in the market. We tried to determine what factors influenced value. We decided consistent growth in earnings was the principal feature." After graduation in 1938, he went to work in the petroleum business

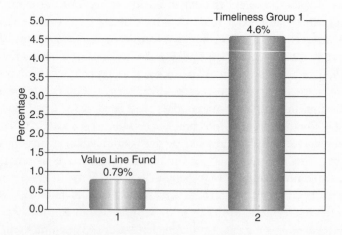

Figure 10.3   Value Line Fund versus Timeliness Group 1, 1987–2001.
Source: **Mark Hulbert. Used with permission.**

in Venezuela, but continued to study the stock market. He heard about Value Line in 1944. "Sam [Eisenstadt] had almost the same approach as I did. But I was having a hell of a time following 20 stocks by hand, and he had a computer. That was the last time I did any work" on picking stocks.

Hill says he has a solid wall of account transaction records that impressed the CPA sent down by *Money* magazine to audit him for an article three or four years ago. Until recently, he bought all 100 of the Timeliness Group 1 stocks, rebalancing his portfolio every week. "Five or six years ago, when Sam [Eisenstadt] checked on the technical rankings, it looked like there would be some advantage to confining ourselves to stocks ranked Group 1 from both the Timeliness and Technical standpoints." This reduced the stocks in his portfolio to between 18 and 46. "It made it easier to manage the account."

In 1999, facing a serious illness and concerned that his wife, Ollie, would find managing the account burdensome, Hill liquidated his stocks and bought Treasury bills with the proceeds. As it happened, the market was about to begin its worst downturn since the 1970s. The account now provides a tax-free income of $1 million a year.

Thus, the practical implementation of Value Line ratings has made Mr. Hill rich.

A Mind Still Open after 58 Years

As Will and Ariel Durant wrote in *The Lessons of History* after a lifetime of studying the panoply of world history, it is appropriate to ask at the end of a seminal study what use the study has served. Have you found in your work only amusement, only a method of scratching out a living amid a stormy market, a way of finding some good and bad stocks? Have you learned anything about the nature of markets, of companies, of science?[9]

Sam Eisenstadt is alive and kicking after 58 years of continuous service at Value Line, and well able to reflect on his record. In 2001, in fact, he attended a swing dance night at the Niederhoffer house and danced circles around most of the younger attendees—including Victor, who still fancies himself something of an athlete. In October 2001, Eisenstadt graciously consented to an interview to look back over his career. We started by asking him why he feels the timeliness classification has worked and whether he was discouraged by recent results.

"The rationale behind using earnings momentum and earnings surprise is their tendency to persist, which does not get fully priced into the stock," he said. "At least, that is what academic studies seem to show. The fact that they have not worked well recently is more a reflection of a 'value' bent to the market than the argument offered. I daresay when the market reverts (as it always has) to a growth orientation, you'll see a revival in both earnings momentum and surprise."

We asked him if he is pleased by what he has accomplished. "To some extent, I am pleased—primarily by questioning the efficiency argument. In the late sixties, Wall Street was on the defensive with an onslaught from the University of Chicago claiming that we were all in effect wasting our time. There was no response forthcoming from the financial community. We had a record, albeit a short one at the time, that indicated we were on to something. Since then, the efficient market adherents have softened their arguments, and I daresay Value Line had something to do with it."

Value Line initially placed much importance on time series analysis, but changed its approach in 1964–1965. We asked Eisenstadt why.

"We were trying to separate stocks from one another. Time series separates years from one another—finding years of over- and undervaluation. Our problem was to differentiate stocks. In order to do so, we had to measure all stocks with a common yardstick, rather than a different formula for each company, which resulted from time series analysis. Since we assumed we could not predict the market, it made sense to reduce everything to a relative basis and bypass the market forecast. There were always relatively underpriced or overpriced stocks—regardless of the level of the market."

Then we asked the hard question. What would he have done differently?

"In the early years, we spent almost all the time working with time series analysis—a leftover from the visual fittings that Arnold Bernhard had devised in the early thirties. Early on we started to use multiple regression analysis to increase the number of factors and years to get better fits—which, of course the process produced. Despite the better fits, we did not get the kind of results we were striving for. We were attempting to predict absolute prices for individual stocks using their own histories of prices, earnings, dividends, and book values, and so on. Because we were dealing with absolutes, we had periods of time when most stocks were undervalued or overvalued, without saying much about individual stocks.

"We spent many years [until 1965] working in this environment. It's difficult for me to take myself back, since at this point I know the future, but I should have gone to cross-sectional analysis at a much earlier time and changed the system to a relative [ranking] basis.

"As for the future—50 years from now—I think stock selection will become increasingly difficult. We will become more and more dependent on accurate earnings forecasts, which I suspect have not improved much over the years. With computers humming and quants concentrating on the field, I can only see the problem becoming increasingly difficult. We'll have to keep up with the development of new statistical techniques and high-powered computers to provide us with an edge."

He concluded with some enduring guidance:

> I have learned that stock selection is not a random process. The application of statistical methods can be helpful, but it is very difficult to outperform the market. We are working with very low information coefficients that become statistically significant when the universe is large. Nor does the system work equally well in all phases of the market. There are times when a "value" approach produces better results. The system is adaptive, however, and adjusts to a changing environment. If the environment changes rapidly and frequently, it creates difficulties for the system. Nevertheless, over the 36-year history of the system, it has had a respectable batting average and attracted the attention of the academic community.

His advice for future investigators: "Don't give up and become complacent. We're only explaining a tiny amount of the unknown. Be curious, keep an open mind, and persist."

11   WHEN THEY SWING FOR THE FENCES, WE RUN FOR THE EXITS

What Should I Trade?

Lyrics by Victor Niederhoffer and Laurel Kenner. To the tune of "What Is a Man?" from *Pal Joey* by Richard Rodgers and Lorenz Hart.

There are so many, so many ways to trade
But baseball is the model that's for me
It tells the Average Joe
How he can make some dough
The times change far too much to trade without it

1. What's a good trade?
Should I buy stocks now?
Am I a bull? Am I a bear?
Am I the value or the growth kind?
Am I the old or the tech kind?

What's a good trade?
Trading's like baseball

Win with a bat, or win with a glove.
Value has lagged since the world began
What should I buy? What should I sell?
What makes a winning trade?

2. First, runs expand
Stocks set to fall then
Next, runs contract—bull's horns are sharp
It's all so easy after the fact
Vol first goes down, Bulls are set to frown

When balls are dead, Time to steal bases
When balls are live, Swing from the heels
Cycles have changed since the world began
Offense at times, Defense at times.
That makes a winning trade.

One afternoon in March 2002, we were sitting on a bench on 81st Street with Larry Ritter, dean of baseball history, talking about players and seeing how far Vic could hit a tennis ball down Broadway. We both knew we were in the presence of one of the greats, and requested Larry's advice on how to begin this chapter. He told us to always begin with Babe Ruth. There really is no better way to begin, because the Babe epitomizes an important predictive relation between baseball and the stock market. We call it the Home Run Indicator. Consider:

- In 1927, two years before the Crash, Ruth hit a record 60 home runs. Similarly, in 2000, two years after Mark McGwire broke Roger Maris' record of 61 home runs in 1998, the market began to decline drastically.
- In the 1930s, Ruth's slugging dropped to .500 and lower; and America slid into the Great Depression. (We'll return to this pattern of home runs and market moves.)

Unlike the well-known Super Bowl Indicator (mentioned as a spurious correlation in Chapter 8), the Home Run Indicator does not rest on the outcome of a single game. Rather, it relies on the tendency of long-term trends in the market and society to show up first on the baseball field. Two examples:

1. The internationalization of baseball preceded that of the stock market by more than 100 years. Baseball teams toured the world starting in 1888, but the New York Stock Exchange listed its first foreign company only in 1990.
2. Baseball was integrated in 1944, with Jackie Robinson breaking the barrier. The NYSE didn't admit its first black member until 1967. (The first female member was admitted in 1970.)

The foreshadowing quality of baseball is detailed in the time line at the end of this chapter. But for the investor, it is the game itself—home runs, in particular—that bears the most watching.

Win with a Bat or Win with a Glove (Artist: Milton Bond, © 1993).

To explain, we need to go back to the first two decades of the twentieth century—"the dead ball era"—before the Babe gave up pitching and took up batting in earnest. The balls were called "dead" because they did not carry long distances no matter how hard they were hit. Spitballs and doctored balls were permitted, favoring the pitchers. Earned run averages of 3 were the norm. The offense was fought with bunts, slides, sacrifice flies, place hitting, and base stealing. "Brains were as important as brawn," wrote Ritter, "maybe more so." Home runs were rare. From 1901 to 1918, total home runs declined from 455 a year to 235. In 1908, Sam Crawford led the league in home runs—with seven. Outside the ballpark fences, the market languished. In 1918, the Dow closed at 82.20, little more than double the 40.94 at which it began life in 1896.

After the hard days of World War I, authorities eliminated spitballs and other doctored balls, put cork in the ball to liven it up, changed the balls more frequently, and outlawed trick pitches. The Babe started swinging from the heels. His slugging percentage went from the .400-to-.500 level to .847 in 1920, and stayed at .600 or higher for the next 10 years. Ruth's transformation from pitcher to batting star serves as the starting point of the no-holds-barred spirit of the 1920s. "I swing big, with everything I've got," said Ruth. "I hit big or I miss big." From 1918 to 1930, home runs increased from 235 to 1,565 a year. In the world beyond the fences, business was expanding. In 1924, after treading water for the prior decade, the Dow had five years of unbroken gains, rising 260 percent through the end of September 1929.

As the century progressed, home runs continued to predict and reflect the stock market and society:

1935 to 1943: The number of home runs diminished. Bunting and sacrificing again came into fashion—appropriate to the Depression-era psychology that gripped the market.

1943 to 1952: Home runs expanded. Stars like Ted Williams came to the fore. From 1948 to 1965, the Dow soared from 119 to 969.

1963 to 1991: Home runs diminished. A major star of the period was Lou Brock, who stole a record 118 bases in 1974. "Brock," wrote Ritter, "represented a return to the old-fashioned style of baseball: bunting, stealing, trying to out-think the opposition." In the world outside the ballpark, recessions and market crashes became the rule.

After major setbacks in 1966, 1969, 1973–1974, and 1977, the Dow finished 1981 at 875, or 9 percent below its 1965 close.

After a players' strike in 1994 threatened interest in the game, a general move toward immediate gratification came about in the area of sports and, dare we say it, in the offices of the nation's capital. Home runs once more began to

Table 11.1 Home Runs by Year

Year	Baseball Leagues	Dow League
1990	3,317	2633.66
1991	3,383	3168.83
1992	3,038	3301.11
1993	4,030	3754.09
1994	3,305	3834.44
1995	4,081	5117.12
1996	4,962	6448.27
1997	4,640	7908.25
1998	5,064	9181.43
1999	5,528	11497.12
2000	5,693	10786.85
2001	5,458	10021.50
2002	5,059	8341.63

climb. The market, too, slowed down a bit in 1994 when the Federal Reserve doubled the federal funds rate; but after that it was up and away for the averages.

Table 11.1 shows the combined home run totals for the American and National Leagues during the 1990s, alongside the Dow league's year-end closing levels.

Playing to the Crowd

Two questions arise: What causes the cyclical shifts in home runs? Why should home runs foreshadow market moves?

We hypothesize that the owners of Major League baseball teams act to anticipate the mood of the fans by adjusting the balance between offense and defense. If hard times are ahead, they tone down the game, making the batters work harder for home runs so that the audience can feel catharsis. If the spirit of the times is expansive, they liven up the action and let the home run records roll. The owners can make these changes by changing the rules in myriad ways: Balls, bats, and gloves change; the surface and size of the fields change; the strike zone changes; pitching rules change. These things can occur gradually, over several years. In the meantime, the market is likely to catch up.

We see another element at work. The scientific play that dominated in 1900–1918, 1932–1946, and 1970–1977 represented the kind of attention to detail and hard work that is apparently a precondition to success. A period of small gains leads, both in baseball and markets, to a desire for home runs. In baseball, it led to Babe Ruth in the 1920s, and to Mark McGwire and Barry Bonds in the 1990s. In the market, we had the Roaring Twenties, the postwar boom of the late 1940s and 1950s, and the great bull market of 1982–2000. After each period of scientific baseball, the market was ready for a sustained rally. Conversely, after the end of each period of home run "hitting-from-the-heels" baseball, the market was ready for a drop.

Before the 1990s, it was customary after a home run for the hitter to quietly run around the bases with his head down so as not to embarrass the pitcher. When he reached the plate, he might discreetly doff his hat to the fans. As the bull market of the latter half of the 1990s rolled on, it became common for home run hitters to indulge in a bit of trash talk, a shuffle to first base and then a roll of the bat. Some longtime fans were appalled.

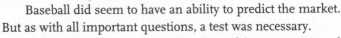

Baseball did seem to have an ability to predict the market. But as with all important questions, a test was necessary.

Although the beginning and ending of the expansion and contraction periods in home runs were somewhat arbitrary (Is a one-year spike to a new high preceded by two down years a high, or a temporary reversal?), we started with five-year highs in home runs over the past 100 years. We then looked to see what happened in the stock market the next year.

When home runs were not at a five-year high, the market went up 12 percent the next year, on average; when they were at five-year highs, the next year's average move was a 2 percent gain (see Figure 11.1).

Next, we studied the relation between five-year changes in home runs and the next five years' performance in stocks. The correlation was −0.20, with 20 observations, a level fairly unlikely to have occurred through chance variations alone.

Finally, we looked at the correlation of home run changes one year and stock market changes the next year. The correlation was −10 percent. The bottom line was that every extra 10 percent increase in home runs knocked 1 percent off the market the next year.

Taken together, the three relations provide confirmation that overly numerous home runs presage poor stock performance.

New Century, New Game

The late 1990s differed in an important aspect from previous periods: While the home run records kept coming, so, amazingly, did record strikeouts. Bill

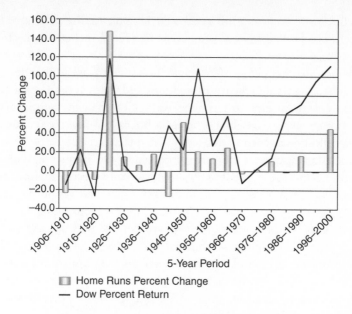

Figure 11.1   Home Runs and Dow Change

James attributes the conjunction of record strikeouts and homers to smaller bat handles, aluminum bats, strength training, and abbreviated pitcher motions. On the one hand, we had fundamentalist primitives who didn't understand the value of compound growth (10 percent for 20 years = eightfold return); and on the other, day traders with microterm mentalities and a quest for immediate gratification that deflected us from the hard efforts required for a proper base of operations in the market.

In keeping with our hypothesis, the market followed suit. Huge swings that previously might have occurred once a year became commonplace in the first three years of the new century.

A favorite theme of ours is that the common man often provides a better reflection of what the future holds for the market than the more sophisticated experts and professionals at the higher levels of the feeding pyramid. As popular as basketball and football are, baseball holds a unique position in the American psyche because it is a game that ordinary Joes and Janes can relate to. Baseball is the only sport where people of average height, weight, speed, and strength can play at the highest level. The median height and weight of American baseball players is 5 feet 10 inches, 190 pounds—the average for all U.S. adult males.

As the late team owner Bill Veeck said, "Baseball is the only game left for people. To play basketball now, you have to be 7 feet 6 inches. To play football, you have to be the same width."

It is not just that people of average physique can rise to the top in baseball. Baseball is geared to the future volitions and tastes of the average Joe. Because markets themselves are in many ways affected by the normal activities of the average person, baseball provides a forecast of the market and life as well as a reflection of current times (see Table 11.2).

From Mark Twain in the nineteenth century to Jacques Barzun in the twenty-first century, everybody agrees that baseball reflects American society. Paul Dickson found the thought so obvious that when he was putting together *Baseball's Greatest Quotations,* he rejected all observations along those lines.[1] For Mark Twain, baseball was "the very symbol, the outward and visible expression of the drive and push and rush and struggle of the rising, tearing, booming nineteenth century," as he put it at an 1888 dinner at Delmonico's sponsored by Albert Goodwill Spalding, an early impresario of the game. More than a century later, in 2001, Major League baseball played to some 75 million fans, more than any other sport.

Baseball has always reflected America's sorrows and flaws along with its good. Abner Doubleday, who would become a heroic general in the Battle of Gettysburg, invented the game in 1839 at Cooperstown, New York. African Americans were barred from the game, a taboo not broken until Jackie Robinson played for Brooklyn in 1944. A strike closed the gates in the recession year of 1974. The World Series was postponed as the nation mourned the attack on the World Trade Center on September 11, 2001, and the resumption of play six days later was seen as a necessary step toward getting back to normal. Newspapers noted, for once without cynicism, that President George W. Bush watched the first two games of that Series at Camp David with his family, and that he was in New York for Game 3 to throw the first pitch. It was a strike, and New Yorkers gave the president a thunderous cheer. "It means a lot that he's here today. It shows that this guy is a real man," Al Meditz, 58, a mail carrier from Rego Park, Queens, told the *New York Post.*

After all the ribbing Bush received about his inability to speak with proper grammar, his short work weeks, and his supposed general lack of intelligence (he graduated in the top half of his class at Harvard Business School and received an MBA while Vic was there), one can imagine that his pitching would have been the object of great ridicule in any other circumstances.

The only other two presidents to attend a World Series game, Ronald Reagan in 1980 and Calvin Coolidge in 1920, did so at the beginning of gigantic bull markets.

Table 11.2 Time Line of Baseball and Financial Markets 1792–2001

Baseball	Date	Markets
	1792	Five securities traded
	1829	380,000 shares traded
	1830s	Railroads dominate
	1836	Trading prohibited in streets
First formal rules created	1845	
First official game between two clubs	1846	
	1853	Complete statement required
First league	1857	
First admission fee (50 cents)	1858	
First betting scandal	1865	First permanent home for NYSE
First all-pro team (salaries $1,400)	1869	All shares must be registered
Nat'l Association of Baseball Players	1871	Specialists are created
First no-hitter	1875	
First Nat'l League home run	1876	
First scandal in major leagues	1878	First telephone on the floor
First players' union	1886	First million-share day
	1896	Dow Jones average introduced by *Wall Street Journal*
First modern World Series	1903	NYSE moves to current site
	1907	Wall Street panic
	1913	Federal Reserve System created
First game to draw 1 million fans	1920	Dow ends year at 71.95
"Lively ball" introduced; Babe Ruth hits 54 home runs in single season First player earns $50,000	1923	
Babe Ruth hits 60 home runs	1927	
First player hits 500 career home runs	1929	Crash
	1932	Dow hits bottom
First All-Star game	1933	Securities Act of 1933
	1934	SEC formed

(continued)

Table 11.2 *Continued*

Baseball	Date	Markets
First night game	1936	NYSE President R. Whitney jailed for embezzlement
First election to Hall of Fame	1936	
First televised game	1939	
	1942	Lowest price for NYSE membership
First $100,000 player salary Jackie Robinson is first black major league player	1947	
	1953	Daily volume reaches 1 million First NYSE member corporation
First perfect game in World Series	1956	
	1957	S&P index first calculated hourly
Roger Maris first player to hit 61 home runs in a season	1961	
First domed stadium, Astroturf	1965	
	1967	First woman member
Pitcher's mound lowered 10 inches Strike zone defined armpits-knees	1969	
	1970	First black NYSE member
	1971	Nasdaq opens
First players' strike	1972	DJIA closes above 1,000 CBOE opens
First player hits 715 home runs	1974	Trading hours extended
First game to draw 3 million fans	1978	
	1982	First 100 million-share day
	1987	Dow has largest one-day point drop
	1988	"Circuit breakers" introduced
First game to draw 4 million fans	1991	Off-hours trading Dow tops 3,000
First non-U.S. World Series winner	1992	Average daily volume tops 200 million shares
Players strike, World Series canceled	1994	Internet trading launched
	1995	First Internet IPO
	1996	NYSE volume exceeds 1 billion

Table 11.2 *Continued*

Baseball	Date	Markets
Mark McGwire first to hit 70 home runs in a season	1998	
	1999	Dow closes above 10,000
	2000	First global index Dow has biggest up, biggest down days
Barry Bonds first to hit 73 home runs in a season	2001	NYSE volume tops 2 billion Decimalization replaces eighths

Baseball's freedom from the tyranny of the time clock harkens back to the pastoral past recalled by the green field itself. The game originated in the days when Americans began coming en masse from the farm to find jobs in the cities. The game continues at its own pace, regardless of the demands of sponsors. In the shortest game, the New York Giants beat the Philadelphia Phillies 6–1 in 51 minutes on September 28, 1919. The longest game, between the Chicago White Sox and Milwaukee on May 9, 1984, lasted 25 innings and took eight hours and six minutes. While variations in tennis games often range to similar multiples, the length of the matches offer no competition.

We note with admiration the average American's delight in the amazingly detailed record of statistics concerning every aspect of the game. When a player hits a home run, before the batter has rounded third, fans can expect a recap of how many similar blows have been struck, classified by inning, score, handedness of pitcher and batter, and whether the event occurred at home or away. At a 2001 Yankee playoff game co-announced by New York Governor George Pataki, it was mentioned as a matter of routine that a certain batter had the third highest percentage of foul balls per pitch with two outs during playoffs of all American League players. If only market practitioners were to keep at their fingertips one-thousandth of that kind of knowledge about the picks of their favorite analysts—returns to be anticipated, winning streaks, balls, strikes, and so on—the market would be a far more sensible and profitable place.

12   BOOM OR BUST?

That land speculation is the true cause of industrial depression is clearly evident. In each period of industrial activity land values have steadily risen, culminating in speculation, which carried them up in great jumps. This has been invariably followed by a partial cessation of production, and its correlative, a cessation of effective demand, and then has succeeded a period of comparative stagnation, during which the equilibrium has been again slowly established.

—Henry George, *Progress and Poverty*[1]

Real estate, fixed and immovable, might seem an ideal alternative to a roller-coaster stock market. Yet real estate prices are every bit as subject to violent price swings. Real estate investment trusts (REITs)—the main way that small investors can invest in large-scale income properties—have failed to measure up to stocks as long-term investments. Of course, a $17 trillion market that includes office buildings, residences of all types, farmland, warehouses, industrial property, and hospitals offers endless variations, niches, and opportunities for profit; and it is impossible to quantify all the benefits of owning a home. The investor, however, may find that the best profits will come from studying the patterns linking real estate and business cycles.

Begin with the big picture. At once a source of wealth, a factor in business production, and a consumer good, real estate is the largest of any asset class. Federal Reserve statistics show the value of U.S. commercial property at $5 trillion and U.S. residential property at $12 trillion. This compares to some $11 trillion in stocks and $5 trillion in corporate bonds. About 50 million people own homes in the United States, but that is not the end of the story. Because real estate represents about 20 percent of the assets on every corporate balance sheet, anyone who holds stocks has an interest in real estate. Americans have a large part of their wealth in real estate, probably more than they realize. Real estate absorbs a sizable portion of the money that people spend—some 10 percent to 20 percent of typical business operating expenses, and at least one-third of a typical family's income. It is a factor in all production and spending decisions.

Everything that happens takes place on real estate. Like the grinding of tectonic plates across the earth's surface, changes in real estate prices affect everything above, causing earthquakes; volcanic eruptions; and continental drift in business activity, personal wealth, and the stock market. Fortunes are made and lost in such epochal real estate slumps as occurred in the periods 1972–1974, 1989–1990, and 1998–1999.

Several theories attempt to pinpoint the cause of real estate cycles. David Ricardo and Henry George observed in the nineteenth century that rents and land prices rise when business is good, absorbing the extra profits generated. The price rise is exacerbated as speculators jump in near the top. Eventually, business staggers under the burden, rents and mortgage payments go unpaid, and land prices crash. But hope springs eternal, and real estate eventually becomes cheap enough to let entrepreneurial business plans pencil out.

Going back into history, the demise of great speculative land operations—the South Sea Company in England and the Mississippi Company in France—created wholesale financial panics. The memoirs of the great eighteenth-century speculator Giacomo Casanova detail how he used such excesses for the mutual benefit of himself and his *amours*. In modern days, who can forget 1980s Japan, when the few acres around the imperial palace in Tokyo commanded a higher price than all the real estate in California? Or the 1990s tech boom that drove Silicon Valley rents and land prices up hundreds of percent? In both cases, as in so many others, disaster soon followed.

Yoon Dokko, of Korea's Ajou University, and colleagues at University of California Berkeley note that many explanations of real estate cycles feature "the greedy developer" and "the bumbling lender." This is because bankers apparently like to lend as long as business conditions are good, whereas developers have a complementary tendency to borrow so long as credit flows. The resulting oversupply brings down prices.[2]

Both of us have firsthand experience with the real estate cycle's power to turn life upside down. After first losing their stake in the stock market, Vic's family tried to rebuild by buying depressed properties at foreclosure sales in the 1930s. When the investments failed to pay off, speculation became a dirty word in the Niederhoffer family until the late 1950s, when Vic gingerly took his first steps into buying mining properties on the American Stock Exchange. Almost four decades later, a financial collapse in Thailand brought about by massive overbuilding forced Vic to close his hedge fund and mortgage his home. Nobel Prize winner Joseph Stiglitz, asked about the causes of Southeast Asia's market collapse in a June 2000 interview with the *Progressive,* went to the heart of the problem: "The biggest problems were the misallocations of lending to speculative real estate, and risky financing, especially borrowing short-term debt on international markets."[3]

Laurel's father, John Kenner, a mortgage banker, had a quick eye for value. But he lost his livelihood in the 1972–1974 REIT collapse, after refusing to sign off on what he considered to be inflated appraisals of commercial properties. Unfortunately, most of his wealth was tied up in the company REIT.

Promoting REITs

REITs originated in 1880 as tax-advantaged vehicles for purchasing real estate. The tax advantages have been removed and restored over the years, but under current law, REITs can avoid corporate taxes if they distribute at least 90 percent of net taxable income. The main idea behind REITs is to give small investors opportunities to invest in office buildings, warehouses, hospitals, shopping centers, apartment houses, and other large properties. REITs are thus similar to stock mutual funds, which let investors hold interests in a greater number of stocks than the size of their stake would otherwise permit.

In addition to the tax benefits, REITs offer improved liquidity over direct investment in real estate because investors can easily sell their shares. Dividend returns for REITs generally vary from 6 percent to 8 percent. REITs and real estate mutual funds experienced a tremendous surge in 2000–2002, when the Nasdaq—consisting mainly of growth stocks that pay no dividends—lost three-quarters of its value, and investors sought safety in dividend-paying stocks. As of mid-2002, there were some 300 REITs, 190 of them publicly traded, with a combined market value of about $300 billion, up from $13 billion in 1992. In addition, some 130 open-end U.S. mutual funds are devoted to real estate, with holdings consisting of REITs, real estate operating companies, or a mixture of the two. The largest are run by Cohen & Steers, Fidelity, and Vanguard (see Table 12.1).

Like all dynamic fields, the REIT industry undergoes constant innovation and turmoil. In the late 1990s, existing properties were transferred to umbrella REITs, but these vehicles proved unpopular because they subjected investors to unrealized gains. The turn of the millennium brought master partnerships to invest in assorted REIT mutual funds; some feared that this development was symptomatic of a top.

Promoters seized the opportunity to capitalize on the growing popularity of REITs. One well-publicized study after another presented REITs as ideal components of a diversified portfolio. It was claimed that the industry had outgrown the massive liquidations and boom-and-bust cycles of the 1970s and 1980s, and that the problems of those days—too much debt, too little transparency, and too many conflicts of interest involving management—had been overcome. As discussed in this chapter, real estate cycles have existed for centuries. It is unlikely that they have suddenly disappeared for good.

To objectively evaluate even past REIT performance is no easy task. It is difficult to find good data on real estate and REITs. Many figures on real estate prices are based on appraised values, not on transaction prices. Using appraised values tends to smooth out variations in returns while creating spurious correlations. The difficulty is that transactions in the same properties are relatively infrequent, and prices vary with respect to property type and locality.

Survivor bias, as discussed in Chapter 3, compounds the data problems. The data that get reported and saved tend to relate only to properties that manage to escape bankruptcy, disuse, or drastic change. The National Association of Real Estate Investment Trusts (NAREIT) has data on REIT returns

Table 12.1 Morningstar Ratings

Fund	Net Assets (in Billions $)	Morningstar Rating
Cohen & Steers Realty	1.38	★★★★★
Vanguard REIT Index	1.33	★★★★
Fidelity Real Estate	1.26	★★★

Source: Morningstar.com

and appraised values of real estate held by selected institutions going back to 1970, but apparently only companies that have continuously provided data to NAREIT are included in the database.

An exhaustive study of REIT prices by Jun Han of CIGNA Investment Management in Hartford, Connecticut, and Youguo Liang, a managing director at Prudential Real Estate Investors, included data on all publicly held companies that were classified as REITs during the period 1970–1993. Han and Liang concluded that the survivorship bias of NAREIT data compared with their own was in the range of 2 to 3 percentage points a year.[4]

Brokerage house reports do not help investors evaluate REITs. The three key metrics that tend to be analyzed are:

1. Price to funds from operations.
2. Dividend yield.
3. Discount to net asset value.

These are combined by the analyst in some fuzzy way, with high values of the first being bearish and high values of the latter two being bullish. This number is compared with an expected growth rate, and if the comparison is good, it generates statements like the following from a major brokerage house in early 2002:

> We estimate REITs are trading at 93 times our 2002 FFO estimates at a 5 percent discount to net asset value, and are sporting an average dividend yield of 7. We are forecasting a 5 percent earnings growth, with earnings rates likely to accelerate if occupancy levels rise or interest rates continue to fall. We believe the REIT institutional and retail investor base will continue to expand.

A fourth metric that REIT analysts like to use is the spread between a REIT's dividend yield and bonds. During volatile times in the market, such as the credit crunch of 1998 and the period after September 11, the spread widens. According to Bank of America research, inordinate duration of high spreads is indicative of future superior performance for REITs. The trick is to differentiate a high spread that might illustrate undervaluation from a high spread that appropriately takes increased risk into account.

REITs versus Stocks

Given all the booms and busts in real estate over the centuries, the vast divergences in prosperity among sectors ranging from apartments to farmland to warehouses, the vicissitudes of regional cycles, and the grave difficulties in obtaining accurate price data in an industry characterized by bankruptcies, closings of real estate enterprises, and the tearing down of buildings—is there anything we can say about the long-term returns from holding REITs, compared with common stock?

Our studies show that, until recently, the performance of stocks and REITs had been strongly linked, with a 50 percent correlation on an annual basis. The relation broke down in the late 1990s. REITs tumbled as the S&P 500 doubled in 1997–1999, but gained 43 percent in 2000–2001 when the S&P 500 declined 22 percent (see Table 12.2).

This led the REIT industry to loudly proclaim that the correlation between the two asset classes was decreasing. The implication was that institutional portfolio managers must buy REITs to achieve a proper balance of risk and reward. Such a development has been the goal of the REIT industry for decades. One industry-sponsored study after another has tried to prove that a diversified portfolio of REITs and stocks is better than a portfolio of stocks alone. On May 29, 2001, the National Association of Real Estate Investment Trusts published a study by Ibbotson Associates Inc., the dean of market return statistics, purporting to show that REITs "represent a strong source of diversification for a wide range of investment portfolios by increasing return and decreasing risk."[5]

Regrettably, all the careful studies of these phenomena show very small, if any, incremental returns from such diversification. Ronald Kaiser, a principal in the Foster City, California, real estate advisory firm of Bailard, Biehl & Kaiser, considered this exact question.[6] Using nine different academic and industry sources, he constructed a series of real estate returns from 1919 to 1997. He concluded that real estate returns were similar to those produced by domestic stocks over this 86-year period,

Table 12.2　Performance of REITs versus S&P 500

Year	Morgan Stanley REIT Index Change (%)	S&P 500 Change (%)	Divergence (Percentage Points)
2001	12.83	−13.04	25.87
2000	26.81	−10.14	36.95
1999	−4.55	19.53	24.08
1998	−16.90	26.67	43.57
1997	18.58	31.01	12.43
1996	35.89	20.26	15.63
1995	12.90	34.11	21.21

Source: Bloomberg L.P.

ranging between 10 percent and 11 percent a year compounded. This is as it should be, since both asset classes are equity investments. Both the S&P 500 and REITs yield returns that both exceed inflation and significantly outperform corporate bonds, Treasury bonds, or direct unleveraged investment in real estate assets. Stocks certainly have the advantage over real estate in terms of liquidity, but real estate compensates with lessened within-year volatility, Kaiser concluded. However, Kaiser's own figures show that stocks return about one percentage point a year more, compounded, than real estate. This is consistent with the careful work of William B. Brueggeman and Jeffrey D. Fisher, in their excellent textbook, *Real Estate Finance Investments*.[7]

Brueggeman and Fisher studied quarterly returns for REITs and other investments, including the S&P 500, from 1985 to 2000. They found that the S&P 500 produced quarterly geometric returns of 4 percent, whereas quarterly returns of equity REITs were 2.6 percent. The difference of some 1.4 percent a quarter is not so minuscule as it may seem. One hundred dollars compounded at 4 percent comes to $189 in 15 years, whereas 2.6 percent compounded comes to only $151. By comparison, institutional real estate holdings yielded 1.73 percent quarterly, corporate bonds yielded 2.24 percent, and T-bills yielded 1.4 percent. The Consumer Price Index rose 0.79 percent a quarter during this period. (The geometric mean measures the compounded rate of returns that an investor would have earned on $1 invested in the index during the period. Portfolio managers evaluating the performance of an investment use the geometric mean, rather than the arithmetic mean, which is a simple average.)

Because Brueggeman and Fisher used the problematic NAREIT data, with the survivor bias discussed earlier, their estimate suffers from an upward bias. Considering the highly superior returns of stocks over REITs, the potential for improved portfolio performance by combining REITs and stocks seems most unlikely. Furthermore, a careful study shows that quarterly REIT returns are correlated 60 percent with quarterly S&P 500 returns. Nevertheless, after making heroic assumptions using such things as arithmetic returns instead of geometric returns, Brueggeman and Fisher concluded that some very small diversification benefits could be achieved by investing in a combination of stocks and real estate.

Interlocking Gears: Real Estate, Business Cycles, and Stocks

Although investing in REITs is unlikely to significantly improve returns, the speculator will find real estate a highly profitable field of study for understanding stock market cycles. According to a widely respected economic theory first put forward by Henry George and David Ricardo in the nineteenth century, business cycles are caused mainly by movements in real estate values.

George and Ricardo began with the observation that rents and land prices rise when business conditions are good. Eventually, rent-seeking landlords absorb all the excess profits that businesses can make. Businesses fall behind on rents and mortgage payments; defaults begin, and bankers call in loans. Land prices begin declining because fewer tenants can be found to lease property at current prices. As these developments reduce lending for other business activities, general business conditions worsen. Just at this most inauspicious time, an abundance of new development comes on the market. Developers had broken ground on new projects back when business conditions were good, acting on the assumption that property values would keep rising. Now that the projects are complete, there are few takers.

The net result is that rents and land values are driven down still further. Similar patterns are observed in many other areas—venture capital and agriculture, to name but two. In the real estate cycle, prices eventually fall to a level low enough to permit entrepreneurs to start profitable businesses on these properties once again. Expansion of these new businesses spurs real estate prices higher, and the cycle is ready to repeat.

This simplified model is so obvious and so elementary that it almost seems naïve to present it, except that throughout history and across countries the cycle George and Ricardo described seems to repeat over and over again.

Homer Hoyt was the first to study these cycles systematically. In *One Hundred Years of Land Values in Chicago: The Relationship of the Growth of Chicago to the Rise of Its Land Values, 1830–1933,* Hoyt documented dramatic swings in the total value of Chicago land values (see Figure 12.1).[8]

The most thorough and thoughtful real estate research that we have found—that of Kaiser, Liang, Prudential, and the research firm Torto Wheaton—confirm the economists' hypothesis of real estate cycles.

Kaiser, for example, found tremendous boom/bust cycles in investment property, with peaks in the early 1800s, the 1870s, the 1920s, and the late 1980s. In each case, a rapid run-up of rents, usually preceded and accompanied 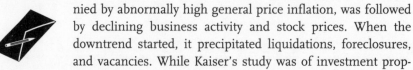 by abnormally high general price inflation, was followed by declining business activity and stock prices. When the downtrend started, it precipitated liquidations, foreclosures, and vacancies. While Kaiser's study was of investment property, he concluded that the underlying forces in all real estate sectors are similar in their effect and timing.

The conventional wisdom is that gains in stocks drive up real estate prices because people have more money to invest. It has not always worked that way.

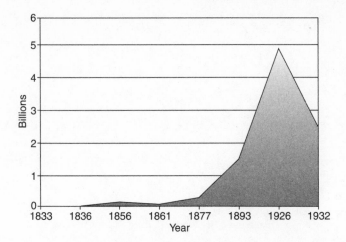

Figure 12.1 Total Value of Chicago Land Peaks and Valleys, 1833–1932. *Source:* **Fred E. Foldvary, "Real Estate and Business Cycles: Henry George's Theory of the Trade Cycle," paper presented at the Lafayette College Henry George Conference, June 13, 1991.**

Using an index of REIT prices as a proxy for real estate prices, we found that from 1993 through 2001, REIT prices led stock market prices. The correlation between changes in REIT prices in one quarter and the S&P change the next quarter was an amazingly large −0.5. As we explained in Chapter 8, our general formula for usefulness is that the correlation coefficient multiplied by the number of observations should be greater than 10. With our formula, 36 quarters and a correlation coefficient of 0.5 is a highly useful 18. The correlation between the change in stocks in one quarter and the change in REIT prices in the next quarter, however, was close to zero.

The average quarterly gain for the S&P 500 after a quarter in which the Bloomberg REIT Index declined, or rose less than 0.5 percent, was 7 percent. That is more than twice the average 3 percent quarterly gain for the S&P during the 1993–2001 period. When the REIT Index rose more than 3 percent in a quarter, the average subsequent change in the S&P 500 was −0.5 percent. When the change in REITs was between 0.5 percent and 3 percent, the average change in the S&P was 1 percent.

A scatter diagram of the relation between these quarterly changes appears in Figure 12.2. Note that the quarters after declines in real estate prices tend to be followed by big increases in stock prices (the northwest quadrant of the

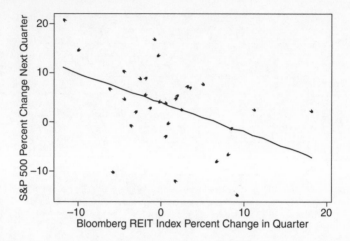

Figure 12.2   How Real Estate Leads Stocks: REIT Performance versus S&P 500 Performance in Next Quarter. *Source:* Niederhoffer Investments.

chart). Similarly, the large increases in real estate prices tend to be followed by relatively muted moves in stock prices (the southeast quadrant).

We next looked for cyclical patterns in real estate prices themselves. We found, going back to 1971, a significant −0.35 correlation between the return in REIT prices in one year and the return two years later. When REITs gained 25 percent or more in a year, the gain falls to an average 8 percent two years later.

Eight declines in REIT prices occurred during the period from 1971 to 2001, and the REITs returned 24 percent, on average, two years later (see Table 12.3). Results show total return, including reinvested dividends and capital appreciation.

We Make a Bearish Call

In February 2002, we put these findings to use in the market. The divergence of some 65 percentage points in favor of the REITs in the period 2000 to 2002 had been the greatest in recorded history. Not only were real estate prices at a high, but business conditions were at a low, the September 11, 2001, destruction of the World Trade Center having exacerbated an economic pullback that had been under way since March.

Table 12.3 Annual REIT Returns Two Years after Decline

Period	REIT Return (%)	Period	REIT Return (%)	REIT Return Two Years after Decline (%)
Dec-01	16.0			
Dec-00	26.0			
Dec-99	−6.0	Dec-01	16.0	16.0
Dec-98	−19.0	Dec-00	26.0	26.0
Dec-97	19.0	Dec-99	−6.0	
Dec-96	36.0	Dec-98	−19.0	
Dec-95	18.0	Dec-97	19.0	
Dec-94	1.0	Dec-96	36.0	
Dec-93	19.0	Dec-95	18.0	
Dec-92	12.0	Dec-94	1.0	
Dec-91	36.0	Dec-93	19.0	
Dec-90	−17.0	Dec-92	12.0	12.0
Dec-89	−2.0	Dec-91	36.0	36.0
Dec-88	11.0	Dec-90	−17.0	
Dec-87	−11.0	Dec-89	−2.0	−2.0
Dec-86	19.0	Dec-88	11.0	
Dec-85	6.0	Dec-87	−11.0	
Dec-84	15.0	Dec-86	19.0	
Dec-83	25.0	Dec-85	6.0	
Dec-82	32.0	Dec-84	15.0	
Dec-81	9.0	Dec-83	25.0	
Dec-80	28.0	Dec-82	32.0	
Dec-79	31.0	Dec-81	9.0	
Dec-78	−2.0	Dec-80	28.0	28.0
Dec-77	19.0	Dec-79	31.0	
Dec-76	49.0	Dec-78	−2.0	
Dec-75	36.0	Dec-77	19.0	
Dec-74	−42.0	Dec-76	49.0	49.0
Dec-73	−27.0	Dec-75	36.0	36.0
Dec-72	11.0	Dec-74	−42.0	
Dec-71		Dec-73	−27.0	
		Dec-72	11.0	
		Dec-71		

Source: Niederhoffer Investments.

In 2002, dividends of REITs were averaging 7 percent a year. These dividends obviously looked very good compared with alternative yields of about 1.5 percent on stocks and 2 percent on Treasury bills. Advocates for REITs point to dividends as an overriding positive for the industry. Yet this same argument was made in 1987, when REITs underperformed the S&P 500 by some 50 percent. It seemed clear to us that highly leveraged REITs would be unable to maintain their current dividend payouts in a weak real estate market. After all, office vacancies in 2001 had increased at the greatest rate on record and were widely expected to be heading to heights unseen since the late 1980s—levels that had been followed by dismal performance for REITs, bankruptcies, and related bank failures. At year-end 2001, the national office vacancy rate was 13.1 percent, up from 6.2 percent in the third quarter of 2000. The Grub & Ellis brokerage was projecting a 15 percent vacancy rate by the end of 2002.

Increasing vacancies are a crucial negative signal. A definitive PricewaterhouseCoopers study indicates that rising vacancy rates are the most accurate signals of a decline in prices. The study was based on 20 years of prices for every major metropolitan statistical area broken down by type (i.e., office, apartment, industrial, residential, hotel, and warehouse). Numerous academic studies backed up the conclusions of PricewaterhouseCoopers.

We saw numerous other early warning signs that REITs were headed for a decline:

- **Fuzzy accounting:** A report from Green Street Advisors, the most scholarly and studious firm in the field, found evidence that REIT funds for operations, the measure most investors look at, were lower in 2001 than in 2000, but that some REITs were excluding nonrecurring charges and write-offs from their financial statements, making results appear better than they were.[9] We feared that some REITs, especially highly leveraged ones, would not be able to maintain their dividend payouts in a weak real estate market.
- **Popular books:** A trip to the local Barnes & Noble revealed that real estate was the hot new growth area in the financial publishing industry. *Investing in Real Estate,*[10] *Rich Dad, Poor Dad,*[11] and *J.K. Lasser's Real Estate Investing*[12] were selling particularly well. Because of the long lead times involved in writing and publishing, book sales tend to be a lagging indicator of what is likely to make money. We were reminded of the rash of Dow 40,000 and day-trading books that proliferated at the millennium, just before the stock market's debacle.
- **S&P 500 membership:** The arbiters of Standard & Poor's, after intensive lobbying from the real estate industry, added three REITs to the

S&P 500 Index in late 2001 and early 2002: Equity Office Properties, Equity Residential Properties, and Plum Creek Timber Company. As our colleague and CNBC Money editor Jon Markman has shown, however, stocks removed from the index typically outperform the ones that are added.[13]

- **Doc Greenspan:** The much-venerated Fed chairman had been tooting the horn for real estate, noting in his February 28, 2001, monetary policy report to Congress that the wealth effect from rising residential real estate values had cushioned the economy from the violent declines in consumer spending triggered by layoffs and the drop in the stock market. We could not help but wonder why a wealth effect from real estate values was more virtuous than a wealth effect from Nasdaq stocks, which had elicited the chairman's full firepower in 1999–2000. We had also learned to be wary of Greenspan's Mr. Magoo-like knack for bad timing. His sightings of irrational exuberance in the stock market in December 1996 at Dow 6437 and inflationary danger in the market in 2000, well past the end of the capital spending boom that engendered the Nasdaq's rise, are only two outstanding examples.

A January 31, 2002, *Wall Street Journal* article noted that 2001 had brought the sharpest jump in office vacancies ever recorded.[14] On top of all this, well-connected, highly respected firms with every reason to be as friendly as possible to the REIT industry were beginning to lower their opinions of real estate's prospects. Merrill Lynch, in a December 19 research comment, saw "muted price appreciation" in "this late-cycle sector."

Wrath of the REIT Advocates

Despite all these warning signs, REIT shares had held up extraordinarily well. At the end of February, the Bloomberg REIT Index was still up 17 percent from its year-earlier level. All things considered, it seemed like a good time for us to predict that a decline in REIT prices was imminent. Yet when we presented our findings in a series of columns for CNBC Money in February and March 2002,[15] we were vilified like never before in our career. Letters from the REIT industry poured in for us and our bosses. Some samples of our e-mails:

> Victor, Victor, Victor . . . It was with horror that I read the piece that you and Laurel wrote on REITs. . . . Your article belongs in the trash compactor! (Barry Vinocur, editor-in-chief, *Realty Stock Review and Property* magazine)

> Your REIT article was the most poorly researched and written article on this sector in the past eight years. . . . I'm not alone in this view. I've spoken to ten institutional clients this morning who are all incredulous that this article saw the light of day. (Louis W. Taylor, senior real estate analyst, Deutsche Bank Alex Brown)

Mr. Taylor added that the industry's reaction to our article indicated our "incredible arrogance, unprofessionalism, and cowardice," and that we and our editors were all a disgrace to our profession.

Those comments were typical of what we received from experts who know infinitely more about the subject than we do. We also received a raft of critical comments from what appeared to us to be more typical readers, such as:

> It is people like you that create panic and people begin to sell. I hope your poor judgment falls on deaf ears.

The article elicited some notice on the Motley Fool real estate message board, where "fatuous" was a typical comment. Our credentials received considerable negative scrutiny—it was noted with derision that Laurel had been an aerospace reporter and that Vic had played squash. "This guy is as bad a columnist as he was a hedge-fund operator," one wrote. We would have added only that most of the companies Laurel covered from 1989–1994 had been sold off, and that the hardball squash game that Vic ruled for a decade is extinct.

Untimely Optimism

The torrent of vituperation directed at us is instructive in many ways. As economists who study the subject invariably conclude, contractions are likeliest just when developers and banks are most convinced that business conditions warrant expansion. Real estate decisions take a relatively long time to reach the marketplace, and when they do, it is all too likely that conditions will have changed dramatically. Rent rates and demands fall at the same time. Similarly, just when investors are most optimistic about real estate securities, the peak is near. The psychological bias at fault in these upheavals is called the "recency effect." The last few levels and the last few changes are remembered too vividly, to the exclusion of other changes that have since faded from memory. A related problem in decision making is the human proclivity for going along with the herd at exactly the time it would be appropriate to stand alone.

Even those who agreed with us had bones to pick. Ron Kaiser reviewed our work and pointed out that we omitted "the single most impressive reason for being bearish: REITs usually trade at about 20 percent below net asset value, and they are currently closer to 100 percent of NAV."

More typical was the disagreement of William Wheaton, a principal in the respected Torto Wheaton real estate consulting firm, source of the best statistics of office vacancies and completions going back to 1967. In a February interview, he told us he believes that the real estate markets are "really healthy." He predicted an upturn spurred by economic recovery in the middle of this year.

But office vacancies continued to climb in the third quarter. On September 19, 2002, Torto Wheaton predicted that demand would not rebound until mid-2003.[16]

Jon Fosheim, cofounder of Green Street Advisors, an independent research house that produced a study we had cited approvingly, also found many areas of disagreement with us. Fosheim noted that while REITs had had two very good years, this followed on the heels of two years of underperformance, and that REITs had done about as well as the S&P over the past 5- and 10-year time frames. He emphasized that while his firm had indeed noted accounting hocus-pocus, nothing suggested that REITs were any worse in this area than other companies. His most important quarrel with us was the contrary evidence provided by "the collective opinions of thousands of investors on Main Street who risk their capital every day buying and selling real estate . . . we place high faith in their opinions as to how to price REITs." Apparently Fosheim, whose clients include major mutual fund firms, institutional investors, and REITs themselves, was not overly enthused by our conclusion that REITs were headed for a sharp contraction.

We were reminded of the old Hungarian proverb that, roughly translated, means, "The more he talks about his honesty, the more I check my change." This would seem to apply when industry analysts talk about correcting negative statistical information.

The Ground Shifts

Purely by coincidence, of course, and without citing us, the *Wall Street Journal* ran an article on Monday, February 25, 2002, entitled "Commercial Real Estate May Damp the Economy."[17] After reciting a litany of negatives that made our own piece sound quite muted by comparison, whom should they trot out to confirm the negative but Green Street Advisors. "We haven't seen the bottom," Green Street analyst John Lutzius told the *Journal*. "Quite a lot of jobs were lost in the last quarter of 2001, and that may not be reflected yet in the vacancy and rent statistics."

Doubtless because of our shocking bearish views, Laurel was asked to defend our position on Money Matters Radio Network. Talk show host Barry Alexander, president of the $2.5 billion New England Advisory Group, said right off that he had been telling people since 1997 to buy REITs. Perhaps as a sop, the show's detail man later told Laurel he liked what we said about the vacancy factor. "We are located in an office park. Two years ago you would have to circle the parking lot forever to find a parking space, or park in the overflow lot well over a football field away. Today, you can park almost anywhere you like at any time of day. Also, the 'space for lease' signs are popping up faster than the crocuses."

We felt vindicated when REIT indexes dived two months after we ran our initial article on February 14, 2002. Between April 12, 2002, and October 9, 2002, the Bloomberg Office REIT Index fell 24 percent.

Altogether, the developments in REITs reminded us of the remarkable week in March 2000 when Vic received five proposals, including two from his daughters, to fund Internet companies. We promptly predicted a crash in Internet stocks, based on the law of supply and demand, in a column that turned out to be our last for the publicly held Internet site we were then writing for. The crash came as if on cue; thestreet.com's Internet index, DOT, peaked on March 10, 2000, and by mid-2002 had lost 95 percent of its value.

The near-unanimous negative sentiment that our article on REITs elicited is all too typical of what happens at market peaks. Such virulent reactions explain why the public consistently loses, over and over again, much more 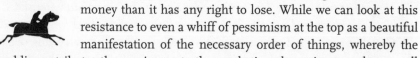 money than it has any right to lose. While we can look at this resistance to even a whiff of pessimism at the top as a beautiful manifestation of the necessary order of things, whereby the public contributes the maximum to the market's upkeep, it was sad to see all these forces once again coalescing to induce all too many to ruination.

13 MARKET THERMODYNAMICS

Nature's rules rules apply for all particles and interactions.

—Gordon Kane, *Supersymmetry: Unveiling the Ultimate Laws of Nature*[1]

Most weeks, Vic knows exactly how his youngest daughter, Kira, spends her time. There are four hours a day when she is not at school, eating, or sleeping. In those four hours, she has to complete an hour of sports (usually a game of squash with Daddy), an hour of ballet, and an hour of piano practice. She also has an hour for play, which she often spends diving for dollars with friends in the pool.

The distribution of these pastimes can be expressed by a simple formula, which we shall call the Kira Equation:

$$Sports + Ballet + Piano + Diving = 4$$

Occasionally, Kira requests that she be allowed to trade ballet practice for sports, or what have you, and being an agreeable father, Vic is always amenable. But he insists that she make up the deficit in the weeks thereafter.

Thus, by counting how many hours Kira has spent on any three activities, Vic can figure out how many she has spent on the other one. And by looking at Kira's activity record in one week, Vic can generally predict the distribution of her activities in the weeks to come.

The Kira Equation was inspired by an ingenious example invented by the Nobel Prize winner Richard Feynman. In Feynman's story, a mother is hunting for wooden blocks missing from her son's 28-piece set. She uses some clever calculations of mass to discover all the hiding places: a little locked box, the space under the bed, and the fish tank, where the water level was the giveaway. Feynman used the example to illustrate the law of conservation of energy, one of two basic physical laws (the other being the law of entropy). The laws of conservation of energy and entropy are the cornerstones of our understanding of everything that happens in the physical world and much else in life.

But what does physics have to do with the understanding the market? It can be as useful as it is in helping Vic guide Kira in making the most of her time.

Market Experiments versus "Market Feel"

 Many traders tell us that they base trading decisions on their "feel" for the market. Unfortunately, we have no market feel and are forced to compensate by using scientific research and methods to help with our decisions. Our own trading style has been developed over four decades of continuous use of the scientific method.

Of the many ways people have devised over the centuries to understand humanity's place in the cosmos, science holds a special place. In essence, science is a process of inquiry designed to ask and answer questions about the great principles underlying the physical world. Progress in science has led to enormous increases in human betterment. One of the best things people can do to improve their investing results and their lives is to become familiar with the truth-seeking method that has permitted these achievements: gathering facts, discovering regularities and patterns, forming theories, and testing predictions. Odd though it may seem, given the scientific method's successes, the investment field has not universally embraced it. Thomas Kuhn observed in his 1962 classic, *The Structure of Scientific Revolution,* that science does not always progress smoothly. Members of the old guard tend to resist ideas that threaten paradigms on which their livelihoods and reputations are based. Too often, a new theory's acceptance results not from acclamation, but from funerals.

This regrettable tendency to reject fresh insights shows up in spades among market gurus. In science, great breakthroughs are often made by scientists attempting to verify theories that turn out to be untrue. The first capacitor, the Leyden jar—a device that could store large amounts of electrical charge—was invented by Pieter van Musschenbroek, a physicist and mathematician in Leyden, Netherlands, as he tried to prove the fluid theory of electricity, which turned out to be a fallacy. This fruitful trial-and-error method is seldom practiced in the investment field, however, because few propositions are ever stated in verifiable form. Francis Bacon is credited with saying, "Truth emerges more readily from error than from confusion." Too much market forecasting is built on a framework of confusion akin to the forecasts of palm readers and storefront psychics. Kuhn's summing-up of the state of optics before Newton is apropos: "[O]ne may well conclude that, though the field's practitioners were scientists, the net result of their activity was something less than science."

In sticking to the scientific method, we have attempted to follow in the footsteps of generations of scientists who sought the spark for new ideas from the stores of knowledge accumulated in other disciplines. Although academic science is conventionally divided into the four major disciplines of physics, chemistry, biology, and earth sciences, the natural world recognizes no such boundaries. Inventions and concepts often resonate far beyond their field of origination. The invention of the microscope, a triumph of optics, opened up for biologists and chemists worlds of objects invisible to the naked eye. Einstein's grasp of geometry and certain invariances of right-angle triangles led to his discovery of the theory of relativity. Such cross-pollination among disparate fields is so frequent and important that we have collected some outstanding examples in Table 13.1.

Social sciences, too, have benefited from cross-pollination. Adam Smith, the Newton of economics, modeled his idea of the invisible hand on a parable by the Dutch poet Bernard de Mandeville, *The Fable of the Bees; or, Private Vices, Publick Benefits*. Given the accelerating pace of interaction among the sciences, it is likely that more and more great discoveries will be made within a few generations as scientists apply rules and ideas from other fields to their own. Entirely new disciplines can be expected to emerge. We already have seen the sciences of optics, electricity, and magnetism merge into electrodynamics, then combine in turn with other strands of knowledge into modern particle physics. Is it possible to think of a surgeon in 50 years' time who will be unfamiliar with genetics, electronics, and computer science?

Can investment in stocks be guided by fundamental concepts used to explain the structure and energy of matter? We think so. Experiments already are

Table 13.1   Idea Transfers

William Harvey	**Blood circulation** William Harvey, physician to James I and Charles I of England, discovered that the heart pumped blood through the body and that veins contained valves, a model drawn from the principles of hydraulics.	1628
Alessandro Volta	**The electric battery** Volta theorized that electricity was created by the difference in potentials between two dissimilar metals after reading about the involuntary twitching of a dissected frog's leg when it came into contact with two different metals.	1800
Horace Wells	**Anesthetics** Wells, a dentist, was observing people inhaling laughing gas at a carnival, when one man fell and injured himself. Remarkably, he did not appear to experience pain. Wells decided laughing gas might be useful in his dental practice.	1844
Louis Pasteur	**Left-handed and right-handed molecules** Pasteur noticed that salts of racemic and tartaric acids had different effects on polarized light. This led to his discovery that organic compounds exist in mirror image forms at the molecular level.	1848
Elihu Thompson	**Welding with electricity** In an experiment to demonstrate the movement of electricity as a spark, Thompson noticed two wires had fused, welded together.	1876
Hilaire de Chardonnet	**Rayon** Chardonnet, while developing photographic plates, spilled one of the chemicals. Wiping it up, he noticed it made silk-like strands. Within six years he had produced artificial silk (Rayon) from collodion.	1891
Wilhelm Röntgen	**X-rays** Röntgen's studies with cathode ray tubes led to the discovery of X-rays.	1895
Henri Becquerel	**Radioactivity** Becquerel discovered radioactivity while investigating substances made phosphorescent by visible light.	1896

Table 13.1 *Continued*

Alexander Fleming	**Penicillin**	1928
	Here's an example of a cross-fertilization that literally drifted in. Fleming was growing a plate of Staphylococcus bacteria when a spore of a rare *Penicillium notatum* mold wafted up from a lab studying fungi one floor below. When Fleming returned from vacation two weeks later, the Staph bacteria were flourishing, except for the spot where the penicillin mold had taken hold.	
Watson, Crick, Wilkins, and Franklin	**DNA double helix** Combined insights from biology, physics, chemistry, and x-ray crystallography led to the discovery of DNA's form.	1962

proceeding. Charles Sanford, a former president of Bankers Trust, developed a concept he dubbed "particle finance" based on the science of the particles that make up matter. Sanford identifies and splits the different risks embodied in a single financial instrument to gain protection from the unpredictability of financial events—the equivalent of chaotic phenomena in physics. A practitioner of particle finance, instead of simply buying the collection of risks called a bond, might choose a different risk mix. His portfolio might consist of X amount of credit risk, Y amount of exchange risk, and so on.[2]

In another experiment, Charbel Tannous and Alain Fessant of the Universite de Bretagne Occidentale in Brest, Belgium, used combustion models from high-energy physics to predict future values of stocks. The professors observed that some stocks tend to jump suddenly after a long period of stability, in the same way that combustion sometimes seems to occur spontaneously. Noting that ignition takes place when fuel concentration reaches a certain level, the professors modified fuel combustion equations by replacing fuel concentration with share prices of real companies.[3]

Money as Energy

Markets are filled with different energies and transfers. Money can be viewed as energy, efficiently moving from person to person in free capital markets. Like energy, money exists in many different forms: currency, land, goods, stocks, and bonds, to name a few. Commerce transfers this wealth around the world from person to person and country to country in a circular flow of goods, labor, land, and capital between households and businesses. This simple model can be expanded to include the effects of government and international trade. Just as potential energy exists in the world of physics, potential wealth energy exists in the form of oil wells yet undiscovered, seeds stored in farmers' sheds, and technologies visualized in inventors' minds.

In physics, the concept of energy transfer is expressed in the first two laws of thermodynamics.

These special laws provide the foundation for all other laws governing the physical world. They are fundamental to understanding not just physics, but life. In the following pages, we set forth some variations on the themes embodied in these two great laws.

The First Law of Thermodynamics: Conservation of Energy

The first law of thermodynamics—conservation of energy—has nothing to do with preserving trees, avoiding gas guzzlers, or turning off the lights when leaving the house. In essence, the first law says that while all real-world processes involve transformations of energy, the total amount of energy stays constant, or is "conserved." The first published expression of the law came in 1842, when Julius Robert Mayer, a German physician, asserted that energy could not be destroyed, only transformed. Mayer demonstrated the equivalence of heat and other forms of energy. Albert Einstein extended Mayer's work in the twentieth century by showing that matter and energy also are equivalent.

Social scientists such as Herbert Spencer used the conservation concept to develop a theory of human society. Marxists appropriated it in an attempt to bolster the fallacious argument that economics is a zero-sum game. For purposes of practical speculation, the first law provides an excellent working model of financial markets, with numerous fruitful hypotheses and insights into market forces.

Conservation of Energy, Variation 1: The Kira Equation

Let's go back to Vic's daughter, Kira, and the equation of her extracurricular activities. We will substitute U.S. bonds for Ballet, U.S. stocks for Sports, German bonds for Piano (in honor of Beethoven), and the U.S. dollar for Diving.

We will move from the realm of time, where Kira's minutes add up, to that of two-dimensional counterbalancing moves in market prices. When the Kira Equation is applied to markets, the movements in bonds, stocks, German bonds, and the dollar in a period sum to zero. For those who follow the market on a day-by-day basis, the idea is somewhat intuitive: Time and time again, a strong move in the bonds is counterbalanced by an equal and opposite move in stocks.

Next, we separate out two elements in the equation: daily moves in bonds and stocks over the last five years. The correlation between the two is shown in Figure 13.1. There is a slight positive correlation between the two.

The counterbalancing holds true from week to week. As illustrated in Figure 13.2, when U.S. bonds are up more than two points in one week, then the S&P 500 tends to go up 3.5 points in the next week.

The predictive connection between stocks and bonds illustrated by the scatter diagrams in Figures 13.1 and 13.2 is one of the most useful regularities that we have discovered in many hundreds of thousands of hours in studying such interrelations. For traders, a few points a week in the S&P 500 adds up to pretty big money over time. After all, 11 percent a year, compounded continuously over 20 years, amounts to an eightfold increase.

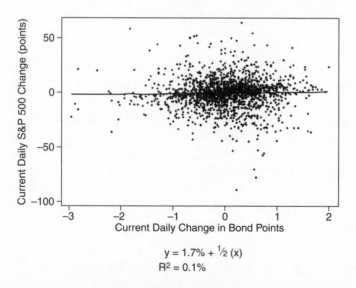

$$y = 1.7\% + \tfrac{1}{2}(x)$$
$$R^2 = 0.1\%$$

Figure 13.1 Correlation of Daily Moves in U.S. Bonds and U.S. Stocks, July 1994–May 2001. *Source:* Niederhoffer Investments.

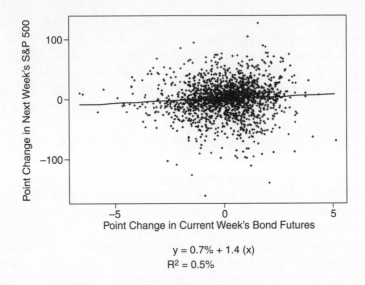

$$y = 0.7\% + 1.4\ (x)$$
$$R^2 = 0.5\%$$

Figure 13.2   Correlation of Weekly Moves in U.S. Bonds and Stocks, July 1994–May 2001. *Source:* **Niederhoffer Investments.**

Moreover, the results are highly significant from a statistical standpoint; mean changes this far from zero are less likely than 1 in 1,000 to have been obtained by chance variations alone.

The total amount of energy in the market is constant vis-à-vis the closed system of bonds and stocks. It is possible to exchange between time periods, borrowing, if you will, from the total energy, with a certain lag for repayment. Einstein's special theory of relativity casts further light on these borrowings and repayments. The special theory explains that mass and energy are equivalent and that energy is forever being converted to mass and then back again. When you wind a watch, the spring's mass increases ever so slightly as energy is stored in it. As the spring unwinds, this barely perceptible amount of mass is converted back to energy. The market, too, can "store" energy. The energy, however, must always be repaid, just as Kira must make up a missed piano practice session in subsequent weeks.

Conservation of Energy, Variation 2: Disappearing Money

Hope springs eternal for humans. Well it should, given the human capacity to improve well-being and happiness, as evidenced by the contributions to civilization of such giants as Leonardo da Vinci, Isaac Newton, and Thomas

Edison. The everlasting, renewable nature of hope seems to be a necessary ingredient to our ability to deal with the hardships and disappointments of life. And nowhere do we see hope better exemplified than when we turn on our television after a dismal period for stocks and find an attractive reporter removing her glasses and saying, "Tech is back!"

Perhaps Intel just reported better-than-forecast earnings, prompting a buying rush among investors. The resulting price rise in Intel makes other stocks in the tech sector relatively cheap, and money comes in to buy these as well. The process continues, sometimes for years, as it did in the 1990s, when a tremendous river of money flowed into the field from savings accounts, money-market funds, and foreign investors, and the Nasdaq rose from 374 to 4069.

More important than any particular company's earnings report in this process is an underlying perception that technology is good, that profits are available, and that entrepreneurship leads to a beneficial horn of plenty that is constantly being replenished for investors, suppliers, customers, and employees.

Ah, but always the seed of discontent. Enthusiasm has a tendency to wax and wane. Ultimately, potential energy in the world of savings, alternative investments, or even credit card borrowings will be drawn down to the point that there won't be enough to continue the rise or even to sustain the rise that has taken place. At that point, confidence is shaken and doubts that had long seemed unrealistic suddenly assume an alarming aspect.

The events of 2000, discussed in the introduction to Part One, illustrate this well. When the point of maximum drawdown of potential energy was reached in early 2000, the chairman of the Federal Reserve, who had been concerned with irrational exuberance for more than three years, chose that inopportune time to ratchet up the federal funds rate from 5.50 percent to 6.50 percent. The increase was accomplished in three steps. The first two increases, of one quarter-point each, took place February 2 and March 21. The final, half-point increase was made May 16—after the Nasdaq had already fallen 26 percent from the high of 10 weeks earlier. Confronted by the powerful force of the Fed, large investors who had recently converted to tech began selling their inflated holdings. New tech firms had only lately been besieged by investment bankers seeking the privilege of underwriting their initial public offerings. Suddenly they found it impossible to sell stock. Without capital, they could not order equipment. Manufacturers of the equipment saw a precipitous drop-off in orders. Tech shares fell, so the public withdrew money from tech and put it into growth stocks. When growth stocks began to succumb, the public bought value stocks. When the revered value investor of Omaha allowed in his annual letter to shareholders on February 28, 2002, that he had "decidedly lukewarm feelings about the prospects for stocks in general over the next decade or so," the public began to convert any remaining shareholdings into cash—and waited for the attractive TV reporter to stop furrowing her brow and start removing her eyeglasses again.

The same sort of transfers happens constantly in the natural world. The sun generates energy, a plant uses the energy to make sugar, a jackrabbit eats the plant, a coyote eats the rabbit, the coyote dies, and nutrients from the carcass leach into the soil to become fertilizer for plants.

The important thing to know is that at any point in such stories, the quantity of mass and energy is exactly what it was at the start. Any amount that seems to have gone missing can be found somewhere.

The conservation of energy law is helpful, for example, in deflating fallacious news reports about the trillions of dollars that "disappeared," "evaporated," or "vanished" in stock market declines. Money, like energy, does not disappear; it always goes somewhere. From its peak in March 2000 to the lows of October 2002, the U.S. stock market, as measured by the inclusive Wilshire 5000 index, lost 50 percent of its value, or $8.15 trillion, based on Wilshire Associates' formula of $1.1 billion per point. But the money did not disappear. For every investor who bought at the top, a seller on the other side of the trade got out at the top.

Our story about the attractive TV reporter is a qualitative tale about a single move in a single market. Other explanations could be developed. The stories regarding the markets of other countries and other periods of U.S. history would doubtless be different. Our model is not an exact depiction of all the forces that affect markets. All models are necessarily simplifications of reality. The key question for any particular model is whether it leads to fruitful predictions and insights, and then based on tests of these, whether it is possible to develop a better model.

The amazing thing about the model that we have posited is that many of the specific regularities embodied in it appear to be consistent with actual relations that have appeared during the past 20 years.

Conservation of Energy, Variation 3: Where Does Money for IPOs Come From?

Assume that money available to buy stocks is fixed, and that it depends to a significant degree on the money taken up by initial public offerings. Money to buy new stocks must come from somewhere. A good working model is that it comes from the money that would otherwise be available to buy stocks that already exist. And that leads to a working hypothesis:

- When IPOs are numerous, little money is available to buy existing stock.
- When IPOs are few, much money is available to buy existing stock.

In fact, declines in IPOs are highly bullish. Figure 13.3 shows the total number of IPOs in each of the past 20 years contrasted with the S&P's performance.

Statistically speaking, the correlation between the change in the number of IPOs in one year and the percentage change in the market the next year is −36 percent—a strong negative association that reminds us of the transfers of energy we see in the bounce of a ball or the movements of a roller coaster, something that market participants are all too familiar with these days.

We next looked at the correlation between the total dollar value of IPOs and market results in the next year, and found similar results going back to 1991, the earliest year for which data were available. The correlation was −33 percent.

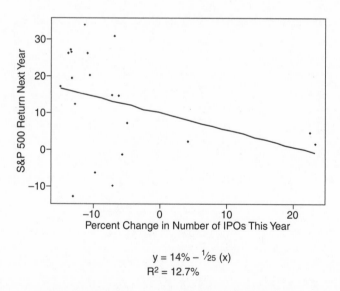

$$y = 14\% - \tfrac{1}{25}(x)$$
$$R^2 = 12.7\%$$

Figure 13.3   Fewer IPOs Lead to Better Market Performance. *Source:* **Niederhoffer Investments.**

Conservation of Energy, Variation 4: Transformations of Energy

In considering energy in nature or markets, it is helpful to think of potential energy, on the one hand, and "working" transformations of energy, on the other. Active forms of energy include kinetic, chemical, electric, electromagnetic, elastic (as in a bouncing ball), nuclear, heat, and sound.

Money available to buy stocks may be thought of as a form of potential energy. When cash piles up in money-market accounts and investment in stocks dwindles, as it did in 2001 and 2002, the situation is similar to a pendulum pausing at the top of its arc. At that moment, the energy seems to have disappeared. In reality, it is there in potential form and quite likely to be converted into movement.

When movement begins, one possible route is into equity funds. At the beginning of 2002, the ratio of assets in equity funds relative to money market funds was 1.5, close to a four-year low of 1.4. A high of 2.6 occurred in the spring of 2000 just as the market was embarking on its terrible 18-month descent.

Our study of the equity/money-market ratio indicates that the best prediction for the return the next month as determined by regression analysis is 5.8 percent less 2.4 percent multiplied by the level of the ratio (see Figure 13.4).

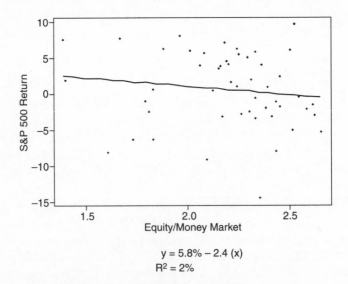

$$y = 5.8\% - 2.4\,(x)$$
$$R^2 = 2\%$$

Figure 13.4   Equity/Money-Money Ratio as a Predictor of Next Month's S&P 500 Return. *Source:* **Niederhoffer Investments.**

The Second Law of Thermodynamics: Entropy

In the middle of the nineteenth century, Rudolf Clausius and William Thomson (Lord Kelvin) formulated the second law of thermodynamics—entropy. In essence, the law says that whenever an energy distribution is out of equilibrium, a potential force exists that the world spontaneously dissipates or minimizes. Clausius coined the term "entropy" to refer to the dissipated potential. Whereas the first law explains that the total amount of energy remains constant, the second law observes that the world is inherently active, always acting to minimize potential (or, to say the same thing in a different way, to maximize entropy).

The second law is easy to demonstrate empirically. Place a glass of hot water in a cold room. Heat from the water will spontaneously dissipate into the room until the temperatures of water and room are the same. Thus, the potential energy of the water's heat is minimized, and entropy is maximized.

Entropy, Variation 1: Maximization of Transfers

The stock market, too, has a way of maximizing entropy: It transfers wealth. The percentage of NYSE stocks traded that close unchanged on an average day is about 2 percent, much higher than would be predicted by chance. The stock price moves in such a way that it maximizes entropy while going nowhere. This holds true for longer periods as well. When a stock has a big move in the beginning of a week, the best guess for the second half is exactly the opposite.

The types of orders used by traders are comparable to different forms of energy. Market orders can be compared to kinetic energy, while limit orders and stops correspond to potential energy. A sharp up move triggers stop loss orders. After the usual retracement, the market encounters less resistance on its next rise, and is able to move up with greater ease. That is why double and triple tops tend not to hold. The removal of limit orders maximizes the entropy in the system.

To illustrate, take any ordinary piece of paper and crumple it in your hand. As the paper crumples, energy is stored in all the creases. These resist the force you are exerting. If you can overcome this resistance, the crumpled ball of paper must collapse, forming more and more creases and points. Eventually, the energy stored in the crumpled ball will be so great that you would need to exert a huge force just to make it even slightly smaller. Thanks to research being carried out on this phenomenon, scientists may better be able to understand how a blood cell's membrane contorts to pass through the smallest capillaries, how a car's bumper absorbs the energy of a crash, and how the earth's tectonic plates collide and buckle to form a mountain range. This phenomenon also appears in markets. Sharp downward moves in prices require a lot of energy. When these sharp movements occur, the energy required to take the price lower is so great that prices tend to take the path of least resistance and move up.

Entropy, Variation 2: Friction and Heat Dissipation

Friction is an obvious example of entropy in everyday life. As with any real-world system, some of the energy in the market is not captured by the trader, but is dissipated in the form of friction. In the market world, perhaps $15 billion a year is extracted by the infrastructure in the form of bid-asked spreads, brokers' commissions, and National Futures Association fees.

The profitability of the market infrastructure may be gauged by the value of seats on major trading exchanges. The number of seats on the New York Stock Exchange, American Stock Exchange, Chicago Mercantile Exchange, Chicago Board Options Exchange, Chicago Board of Trade, and New York Mercantile Exchange totals more than 8,000, with a combined value in early 2002, based on the most recent seat sales, of $6.4 billion (see Table 13.2).

Average people who do average things are the ones who make seat ownership a lucrative business. If you conform to all the customs in the markets, you will be a valued contributor.

Different traders must deal with different amounts of friction, depending on their place in the infrastructure. Friction is minimal for a trader on the

Table 13.2   Value of Seats on Selected U.S. Exchanges

Exchange	Number of Seats	Last Sale Price ($)	Date
NYSE	1,366	2.5 million	Feb. 2002
AMEX	203 (options)	300,000	Feb. 2002
AMEX	661 (regular)	270,000	March 2002
CBOT	1,402 (full)	400,000	March 2002
CME	625 (full voting)	800,000	Jan. 2002
CME-Index and options market division	1,287 (voting)	550,000	March 2002
CME-International monetary market division	813 (voting)	380,000	Feb. 2002
CBOE	930	365,000	Jan. 2002
NYMEX	816	875,000	Jan. 2002

Source: NYSE, National Association of Securities Dealers, Chicago Mercantile Exchange, Chicago Board of Trade, Bloomberg News.

floor of an exchange and is highest for retail customers who enter trades through a traditional brokerage firm. A trade that is profitable for floor traders or institutional traders may be a losing proposition for retail investors. An easy way to improve your returns in the market is to reduce trading expenses. There are many ways to do this. Start by negotiating lower commissions, or by finding a discount broker. High-volume day traders, who typically pay very low commissions but nevertheless pay out 50 percent of their profits as commissions, should consider adjusting their trading style. High-cost investments such as load-bearing mutual funds, foreign securities that require higher commissions, penny stocks, and structured notes are best avoided in favor of less expensive alternatives.

Entropy, Variation 3: Sector Rotation and Maximum Entropy Production

The reader may wonder why, if the law of entropy rules the market, some sectors manage to stay "hot" for long periods. A similar apparent conflict exists in science, where physics says energy dissipates, while biology observes that life tends to become more ordered.

The answer is that an ordered flow—a flame, for example—can be more efficient at dissipating energy potential than a disordered flow. In the market, hot sectors exist because they feed off potential energy in their environments. Once the sector matures and becomes predictable, quick profits disappear like a candle burning out.

A further everyday illustration of this principle, known as maximum entropy production, is provided by a pot of boiling water. Given the law of entropy, we might expect the movement of the water to be random and unpredictable. Instead, the movement is quite orderly. When the burner is turned on, the heated water at the bottom moves up the center of the pot to the surface. Some water escapes as steam, and the rest cools and moves back down to replace the hotter water rising to the surface. This orderly process efficiently transfers the heat from the gas burner into the atmosphere, thereby maximizing entropy.

The same principle allows the persistence of heat in certain sectors of the stock market, with happy consequences for some investors. Some mutual funds tend to invest in industries that are showing relatively strong performance and ride them until they lose steam. Mark Hulbert, dean of fund evaluation, concluded that these "sector rotation" funds outperformed the average mutual fund in the five years ending in 2001. We see no evidence as to whether the superior performance of sector-switchers will continue in the future, or whether their success was a by-product of the market conditions peculiar to the 1997–2001 period. At the end of November 2001, some $173 billion was invested in such funds, up from $92 billion in November 1997. Assets in industry-specific funds totaled less than $100 billion in late 1997; they peaked at $301 billion in August 2000.

We performed our own studies of sector rotation and found that the relative rankings of at least some classifications show negative correlation between years. From 1987 through 1998, the average annual move for a Nasdaq industry group after a year in which it suffered a 10 percent decline was +25 percent.

In 2000, and 2001, the reversals of fortunes in the performance of the S&P 500 Economic Groups were almost complete. The two best- and two worst-performing groups of 2000 switched places the following year, with the rank correlation between them −0.8 (with −1 being a perfect inversion).

This is consistent with the idea that a limited amount of energy is available for the purchase of stocks (the first law of thermodynamics), and with the key insight of the second law of thermodynamics, or the law of entropy, that the world acts spontaneously to release potential energy.

Entropy, Variation 4: The Law of Ever-Changing Cycles

An options-trading associate of ours, Leonard Kreicas, made some observations on the second law—entropy—in a January 3, 2002, post to the Spec List:

It seems generally when the investment community has figured out a sure-fire way to make money, the system collapses due to the law of entropy. Most commentators blame it on a random event, a 100-year flood. The market conditions now are all in a consensus for a 2002 stock market recovery, which means the bets have already been placed. What I'm expecting is a random event that sets the balloon to go off in a entirely different direction. When a balloon full of air is let go, it's impossible to predict which direction it will go as the air escapes. We do know that the process is very fast, follows a random path and increases entropy. The same could be said for markets as they lose air.

Entropy and diversification can be considered kin. In the late 1990s, the public had a mania with stocks. Figures showed record numbers of shareholders. This meant people were not putting money in bonds, savings accounts, gold, etc. They were concentrating their money in one asset class: Nasdaq stocks. The last two years showed the consequences. Perhaps now investors will diversify their portfolios. Put another way, entropy will increase. Mutual funds and brokers will keep on talking up stocks, but increasing entropy predicts money will randomize and spread out more. Maybe the euro, real estate and money markets will receive some funds as investors reduce risk. I can't predict the eventual distribution. However, when money rushes into one spot as it does during a bubble, eventually it bursts in a dramatic show of entropy.

Conclusion

The first two laws of thermodynamics are not the Holy Grail. They do not explain how a system operates or what causes it to change, either in physics or in finance. They do not account for psychic energy or productive energy—key elements in markets. They apply only to closed systems. They cannot address all the unpredictable ways in which potential energy can be converted to kinetic energy (or waste heat). There is a basic problem in measuring potential energy. As our friend Jack Tierney, a plainspoken Tennessee philosopher, says, "In the realms of biology and physics, it might be possible, but in a realm with Alan Greenspans and printing presses, you can't."

The laws of conservation and entropy are amazingly helpful, however, in making predictions in a world of seemingly constant change. The usefulness of any model is measured by the verifiability and falsifiability of its predictions. We believe that our applications of the laws of thermodynamics will be fruitful, although they certainly have many holes and many areas for improvement. As always, knowledge is acquired through continuing observations, experiments, and theoretical reasoning. The application of physics to investment has great potential.

14 PRACTICAL MARKET LESSONS FROM THE TENNIS COURT

In order to gain a win against me, you have to beat me in the opening, the middle game, and the endgame.

—Alexander Alekhine, Chess World Champion 1927–1935, 1937–1946

The roads to victory and defeat cross the same ground in games and financial markets. The fundamental goal in each pursuit is to win, given the resources brought to the table, expected edge, potential variability, duration of the game, and the point at which the game ends in victory or ruin.

It is no accident that games and trading are so similar. Games were created to mirror the crucial risk-reward decisions that we face in life, whether they relate to finance, marriage, jobs, education, or sports. As Paul Heyne points out in *The Economic Way of Thinking*, in a quote we cannot repeat too often, "Everyone who makes a decision in the absence of complete information about the future consequences of all available opportunities is a speculator. So everyone is a speculator."

Throughout my trading career, my experiences in competitive squash, tennis, and other racquet sports have provided me with a rich source of insights. I was undefeated for 10 years as U.S. squash champion, won a few national titles in paddleball, and was winner or finalist in a handful of state tennis and ping-pong tournaments. Steve "Hobo" Keeley, the holder of numerous national titles in paddleball and racquetball, kindly refers to me as the greatest all-round racquets player of all time, which may be stretching it some. I did defeat Marty Hogan, the greatest racquetball champion, in a world series of racquet sports a few years ago when I couldn't move more than a few steps because of a bad hip. True, Marty let up a bit. But here is Lesson 1: A player should never let up, in sports or in markets.

In this chapter, we point out what investors can learn from how champions prepare for and play their game.

Before the Game

Pick Your Spots

On the court: The beauty of both sports and markets is that you can choose when and where you want to play. If you are a tennis player, you might choose to stay away from the relatively uncontrolled conditions of grassy courts, the surface on which Goran Ivanisevic, who was not even seeded in the top 100, won Wimbledon.

In the market: According to the academics, the market enjoys a 10 percent annual upward drift, with random movements from all previous paths of price change. For those with satisfactory long-term staying power, buy-and-hold is therefore a winning strategy. Most people find it difficult to make two timing decisions that both carry above-average expectations. Additionally, a stake can be substantially reduced by capital gains taxes; ask any veteran day trader.

Even an old dog sometimes learns new tricks, though. If I have learned anything over the past several years, it is that opportunities resulting from substantial event-driven declines are occurring with increasing frequency—and conversely, there are certain times when it is best not to enter the market tournament. Certain indicators have proved reliable in identifying such times:

- An increase in the stock-bond ratio (the number of 30-year Treasury bonds it requires to "buy" the level of the current S&P 500 futures contract).
- A decline in the Chicago Board Options Exchange Volatility Index below 25.
- A 20-day high in stock futures.

Decide How Much Risk You Will Take

On the court: All great players will tell you that the thing they hate most is when an inferior opponent plays a risky game—creating confrontation, going for broke, going for the lines on every shot. That is the only way the better player can lose.

In one of my early squash tournaments, I played against Sam Howe, then U.S. champion. Sam called "one point set" at 14–14 in each of three consecutive games to fray my nerves. (Sam had the option of extending the game by three points, or letting the game be settled in the next point, "one point set.") I was not overly averse to risk, and won each game 15–14. What Sam did not appreciate fully is that younger players frequently react much better to handling risk. Older players are more fearful of not making it back should they fall behind the eight ball.

Art Bisguier, a chess grandmaster who has won every conceivable U.S. championship, tells the story of how he once made a sharp move in a game against then-world champion Tigran Petrosian, and Petrosian asked for a draw. Bisguier, who believed Petrosian had an edge, accepted, and then asked him why he offered a draw. Petrosian said rivals Mikhail Tal and Paul Keres were walking by and he was afraid that if did not accept Bisguier's challenge, they would consider him a coward—but if he did, he might get beaten. So he took the middle road. That was the right thing for a world champion to do. The bottom line is that when you have an edge, you should play a conservative game. When you do not have an edge, you need to take risks.

In the market: In speculation, the house almost always has the edge. The "house," of course, is the operator of the casino—the Nasdaq market maker, the NYSE specialist, the broker. That is why the speculator should go for big profits. Only the house can grind small profits day in and day out. If your gains are limited relative to your capital, then the only constant will be the vigorish extracted from you in commissions and bid-asked spreads: a sure formula for losing. That said, I do not advise crazy gambles. My own approach to risk taking is based on statistical analysis.

Have a Game Plan

On the court: Prepare before the game; there is no time once the play starts. I loved it when my opponent had to take an extra few minutes in the warm-up to practice a shot. I was always at the court two hours before I played. All good players know that the action during a game is too fast-paced to rely on improvisations. Practice and plan for all possible scenarios in advance; expect your opponent to have done the same.

In the market: Do all your studies at least two hours before the open. Run the various scenarios that can occur unexpectedly during the trading day. Prepare for the myriad situations that may result from a government or corporate announcement. Once a major contingency happens, there will be little time to think before you react. While you should always be aware that plans are subject to the law of ever-changing cycles, it is important to have a certain stick-to-it-iveness if your plan gives you an edge.

Have Sufficient Stamina

On the court: There are very few things you have complete control over in sports, but stamina is one element that is completely in your hands. After a match, it is also the one element you would hate to kick yourself for having let slide. Make your opponent beat you . . . do not beat yourself.

In the market: The larger your asset base relative to the fluctuations in your holdings, the better able you will be to take advantage of the situations when your studies tell you that you have the edge.

Have Backup Equipment

On the court: No matter what, if you do not have the proper equipment, you are a sure loser. Good tennis players can be observed carrying six identical racquets to their matches, each one strung to the same tension. Strings and racquets have a way of breaking down, and if they do, the change to unfamiliar equipment can be calamitous.

One of my favorite squash victories occurred against Mike Desaulniers during the Canadian Open in Toronto in 1975. After the game, I struck up a conversation with Mike's mother:

> **Vic:** Mrs. Desaulniers, your son did very well. One little point would have made the whole difference in the match.

Mrs. D: Yes, I was very proud of him. I thought he did pretty well considering he lost his racquets yesterday and was playing with borrowed shafts.

Vic: In that case, Mrs. D, we'll give your boy a "but-for" victory on that one.

In the market: How many traders do you know who have confided to you that they lost a fortune when their Internet connection went down, their broker's line was busy, or, worst of all, they were engaging in an activity they were unwilling to interrupt by indelicately answering the telephone?

During the Game

You have picked your spot, you have decided how much risk to take, you have laid plans for every possible scenario, you have enough in reserve to keep you from going under, and you have your equipment and backup plan in order. Now you have to play the match; and in my book, the first blow is nine-tenths of the game.

Win the First Point

On the court: In squash, the accepted strategy used to be to save the best, most powerful serves for the last few points of the game. My way was to hit the hard serve for points at the start, thus getting off to a lead that my opponent could not overcome. Doing so can lower an opponent's self-confidence and encourage him to take risks to catch up.

In the market: To reduce the chances of starting out with an immediate loss, consider using limit orders. For example, you might buy at 0.25 percent below the bid and sell at 0.25 percent above the asked. Or buy 5 percent below the current market price. I used to like to place my buys at 1/8 above the round number and sell at 1/8 below, a tested method for profit when I wrote on the subject in the 1960s with M.F.M. Osborne, the Pasteur of the field. However, fast-moving day traders tell me that these days, this strategy is naïve, and they have ways of making fixed-rule followers of the old school like me eat my own rules.

Maintain a Strong Base of Operations

On the court: Other things being equal, the best position in all games seems to be the center. Being in the center minimizes the longest distance you have to travel to hit an opponent's shot. I am not graceful, and when someone watched me play for the first time I would invariably hear "That's Niederhoffer?" *sotto voce* in the stands. But after the game, it would be, "He's not even sweating."

In the market: Maintain a financial position that lets you maneuver easily into good opportunities. Take a lesson from chess master Bobby Fischer, whose favorite proverb was, "I never want to get in a position where I can't put my hand around all my pieces." A hand can fit around 10 or 15 stocks, and that is enough to achieve all the reasonable benefits that diversification can provide. This does not conflict with investing in index funds, where low costs, diversification, and the long-term forward movement of the market work in your favor.

Do Not Create Crises

On the court: If you have the edge, do not take risks. Do not force your opponent to hit good shots. If you force him into a crisis, he may rise to the occasion and come up with a winning shot. For example, if I were to hit a drop shot, my opponent could lunge and hit a very hard shot that I might not be able to return. The same thing holds in poker. If you are a better player than your opponent, the last thing you want is to play him a hand where you both have all your chips in but you have a very small edge. He just might draw the lucky card.

In the market: Never put all your chips on one thing, no matter how good. Failure could keep you out of the market, and there is always an edge for you in the market if you buy and hold, derive your own method, or follow one of ours. Once you have an edge, maintain it and accumulate steady profits.

Rome Was Not Built in a Day

On the court: Play your points one at a time. Do not go for the total win with one shot; games are not designed that way, and trying to do so puts you too much on the defense. Break your opponent's game down bit by bit. First try the forehand, then the backhand, then the net. Ultimately, you will find a weak spot, and your chance to put him away will arise.

In the market: The mouse with one hole is quickly cornered. Do not commit too great a percentage of your assets to one situation. A profit from stocks is good. So is a profit from mutual funds, and do not forget the friendly bond market.

Hit Them on the Half-Volley

On the court: The best time to hit the ball is on the half-volley, when it is just starting to bounce up from the court. The technique works because it lets you take maximum advantage of the ball's momentum. Your opponent is not able to read your next move well, and has less time to recover. My squash rival, Sharif Khan, held a plus record over me because he followed this method, even though he often made five times as many errors as I did. Rene Lacoste, master tennis tactician and businessman, wrote that when he hit every shot on the half-volley, his play improved 40 points a set. Today, Andre Agassi owes much success to such shots.

 In the market: After a big down day, come right in the next day to pick up a line of stocks. When the market starts moving up, the shorts will not have time to recover. A test we ran in December 2001 showed that the last 30 times the stock market dropped 2 percent or more in a day and then opened lower, the average change from that open to the next open was up 0.5 percent, with an average variability of 0.25 per- cent. (But beware the ever-changing cycles. We strongly recommend that you test any patterns mentioned in this book before acting on them.)

Come Up Front

On the court: The least-used weapon in racquet games is to go up front. At the net, you can hit much sharper angles and force your opponent to run faster and farther. Too many players spend 99 percent of their time perfecting ground strokes and just 1 percent of their time on the net game. In fact, the best way for the average player to improve is to develop a net game, as the benefits and rate of improvement are much better there.

In the market: Train yourself to react instantaneously to opportunities. That will give you the greatest chance of making a fast profit. But be sure that you do not follow the herd in trying to react to a news announcement, as the big boys, the market boys, and top predators are likely to get there ahead of you.

Attack on Both Sides

On the court: Create pressure on both sides. Good players often attack on one side and then the other. By forcing the opponent to defend on both sides, you can often move in for the finish.

In the market: An initial rise is often followed by a decline that gives way in turn to a final rise. On the 193 occasions in 1994–2001 that S&P 500 futures were up from close to 11 A.M. and down from 11 A.M. to 1 P.M., the expected move from 1 P.M. to the close was 0.2 percent, with a variability of about half as much and a batting average of .530.

Be Aware of Changing Cycles

On the court: Between games, your opponent will adjust his strategy to your play. In tennis, if you have been staying back on the baseline after your serve, he will expect you to keep doing that, so surprise him by coming up to the net. (But don't change during the middle of a game if you are winning.) Tom Wiswell, a longtime world checkers champion, once said: "The wise player can see the handwriting on the wall before there is any."

In the market: After trend-following has worked for a while, be prepared to reverse. After reversalists like me have had their day, be prepared for a major trend. The winners in one month are the losers next month, according to a

study I made of trend-following funds versus reversal funds during the 1990s. The average difference in performance was 4 percent.

Pick Up the Pace

On the court: At the beginning of a game, when your opponent is not yet warmed up, slow drop shots are often effective. Near the end of the match, however, your opponent will be faster on his feet; so make sure all your shots are much harder and faster than at the beginning.

In the market: Reversing is usually grand at the beginning of months or years, but beware of reversing at the end. From the end of 1989 through 2000, a rise in S&P 500 futures over the first 11 months of the year has been followed by an average change in December of 4 percent. If there was a loss over the first 11 months, the expected December move was just 2 percent. At the start of the year, however, industry groups tend to reverse direction, as professionals

**UNITED STATES
SQUASH HALL OF FAME**
Inaugural Class
Inducted April 15, 2000

Victor Niederhoffer
1943-

**National Champion 1966, 1972, 1973, 1974, 1975
National Doubles Champion 1968, 1973, 1974
North American Open 1975**

One of the more analytical and intense players ever, Vic Niederhoffer was perhaps most famous for being the only player to interrupt Sharif Khan's thirteen-year-run as North American Open champion, in a stirring match in Mexico City in 1975. Born and raised in Brighton Beach, Brooklyn, Niederhoffer was taught the game as a freshman at Harvard by coach Jack Barnaby. He won the national juniors in 1962, the intercollegiates in 1964 and two years later his first nationals. After a five year hiatus from the nationals, he came back and became the first man to win four nationals in four consecutive years. In tournament play he took both the Gold Racquets and the Harry Cowles six times (both for the first time as a junior in college in 1963). He won the national doubles three times, with Vic Elmaleh, Jim Zug, Sr. and Colin Adair. Vic Niederhoffer, at one stretch, practiced or played a match on 3,500 consecutive days without exception. "His opponents did little but gasp, sweat and run," wrote *Sports Illustrated* in 1975. "But Niederhoffer seemed to play effortlessly. His shots were not always brilliant, but he patiently waited out long rallies and his frustrated opponents consistently found themselves in situations where most of their moves were of high risk. And then they were forced to make mistakes which ruined them."

"His shots were not always brilliant, but he patiently waited out long rallies . . ."

regroup and reallocate to capture all the easy money made by the public during the previous year.

The Endgame

On the court: Whenever I was ahead in a squash game, I liked to imagine that the score was against me by my margin of victory. Near the end of a match, I redoubled my energy and never hit slow shots. The opponent is always at a do-or-die stage at that point, and will run his hardest to catch anything without pace.

En garde: Jamie Melcher, a former Olympic fencer who now runs Balestra Capital in Manhattan, said he became more cautious about finishing games after losing a number of early matches. As he matured, he said, "I would fence defensively, determined not to lose a single point, rather than trying to win points. This shift in attitude enabled me to win those bouts almost every time."

In the market: The idea reconciling these apparently conflicting pieces of advice might be to avoid undue risks when you are ahead. This thought is consistent with the idea of taking gains after a good run in the market. An extraordinarily wise old rule says, "Never underestimate your opponent." The market might be considered the toughest opponent of all. It certainly has been for us.

Laurel and I followed our own advice in 2001 by taking profits on several portfolios after short holding periods ranging from one to three months. We bought a group of beaten-up Internet stocks in late December 2000 and sold them about a month later after doubling our money. Before the summer crash of 2001, we sold various groups of volatile stocks we had recommended at the start of the year. In November 2001, we sold a portfolio of below-$5, high Value Line-ranked stocks, for a 20 percent monthly gain. At the start of December 2001, we mopped up a 21 percent profit on a biotechnology portfolio with insider buying, recommended October 25, 2001, to readers of our column.

Mopping up by taking profits may have drawbacks. As noted, most of us find it difficult to make two timing decisions—buy and sell—that both have above-average expectations. If academics are right about a 10 percent annual upward drift with random movements from all previous paths of price change, you will not be participating when you are out of the market. However, it is always wise to have a cushion while waiting for the market to offer another chance for an edge. As my chess teacher, Art Bisguier, likes to say: "Do to them before they do to you." Therefore, we were delighted to accept 20 percent short-term gains, regardless of the wisdom of the academics.

15 THE FINE ART OF BARGAINING FOR AN EDGE

> **The handshakes** are followed by shouting, the shouting by insults, the insults by impudence and more insults, shouting, and handshakes until the business is finished.
>
> —Joseph De La Vega, *Confusion de Confusiones* (describing the Amsterdam bourse of 1688)[1]

TRADERS!

- Do you have an inordinate tendency to sell at the low of the day and buy at the high?
- Do you find yourself behind the eight ball in many of your trades five minutes after you get a fill?
- Do you ever wonder why the average price you pay is always higher than the average price for the day and the average price you sell at is always lower?

- Do you find that the trades you feel most certain of and that you have most of your chips in are the ones that turn out to be the greatest disasters?
- Have you ever, at the end of a day or a week, thrown up your hands in disgust and shouted, "Damn my broker!"

If the answer is "yes" to two or more of these questions, then please read on. You are a candidate for the Kennerhoffer School of Bargaining.

Almost everything that happens in life is a negotiation. It starts when one person induces interest in another person. They meet and begin a process that moves them both in the direction of the other side.

The most important thing in any negotiation is to create a sense of urgency in the other side that is greater than your own. The purest example of this would be the nineteenth-century art of cornering stocks practiced by operators like Jay Gould. Quiet accumulation would be followed by discreet tips to the press; the manipulators would unload at the top and the public would be left with plummeting shares. Today, a piece of information hits the market electronically; traders jockey for position and finally reach a stopping point, a meeting of the minds.

To gain insight into negotiating, the directors of the Kennerhoffer School of Bargaining took a train trip to the Wharton School of Business in Philadelphia to visit Professor Richard Shell, director of the Executive Negotiation Workshop. Shell described the common mistakes people make in negotiating:

- They talk rather than listen.
- They are unclear about their goals.
- They think about minimizing risk more than maximizing opportunity.
- They assume that negotiating is inherently unethical and manipulative.

His advice:

- Always be willing to ask, respectfully, for a better price.
- Practice negotiating in everyday life.
- Learn about the hidden patterns in the negotiating process so you can get past the caricatures associated with negotiators and apply your intelligence.

On a practical level, he said, the first mistake in negotiating is to quote a price first. The second is saying yes immediately. To illustrate the point, Shell told the tale of a businessman kidnapped in Mexico. The kidnappers demanded $1 million from his family. The family agreed to pay. An exchange was arranged, after which the kidnappers immediately rekidnapped the man and demanded another $1 million for his release. This time, the family hired a professional negotiator, who offered $25,000. Eventually, the two sides settled at $250,000, and the businessman was freed.

"People often expect to bargain. When they do, and the other side says yes right away, the one who quoted the initial price may feel regret," Shell said. "When bargaining is done well, people can be very satisfied with even a lousy deal; if it has been set up poorly, they will feel unsatisfied even though they did very well."

If the other party fears being worse off if the deal does not go through, that translates into leverage for you. The prospect of loss need not be only material; the fear of loss in self-esteem or reputation can be equally leverage-enhancing. In the stock market, the speculator does well to keep in mind that the movements of a stock are designed to show attractiveness and scarcity to potential buyers.

The day after the October 1987 crash, Shell's late father, a retired Marine Corps general, came home from his job as the head of the Virginia Military Institute and called his broker. He assessed the panic selling going on and concluded the situation was not as severe as other crises he had endured during war and depression. He calmly placed orders. As a buy-and-hold investor, he was rewarded with large gains as the market recovered and went on to greater heights.

Professor Shell, while emphasizing that he is no expert on stock market bargains, sees the keys to speculation as "having disciplined goals, defined limits and understanding of the market, and a fearless willingness to make commitments when others are faltering." Not to be forgotten, he adds, is the importance of "keeping your spouse from cutting off your access to funds." He hastens to add, however, that in his case the wife knows best—she is a journalist and the former managing editor of *Inc.* magazine.

Shell often sees loss aversion, the irrational quirk that keeps investors from selling their losers, come up in bargaining. A $5 bill auction illustrates the principle. A group of people has the chance to bid for a $5 bill. The bidding may start at 10 cents. When it gets to $4.99 and $5, everybody tends to drop out except for two people; the usual closing price is $12. "Both sides are willing to go much further than is rational because of unwillingness to give up their investment."

Which brings us to the first lesson at the Kennerhoffer School of Bargaining.

Watch Your Costs

Vic's former partner, Steve Wisdom, uses the following technique when buying a car. "The way to beat car dealers, I learned many years ago, is to show up looking indigent, then fanatically beat down the purchase price while appearing indifferent/uncomprehending of the finance angle. Dealers will assume they can sell you the car for no margin and make it up on the back end by putting you 'on the chart' (i.e., expensive financing). Then show up the next day in normal clothes, take out your checkbook and buy the car for cash."

Steve's method can be directly applied to the market. A similar technique has been adopted successfully by George Soros, who, to hear him tell it, has never had a successful trade in the market. When Vic used to trade for him, Soros would bemoan his mistakes every day. At the end of each year, at their annual tennis game, Vic would ask, "How bad was it?" Soros would sheepishly smile and murmur something like, "Oh, we were up 87 percent."

In all candor, Vic has never had a satisfactory day of trading either. If Vic makes money on a particular day, it is never enough; he should have traded more heavily. If he loses money, it is even more terrible because he has six kids to support.

The point is, always let your counterparts know about your bad trades. Perhaps they will accommodate with you with a better fill next time, just to keep you in the game. More important, if they feel that you are in the chips, they may not be able to resist the all-too-human tendency to endeavor to relieve you of some of the overplus thereof, as they used to say in the nineteenth century.

Someone once asked J. Paul Getty, the richest man in the world in the 1960s, why he installed a pay phone in his London home. He answered that a businessman makes a few cents on every dollar of revenue, on average, after paying suppliers, employees, taxes, and debt holders. If he gets in the habit of paying 10 cents more than he receives for each item, he will quickly go out of business. Not only will he lose everything, but a few hundred thousand employees and suppliers also will be out of work. Like most people, Getty found it hard to behave differently in his personal life than he did in his business. So he ran his personal affairs in a businesslike way and did not pay out an inordinate amount.

The world's richest people today—Buffett, Gates, and Soros—seem to follow a similar path. If they find it useful to be economical in their activities, it is probably good for the rest of us.

In stock trading, the biggest mistake people make is paying an extra 10 cents or 25 cents out of every dollar in revenue they take in. Time after time Vic has had some manager working for him who loses 100 percent of capital. Invariably, the trades of such managers are highly profitable—before commissions and bid-asked spreads. What happens is that the market and their own money management outmaneuver them. They take in $1, but they pay out $1.10. If they trade often enough, that can be significant by the end of the year, and unfortunately most people do that.

Vic has been a relatively active trader for years. During that time, he estimates, he has made well over half a million trades, and has never bought or sold at the market. He always buys at a limit a few ticks below the current bid price and sells a few ticks above the current offer price. Try it, especially on the electronic markets, and see if you do not start out with a better feeling.

Pick Your Time and Place

You will get a better price if the car dealer wants to meet a month-end quota or win a prize, and is hungry for a sale. One of the most successful speculators of our generation, Mr. P himself, often featured in the columns of our editor, Jon Markman, has kindly shared for the benefit of our readers his patented method of buying a Jag on the cheap. He waits until 5 P.M. on Christmas Eve. Then he goes into the showroom:

"You must be very tired tonight." (To initiate a query here is key.)

"No, in fact, you're the first customer I've had." (The dealer's downfall.)

"What's your best price on that silver model?"

"Forty-five."

"Oh my, I'm afraid 35 is it for me. Goodbye." (Walks toward door.)

"Just a minute. I haven't sold one all day. It's yours."

"Very good. I need the keys right now. That's the very car my wife wanted, and she needs it tonight as a special surprise." (Had the dealer known that in advance, Mr. P would have had to pay the full price.)

Similar opportunities often come up in markets. The bonds have an inordinate tendency to rise at the end of the month, and on days that futures expire. After all the bulls have evaporated, there is often the opportunity to provide liquidity to the bears at the end of the day.

Our anecdotes illustrate two fundamental laws of bargaining that the academics have locked into. When a buyer and seller have room to maneuver to complete a trade, who is going to get the better deal? Whoever is more patient and is willing to take more risk of the deal falling apart. By watching your costs and waiting until the key moment, you make the other side impatient, and thus get the edge. By downplaying your success, you show awareness of your own fallibility and willingness to let the deal fall apart. These principles are well covered by Theodore C. Bergstrom in an upcoming article for the *Journal of Economic Literature,* "Economics in a Family Way,"[2] available now on google.com, as well as by such books as *Bargaining Theory with Applications* by Abhinay Muthoo,[3] and *The Strategy of Conflict* by Thomas C. Scheling.[4]

When we write our columns, our editors are always after us to tell readers what stocks to buy right now. This is an error, as a close reading of the first lesson indicates. We often feel we are in the position of King Canute, the Viking conqueror of 1,000 years ago whose noblemen demanded that he use his considerable powers to do something about the poor harvest. Canute objected that just because he had conquered England that did not mean he was omnipotent, but the nobles would not listen. So he had his throne brought to the seashore and commanded the tide to stop coming in. As waves lapped over his feet, the nobles presumably got the point.

Even on days when we possess the wisdom and resolve of Canute, our editors demand that we improve the harvest. We therefore came up with a practical application of the principles of bargaining, using IBM as the example. The advantage of choosing a bellwether like IBM is that a large number of competing market makers are always offering quotes, with the happy result that the typical bid-asked spread is very narrow, perhaps a penny. Being able to get in and out for 1/100 of a percent minimizes the grind of paying excessive costs—that inevitable albatross of excessive frivolity on the cost side alluded to earlier.

What happens when you buy at the close of a day in which IBM declines 3 percent and hold two days? It seldom occurs, but over the past decade it happened enough times to give a significant sample, both from a practical and statistical standpoint.

In fact, a 3 percent drop in IBM occurs a little more frequently than once a month. Table 15.1 shows the average expectation and the number of trades you make per year by varying your filter.

The results show that you make 0.6 percent after a 3 percent drop, and 1.6 percent after a 5 percent drop. You lose about a third of the time. The variability is highly unlikely to have occurred through chance variation alone, about 1 in 500.

Making 0.6 percent in two days in 8 to 12 months will not make you a Getty, but it is a good start. Before too long, such trades could amount to some serious money—at least enough to pay for your next lesson at the Kennerhoffer School

Table 15.1   Average Profit per Trade after Big Daily Drops in IBM

IBM Trade	After 3% Drop	After 5% Drop
Percent change after 2 days	0.6%	1.6%
Approximate number of occurrences	Once a month	Once a quarter

Source: Niederhoffer Investments.

of Bargaining, especially since it is free. The value of watching your costs and picking your times is illustrated. Such trades will make you less hungry.

Keep a Doleful Mien

> To the question, "How do you do?" Beethoven would often answer, "As well as a poor musician can do."
>
> Norman Lebrecht, *The Book of Musical Anecdotes*[5]

Vic's friend and mentor, Steve "Hobo" Keeley, has a technique that applies to all situations. When buying a product, he invariably puts on a doleful expression and after looking the purveyor in the eye, sighs, "Look, we're both God-fearing people. How much do you need over cost on this?" Or, "What's your best *dealer* price on this?"

The important thing to remember is that you do not have to take the first price quoted.

Duncan Coker, an investor friend of ours who has had occasion to bargain with real experts—Third World merchants—says his greatest challenge is getting his opening bid low enough.

"I often think I will insult the seller going in too low, but this is not the case," Coker reports. "Once when I was looking at rugs in Turkey I went in with an opening offer half the price I was willing to pay. After many mint teas, we settled somewhere in the middle. Later, a Turkish friend told me that the correct opening price was one-tenth of my offer."

Do not worry about offending the seller, or in the stocks bazaar, the market maker. After all, even a transaction below average cost may benefit a seller with excess inventory, as the Generation X economist N. Gregory Mankiw observes in *Principles of Microeconomics*.[6]

Information Is Valuable

Coker's tale illustrates the truth that not everyone has all the information necessary to make decisions. Information is scarce, and a cost arises in acquiring it, whether it is direct, is the subscription fee for an investment advisory service, is the opportunity cost of taking the time to read a book like this or obtain a few extra quotes on a car.

Bargaining received serious attention from George Stigler, who won the Nobel Prize in Economics in 1982 for his 1961 paper on the subject.[7] Stigler's pathbreaking theory, in a nutshell, is that consumers should seek information up to the point that the expected marginal benefits from additional search are equal to or less than the marginal cost. Say it costs you $100 in time and transport to visit a car dealer. Compare the additional reductions you get each time you visit a new dealer. When the average of the last two reductions is below $100, then stop searching. Stigler also developed a formula for estimating expected high and low prices based on the assumption that prices would follow the uniform distribution of equally divided ones to sixes that you get when you throw a single die.

Stigler's paper set off an explosion of interest in the role of information in economics that continued for decades. In 2001, the theory of asymmetric information gained three economists the Nobel Prize. It also gained us a 20 percent profit on a group of biotech stocks that we chose because of inside buying by corporate officers and directors. We reasoned that these insiders must have had information that outweighed the overwhelmingly bad odds of winning approval for their product from the FDA.

It happens that George Stigler's son, Stephen M. Stigler, is a friend and mentor of ours. We thought it appropriate to ask Steve whether any of his father's practical techniques of bargaining had helped him. He wrote that he employed an effective strategy on his last car-buying trip by taking his wife, son, and daughter along. "My son did the bargaining. He was ready to walk if they didn't come down. My wife and daughter were along to choose model and color. I was paying, but not until my son gave the nod. The salesmen, managers, and so on, didn't know who to sell to. We got the car, but they were still muttering as we left."

Sex and Bargains Do Not Mix

One of Vic's traders, Patrick Boyle, in his previous career as a hotelier, says he rarely admitted to a customer that more than one room was available even if half the hotel was empty. His first price quote was much higher than he thought the customer would accept. "Sometimes the person would pay, and if they wouldn't, they were much happier when the price dropped," Boyle says.

"Often I would have customers in the exact same types of rooms, some paying $40, some paying $400.

"The greatest mistake people could make was to come in during busy season and say, 'Please tell me you have a room.' That automatically tacked an extra $75 on to their room rate. The only bigger mistake was for a young guy to come in with his new girlfriend. He would never want to appear cheap by bargaining, and that was always worth $100."

Boyle also took advantage of the attractive properties of round numbers, well known to stock traders. "Usually people looking for a room have a price in mind, for example $200 per night. If you priced rooms a little above round numbers like that you could increase profitability, because they would happily pay $210 rather than drive around any more."

Those lessons—the flexibility of price, the undesirability of being eager, and the exercise of care around numbers—are all eminently applicable to buying stocks.

"It is important," Boyle concludes," to always be friendly. No one wants to reduce the price for someone they dislike."

Remember that it is a free society, and it is not shameful for people to say at what price under the quoted one they would buy.

16 AN AMIABLE IDIOT IN THE BIOTECHNOLOGY REVOLUTION

The ability to manipulate the genetic codes of living things set off an unprecedented industrial convergence: farms, doctors, drug makers, chemical processors, computer and communications companies, energy companies and many other commercial enterprises will be drawn into what promises to be the largest industry in the world.

—Juan Enriques and Ray A. Goldberg, *Harvard Business Review* (March–April 2000)[1]

Vic's 10-year-old daughter Kira talking:

"Daddy, tell me a story. About great heroes and what happens to them today."

"Very good. You've been hearing in school about the heroic exploits in mythology: how Perseus had to cut off Medusa's head, how Theseus killed the

Minotaur, and how Jason sailed to capture the Golden Fleece. Jason had to work like a demon to get it from King Aetes."

"That's right. First he had to build the Argo with 50 oars. Then he had to round up Hercules and 49 other heroes to stand a chance."

"And then, they had to overcome the water nymphs, the harpies, the clashing islands, the fire-breathing bulls, the armed men who sprang up from dragon's teeth, the dragon itself, King Aetes' pursuing army, Medea's brother, the sirens, the rock-throwing giant. And Jason had a broken heart from seeing his father and mother slain on his return."

"And what did he get for it, Daddy? Not much."

"Yes. He ended up penniless and homeless. And one day when he returned to look at the Argo once more . . ."

"The prow fell on his head and he died. Thank goodness we don't have to do such hard things today. When you do want to do something heroic you get rewarded, not killed."

"On the contrary. There is one thing even harder than Jason's quest for the Golden Fleece. That is for a biotech company to get a product approved by the government. It is very sad, because biologists know more now about the effectiveness of molecules and their side effects than they ever did before. They spend a good $50 billion a year researching new ones, and they have filed patent applications for 30,000 of them. If they win a patent, then they have to show that the inventors are qualified, search the literature, and do some preliminary studies. About 1,500 to 2,000 of these new drugs make it through that process each year, and then they are ready to be tested on humans. At that stage, they are called I-N-Ds, Investigative New Drugs."

"Sounds pretty hard, sort of what Jason had to do to get to Colchis," Kira said.

"Good point. That's when the Phase 1, Phase 2, and Phase 3 studies that you're always hearing about start."

"How much does it cost?"

"Well, Tufts, in Boston, where your dentist went to school, has a center for studying this. Their current estimate is that it takes 18 years and $800 million to get one drug approved by the FDA."

"Daddy, I have a question. If they come up with 2,000 new INDs a year to test, how many of them reach the final destination?"

"Great question. Fewer than one in 100. About 15 or 20 each year. Not very good odds."

"And when they do get approved, is the Golden Fleece very valuable?"

"Oh, yes. They get 17 years without any competition from the same molecule, and the nice warm feeling that they don't have to worry much about others going through the same journey they took, because they won't have the time or the money."

I Know This Crazy Guy . . .

Roger Longman: You wouldn't believe it, but I know this guy. Rich trader in Connecticut. Went to Harvard, got a PhD in economics from University of Chicago. But he thinks the FDA should be abolished.

Drug company big: You're killin' me.

Longman: Yeah. He goes around saying that. He runs some kinda fringe group. Meetings. Slogans. You know. Buzz words. "The FDA stifles innovation." "Big Pharma is keeping out little companies." "Each year the FDA's failure to approve drugs costs 100,000 lives." "The FDA would never have allowed Windows to be approved if software were under its jurisdiction." Stuff like that.

Drug company big: People like that, nobody pays attention. Everybody knows the FDA is there to protect people from stuff that makes babies get born with flippers instead of arms.

Longman: He talks to a bunch of business school kids over the Internet. Wrote a book on trading that has sort of a cult following.

Drug company big: Well. Maybe he'll convince Chile to fire its drug regulators. What do guys like that say when you bring up thalidomide babies?

Longman: He came right back and said no way would the FDA approve aspirin today, since it causes deformities too. And then he said the FDA wouldn't let anybody advertise that taking aspirin brings heart disease down by 40 percent. I didn't want to go there. Thing is, people like him exist. They're out there, you know what I'm saying?

The Old Phase 2

Despite irreconcilable differences on the subject of drug regulation, Roger and Vic are good friends and have tremendous admiration for one another. Whenever the two of them meet, Vic takes his arm. "Roger, let's do the amiable idiot routine," he says, doing a bit of soft-shoe. "Have you had occasion to mention me in any of your talks with Big Pharma lately?"

Roger falls into step. "Oh, it's not that, Vic," he always says. "It's just that you need to realize that there's no requirement for approvals to take 20 years. The drug companies and regulators do it to make sure the drugs are safe."

It is all too typical of those totally immersed in a milieu, be it an industry, a political culture, or a profession, to defend its norms. Roger is editor and managing partner of Windhover Information Inc., publisher of a respected group of magazines that are must reading for drug industry venture capitalists. The "drug company big" in the preceding dialogue is an actual person, a top executive at a major pharmaceutical firm. We withhold his name in the interest of diplomacy.

The Trader's Apprentice

"Registered letter here, Vic."

"Not another garnishing from the Infernal ones regarding that $40 dispute on our 1970 returns."

Rob, my office manager, hands me the letter. "No. It's from that Chinese guy you turned down for a job because you didn't think he understood American markets well enough to help."

"What does he want, reimbursement for a first-class ticket?"

"He says he read in those nineteenth-century investment books in your library that old-time speculators started out on Wall Street as apprentices. They did menial work for free and after they'd proved themselves, they'd be given a chance to trade. He wants to do that for you. He sent his e-mail address."

I tap out the address on my computer monitor. "Let's go," I write, and push the send button to Shi Zhang.

Shi appears at the trading room door a few days later. He calls me "Sir." The traders in my office, unaccustomed to such displays of deference, nickname him "Mr."

For Mr.'s first project, I ask him to classify five years of monthly prices for the 150 companies in the Russell 2000 Health Care Index according to the level of insider trading in the preceding two months.

Shi proved himself a worthy apprentice. His biotech study and many other contributions appear throughout this book. Moreover, several weeks after his arrival, after Shi had racked up a 46-trade win record with his first 48 forays into the German bund market, my other traders formed a line, bowed in unison, and called him "Master," over his outraged protests.

The Invisible Victim

Jim Lorie, one of the original directors of the Center for Research in Securities Prices, talking to the Friends School at Chicago 35 years ago; Vic audited the class before their first squash match together.

"Kids, there is not one economist who has ever studied the FDA who hasn't concluded that they'd do much better if they speeded up the approval process. As George Stigler says, industry co-opts regulations to make sure they are designed and operated primarily for its benefit. By driving up the cost of pharmaceutical research and delaying drug approvals, the FDA reduces the supply of new, effective drugs."

"But what about safety, consumer protection, and imperfect information?" asks a student.

"Yes, but at what price?" says Lorie. "You have to balance the costs against the benefits. Let's look at this diagram of what happens if the FDA allows or rejects a drug, classified by whether it's beneficial or harmful."

He chalks Table 16.1 on a blackboard.

"FDA officials know they'll be punished for approving a harmful drug (Type I error), but not for failing to let a good one go on the market (Type II error)," Lorie says. "If a harmful drug is inadvertently allowed to go to market, the victims are identifiable and might appear on Oprah. But if a beneficial drug is rejected, the victims are faceless, nameless, and rarely acknowledged even in the abstract. Is it any wonder, then, that the FDA places too much emphasis on avoiding Type 1 errors and not enough on avoiding Type 2 errors?

"Although many lives are lost because of FDA delays and failure to approve good drugs, from the agency's standpoint it's much worse to let a bad drug slip through. They always say that economists can never agree on anything. But every economist who has studied the FDA has concluded the same thing: The FDA needs to approve drugs faster. The economists also agree as to the reasons for erroneous decision making at agencies like the FDA.

"You have to balance disasters like thalidomide, which by the way was never approved in the United States, against things like aspirin and penicillin which could never make it by the FDA at all today under the current setup," Lorie concludes. "The net result of all this misplaced emphasis on minimizing the Type 1 errors at the expense of the Type 2 errors is 50,000 extra deaths a year, according to the best estimates."

With just three minutes left before our game, Jim winds up his talk. "From Adam Smith to Sam Peltzman—who first studied the lives lost by delays in

Table 16.1   FDA Decision Making

		Drug Is Beneficial	Drug Is Harmful
FDA reviewers . . .	Allow the drug.	Correct decision	Type 1 error
	Reject the drug.	Type 2 error	Correct decision

approval—to Milton Friedman, every economist who studies this has concluded that the cures for the market's woes are often worse than the disease. Nowhere is this more harmful, nowhere is this more tragic, than in the case of our current system for deciding which drugs get approved."

Things have not improved since Lorie's talk. I found numerous examples of deadly FDA delays:

Septra: The FDA delayed approval of the antibacterial drug Septra for five years, taking three years longer than European regulators. Nobel Prize winner George Hitchings estimated that the five-year delay cost 80,000 lives.

Beta Blockers: Beta blockers regulate hypertension and heart problems. The FDA held up approval for eight years because it believed they caused cancer. In the meantime, according to Dr. Louis Lasagna of Tufts University, 119,000 people died who might have been helped by the medication.

Clozaril: Clozaril is effective in treating 30 percent to 50 percent of schizophrenics who don't respond to other medicines, according to *The New England Journal of Medicine*. The effect was discovered in 1979, but Clozaril was not approved in the United States until 1990. Companies believed the FDA would reject it on the grounds that 1 percent of patients who take the drug develop a blood ailment. As a result, some 250,000 patients suffered needlessly.

Mevacor: A cholesterol-lowering drug that reduces heart disease deaths by about 55 percent, Mevacor was available in Europe in 1989. It was not approved in the United States until 1992. As many as 1,000 people died from heart disease because of the FDA's delay.

Havrix: The first vaccine to prevent hepatitis A, Havrix was available in Europe and 40 other countries three years before being approved in the United States.

Interleukin-2: European regulators approved Interleukin-2 in 1989 for the treatment of kidney cancer. Three years later, it won approval for that use in the United States. In the interim, 3,500 people died who might have been saved.

The Trial

As I told my daughter, and as Lorie made plain, biotech companies' quests for the Golden Fleece are fraught with many dangers. Bringing a product to market demands a combination of research, manufacturing, scientists, doctors, consultants, and government affairs people. *Forbes ASAP* editor Michael S. Malone gave a firsthand report of a few crucial moments of one typical quest in a report for ABCNEWS.com:

> As it happens, two years ago for a magazine story, I followed a biotech company as it ran the gauntlet of final FDA approval on a new heart drug. Now, in my career as a journalist, I've seen new product design teams sweat and fight and break their health trying to get a new model to market. I've seen CEOs with bad quarterly numbers get ripped to pieces by packs of howling analysts. And I once watched a corporate chairman nearly collapse from a stroke while trying to drive a merger vote through an angry shareholders' meeting.
>
> But nothing prepared me for the FDA Star Chamber. The company I was watching had spent two years field testing their drug, then weeks preparing its FDA presentation. Then the entire senior staff of the company moved to a hotel near Bethesda, Maryland, set up a full communications center in a conference room there, and spent four days running rehearsal after rehearsal, rewriting the entire presentation a half-dozen times.
>
> Meanwhile, back home, the company froze, knowing that its stock value and its future sales all depended upon what happened inside the FDA chambers at the National Institute of Health.
>
> The hearing itself had all of the elements of a nightmare: the terrified presenters, the panel of doctors on stage, each with their own prejudices and agendas. Eight hours of misery, until the final vote. . . .
>
> The company gained approval by a single vote. General cheering and back-slapping. The presenters went home to a gigantic company party—only to learn a couple days later that one of the approving doctors had changed his mind.
>
> The company stock collapsed, morale imploded, and the company reeled under the shock for months. It is only now regaining its footing.[2]

Who would be foolish enough to buy stocks in a company subjected to these perils? Amazingly, numerous investors are willing to share in the risks. These hardy souls may be likened to the Dutch entrepreneurs who braved similar odds to finance a new company in America some 350 years ago. Certainly the incentive for buying such stocks is the spectacular profit that may be realized by those who pick the products that make biotech the likely choice for the breakthrough industry of the twenty-first century.

Even more surprising, however, is that executives in such ventures often take bullish positions by buying their own company's stock. Presumably, these purchases are engendered by something more than pure optimism that the quest will end by capturing the prize. One such motivation must be information. Executives have to know by the time they spend 10 years of effort and $800 million of expense whether Big Pharma is likely to help them get through the final rocks. They have to know from their scientists and their doctors how the treatments are going. Their well-connected consultants must give them feedback as to how the winds are blowing with their current or former colleagues at the FDA.

Human nature being what it is, the wheels of commerce have a way of lubricating the flow of information. There are meetings, studies, and letters. Consultants are hired, often those who will eventually opine on the product's effectiveness. No matter how blind the double-blind study, somewhere along the path a company may chance to come by some knowledge as to the likelihood of success, however tenuous the approval process.

Profit from Asymmetry

George Akerlof, Michael Spence, and Joseph Stiglitz won the Nobel Prize in 2001 for writing about such situations. In their branch of the dismal science, known as the economics of information, they study how much information people demand in determining what they will buy and sell. Among their areas of focus are situations of asymmetrical information, where the buyer and seller have different degrees of information.

Akerlof used the example of the sale of a used car. The seller knows whether it is good or bad, and consequently the price drops because the buyer fears buying a lemon. Similarly, Stiglitz observed that a person buying insurance knows how sick or how likely he is to avoid calamity much better than the company selling policies.

Stiglitz, like most economists, is much more concerned about how imperfect and asymmetrical information can lead to violations of the competitive model that can only, according to his lights, be fixed by government action to correct the asymmetry. Indeed, after the September 11, 2001, attack on the World Trade Center, Stiglitz figured prominently in urging the government to expand its role in assuring security at airports. We will refrain here from a discussion of the virtues of competition and innovation that would be stifled by such interference, except to note that we would gladly pay $15 a ticket extra to fly on a plane manned by armed guards should the government ever deign to let airlines compete by offering additional security.

Now consider those biotech and pharmaceutical executives who, with full knowledge of the difficulty of threading their product through the FDA needle, are courageous enough to buy shares in their own company. Are they doing so thinking that their product is likely to be rejected? We would hazard they are not. Moreover, since a substantial part of their own wealth is tied up in the options and shares they already own, our guess is that they are not doing it to throw good money after bad. The information that is revealed by their insider purchases and sales contains, to us at least, as much of value as the advertisement that a car is for sale or an individual's inquiry about buying insurance.

That said, we would not use insider sales as a signal to short stocks. We generally don't believe in shorting individual stocks. It is too difficult for us to overcome that 15,000 percent-a-year arithmetic updraft against the shorts documented in Chapter 9. As far as we know or can predict, others suffer from this same failing.

Trading on insider purchases has risks as well. Some executives might be deceiving themselves as to their company's true prospects. Worse still, they might be buying shares to throw the public off the scent. An executive might buy a minimal number of shares as a setup for a huge sale, timing the transactions to take advantage of the lags in required reporting times. He might escape disclosure altogether, as did CEO Chairman Kenneth Lay, by selling large, equal numbers of shares as part of a "long-term" plan. On balance, however, we have found insider buying to be a profitable signal.

The Niederhoffer-Kenner-Zhang Drug Trials

Inspired by the rather draconian requirements of the FDA, which involve double-blind studies by accredited investigators at designated centers, we decided to follow to as great an extent as possible their own standards of proof. However, because we did not have $800 million available to perform a complete double-blind study, nor did we find it appropriate to wait 18 years before making a decision as to our financial health, we took certain shortcuts for which we beg the indulgence of all parties.

It is common for companies submitting protocols to the FDA to compliment the regulators on their acumen and fairness (need we inquire as to why this grotesque servility seems to be so prevalent?), and we would similarly compliment the regulatory agency for the high test standards that they have set for the companies under their jurisdiction, including the requirements that the drugs be administered in double-blind studies on patients with no other condition besides the ones being tested, and who are available to take the full course of treatments at locations approved and monitored by FDA consultants.

Although we are firmly convinced that these stringent requirements and others that we have doubtless left out have added immeasurably to the loss of human life by requiring pseudoscientific results that have no relation to the way patients actually take medicines in the real world, we have tried to follow the spirit of the FDA's requirements in our own work to as great an extent as feasible with our own financial results and proper reporting of those results to our readers.

To test our theory that a dose of insider buying leads to healthy profits for biotech investors, we conducted, with the assistance of Vic's aforementioned apprentice, Shi Zhang, a comprehensive three-stage study of all subjects enrolled in the Russell 2000 Health Care Index over the six years 1996–2001. The first stage involved a Phase 1 study of the safety of such a procedure. We looked at the performance of 50 companies in the year 2001. The results showed that these companies displayed healthy returns in excess of 20 percent, greater than the Index's returns during that year.

Consultants who oversee our work pointed out that these results could well have been affected by special factors relating to the 2001 cohort, and they suggested a more complete study involving a six-year period. This led us to roll out a comprehensive Phase 2 trial. In compliance with currently required FDA protocols, we enrolled 1,000 healthy subjects who registered positive for insider trading within a two-month period. We followed their health during each of the next 12 months, as measured by their average percentage change in price. While this was not a double-blind study, we did, in accordance with standard procedure, compare this with a much larger control group of 1,800 subjects that were afflicted with insider sales. (Many subjects received these dosages in separate months, and each administration of a dose of buying or selling in a month was treated as a separate subject.)

The results for healthy and unhealthy subjects (i.e., insider buys versus insider sales) for all six years combined appear in Table 16.2.

The results of the Phase 2 studies were highly encouraging, and yet the variability in the results by years shows that, as for most treatments, there is much uncertainty as to the actual outcome. Note, in the years 1998 and 1999, the differentials of 30.2 and 39 percentage points, respectively, between returns for buys and sells. Aside from these two years, the results appear relatively random.

In the tradition of early investigators of medical treatments, we decided to try the treatment ourselves on a real-time basis. The results were carried live on CNBC Money, starting with our October 25, 2001, column, where we reported the enrollment in our portfolio of 10 insider-positives. After just one month in the study, they showed improvements in their health, as illustrated in Table 16.3.

The 25 percent average improvement was so drastic that we immediately closed out the companies from our portfolio and took profits.

Table 16.2   Follow the Insiders in Biotech

Year	Mean % Return for Insider Buys	Number of Buys	Mean % Return for Insider Sales	Number of Sells
2001	−3.4	80	4.9	124
2000	3.1	209	−6.8	480
1999	149.0	197	109.8	278
1998	50.3	207	19.1	280
1997	8.2	140	−5.9	244
1996	30.9	15	20.1	14
Weighted average percent return*	49.2		22.6	
Total transactions		848		1,420

* Note the weighted average percent return cannot be calculated by simply averaging the mean annual returns.

We decided to conduct a confirmatory trial in 2002 with twice as many patients. The patients were fragile to begin with, and it would be impossible at this point to separate the effects of the insider dosages from the Great Market Virus of 2002, Type "Meme." However, we have concluded that our first study was what they call in the trade "a false positive," and reluctantly pulled the plug. Our tests resulted in what is called a negative study in the medical literature. The patients taking the medicine actually died

Table 16.3   Improvements in Health

Stock	Change (%) (October 25–November 21, 2001)
Corvas	−0.4
Dyax	64.4
Genelabs	−10.1
Genzyme Transgenics	1.1
Guilford Pharmaceuticals	15.6
InKine Pharmaceutical	30.4
Large Scale Biology	45.8
The Medicines Co.	54.2
3-Dimensional Pharmaceuticals	19.9
Triangle Pharmaceuticals	−2.9
Average	25.1

Source: Niederhoffer Investments.

at earlier ages than those with no treatment. Indeed, the authors of this book enrolled in the study themselves for the purpose of science, financial health, and this book. Suffice it to say that their financial health was injured to the tune of 50 percent by their purchase of these stocks in 2002 (versus an approximately 30 percent decline in the biotech index itself).

Which, once again, shows the necessity of counting.

17 EARNINGS IMPOSTORS

To the tune of the Duet of the Captain and Little Buttercup in *H.M.S. Pinafore*, by W.S. Gilbert and Sir Arthur Sullivan:

Things are seldom what they seem
Public's wrong at the extremes.
Prices climb on Wall Street hype
Execs sell when time is ripe
Very true
So they do.

Mergers work accounting gimmicks
Analysts are only sidekicks
Profit forecasts are precut
CEO has time to putt.
Even so,
No cash flow.

Managed earnings laid on thick
Inventory hides the trick.
Statements obscure bottom lines
Accruals shroud cash flow declines
So they are
Never at par

Hide the debts in towns offshore
Then go out and borrow more
Option costs they don't deduct
Public is the goose they pluck
So they do
In full view

Worst of all is the write-down
Officers they all leave town
Pay their bonus, then go under
Only bad folks get to plunder
First they fake
Then they take.

Big execs retire like kings
Eliot Spitzer has his fling
Gild the earnings, steal the till
What is left is sure to kill
Yes, I know,
Dow will go.

Pictures of corporate executives and accountants in action in the good old days were more likely to show them hitting a drive at an important conference at the Greenbrier Resort than taking a perp walk before an indictment for corporate fraud.

Lists of those in the Rogues Gallery were more likely to include bank robbers than executives charged with crimes from such companies as Adelphia Communications, Arthur Andersen, Enron, HomeStore, ImClone, Tyco, or WorldCom. Security analysts, rather than Attorneys General, were more likely to be studying financial statements. Income statements were more important than balance sheets.

But in the early years of the twenty-first century, all that has changed. Executives are depicted as impostors. The attractive members of the opposite sex at cocktail parties no longer surround the venture capitalist. The bullish analyst is laughed off the television set. As Gilbert tells us in *Pinafore:*

> Highlows pass as patent leathers
> Jackdaws strut as peacock feathers.

Yes, indeed, training in detecting the impostors is becoming more important for the investor than the study of the principles of scientific management. The study of balance sheets has become more important than the study of income statements. Within the balance sheet, the "cash and cash equivalents" is king. You can talk, you can bicker, you can boast about the earnings, but when profits don't show in cash flow from operations, you've got to be careful.

We found four questions to be helpful in differentiating between the real and the distorted, and the true and the false:

1. Has the company announced a stock buyback? Buyback announcements preceded highly superior performance in all periods we tested.
2. Does the company pay dividends? Giving cash back to shareholders has been associated with superior long-term returns for at least the past century.
3. What's happening with inventory and accounts receivable? Decreases in these two indicators lead to good performance. Increases are bad news.
4. Does the company pay taxes? The bottom line may be a chimera, but if the company is so profitable that it has to bite the bullet and pay cash to the IRS, that's a good sign that the earnings are real.

Not all of these measures are good for all seasons. Companies with high dividend yields have performed significantly better than companies with low dividend yields over the very long term. But they held no advantage in the 1990s, or even in the difficult market year of 2002. Buybacks can signal that a company is willing to back up its good intentions with cash—but sometimes, it works out best for all concerned if the company keeps the money to invest in the business. Accounts receivable, inventory, and cash taxes paid may be of more enduring value, particularly combined with the buyback or dividend signals.

We discuss each of these findings in this chapter. But first, we will explain the accounting issues in a bit of detail. You don't need a green eyeshade to understand this stuff, and an investor who knows a cash profit from an accrued profit will have a meal for a lifetime.

Cash Money

Cash is the first item on the balance sheet. By looking at a company's audited statement of cash flows from one year to the next, you can tell whether cash increased or decreased. But where did that cash from, and where was it used?

In a nutshell, cash flow from operations is designed to show the cash effects of revenues and expenses. If a business is to survive, it must in the long run generate such cash flows. If a business constantly loses cash from its operating activities, who would want to own it?

The record that keeps track of these increases and decreases is called an *account*. The left side of an account is called a *debit,* and the right side is called a *credit.* The rules for financial bookkeeping are designed so that the debits on any transaction are equal to the credits. That is what is meant as *double-entry bookkeeping.*

The double-entry bookkeeping system, followed by all major companies, is designed to reflect the fact that economic transactions have impact on two or more than two accounts at the same time. For example, if you go out to buy a box of cereal, your cash decreases and your stock of cereal increases. An increase in an asset or expense is a debit, and an increase in a liability or revenue is a credit.

The basic equation that keeps the debits and credits equal is

$$\text{Assets} = \text{Liabilities} + \text{Owners' equity}$$

For this equation to remain in balance, all changes on the left side must be balanced by an equal change on the right side. Also, any increase in an account on the left side must be balanced by either a decrease in an account on the left side or an increase on the right side.

If we divide the left side of the equation into cash and noncash assets, we get the new equation:

$$\text{Cash} + \text{Noncash assets} = \text{Liabilities} + \text{Owners' equity}$$

Then we can see that any increase in noncash assets must be balanced by a decrease in cash assets, or an increase in liabilities. Any decrease in noncash assets must be balanced by an increase in cash, or a decrease in liabilities.

By working through the transactions that cause an account to increase or decrease, an accountant or an educated reader can calculate the difference between the cash flows and the net income of a business. They are all summarized and reported on the statement of cash flows. All public companies have been required to report this in their annual reports to shareholders and in SEC filings since 1987.

Table 17.1 shows some selected financial figures from General Electric for the calendar years 2001 and 2000 to put this in perspective.

Table 17.1   General Electric: Selected Financial Items

	Year Ended	
	2001 (in Millions)	2000 (in Millions)
Inventory	8,565	7,812
Accounts receivable	9,590	9,502
Sales	125,679	129,417
Net income	13,684	12,735

Source: Bloomberg L.P.

Bear in mind that these are just selected figures, and that we have not queried General Electric about these items because the company refuses to grant us an interview. Note, however, that on a sales decrease of $3.7 billion, General Electric was able to increase net income by $949 million. This is highly commendable. However, of this $949 million, $753 million came from an inventory increase, and $88 million came from an accounts receivables increase. Taking this $841 million away, the net increase in earnings was just $108 million.

Accountants and analysts use that exact procedure with all asset and liability accounts to compute the difference between cash earnings and accrual earnings. (We emphasize that this is merely a partial picture of General Electric's financial statement, and that the company actually generated cash flow of $32.2 billion in 2001, up from $22.7 billion the previous year. Other items on the statement of cash flow account for this difference, such as an increase in insurance liabilities and reserves of $9.2 billion). While we hesitate to opine on these matters because of our lack of direct contact with GE, may we speculate that fear that such items might be signaling that all was not well was responsible in part for the 47 percent decline that GE experienced from top to bottom in 2002?

Buybacks

Let's turn to buybacks and dividends—the two main ways for a company to return cash to shareholders.

Nothing is inherently better about companies that pay dividends or buy back stock. A growth company may decide to invest the cash in its business.

When a company perceives that the rate of return in its own business is less than shareholders could achieve on their own, it's prudent for all concerned if extra cash is distributed. Moreover, in an investment atmosphere that is poisoned by mistrust and fraud, distributions show good intentions in a way that mere reassurances never could. A company that gives cash to stockholders can't waste it on ill-considered mergers, grandiose buildings, outlandish executive perks, and other hubristic activities.

As Paul Fels, a reader of our CNBC Money column observed: "You can fake or inflate earnings, but if you pay out cash, you had to have it in the first place."

Share buybacks increased rapidly starting in the mid-1980s as the percentage of companies paying dividends dwindled. In 2000, companies spent as much on buybacks as they did on dividends, according to an admirable study in the August 2002 *Journal of Finance* by Gustavo Grullon of Rice University and Roni Michaely of Cornell University.

Buybacks have three major virtues:

1. **Signaling.** By authorizing a stock buyback, a board signals to shareholders that it feels the stock is undervalued.
2. **Better income ratios.** Other things being equal, the reduced number of shares will improve earnings per share and return on equity.
3. **Flexibility.** Investors can interpret the elimination or reduction of a dividend as extremely bad news. Because a stock buyback is a one-time event, no embarrassment results from failing to repeat it.

The classic study on share repurchases was conducted by David Ikenberry, a professor at Rice University; Theo Vermaelen, professor of finance at INSEAD, a French business school; and Josef Lakonishok, a finance professor at the University of Illinois. The study, published in the *Journal of Financial Economics* in 1995, found that companies buying back their own shares perform some 4 percentage points better than the averages. Studies of companies in India, England, and Canada confirmed the professors' findings.

At least two funds are putting the study's findings to profitable use. David Fried's *Buyback Letter* has enjoyed one of the best ratings from *Hulbert Digest*, the acknowledged arbiter of newsletter performance. Professor Vermaelen's own buyback fund that he manages for a Belgian bank, KBC, reported a return of 40 percent from the fund's inception in July 1998 through April 2002.

We verified the academics' conclusions ourselves in April 2002 by compiling a list of every company in the S&P 500 that had announced a buyback since the beginning of 2000. We tracked each company's performance over a full year, using the close on the day after the announcement as the buy date.

The 224 companies we identified outperformed the S&P 500 by an average of 30 percentage points a year, a 1-in-100 million shot by chance alone.

By October 2002, we had added 15 additional companies. The advantage dwindled to 6 percentage points—still a very respectable edge.

When we reported our findings, many readers wrote in to express concern that companies would fail to follow through after announcing buybacks. The worry is misplaced. A company's buyback announcement signals that management believes the stock to be undervalued. If the stock immediately rises based on this signal, the job has been done. We found no evidence that companies that do implement buybacks perform better than those that don't. (Investors can monitor actual repurchases by watching the shares outstanding reported in consecutive quarterly financial statements.)

Dividends

When mutual funds statements are too depressing to watch and every week brings news of a new major accounting fraud, few things seem more reassuring than dividend checks in the mail. Not only do the payouts offer a cushion against stock declines; a company that must come up with hard cash to pay higher dividends quarter after quarter has less latitude for accounting shenanigans. A dividend offers tangible proof to shareholders that they exercise at least some control over the assets they own.

Older generations of investors knew this well. "My father-in-law (now deceased) looked only at dividends for his personal support and never concerned himself with the value of his portfolio," wrote reader Patricia K. Schwabacher. "During market downturns, he worried not at all. He just didn't buy a new car or a new boat at those times. He only concerned himself with the security of the dividends. He retired at 50 and died at 90, having lived a very nice lifestyle, with a net worth that increased 10-fold during that period of investment."

Regrettably, the number of companies paying dividends steadily dwindled from 70 percent in the 1970s to about 20 percent in 2000. U.S. tax policy is partly to blame. Dividends are taxed at the corporate level of 20 percent, and when they reach the investor's pocket they are taxed again at 40 percent, on average. If the company holds onto the money and invests the money wisely, or buys back its own shares, investors can enjoy capital gains taxed at only 20 percent. That's why the retention ratio—earnings retained versus total dividends paid—has increased from 30 percent in the 1950s to 70 percent today.

But the double tax is not the only skewed incentive confronting management. Congress has done further mischief by permitting deductions for interest but not dividends. In effect, companies are encouraged to go into debt. As ratings agencies and investors frown on highly leveraged balance sheets, some companies—Enron comes to mind—go to great lengths to hide their debt with dubious or fraudulent accounting.

Moreover, executive options decrease in value along with stock prices when a company pays dividends. The rise in executive pay over the past 50 years has been accompanied by a decline in dividends.

We wanted a fresh look at the question of whether dividends actually are predictive of superior stock returns. As has become our wont, we began by consulting that magnificent analysis of 101 years of stock market data, *Triumph of the Optimists*.

Dimson, Marsh, and Staunton, the authors of *Triumph*, examined the performance of the 30 percent of companies with the highest dividend yields at the beginning of each year and compared it to the performance of companies that were in the lowest 30 percent of dividend yield. From 1900 through 2001, companies with the highest yields returned 12.2 percent a year. Companies with the lowest yields showed an annual total return of 10.4 percent.

A difference of 2.2 percentage points a year may not seem like much. But over time, it becomes a gigantic differential. Over the 101 years of the study, $1 invested in the highest-yielding companies could have come to $4,948, while $1 invested in the lowest-yielding companies would have grown to a mere $1,502.

The margin of superiority for high-yielders versus low-yielders, however, has been close to zero since 1990. To determine if the regime shift had set in, we updated the *Triumph* data by considering the S&P 500 companies that showed the highest yields at year-end 2000 and year-end 2001, along with their performance in the next year.

We found that the 10 high-yield stocks outperformed the market in 2001 with a positive return of 8 percent versus a 10 percent loss in the S&P 500 and a 39 percent loss in the Nasdaq. But in 2002, the effect did not hold up. The top 10 high-yield stocks were down 34 percent as of mid-October, even worse than the 24 percent loss in the S&P 500 and exactly even with the 34 percent loss in the Nasdaq.

The numbers were similar for the top 30 high-yielders. These stocks were little changed in 2001 and were down 25 percent as of mid-October 2002, as Table 17.2 shows.

The great danger in buying a stock with a high dividend yield is that dividends can be cut. Ford Motor Company, Dynegy, Goodrich, Transocean, and

Table 17.2 Changing Cycles: Performance of Top 10 Dividend-Yield Stocks (2001 vs. 2002)

Company	Yield at Year-End 2001	January–October 2002 Performance (%)	Company	Yield at Year-End 2000	2001 Performance
Plum Creek Timber (PCL)	10.05	−27.1	Sabre (TSG)	12.06	−1.8
Dana (DCN)	6.77	−23.7	J.C.Penney (JCP)	10.47	155.79
Ford Motor (F)	6.68	−46.6	Rockwell Automation (ROK)	8.48	−15.51
J.C.Penney (JCP)	6.44	−45.5	Dana (DCN)	8.1	−3.34
Rockwell Automation (ROK)	6.34	−10.4	Ford Motor (F)	7.68	−29.27
CMS Energy (CMS)	6.08	−70.0	Deluxe (DLX)	7.33	116.65
Eastman Kodak (EK)	6.01	−10.8	Winn–Dixie Stores (WIN)	7.09	−23.52
Ameren (AEE)	6	−1.8	Thomas & Betts (TNB)	6.92	34.92
RJ Reynolds Tobacco (RJR)	5.86	−39.1	Wachovia (WB)	6.9	16.47
CenterPoint Energy (CNP)	5.66	−67.4	Southern Co. (SO)	6.6	31.95
Average		−34.24	Average		8.16
Standard deviation		23.59	Standard deviation		1.77

Qwest Communications were among the companies that suffered declines exceeding 40 percent in 2002 after cutting or eliminating their dividends. There is also a risk in buying a company where management is implying that they have encountered sufficient barriers in their ability to use your capital that they are giving it back to you.

Up with Dividends

We next looked at companies that initiate or increase dividends. The academics have concluded that dividend increases are irrelevant. In the scientific tradition, we vetted their findings. Cycles are always ready to change in markets, racing, and in life—just when they seem "sure as rain." A preliminary study of dividend increases in the year 2002 yielded results contrary to the academics' findings.

We took the 120 companies in the S&P 500 that increased their dividends in 2002, and found in mid-October a cumulative performance of −14 percent. Twenty-two companies decreased their dividends, and their performance was −20 percent. The difference is significant at the usual statistical levels. Companies that declared new dividends beat the S&P 500, as Table 17.3 shows.

We conclude that there is no magic bullet for stocks. High-yield companies seem to show superior performance over time, but that effect apparently vanished in the difficult year of 2002. Companies that increase dividends have had relatively woeful performance in the past, but in these times they augur good performance.

Dividend Yields and the Market

We often hear from gurus of the value persuasion that stocks are too high because dividend yields are too low. Bill Gross, the reigning bond king of Pimco, used 100-year statistics on dividend yields and dividend growth in September 2002 to argue that the Dow should be at 5000. (It was then at about 8500.)

Such an argument is so naïve that we are almost embarrassed to hear it expressed. It leaves out the fact that companies were spending as much to buy back shares as they paid out in dividends. It also leaves out the fact that interest rates on the 10-year note are at the lowest levels since the 1950s. That means stocks don't have to yield much to be attractive, as Tables 17.4 and 17.5 illustrate.

Table 17.3 New Dividends and Stock Returns*

Company	Ticker	Dividend Declared	Change after after 12 Months (%)	Difference versus S&P 500 aftr 12 Months (%)
AmerisourceBergen	ABC	10/31/2001	12	28
FedEx	FDX	5/31/2002	N/A	N/A
Goldman Sachs	GS	6/24/1999	32	22
John Hancock Financial Services	JHF	11/13/2000	32	49
MeadWestvaco	MWV	1/13/2002	−17	0
Metropolitan Life	MET	10/24/2000	10	29
Monsanto	MON	10/18/2000	49	72
Pepsi Bottling	PBG	4/29/1999	7	−3
Principal Financial	PFG	10/25/2002	N/A	N/A
Qwest	Q	5/2/2001	−87	−73
RJ Reynolds Tobacco Holdings	RJR	7/28/1999	5	−2
Rockwell Collins	COL	7/2/2001	6	29
United Parcel Service	UPS	11/18/1999	−9	−9
Visteon	VC	7/14/2000	24	43

*Returns don't include reinvested dividends.
Source: Bloomberg L.P.

323

Table 17.4   Year-End Yields for U.S. 10-Year Notes (1962–2001)

Year	Yield (%)	Year	Yield (%)	Year	Yield (%)
2001	5.051	1987	8.859	1973	6.902
2000	5.112	1986	7.223	1972	6.412
1999	6.442	1985	8.986	1971	5.892
1998	4.648	1984	11.514	1970	6.502
1997	5.741	1983	11.801	1969	7.882
1996	6.418	1982	10.389	1968	6.162
1995	5.572	1981	13.982	1967	5.702
1994	7.822	1980	12.432	1966	4.642
1993	5.794	1979	10.332	1965	4.652
1992	6.686	1978	9.152	1964	4.212
1991	6.699	1977	7.782	1963	4.142
1990	8.067	1976	6.812	1962	3.852
1989	7.935	1975	7.762		
1988	9.137	1974	7.402		

Source: Bloomberg L.P.

We took out the pencil and paper to see what happens to the S&P 500 when per-share dividends fall. From 1938 through September 2002, S&P 500 dividends have declined in only six years. Table 17.6 shows what happened to the market in the year of the decline and then in the next year.

Table 17.5   Selected S&P 500 Year-End Dividend Yields

Year	Yield (%)	Year	Yield (%)
2001	1.4	1990	3.7
2000	1.2	1980	4.5
1999	1.1	1970	3.4
1998	1.3	1960	3.3
1997	1.6	1950	7.2
1996	2.0	1940	6.3
1995	2.2	1935	3.5
1994	2.8	1900	4.3
1993	2.7		

Source: Bloomberg L.P., S&P Security Price Index Record, *The Triumph of the Optimists* (Princeton, NJ: Princeton University Press, 2002).

Table 17.6   Down Years for Dividends

Year of Decrease	Decline (%)	S&P 500 Return	Next Year's S&P 500 Return
1938	–37	25	–5
1942	–16	12	19
1951	–6	15	12
1958	–3	38	8
1970	–1	0	11
1971	–2	11	16

Source: Niederhoffer Investments.

In the six years that dividends declined, the average capital gain in the S&P 500 was 17 percent. The next year, the gain was 10 percent. Including dividends would add 5 percentage points to those results. The myth that stocks can't go up unless dividends do is clearly wrong.

Cash Indicators

In 2002, when confessions and revelations of accounting frauds filled the newspaper pages and the air was thick with the dust of crumbling companies, a friend who invests in Indian companies told us that wild exaggerations in financial reporting are the rule there. The only way to tell the genuine companies from the frauds was to find the ones that actually paid taxes.

On investigation, we found that many U.S. accounting disasters—WorldCom and Global Crossing being notable examples—had reported splendid earnings right up to the moment they imploded. There was, however, one sign of trouble that in retrospect seemed intriguing. Relative to the actual cash taxes that the companies paid, both companies had reported very high annual earnings before interest, taxes, depreciation, and amortization (EBIDTA) and taxes.

We wondered if the amount of taxes actually paid by a company relative to reported earnings might provide a clue as to whether financial chicanery was occurring behind the scenes. After all, few companies would go so far as to pay taxes on money they never made in the first place.

The mobsters of early Las Vegas understood this. Susan Berman, in her book, *Lady Las Vegas,* reports that when casino operators divided up the profits, there would be a pile for themselves, a pile for the government, and a pile for the mob bosses. Bugsy Siegel's bosses knocked him off when he didn't have a pile for them. They figured that if they didn't get their pile from Bugsy, he was either mismanaging their assets or stealing from them.

Nothing is wrong in principle, or is even suspicious, about a company reporting one income to the government and another to the public. Companies have two opposing goals: reporting as little net income as possible to the IRS—thereby limiting tax liability—and reporting as much net income as possible to the investing public. The rules that the IRS uses to calculate a company's income and tax liability can differ significantly from the Generally Accepted Accounting Principles (GAAP) the SEC requires companies to follow when calculating the income they report to the public.

A company's taxable income may differ significantly from the income it reports to shareholders for many legitimate reasons: the depreciation method used, the treatment of amortizing intangibles, the way revenues are booked, and whether and how stock options are expensed.

Tax accounting is one of the most technical, controversial, and fuzzy of all accounting areas. One generalization we can make is that growing companies tend to have increasing deferred tax liabilities. That's because they are continually making capital expenditures (buying computers or trucks, for example). Estimates of when deferred liabilities (or credits) are likely to be realized can vary substantially under GAAP and IRS guidelines. The difference in timing can occasionally—though not always—be material.

A back-of-the-envelope study seemed in order. Using the 30 Dow Jones Industrial stocks, we compared the EBITDA from their income statements to the cash taxes paid figure in their cash-flow statements. We separated the companies into high-tax payers and low-tax payers, and compared their stock performance. The results are shown in Tables 17.7 and 17.8.

Counterintuitively—which suggests the finding deserves closer scrutiny—the companies that paid less tax on the same amount of income did worse than the companies that paid more. You would expect that companies better able to avoid, or at least put off, paying taxes would be better managed and thus have higher performance. Our studies suggest the reverse at a statistically significant level.

To make sure our results were not due to chance, we ran the same test on a sample group of 50 S&P 500 stocks. As Table 17.9 shows, the high-tax payers again significantly outperformed the low-tax payers.

Our studies were very preliminary. It is quite possible that during other periods and other regimes, companies paying less tax would outperform, helped by their greater cash flow.

Table 17.7 High-Tax Payers

Name	Ticker	EBITDA, 2001 (in Thousands)	Cash Paid, 2001 (in Thousands)	Ratio, EBITDA/ Tax Paid	(%) Return 1/2002–9/2002
Hewlett-Packard	HPQ	3,200	1,159	2.8	–37.6
Exxon Mobil	XOM	29,000	9,855	2.9	–13.8
Home Depot	HD	5,700	1,685	3.4	–45.5
Procter & Gamble	PG	7,000	1,701	4.1	13.4
Wal–Mart Stores	WMT	13,400	3,196	4.2	–17.7
Boeing	BA	6,500	1,521	4.3	4.3
Johnson & Johnson	JNJ	9,500	2,090	4.5	–11.8
Coca–Cola	KO	6,200	1,351	4.6	3.4
Philip Morris	MO	18,000	3,775	4.8	5.8
Merck	MRK	11,500	2,300	5.0	–18.8
Walt Disney	DIS	4,600	881	5.2	–32.0
McDonald's	MCD	4,000	774	5.2	–13.4
3M	MMM	3,300	520	6.3	3.3
Alcoa	AA	3,500	548	6.4	–30.1
Caterpillar	CAT	2,500	379	6.6	–17.8
				Average stock performance	–13.9
				Standard deviation	17.5

Table 17.8 Low-Tax Payers

Name	Ticker	EBITDA, 2001 (in Thousands)	Cash Paid, 2001 (in Thousands)	Ratio, EBITDA/ Tax Paid	(%) Return 1/2002–9/2002
IBM	IBM	16,100	2,279	7.1	−43.8
Intel	INTC	8,900	1,208	7.4	−43.8
SBC Comm.	SBC	20,000	2,696	7.4	−35.0
United Tech.	UTX	3,700	497	7.4	1.4
DuPont	DD	3,500	456	7.7	−5.1
International Paper	IP	3,300	333	9.9	−5.5
Microsoft	MSFT	13,000	1,300	10.0	−30.4
American Express	AXP	6,800	545	12.5	−8.5
General Motors	GM	23,000	1,843	12.5	−12.3
Citigroup	C	31,600	2,411	13.1	−37.7
Honeywell	HON	1,100	79	13.9	−8.7
Eastman Kodak	EK	1,900	120	15.8	0.9
General Electric	GE	27,400	1,487	18.4	−24.4
AT&T	T	15,600	803	19.4	−49.2
J.P. Morgan	JPM	11,200	479	23.4	−32.3
				Average stock performance	−22.3
				Standard deviation	

Table 17.9   S&P 500 Sample Results

50 of 500	
High-Tax Payers	
Average performance	−15.7
Standard Deviation	24.9
Count	25
Low-Tax Payers	
Average	−31.0
Standard Deviation	24.6
Count	25

Cash Money

Balance sheets contain gold, but you have to know where to look. We found it buried in the fourth layer from the top, after cash, marketable securities, and accounts receivable—the inventory changes.

Is the company's inventory up? Chances are its stock is going to fall.

Is inventory down? Likelier than not, that stock will rise.

Sounds pretty much like common sense. It's an accounting twist as new as the twenty-first century and as old as trade: If a company puts a high value on a heap of inventory, earnings might be pumped up. But those microchips, routers, and subassemblies that are valued at billions on the balance sheet may have to be unloaded at a steep discount.

You can ignore it. But you can bet the market won't—not when times are tough and trust is low.

Anecdotes about companies that found their inventory building up before precipitous declines in price are legion. For example, Nvidia Corp.'s inventory in the year ending January 2002 increased to $214 million from its January 2001 level of $90.4 million. That's a jump of 137 percent; sales rose only 86 percent. Doubtless Nvidia was building up inventory in anticipation of much higher sales in 2002. Its shares declined 89 percent in 2002 (through October 9).

Or look at Tellabs, which fell 74 percent in 2001. Its inventory at year-end 2000 had increased 131 percent, to $428 million from $186 million, from the year-earlier level, while sales rose just 46 percent. In 2001, sales fell 35 percent.

Motorola provided an especially noteworthy example in 2000. Inventory increased some 40 percent, to $5.2 billion from $3.7 billion, but sales only rose 14 percent, to $37.6 billion from $33.1 billion. Motorola stock's 26 percent decline in 2001 seems somewhat muted, unless we note that in 2000, when the market in its wisdom was perhaps already discounting this, the price dropped 60 percent.

Companies that suffered sharp price declines in 2000 after reporting inventory increases at the end of 1999 are particularly numerous. Start with Amazon.com, where inventory jumped some 650 percent, to $221 million from $30 million. Sales grew almost 170 percent, to $1.6 billion from $610 million, and there were probably good explanations for management's decision to build up inventory. But the market was unforgiving, and Amazon.com fell some 80 percent in 2000.

Table 17.10 summarizes the ending inventory versus sales change and next year's percentage price appreciation. It seems like plain common sense that an inventory buildup relative to sales could be a sign of trouble. Most of us who have been in business have been victimized by rosy estimates of the value of inventory that can be sold only at drastically reduced prices, particularly in industries where products are subject to rapid obsolescence.

Unfortunately, it's not that simple. Many companies that report sharp increases in inventory are merely responding to sharp increases in sales. Often, they go on to show great performance in subsequent years. On the other side, many companies that show sharp decreases in inventory in a year are responding to drastic declines in sales. Instead of being star companies with sound earnings, they go on to dismal market performance.

As readers of our column and all other sober-minded investors know, anecdotes prove nothing. The diversity of stocks is so great that a story can be found to prove any generalization. To settle the issue, what's needed is a systematic and scientific study from an investigator knowledgeable in accounting, statistics, and practical investment.

Fortunately, such a study has been completed by Jacob Thomas, Ernst & Young professor of accounting and finance at New York's Columbia University, and one of his former students, Huai Zhang, now a professor at the University of Illinois.

Table 17.10   Inventory Buildups, Stock Takedowns

Company	Year	Ending Inventory (in Millions)	Inventory Change (%)	Sales Change (%)	Next Year's Stock Change (%)
Nvidia	2001	213.9	137	86	−84
Tellabs	2000	428.3	131	46	−74
Motorola	2000	5,242.0	41	14	−26
Amazon.com	1999	220.6	650	169	−80

Source: Bloomberg L.P.

Empty Shelves, Rising Stock

In their paper, "Inventory Change and Future Returns," Thomas and Zhang use as their starting point the well-documented finding that a company's stock performance tends to suffer after a period in which accrued earnings exceed cash earnings.[1] Accrued earnings are those that are reported in the annual report and the earnings statement, and they're what the media report. The main difference is that accrued earnings recognize revenues when a sale is legally binding and match expenses against the revenues. Cash earnings recognize sales and expenses in the period during which the money arrives and the expenses are paid. Companies have been required since 1988 to reconcile the difference between cash and accrued earnings on their statements of cash flow, one of four required financial statements that every company must submit to auditors.

More and more investors and analysts are focusing on the cash flow statement. Thomas, an immigrant from India, and Zhang, an immigrant from China, have made an important contribution to financial analysis by systematically testing which items on the cash flow statement are most predictive of future returns. After analyzing 39,315 firm years from 1970 to 1997, they conclude: "We find that inventory changes represent the main component that exhibits a consistent and substantial relation with future returns."

Companies with the greatest reductions in inventory (scaled by assets) show a greater price-plus-dividend return of 4 percentage points more than the average for all companies. Companies with the greatest increase in inventory, on the other hand, show a return 7 percentage points less than that of the average company. The difference held in 27 of the 28 years of the study. The usual statistical tests indicate this is a highly unusual event that could only be explained by chance on substantially less than 1 in 1,000 occasions.

Amazingly, the returns in the next year for these chosen companies add another 4 percent differential to the abnormal return.

Two other components of the balance sheet also have a large impact on returns, although significantly less than does inventory: depreciation expense (the higher the better), and change in accounts receivable (the less growth the better). Both these items give an abnormal return differential of 4 percent for the favorable companies versus the favorable ones.

Why do inventory changes matter so much? The professors offer three possible explanations:

1. **Demand shifts.** High inventory could be a signal that demand is declining and future profitability is in danger.

2. **Overproduction.** For manufacturing firms, producing more than initially anticipated causes per-unit inventory costs to be lower this year, which results in lower cost of goods sold and higher profitability. Everything reverses in the following year when fewer units are produced to bring inventory levels back to normal.

3. **Inventory misstatement.** Firms may use inventories to manage earnings. The cost of goods available for sale is determined by previous period's ending inventory and current period's costs for producing and purchasing inventory. At the end of the fiscal period, we have to assign cost of goods available for sale to either cost of goods sold or the ending balance of inventory. If you overstate the latter, cost of goods sold will be understated and earnings will then be overstated. The following year, inventory is written down and profits take a hit.

The professors conclude that earnings management is the likely suspect. They do not, however, attribute the inventory effect entirely to the practice of earnings management. "Consider the following scenario," Thomas wrote in an e-mail to us. "Cisco is running along on all eight cylinders, making routers and such like. There is a sudden decline in demand, but they think they can overcome it. Things get bad enough where they should reasonably be writing down some of the unsold inventory, but they don't because they're a bit optimistic. In the year after the inventory buildup, they finally admit things are bad and take a write-down, and returns fall. Would you construe the reluctance to take a write-down as earnings management? Some people would not call that earnings management, and view it simply as reasonable optimism about one's prospects."

Born in China, Zhang earned his bachelor's degree from Beijing University and came to the United States for his doctorate. "I entered Columbia's PhD accounting program with a blind trust in accounting numbers," Zhang told us. "Four years later, when I got out, I had developed a healthy skepticism. The flexibility offered by GAAP allows a company's management to manipulate the company's earnings while the investor community's steep penalty for not meeting analysts' forecasts sends the management off in that direction. My paper with Jake shows results consistent with investors being misled by earnings management through inventory. It's just another piece of evidence for my view of the world: Accounting can be dirty."

Much gold is hidden in a company's statements of cash flow. In practice, however, the investor is confronted by items beyond the ken of all but the most sophisticated accountants—and even they acknowledge difficulty.

Thomas, acknowledged as being among the giants in the accounting field, wrote: "Combing through the statements of cash flows and footnotes is painful but rewarding. There is no substitute for doing it the old-fashioned way. Unfortunately, the disclosures are often so cryptic and there's so much intentional distortion that most of us remain confused even after reading the damn thing over and over."

Compustat Confusion

The case for relying on cash earning rather than accrued earnings, with particular emphasis on inventory, would seem to be sound as a nut. But wait: the Thomas-Zhang study was based on companies taken from Standard and Poor's Compustat data files. While Compustat's files are widely used, we have grave concerns about them because of their retrospective nature, and what we consider their survivor bias.

MIT professor Andrew Lo, of whom the cognoscenti in this field always speak in superlatives, pointed out that Compustat "backward-revises" its data, posing insidious problems for researchers. With Compustat, "today's values for 1997s IBM current assets need not be the same as last month's values for 1997s IBM current assets," Lo wrote us. "Compustat's backfilling is a problem every single month, including this month. Do the following analysis (I've done it): this month, take all observations in the Compustat files for October 2001 and save it; then next month do the exact same thing for the exact same date; now run a variable-by-variable comparison of the two supposedly identical files—you'll see at least 200 discrepancies, if not more. These issues don't even touch on the quality of the data, spottiness of the coverage, and timeliness of the updates."

Another potential problem is that Thomas and Zhang examined many different balance sheet items and methods of computing them before settling on the specific ones in the paper. This approach may yield statistical bugs related to the correlation of many balance sheet items with each other as well as to the serial correlation in these items between consecutive years.

Thomas agreed that backfilling of Compustat data is a potential concern, but said it hasn't been a problem in the last decade. "As far as I know, the last major backfill was done in the 1970s." He added: "To me, the two big questions are (a) Why did the market not see this mispricing until it becomes very evident in the next quarters' reported earnings? And (b) Does the mispricing occur even now?"

Whom do you call when you want a scientific update? That's right, the Spec Duo. We pencil-and-envelope tested whether inventory and account receivable changes have been inversely associated with subsequent price performance for recent years.

Dow

Since this was an exploratory study, and we wished to use prospective data from a relatively homogeneous sample, we restricted our study to the 30 Dow companies. These companies are important in themselves, accounting for some 28 percent of the total market value of all U.S.-based publicly traded companies.

We took the five best (those with the greatest decreases) and the five worst (those with the greatest increases) in inventory and accounts receivable for 1998, and compared the performance of the groups during 1999. We then did the same for the best and worst of 1999 as shown in Table 17.11.

Table 17.11   Total Return (%)*

	2000	1999
5 greatest inventory increases	−7	−17
5 greatest inventory decreases	−1	12
5 greatest accounts receivable increases	−1	−18
5 greatest accounts receivable decreases	4	6

* Price appreciation + Reinvested dividends.

The results show that in the year following increases in inventory and accounts receivable, performance was highly inferior, with returns of some −10 percentage points.

For the companies with the greatest decreases in inventory and accounts receivable, the performance in the next year was relatively good, with returns averaging about 5 percentage points.

Because only 20 companies were involved, and because the results were highly variable and subject to much in the way of ever-changing cycles, the odds are only about 20 to 1 that these results could not be attributed to chance variations alone.

Nevertheless, we conclude that you have to know the accounts receivable and inventory territory if you're going to make music in the market.

A Combination Tell

Rewards have never been greater for those able to discern truly superior investment opportunities. Yet favorite buy signals such as buybacks and insider buying too often turn out to be misleading in individual cases. In the words of our favorite science fiction novel, *Invasion of the Body Snatchers,* more than one company that seemed to fit our criteria "only looked, talked, and acted" like one that really thought its stock was a good value.

We have designed a new system to weed out imposters. We started by considering imposters in life and nature. The story of 1890s adventurer Louis de Rougement proved particularly inspiring. As told by Sarah Burton in her entertaining book, *Impostors: Six Kinds of Liar—True Tales of Deception,* de Rougement claimed to have survived 30 years in the vast Australian outback by convincing the cannibals that he possessed supernatural powers. Eventually, he found his way back to London and sold his tale to *Wide World* magazine.

The very first installment of the story created a furor. De Rougement's account of riding sea turtles was widely ridiculed. "I have caught and handled some thousands of turtles," wrote an Australian, "and I never yet saw one which when afloat and when touched anywhere on its body did not sink almost vertically." An admiral weighed in on de Rougement's side: "I have considerable experience of turtle-catching, and know of a midshipman who got on a turtle and enjoyed a 10 minutes' ride before he brought the animal to a standstill." In 1906, the self-proclaimed cannibal chief rode a sea turtle at the London Hippodrome, disproving the naysayers. By then, however, investigative reporters had unmasked de Rougement as an imaginative former valet named Louis Grin.

On reading de Rougement's story, we realized we needed more than a mere sea turtle test to avoid being fooled. This point was driven home when we read about the outrageous high-stakes frauds perpetrated by innocent-seeming plants.

European orchids not only look like bees, they smell like sexually receptive female bees—all to seduce male bees into carrying pollen. A bee, after excitedly crawling all over an alluring flower and attempting union, quickly learns to distrust the fraudulent scent—but 100 other types of orchids practice similar shams.

"After visiting four or five different plants, he has learned his lesson—the whole lot that smell in this general way are useless and he visits them no more," writes David Attenborough, in *The Private Life of Plants.* "But by that time, he is likely to have done what the orchids required of him."

So it goes with investors. They are attracted by companies that buy back their stock, or have insider buying, only to be surprised by disclosures of secret debts, vaporous earnings, or magic-trick accounting for acquisitions. After a few encounters with such impostors, investors may be ready to give up on stocks entirely. But by then, they have made their contributions to the market.

Some plants practice deadlier deceptions, pretending to be food for a predator and then making the predator their prey. The pitcher plants of Southeast Asia are shaped like beakers, flagons, decanters, and champagne flutes. Using copious amounts of nectar, they lure insects inside—and then dissolve their trapped victims in digestive acid.

To avoid being fooled, seduced, or eaten alive by our stock selections, we decided to require multiple signals before buying. Our evolutionary grounds for doing so are that no life form (and hopefully, no company) would expend the energy necessary to give off multiple false signals.

Three-Signal Monte

We settled on three signals that we feel have been particularly efficacious:

1. Buyback announcement.
2. Big decrease in inventory.
3. Big decrease in accounts receivable.

As reported earlier, companies that announced buybacks from year-end 2000 through October 3, 2002, outperformed the S&P 500 by some 6 percentage points. The five Dow Jones Industrial Average companies in 1998 and 1999 with the greatest inventory decreases outperformed those with the greatest increases, with the difference averaging out to some 10 percentage points.

Before choosing these particular signals, we conducted many tests that could be classified as negative studies. The buyback companies perform so well that additional criteria are not overly helpful. For example, we found that the percentage of shares bought back as well as insider buying within this group did not add significantly to the returns during 2002.

Our exploratory work showed a slight edge for the 93 companies that announced buybacks in the first three quarters of 2002 and also reported the greatest decreases in inventory and accounts receivable. Table 17.12 illustrates this signal.

Table 17.12   Performance of Buyback Companies Reporting Large Decreases in Inventory and Accounts Receivable

Buyback Companies	Percentage Points over S&P 500's YTD Return (%)
10 largest inventory decreases	3 percentage points
10 largest accounts receivable increases	1 percentage point

It might be useful to consider the returns from buying baskets of companies showing each of these three signals in the future. But it will require much study before the results will be of practical or statistical significance. When we presented our findings in a series of columns on fundamental analysis for CNBC Money, some readers remarked on the irony. Vic, after all, has long traded on price interactions, not financial statements or dividend payouts. One reader wrote: "The Speculator talking about dividends as a valuable investment criterion! Now I know I'm in Kansas."

There's a certain wisdom in that observation. By the time Vic and his ilk are ready to study value, chances are that tech will be back. *It never hurts to know your way around a balance sheet, though.* If investors agree about anything nowadays, it's that we need transparent, nondistorted financial statements to restore trust in Corporate America. You would think that all executives of major companies would lean over backward so as not to be perceived as managing earnings, for the good of the business world as well as their own stockholders.

The time when a company could expect applause for pulling a rabbit out of the hat to meet earnings forecasts—say, by selling one of the businesses it had acquired over the years—would seem to be over. But apparently, some companies don't feel this way.

General Electric, for example, stated on Wednesday, September 25, 2002, that it expected to meet third-quarter earnings projections. Wonderful, the market said. General Electric shares rose 4.3 percent. The next day, it came out at a news conference that the forecast would be met by selling a business unit, Global eXchange Services. Disappointed investors sent General Electric down 2.3 percent. By Friday, when they figured out that General Electric had loaned the purchase money to the buyer and had even taken back a 10 percent interest; they were more than ready to laugh General Electric out of town. The 9 percent loss over those two sessions took some $25 billion off the market capitalization of the world's most valuable company.

General Electric may have a great reason for the sale, but as the company has refused to grant us an interview and advised us to refrain from contacting it again, we can't report any explanation at all. What's clear is that General Electric's decision cost its shareholders dearly at a time when the need to be beyond reproach is more than evident.

Such a reaction wasn't exactly unprecedented. In February 2002, IBM took a 5 percent hit after the *New York Times* reported that the company used the sale of a unit to lower fourth-quarter operating expenses, instead of reporting the sale as a one-time gain. The demise of Enron, WorldCom, and Arthur Andersen after the disclosure of earnings misstatements and cover-ups has made investors skeptical even of squeaky-clean companies with cash from operations soaring to the moon and no nonrecurring items of any kind.

Yet General Electric's skill in managing earnings to meet analyst expectations has been known for years—and until recently, renowned. Carol Loomis, writing in *Fortune* in August 1999, observed that after the *Wall Street Journal* published a front-page story in 1994 detailing the many ways that Welch and his team "smoothed" General Electric's net income, AIG, Champion International, and Cigna called to say, "Well, this is what companies do. Why is this a front-page story?" (We suspect that many other companies read the article to see how it was done.)

SEC chief Arthur Levitt declared war on managed earnings back in September 1998. In a dinner speech at New York University, the audience put down their forks and started taking notes when Levitt said many executives and auditors were playing "a game of nods and winks" to meet or beat earnings projections to pump up market capitalization and increase the value of management's stock options. Levitt asked Corporate America and Wall Street to stop using accounting gimmicks: no more big write-offs for restructuring charges, future operating expenses, or "in-process research" to make future earnings look better, no more stashing profits in "cookie jar reserves" to bring out later, no more booking sales before delivery takes place, no more quibbling over how big a lie has to be before it's "material" under Generally Accepted Accounting Principles.

The "better-than-expected earnings" game has been a long-time favorite for corporations and their Wall Street cheering section. Come recession, come boom, come 100-year interest-rate events, come terrorist attack, some 60 percent of the S&P 500 has consistently "beat" analysts' forecasts. Here is the distribution percentage of positive surprises for S&P 500 companies from 2000 to 2002:

Q2 2002   60.1 percent
Q1 2002   62.1 percent
Q4 2001   55.3 percent

Q3 2001	51.2 percent (even though country was shut down for a fortnight)
Q2 2001	55.2 percent
Q1 2001	54.4 percent
Q4 2000	51.0 percent
Q3 2000	58.2 percent
Q2 2000	63.7 percent
Q1 2000	70.7 percent

The question is not whether they nudge and wink, but how high they'll take you before they drop the ball.

We wonder how many other companies have a choice now of deciding whether to meet earnings expectations by selling a company or asset they acquired long ago. Let us hope they learn from General Electric's experience. Otherwise, there may come a time when their own credibility is on the line. If their response meets the new standards of evaluation, success is assured. If not, investors will be disinclined to accept at face value any official statements at all.

Similar turning points can be observed in politics. If the gap between word and fact becomes so noticeable that even supporters cannot countenance it, an office holder will soon find his power on the downtrend. In sports, the scandal at the Winter Olympics in Salt Lake City indirectly enabled Sara Hughes to finally gain her well-deserved recognition. According to sportswriter Rick Reilly, Sara Hughes had been the best in the United States for some time. Only after the public pantsing of the judges in the pairs skating competition were the figure skating judges able to do the right thing and give the nod to Sara.

Unfortunately, merely vowing to change won't work when credibility has been damaged too badly. Between mid-July and early October 2002, more than 50 companies pledged to treat options as an expense, responding to calls for greater transparency in reporting operating costs. We compared the performance of these "transparent" companies with that of the S&P 500 and found that they actually lagged the index by 3 percentage points. The 52 companies that took the pledge lost −9.6 percent, on average, versus −6.4 percent for the S&P 500.

Vic's father, Artie Niederhoffer, used to say that if a choice came up between giving people in trouble cash or advice, to always give the cash. Artie's wisdom carries the day here. What counts in troubled times is cash. We hope that the indicators we wrote about in this chapter will prove of service.

18   FINALE

> **[I]t appeared** to me that I should do welcome service to all who have to rough it—whether explorers, emigrants, missionaries or soldiers—by collecting the scattered experiences of many such persons in various circumstances, collating them, examining into their principles, and deducing from them what might fairly be called an "Art of Travel."
>
> —Francis Galton, *The Art of Travel*[1]

We get asked four questions regularly:

1. Aren't there any technical indicators that you use in your work?
2. Where do you find all those down-home philosophers and scientists, who from their job descriptions seem like average Joes but who turn out to have wild but useful ideas about the market?
3. How can you say such awful things about Alan Greenspan? Are you so bullish that you didn't realize there was a stock market bubble?

4. What book do you recommend for me to continue my education after reading this one?

We will answer each of these questions.

Technical Indicators

As mentioned in Chapter 3, there are so many different indicators that one always seems to work well in any particular time period. Thus, when we answer this question by observing that almost all technical indicators are untested, and that most are amorphous and unsusceptible of testing, and the results of all of them are completely consistent with a random walk, the person who has found the indicator to be successful in a specific period invariably responds with disbelief.

To prevent this, we have taken another tack. Without boasting unduly, Vic has been programming for more than 40 years and is quite capable of testing any indicators or method. During many of those years, he was a well-respected and potent force in the industry, and technical analysts often visited to get him to finance or test their systems. This was particularly true when he was chief bottle washer and evaluator of scientific systems for Soros, because if the system was a hit, there was the potential for billions to be thrown at it.

Vic has been recording hourly prices on 15 to 20 markets on a real-time basis by hand for the past 40 years. One of his record books, from 1965, appeared in a Japanese television special on him. In Japan, defeated ronins make pilgrimages to Mt. Fuji for guidance and sustenance; in this case, he was shown seeking guidance from his ancient book of hourly price records.

The three universities he was fortunate enough to attend—Harvard, the University of Chicago, and the University of California, Berkeley—were associated with a large part of the seminal research into the behavior of stock prices. The University of Chicago, where he received his PhD, developed the database used by almost all studies of stock market behavior, the Center for Research in Securities Prices. Of the 12 Nobel Prizes that have been given for economics, 10 of them had some association with the University of Chicago, including the Black-Scholes options pricing model, the Miller-Modigliani cost of capital and dividend contributions, Aliber's work on foreign exchange, and Lucas' rational expectations theory. The theory of portfolio insurance that figured so prominently in the 1987 crash was developed at the University of California while he was attending that institution.

In addition to that, the one thing that he has been very good at doing has been attracting smart people to his organization. Almost all of them are highly quantitative. Richard Zeckhauser, who now is considered a leader in behavioral finance, was Vic's partner for 20 years. In those days, he was always willing to apply his expertise developed from being number one in the mathematical actuaries exam in high school to the solution and scientific analysis of technical studies. Between Vic and his highly intelligent current and former partners and colleagues, we have the ability to implement and utilize on a practical basis any techniques of technical analysis that may have merit.

Therefore, the fact that we are not using such a particular system would mean that it has been seriously multiple-comparisoned here and found wanting, Thus, we are the last people in the world who should be asked to opine on one of the 573 indicators.

After all of this, the conversation invariably comes to an abrupt end as the questioner goes away saying, "_____ Niederhoffer, if it's not invented there, he's too vain to even consider it."

Where Do We Find All Our Experts?

Much of the value in our columns, and in this book, has come from the net we cast to catch all the specialized niches of knowledge, technical expertise, and insights in various fields that our readers kindly communicate to us from around the world.

When we started writing a column on the stock market together in January 2000, we realized that no duo, however well informed, could know everything useful about the market. The great lesson of the twentieth century is that central economic planning creates poverty, but the combined tastes, preferences, know-how, and insights of millions of people somehow direct goods from all over the world to store shelves and tables in a beautiful celebration of prosperity and well-being.

Because we were writing for the Internet, we decided to make full use of our medium. Hayek's great insight was that free markets function best because they draw on the knowledge, wisdom, and skills of the many. We put the idea into practice by asking readers for insights, and our hopes were realized beyond our wildest dreams.

It frequently happens that an expert in one field or another writes in with a constructive suggestion as to how we can improve and pass along sharp and valuable information to our readers. We awarded canes as prizes for what struck us as the most outstanding contributions, in a nod to one of our favorite passages about the market, from *Twenty-Eight Years in Wall Street*, written by Henry Clews in 1887:

> But few gain sufficient experience in Wall Street to command success until they reach that period of life in which they have one foot in the grave. When this time comes, these old veterans of the Street usually spend long intervals of repose at their comfortable homes, and in times of panic, which recur sometimes oftener than once a year, these old fellows will be seen in Wall Street, hobbling down on their canes to their brokers' offices.
>
> Then they always buy good stocks to the extent of their bank balances, which they have been permitted to accumulate for just such an emergency. The panic usually rages until enough of these cash purchases of stock are made to afford a big "rake in." When the panic has spent its force, these old fellows, who have been resting judiciously on their oars in expectation of the inevitable event, which usually returns with the regularity of the seasons, quickly realize, deposit their profits with their bankers, or the overplus thereof, after purchasing more real estate that is on the up grade, for permanent investment, and retire for another season to the quietude of their splendid homes and the bosoms of their happy families.[2]

The first cane went to Brett Steenbarger, a State University of New York psychologist who would become a dear, valued friend. On February 25, 2000, just two weeks before the Nasdaq peaked at 5048, Dr. Brett wrote:

> First, the kiss: You and Vic write one of the most lucid and thought-provoking columns anywhere. Your musical analogies to the markets are dead-on.

Now the tell (favorite indicator):

> On a speculative note, I hypothesize that there is a positive and significant correlation between the beats-per-minute of popular music and price changes in the stock market. From post-Depression blues, forties crooners, fifties/sixties rock 'n' roll, late sixties/early seventies psychedelia, late seventies disco, eighties New Wave, and now the electronic dance raves (150 bpm *de rigeuer*), we've seen a steady ramping up of acoustic adrenalin. And what are we to make of the recent resurrection of the twenties dance sound?

In a subsequent e-mail on March 2, he added:

> The market's music is reaching a heightened tempo, at least on the Nasdaq. But even in the clubs of Ibiza, when the pace has become frenetic at 4 a.m., they have to shift the pace and go into "melodic trance" mode with Robert Miles. It's that old A-B-A structure, I guess. . . . We'll have to see if the dancers start stumbling, spent of their Ecstasy.

We messaged Dr. Brett to tell him we were sending him a cane, and the next day received the following note:

Well, it was quite a day. First your most generous e-mails re: the tells and then my return home. I opened the garage and there, greeting me in bright colors, was a large sign hand-drawn by my two little ones. It read: "Congratulations Cane Winner!" That's enough to melt even the most wizened trader's heart.

We told the story in our column, noting the names of Dr. Brett's kids. The next e-mail melted our own hearts:

"I wish you could have been there," wrote Dr. Brett. "I took Macrae to the computer and showed him your article. When he got to the part with his name, his eyes grew wide. 'You mean anyone in the world who goes to this Web site can see my name?' he asked.

" 'That's right,' I responded.

"He turned from the computer and stared into space, his eyes still quite wide. In a tone of absolute wonderment, he whispered, 'I'm famous!'

"It was a priceless moment."

One reader, Don Staricka, sent us excerpts from his forthcoming *Devil's Stock Market Dictionary,* a masterpiece of humor surpassing the work of Ambrose Bierce.

* * *

Balanced Portfolio: A strategy for breaking even over the course of one's investment career.

Buying Opportunity: Any occasion where an equity suddenly and unexpectedly loses value.

Contrarian: One who bets against the winners.

Correction: A distasteful remedy for unwarranted bullishness. When the prices of equities within a sector (or the market as a whole) move downward simultaneously the market is said to have "corrected." This implies that the higher prices were "incorrect." Contrast with **Rally.**

Dividend: A booby prize.

Equity: Ownership in a company through the purchase of stock. As a shareholder one participates in the success of a company without the obligation to attend departmental meetings, company picnics or sensitivity training seminars. And there's no job interview so you don't have to worry about concealing your tongue stud or borrowing a suit.

Franchise: Information culled from a company's marketing literature that investors interpret as evidence of competitive advantage.

Goodwill: The difference between what an equity costs and what it is actually worth.

Interest Rates: An all-purpose explanation for whatever happens.

IPO: The lowest price at which one will be able to purchase shares in a new company until lockup expiration or until the company's true potential is recognized.

Kondratief: According to Kondratief Wave Theory economic cycles lasting 50 to 60 years trump all other factors and render meaningless our futile efforts to resist the inevitable booms and busts. This theory explains why only now, at the beginning of the twenty-first century, have we finally started to pull out of a catastrophic depression.

Linux: A late twentieth-century collectivist religion practiced over the Internet.

Lockup Expiration: The point at which the full complement of shares from a recent public offering hits the market. See **Supply and Demand.**

Momentum Play: An investment decision informed by the theory that what goes up must go up.

Penny Stocks: Extremely inexpensive equities that are worth substantially less than what they cost.

Phrenology: A science that purports to identify behavioral characteristics based upon a mapping of the lumps and depressions in a person's skull. Now discredited. See **Technical Analysis.**

Portfolio: The itemization of an investor's current blunders.

Rally: A distasteful remedy for unwarranted bearishness. When the prices of equities within a sector (or the market as a whole) move upward simultaneously, the market is said to have "rallied." This implies that the lower prices that resulted from the earlier "correction" were "incorrect." Contrast with **Correction.**

Stop Loss: The point immediately below which an equity begins a sustained rally.

Supply and Demand: The one true explanation for the price of any equity.

Sympathy: A manifestation of the grieving process. If an equity loses value because of mismanagement or the announcement of an SEC investigation, other equities in the same sector may lose value "in sympathy." See **Buying Opportunity.**

Technical Analysis: A form of divination practiced by investors to predict the behavior of the market. See **Phrenology.**

Turnaround Play: An investment decision informed by the theory that what goes down must go up.

Value Play: An investment decision informed by the theory that what has been down for a long enough period of time must eventually go up.

We began circulating the e-mails of Dr. Brett, Staricka, and other experts who wrote in. A small feedback group formed. One of the earliest to enter the fray was Mark M. McNabb, a blues-and-barbecue-loving finance professor at Virginia Tech University. It was Dr. McNabb who articulated the approach that evolved into our mantra:

> The imperative to specialize in Western society has always been an effort to improve one's station in life. Walt Rostow, historian and economist, attributes much of the success in capitalism to the early rise of productivity in agriculture, which freed many to carry out commerce and devote themselves to other areas of knowledge, especially scientific and technical knowledge.
>
> Today, we find even the most dominant firms, such as Intel, are motivated to acquire the knowledge of others (despite the depth of talent within their firms) in order to progress and maintain their position in markets that are changing at a pace unlike any time before in our history. In finance and business, specialization requires the talents of many as new problems often materialize in unexpected areas; a cursory look at the resumes of employees at any leading firm or investment bank, no matter how narrowly focused, will reveal a wealth of talent, knowledge and abilities.
>
> Markets today often present the investor with "information saturation" beyond one's own ability to analyze. What is needed to parse through the mass of conflicting bits is the views and experiences of many, to sort and order it into a rational framework. The challenge is that the framework is never static. It's more like a sandcastle washed out to sea by a torrent of new views and events every day and rebuilt to a new form by those employing their best vision. By combining the disparate talents of many, a consensus arises that surpasses the scope of a single view. Through our assimilating and borrowing from past and present, rather than rejecting the unknown on narrow ideology and training, the truth reveals itself.

As our group of corresponding speculators grew larger, a technically savvy reader, James Cornelius Goldcamp, set up a list so that all the readers could see each other's messages to us and from us. The resulting correspondence gave birth to numerous friendships and business relationships. We held a SpecList party one summer so that we could meet one another face to face. The event proved so enjoyable and fruitful that the Spec Party has become a summer tradition.

We have benefited immensely from the exchange. Most of our columns for CNBC Money contain insights, some attributed and some anonymous, from SpecList members. Some members have written guest columns for us. We were so glad to see Dr. Brett land a Wiley book deal and a CNBC Money column of his own that we were able to overcome a slight feeling of having been upstaged.

It was Dr. Brett, in fact, who in 2002 penned the most eloquent explanation of what the SpecList is all about:

> The patron saint of the Speculation List is not Victor Niederhoffer, although he is near and dear to many of us. The patron saint is Francis Galton. Galton is the father of modern statistics and an exemplar of empiricism. He collected data on thousands of individuals to ascertain the genetic determinants of intellectual functioning. He did not begin from revealed truths or first principles, as would our modern-day egalitarians. He collected data and sought to explain the patterns he observed within the data.
>
> The heart and soul of the SpecList is the empirical temperament. It is a desire to discover and know. It is a celebration of the human capacity to apprehend reality through volitional efforts. In seeking to master the markets, we participate in the very essence of the heroic quest: the winning of a boon while struggling against mighty forces. Those forces are many: the complexity of the markets, the perverse nature of our own emotions, and the savvy competition. Arrayed against those are only the human mind and its capacity to transform data into information.

By 2002, the SpecList had grown to 200 members living all over the world, from South Africa to Slovakia to Silicon Valley. It has been through various permutations and bifurcations. One offshoot became an informal School for Speculators, a unique forum for quantitative work on the market.

More about Ever-Changing Cycles

One of the great purposes of the SpecList has been to keep us abreast of the market's ever-changing cycles. As readers of Vic's first book may recall, the profound principle of ever-changing cycles was put forward by Bacon in *Secrets of Professional Turf Betting,* now unfortunately out of print. We quoted from this 1956 classic at the start of our book, but cannot refrain from doing so again:

> In actual racing, the percentage of winners does not remain constant as the public's play beats down the prices of horses picked by any set scheme.
>
> Some well-to-do horsemen who sent their horses out to do their best for probable betting prices of 3-to-1 "cooled off" as the prices sank below 5-to-2. Instead of trying their hardest to win, they sent the horses out to win, if they could win easily. But the boys were told not to punish the animals, told to pull them back out of the money in the stretch if they saw an easy winning was not possible.
>
> The horsemen knew that this pulling back out of the money would make a bad race show as the last outing in the past performance charts, thus putting the public off the horse for next time.

We thought that nobody could improve on Bacon until a reader, Martin Knight, reformulated the principle of ever-changing cycles as a variant of Newton's law of cooling. Newton observed that the change in temperature of an object is proportional to the difference between its temperature and the surrounding air. Knight pointed out that market cycles obey Newton's law of cooling: the greater the regularity, the greater the difference between actual and random results, the more flow of public money there will be to capture it. That flow will bring the regularity back to randomness, or equilibrium, over time just as temperature will tend to level out in a room. But new heat sources will turn up to create new flows. The beautiful thing about Knight's reformulation is that it provides a quantitative estimate of the rate at which cycles will change.

Knight, an Englishman living in California, is a humble 38-year-old master of statistics who became interested in applying behavioral finance theory to his own investments. He achieved a 77 percent return in 2001 and 33 percent in 2000, although he says he feels comfortable with returns less than that.

We have come across two other geniuses who discovered applications of the principle of ever-changing cycles to markets. The first wrote the *Economist*'s end-of-year forecast in 1986. The anonymous author treats the principle as a variant of a game called "Cheat the Prophet." In this game, which repeats every decade, everybody believes that some easily expandable things (say, to name an updated example, Web page views or energy derivatives trading) are going to be immensely profitable. But then, in the next decade, a small movement in prices and the competitive environment caused by these fixed beliefs sends the things that are supposed to be eternally profitable into unsalable, abysmal deficit. "Thus, the areas that are supposed to be immutably set on some particular course go on to precisely the opposite one." The *Economist*'s writer calls this principle "the law of opposites," and presciently states that knowing about this could make readers quite rich, provided others don't believe it.[3]

A few years later, Julian Simon discovered this principle independently. His discovery arose from his attempt to find out why real commodities prices were constantly decreasing and why predictions of commodity shortages are always wrong. He likened the situation to looking at a tub of water and marking the water level, and then observing people putting water from the tub into buckets and taking it away. But when the tub is examined again, the level is higher than it was at the start. He attributes the constantly increasing water to discoveries of improved methods of production of goods that are in shortage and the development of substitutes. "More people and increased income cause resources to become more scarce in the short run. Heightened scarcity causes prices to rise. The higher prices present opportunity and prompt investors to search for solutions. These solutions eventually lead to prices dropping lower than before the scarcity occurred."[4]

On July 13, 2002, we received a brilliant post from the indefatigable Dr. Brett that so eloquently summarizes the evolution of his and our own thinking on ever-changing cycles that we reprint it in full.

Revisiting Complexity in Trading Systems

It seems to me there are three basic positions one could take regarding the stock and equity index markets:

1. They are random/completely unpredictable—This is the stance of the Efficient Market Hypothesis and leads to the conclusion that efforts to time the markets are a waste of time and that placing money in a well-diversified index of companies over the long haul is the best way of participating in the markets' long-term positive risk-adjusted returns.

2. They are predictable—This is the stance of most technical analysts and developers of mechanical trading systems, who believe they can exploit recurring patterns in the market for profit. These patterns are held to be intrinsic to the markets, reflecting fundamental qualities of human nature (e.g., greed, fear) or regularities in nature (e.g., Fibonacci sequences).

3. They vary in their degree of predictability—This is the stance of those who model the markets and adjust their models to changing cycles. Predictability is itself viewed as a variable, with markets changing in the degree to which they can be predicted and in the elements that comprise valid predictions.

For traders subscribing to Position #3, any trading system must exist at a minimum of two conceptual levels. The first order trading system consists of a set of predictors and a hypothesized relationship between those predictors and market outcomes. The second order system consists of a set of conditions for modifying the parameters of the first system as cycles change.

Stated more simply, a trader who ascribes to the notion of changing cycles needs at minimum: (a) a model to trade and (b) a process for remodeling to keep abreast of shifts in the distribution of price changes over time.

It is, of course, possible to conceptualize a third-order trading system that consists of meta-rules for shifting remodeling processes in response to market conditions.

For example, a first-order technical trading model might buy the market when the 12 period RSI moves from below 30 to above 30 and sell when the RSI moves from above 70 to below 70. A second-order trading system would consist of rules for using 21 versus 12 versus 8 period RSI readings for the original trading system, perhaps as a function of market volatility and trendiness. A third-order trading system might consist of rules for categorizing markets based upon volatility or trendiness and assigning unique remodeling rules for each category (i.e., select from 21 versus 12 versus 8 period RSI readings for a nontrending market of high, medium, or low volatility; shift from 30–70 trigger points to 20–80 and 10–90 crossover points for trending markets of low, medium, or high volatility).

Through the layering of conceptual levels and complexity (as Henry Carstens has observed), the trading system gains adaptive potential. Indeed, the trader who adheres to position #3 *cannot* follow a single trading system, as changing cycles force the creation of a branching tree of trading approaches.

In spite of this, most discussions of trading systems focus on the first level of complexity (entries/exits/stops) without consideration of how these are modified in the face of shifting market conditions. To the extent that this second level of complexity is missing, a trader can be expected to do well under one set of market conditions and dismally in others—which is what we're seeing with many traders who made money in the late 1990s and now are having a difficult time.

A straightforward application of evolutionary thinking suggests that the trader who develops more trading systems across levels of complexity stands a greater chance of achieving adaptive outcomes in the markets. Dean Keith Simonton makes this point in his excellent book *Genius, Creativity, and Leadership*. Citing Donald Campbell, he writes:

> [T]he course of cultural evolution is analogous to that of biological evolution. The 'cultural fitness' of an individual creator is dependent upon his or her ability to generate big ideas, each representing a certain permutation of smaller ideas. The more permutations that are generated, the higher the odds that a particular permutation will survive the winnowing process imposed by posterity. A less prolific creator will simply have a lower chance of leaving intellectual progeny that will endure this selection process.
>
> This model clearly predicts that quality is a probabilistic consequence of quantity. . . .[5]

The idea that there are types of markets and trading systems best suited for particular market types allows for a higher number of permutations than the idea that a single set of parameters can be traded across all markets. Jean Piaget held that the development of complexity was the hallmark of the maturing mind. It may also be the hallmark of the maturing trader.

Here's a July 26, 2002, post from a veteran Florida trader, James Lackey:

My father was a Boilermaker. He was a welder. As a kid I was taught not to watch the welders arc. It will blind you.

When using a torch you can heat up metal to shape it. Or you can turn up the heat and cut metal. I find the same with stock prices.

As the velocity of movement in a stock price increases, it cuts through prices. A slow burn, to add heat a little at a time, just bends prices.

I have always been a tape reader. I watch the markets very closely all day. The joke in the office is, if you stare at the screen long enough you will turn into a bad tick. That is something my grandmother would have said.

If enough contracts trade a certain price, the price begins to glow. It is red hot like heated steel. Any trader older than 5 years, knows touching it can burn him. Therefore, that price becomes untouchable, until someone turns up the heat and cuts through that price.

It is good to know that price of hot steel exists. There is no way to see it on a chart. As it has cooled slightly and no longer glows red. The unsuspecting trader will come on to the price and get burned. Until the price has been cut with a torch. By that time sparks are flying and the work is done.

However, after several minutes prices cool. Limit orders are canceled. The energy needed to cut through that price changes with time. Is steel that is hardened with previous heat harder to cut? Are stock prices that trade with more energy harder to break? Are prices forged like steel, hammered and beaten into super strength?

Once that price is broken, it is damaged. A completely different process must take place to repair the price. Like welding steel, after it has been repaired. A weld is much stronger than the original piece or stock price.

Touching a red-hot price has burned me. Worse, I have been cut to pieces. By a false belief that an old price, that was previously broken would somehow support me from a fall. Metal slivers in the behind, are very painful. . . . LACK

Gone Fishing

In the summer of 2001, we found ourselves grim over a broad worldwide decline. We wanted to knock the hat off of the next broker who greeted us with a cheery, "You're filled at your price, sir/ma'am." Taking our cue from *Moby Dick*, we realized it was high time to go fishing. We went looking for rules that hold true in the market's high tides as well as its low tides. Being partial to patient partisans of the pastime, we invited members of the SpecList to weigh in. As always, we were awed by the insights that poured in from all sides. We here present a few samples of the resulting discussion of what traders can learn from fishing.

Reflections on a Lake

—John Lamberg, engineer/inventor; and Mark M McNabb, finance professor, Virginia Tech

1. **Be on the lake when the fish are feeding**. Know what sectors the market likes.
2. **Don't go fishing when the lake is packed with tourists. You probably won't be able to get near your favorite fishing hole, and even if you do, all those churning propellers will scare the fish away.** If everyone is playing the same stock idea, the easy money has been made.

How to Land Them (Artist: Hy Hintermeister, © 1937).

3. **Come prepared with well-maintained fishing equipment, an adequate supply of bait, lures and sharp hooks, and an extra supply of patience.** Give your best ideas time to work, but don't use margin to see them out.

4. **Don't make noise; you will scare the fish away.** Fidelity never speaks; why should you?

5. **Don't fish where there are no fish. Know the structure of the lake and the habits of the fish you are trying to catch. Electronic fish finders can help you locate fish, but it won't make them bite.** If no one else is buying, why should you? Catching falling daggers can kill a dip-buyer.

6. **Despite your best preparations, sometimes the fish just won't bite. Don't be discouraged; go back to shore and enjoy the day, then come back another time.** Even the best traders are only 60 percent right. Just make the winners big ones.

7. **Sometimes you find yourself in the middle of a school of feeding fish. Keep your hook baited and in the water. Correct equipment problems quickly, and get the bait back in the water.** When your stocks are running up, stay with the trend.

8. **When a big one takes your bait or hits the lure, set the hook firmly, keep tension on the line at all times and play the fish until it tires.** Keep the landing net out of sight. Don't sell winners too soon.

9. **When a really big one breaks your line, take it in stride. He may still be in the area, so always have a backup fishing outfit aboard.** If a market decline washes out a group, get ready when the group takes off again.

10. **Know when to come back to shore, particularly when whitecaps start to appear or there are storm clouds in the distance.** If the market gets crazy, go to cash while you figure things out.

Market Lessons I Have Learned while on a River with a Rod in Hand

—Duncan Coker, investor

Casting upstream into a fast current, mending the line, taking in slack and waiting for that dramatic strike of the trout **(preparation and expectations)**.

Finding the right fly, knowing the knots, leaders, when and how to cast and the all-important presentation. **(It is not easy to fool a fish or the markets.)**

Peaceful serenity of bringing in a fish to the bank in the red dim of sunset, only to let him go to fight another day **(the reward for a long-term perspective)**.

Saltwater Flyfishing for Bonefish

—Duncan Coker, investor

Bonefish are incredibly "spooky." When spooked they move at speeds up to 30mph in a highly volatile way, making sharp turns to avoid prey or anglers **(panics)**. The trigger can be internal, aquatic predators or external, anglers **(market shocks)**.

But invariably they return to the same cycle of following the tides and can thus be caught every now and again **(market cycle)**.

The catching part takes practice, research and a methodical and disciplined execution. Of course it is a lot of fun and challenging **(performance)**.

The Message Found in a Bottle

—Devon Malori, 10 years old (Dr. Brett's daughter)

Last night I heard my grandpa and my dad talking about the stock market. They said something about reading about a bottle that had messages about the market. So I went down to the beach and looked for bottles.

I didn't find very much. But there was one interesting one. It had a piece of paper in it. I copied the message down. It said:

> "We fishermen follow the schools of fish, to maximize our catch. A few fish (usually the weak and dying) always swim away from the school. But every so often, the strongest leader fish break away from the school. Wise fishermen follow the strongest lead fish because they know that the school will soon follow."

I don't know what that means, but I thought I should tell you. There are letters at the bottom of the page underneath the words "5-day break away from the school." The letters read CSCO, QCOM, LU, ORCL, T.

I hope that helps you. I'll tell my dad about it too. Bye, bye.

(May 9, 2000)

The Hoodoo Man

—Peter Daniels, retired aerospace engineer

I've just finished Victor's book, *The Education of a Speculator*, which I enjoyed very much and particularly the part about the "hoodoo man." Here is the story about the greatest hoodoo man I ever met.

Between the ages of 8 and 10 (circa '42 to '44), I spent almost every sunny day with one of the greatest men that I ever met. He was over 6 feet tall, straight as a stick and by all accounts was over 100 years old. His name was Uncle Stone and every sunny day during the summer he walked from somewhere in Pittsylvania County, Virginia, across the Staunton River bridge to Campbell County in order to fish. He dressed the same way every day in a black suit, frock-tailed coat and fedora hat. He carried a cane and two bamboo fishing poles.

When I first met him, I was completely mesmerized because he could catch more catfish than one would think was humanly possible. Some days these strings of fish were only 3 feet long but on other days he could catch a string of fish at least 14 feet long. I saw him hold a string of fish (in the middle of the string) with arms extended over his head and both ends of the string touched the ground. He used the same equipment that everyone else used but his results were phenomenal.

When I asked him how he was able to catch so many fish he replied that he had "hoodooed" the fish.

After that I became obsessed with fishing because I wanted to catch a string of catfish that would reach from my arm, extended over my head to the ground and I wanted to learn the "secret of the hoodoo." I started going fishing every sunny day with Uncle Stone and it took me three summers to catch that long string of fish.

In the meantime, I listened as Uncle Stone told me many stories about his long, wonderful life, including the time when he had been a slave (I know this part is hard to believe, but it's true). But he would never tell me the secret of the hoodoo, no matter how hard I tried to get the answer out of him.

After I caught my long string of fish, I became uninterested in fishing and on our last day on the river bank Uncle Stone told me that he had just turned 105 years old and that he was thinking about getting married again, to a "yella gal this time" (and he did!). He also showed me a large tumor on his right side that he kept covered with his frocktailed coat, and he told me that it would never hurt him because he had "hoodooed" it.

A few years later, the most interesting and upbeat person that I have ever met died. But I know that Uncle Stone died happy because he had beaten the stock market of life, and even George Soros hasn't done that! A few years later, I was walking past a black cabaret one night and stopped to listen, because I loved their music. I'll never forget the song that was playing that night. As I listened I heard the refrain over and over again. It was "Somebody Done Hoodooed the Hoodoo Man," and I said to myself, "Nobody can hoodoo a real hoodoo man!"

Bluefish

—Peter Daniels

There is a strong similarity between the mind-set of surf fisherman and stock traders. Here is a story about surf fishermen. The stock trader analogies are in parenthesis.

Before Jimmy Carter was president, big schools of bluefish roamed the Outer Banks.

These schools could be immense. Miles long and God knows how wide they were.

I once saw a single school that stretched from Rodanthe to Nags Head, which is roughly 20 miles.

I hated them because I just couldn't get away from them, to catch anything else, when I was fishing. A three- to five-pound fish almost every cast! No one couldn't catch them! You didn't dare use bait because then you'd catch two at a time as fast as you could reel them in.

When they started to run, the word got out and surf fisherman from everywhere came here to participate in their feeding frenzy (*investors moving into the bull market*). Two "Island Boys" could make thousands of dollars with a gill net and a rowing dory just fishing from shore (*old-time traders reading the tape and scoring big*). You didn't even need a pole when the blues were "blitzing." Tourists would just ride down the beach and pick up beautiful gray trout, still alive and flapping, that had beached themselves in their frenzy to escape being eaten (*stock tips making money*). One day I caught a blue that was so large that for a long time, I actually thought that I had caught a large shark which were also common near the shore at that time (*gap up big-time on good news when you are long*). God how I hated those bluefish!

Well one night, I looked out of my door and thought that someone had built a city behind my house. It was the lights of large trawl boats, fishing right in my back yard as far as I could see in both directions. The next morning, when I got up, I heard on the radio that Jimmy Carter (*Greenspan solving the irrational exuberance problem*) had invited foreign commercial fisherman to fish, not within the 10-mile limit or the 3-mile limit, but almost in the surf in my back yard. They were so close that I could have recognized individuals for a police lineup. For days the small boats would come out and encircle the fish with purse nets and haul them on board. Day after day, this occurred. Jimmy Carter just gave the place away (*Greenspan raising rates*).

Well, the word was out to the commercial interests both foreign and domestic. The foreigners came and commercial fisherman came from other states and they cleaned up the place, except for the minnows. They took the blues and the gray and speckled trout. They decimated the red drum (it became commercially endangered) and the flounder (*tech, communication and Internet stocks all decimated*).

They left the whiting and the croakers (Dow 30). When it was all over and the trawlers left, the people complained to the U.S. Fish and Wildlife Service. But these sweethearts said, "That 's because of normal ecological conditions, fish were just in a down cycle right now. . . . We are working on it and the solution is conservation by limiting the catch and raising the legal size limits until the fish return (*Fed lowering the funds rate*)."

For a few years, fishing on the Banks was like fishing in the Sahara desert (*stock pickers bottom fishing*). Eventually, fishing improved a little but if you wanted a fish to eat, you had to break the law because the size limits were at the extremities of the bell curve (*insider trading increasing*). Well, I don't fish anymore because I don't want to harass fish that are mostly under the legal limit. I'm just hanging back waiting for the big fish to return (*trader waiting for a higher low and a higher high*). And I've been waiting for over 20 years (*traders after the crash of '29*).

But what does the average surf fisherman do: Buy a bigger surf vehicle (one or more faster computers). Install a CB radio (*subscribe to a live data and news wire sources, buy books on fundamental and technical analysis*). Put a rod rack on the top and sides of his truck so he can carry and fish with 15 different rods at the same time (*swing and day trading with multiple entries*) and all paid for with plastic (*margin account*).

I passed on buying the latest fishing paraphernalia, but boy did I bite on the trading trash. I haven't made any money to speak of since I bought it all. In the old days I could make 15 percent to 20 percent just watching CNBC. Now I have so much data to digest that it takes me all day and night. I've been waiting over 20 years for that chop on the water and great flocks of gulls, circling and diving and picking up tidbits, to tell me that the blues have returned. When that happens, I will know that the other big, delicious fish are back and the blues are moving in for their part of the feast.

Frankly, I'm not sure what I'm waiting for as far as this market is concerned but one thing is certain. Surf fisherman and traders are so much alike primarily because of their positive expectations.

Fishing and Risk

—Patrick Boyle, trader

I don't claim to be much of a fisherman, but most weekends in the summer I go in hunt of stripers, bluefish, or anything stupid enough to bite my bait off the shore of Cape Cod. The one thing I learned quickly as a novice fisherman was how important it is to set the drag on your reel right. It is probably more important than choosing the right bait, or spot to fish, as the location of fish, or what they wish to eat on a particular day can be pointless to forecast.

The drag on a reel is what sets the strength with which the fishing line is held. If set too tight, the line will snap when a fish pulls hard; if too loose, you will not pull anything in.

There are many parallels between this and life. Like a speculator deciding on the level of risk he should take on a trade. It's important to strike a balance, and not hold too tightly to things, be they our beliefs and ideas or our wealth. It is also important not to leave things too free so that you find yourself with no control. It is important to use experience and science in order to set this balance, to give the fishing line a jerk to see if it feels right.

How Can You Say Such Awful Things about Alan Greenspan?

Most people we talk to disagree with us strongly about our characterization of Fed Chairman Alan Greenspan as an old-hearted, destructive villain who caused the 2000–2001 market crash. But that is only half of the story. We also think he was, albeit unintentionally, a part of the meme that led to the World Trade Center attack.

We are well aware that the "doctor" is regarded in most circles as a hero for popping the Nasdaq bubble. Few sympathize with our complaint that his actions amounted to an outrageously hubristic attempt to surreptitiously influence the stock market. To us, his actions were the more objectionable in that they were made with full knowledge that the public would erupt in protest if the intent were spelled out.

Was there excess and fraud in the Nasdaq's rise? To be sure. Yet left to its own devices, the market has a remarkable ability to take care of its own bubbles without help from central planning authorities. Many of the more outlandish Internet shooting stars already had crashed to earth on their own. Investors would undoubtedly have adjusted their expectations for telecommunications and computer shares as the capital-spending boom that propelled them to the heights in 1999 had its inevitable denouement.

The Fed's intervention allowed an antimarket, antitechnology meme to flourish. Naysayers who had been bearish throughout the 1990s suddenly had their day. As the Internet journalist Andrew Orlowski wrote in another context:

> Look into the pubs of England—for every Mark E. Smith, who channeled his hate into creating fabulous new vistas of satire, there are ten thousand bitter men who hate anything young or beautiful or talented, because it reminds them of their own failure of courage.[6]

The result was the first recession in a decade and the worst sustained market decline in a generation. The telecommunications equipment companies that had lent money to Internet firms for purchasing their products collapsed, creating a positive feedback loop that contributed to the poisoned atmosphere.

And the United States suddenly found itself at war with a group of Islamic fanatics seeking to abolish religious and economic freedom. This, we suggest, was not entirely a coincidence. The link may seem outrageous. But consider what the Mideast primitives represent themselves to be. They use rhetoric from the Crusades of 1,000 years ago. They wish to destroy American capitalism. They inculcate their children with an intolerant, backward creed and a suicidal mission to destroy all Americans, civilian or military, wherever they are found.

From the primitive perspective, it is sensible to make war on capitalist society. People free to act in their own economic interest dare to prize liberty above obedience to dictators. They take the indeterminate future and the open skies over the totalitarian's promises of economic certainty or a certain eternity. The very values that primitives worry will destabilize their controlled social hierarchies are fundamental to our system.

Today's primitives have a long pedigree. They are part of a history that includes the Catholic Church's resistance to the 1543 discovery by Copernicus that the earth is not the center of the universe. The common thread is an aversion to change and examination of the premises of the ruling elite. Invoking theology and nostalgia, the primitive seeks control through regulation and theocratic authority. Primitives are, inevitably, anticapitalist, because they seek to maintain power and stasis. In a market society, few trends survive; only free thinking and risk taking are rewarded. The market allocates capital through the decisions of millions of people acting independently in their own interest. Repressive societies, with their nationalism, tribal wars, official religion, and lumbering political ideologies, have no marketplace. Instead, such states attempt to control the distribution of resources, manpower, ideas, and goods. The result is a static, illiquid market; goods are allocated not by supply, demand, and the mediating mechanism of flexible prices, but through corruption and the black market.

Primitive thinking characterizes all reactionary response to the development of technology. As Jacques Barzun remarks in *From Dawn to Decadence*, primitivism is a "disaffection from science and technology" running parallel to the development of Western culture throughout the centuries.[7] In the 1990s, the performance of the fast-moving technology companies of the Nasdaq defined our understanding of risk. Tech companies typically pay no dividend and offer little certainty, but their pursuit of new technologies made them magnets for risk capital. Low-risk, low-return "old technology," "defensive," "brick-and-mortar" companies—makers of carpets, ketchup bottles, and soda pop—suffered in this young-hearted period of technological expansion. After the Nasdaq sank, old-economy, low-return investment strategies were dusted off and once again seized the imagination of Wall Street.

Some of today's primitivist manifestations promise to restore a bond between humans and nature by abolishing Western technology and markets. Islamic terrorism represents a new twist—a medieval mentality that parasitically adopts Western technology, markets, and openness in order to destroy them. The World Trade Center terrorists had e-mail, flew planes, lived in middle-class Florida suburbs, ate pizza, frequented strip bars, and shopped at Wal-Mart. These terrorists seemed disturbingly American, and yet despite the pattern of middle-class consumption, they saw themselves as martyrs in a holy war against the United States.

The premise of U.S. immigration policy has long been that the poor, tired, and suffering, presented with the opportunity for material gain and a decent life, will shed Old World prejudices and embrace American democratic culture. This is the idea behind the Latin phrase written on every coin and every dollar bill produced by the U.S. mint: *e pluribus unum,* the idea of the melting pot: out of many, one. America is founded not on sacrifice, but on creation.

The terrorist attack on the World Trade Center was in essence an assault on the mechanisms that let people transcend merely local values and the social desire for certainty. It struck democracy's central mechanism for mediating uncertainty: the market. The three words of the name were well chosen. The *world* came to *trade* there, in the *center* of economic freedom. No matter what your culture, religion, or viewpoint, you were welcome to exchange the best products of your efforts freely with others.

Primitivists, be they suicide terrorists, enemies of scientific truth, or the self-chosen vanguard of "the people," always have answers for anyone willing to listen, and weapons to point at those unwilling to listen. Yet their arguments are drawn from yesterday's carcass, not the emboldened dreams of tomorrow. Their plans offer the certainty of blood and soil, birth and death, but in doing so omit that which makes us truly human: risk, uncertainty, freedom.

And yet that is why attacks on innovation, science, and liberty are bound to fail. You cannot kill the spirit that makes people want to better their lives and draws millions to the United States from around the world. People realize that trade, business, and freedom are better than a life spent under rigid control exercised by the few, be they bureaucrats, mullahs, or royalty. Creativity will always trump old-hearted men who seek to keep everything as it was in bygone days.

What Book Do You Recommend?

When asked a question like "What's the best book?" it is customary for experts to answer flippantly. Rudolf Nureyev, asked whom he considered the best dancer, always answered Fred Astaire. Paul Morphy was the same way in chess; he would never play anyone an even game because that would legitimize the possibility that someone else could be half as great as he was. When Vic ruled the squash courts, he always said the greatest player was Jack Barnaby, his coach at Harvard, who stopped playing in 1950 and couldn't detract from evaluation of his own play.

Previously, when asked to recommend a good investment book, Vic usually responded that Richard Wyckoff's *Magazine of Wall Street,* in the early 1900s, and, before that, *Hunt's Merchant's Magazine* published in the 1870s, were veritable treasure troves, and that since nothing subsequent to those monumental contributions had been at all noteworthy, it would be profitable to go back to those sources to at least get in touch with the roots of the field.

But all that has changed. We can now recommend without reservation *Triumph of the Optimists: 101 Years of Global Investment Returns,* which we wrote about in detail in Chapter 9. This great book tabulates 101 years of yearly returns for markets in 16 countries, with stock-by-stock returns in England and the United States. It compares these returns to Treasury bill rates, Treasury bond rates, inflation, and currency exchange rates. Returns are broken down into dividends, equity risk premiums, and size effects.

With this as a base, the authors touch on every investment topic imaginable, including value versus growth, small versus big, seasonality, cost of capital, correlations between countries, earnings and dividend growth, benefits from diversification, the relevance of valuation models, and likely returns for the future.

Beating Pods and Pessimism

Invasion of the Body Snatchers, based on a novel by Jack Finney, has long been one of our favorite horror films. Vic saw the original 1954 production and one of the two remakes that seemed to hit just in time for each of the next two generations. But the 2002 market crash led us to reread the book. It is great, and aside from *Triumph of the Optimists,* this is the book we would recommend most to those who wish to prosper in the current market environment. The story is about the danger of losing hope and passively accepting the status quo. If you succumb to conformity and stop thinking for yourself, the pod people will get you.

The hero of the story, Miles Bennell, is a doctor in a typical small town. He is confronted by an epidemic of apparent mass hysteria among his friends and patients. One after the other tells him that their relatives, teachers, and friends are not the people they seem to be. Then, strangely, they return to his office to recant. Now they are feeling fine.

The only problem is that Miles' intellectual friend Jack Belicec doesn't believe it. He finds a mannequin-like body in his cellar. He lays it out on a billiard table to inspect it, and invites Miles over for a look. Jack and Miles find that the body is a blank, like an undeveloped photo, with no fingerprints. "It's all there," says Jack. "It has lips: a nose, eyes, skin, and bone structure underneath. But there are no lines, no details, and no character. . . . It's like a blank face, waiting for the final finished face to be stamped upon it."

The one person Miles relies on, his one beacon of light on a foggy day, is Dr. Mannie Kaufman, a respected psychiatrist in a neighboring community. When Dr. Kaufman tells Miles that "the human mind is a strange and wonderful thing" and that what he and Jack saw was a simple delusion, Miles is somewhat persuaded. What gnaws at him is that Mannie is usually a bit more cautious in giving out his opinion. The thought then occurs to Miles that perhaps the person giving him the opinion isn't Mannie at all, but a pod.

It turns out that Miles is right. Mannie is one of "them."

In the new century, we wondered if a similar invasion had taken over the markets. Only a few years ago, we were surrounded by investors full of emotion, eager to drink deeply of the economic miracle that is the United States. Now those same investors seemed drained of feeling, convinced that the miracle was a hoax. They looked the same, they responded to the same names. But they were not the same. Inspired by Miles' example, I sought out a market psychologist, Brett Steenbarger. With relief, I heard excitement in his voice as he talked of crisis and opportunity. I realized that he, unlike Mannie, had not fallen prey to the pods.

"We're dealing with more than body snatchers," he said. "These are mind snatchers as well. Behind all speculative success is a positive triad of extraversion, energized mood, and risk-taking. We know from research that people who take an active interest in the world around them are more likely to experience life with vigor. They are also more likely to assume prudent risks."

"That's not what we're seeing now," he continued. "Investors are responding with the negative triad that psychiatrist Aaron Beck found among depressed people: dampened optimism about themselves, others, and the future."

"What could have snatched people's minds this way?" I asked.

"It's the hubris meme," Dr. Steenbarger offered. "It's the same meme that told the Greeks that they could not fly too close to the sun, lest they meet the fate of Icarus. What is taking investors over is not the idea of a bear market. Those come and go. It's the idea that they *deserve* a bear market."

With that, the doctor pulled out a copy of *BusinessWeek* and turned to an article titled "The Betrayed Investor." It chronicled the dashed hopes of investors whose trust has been broken by the failures of corporate boards, brokerages, and accounting firms to protect their constituencies. He pointed to the headline beneath the article's title: "Americans bought into the idea that stocks could only make them richer. Then the market bubble burst—and then came Enron."[8]

"You see," he said, "investors no longer feel deserving of rich rewards. They feel like arrogant dupes, and they must pay the price of Icarus for their hubris. This is what has taken over the world. Investors dare not hope. They are afraid they will bring an even greater calamity upon their heads."

It was then that we realized that Finney's book held the answer for today's investors. They may feel like the betrayed Miles, or like the betrayed lover. But there is an important difference. Although dashed expectations may portend a poor relationship, they are a favorable indication for markets. Hitting a 40-day low point in the markets has led to an average rise of 1.5 percent the next day, over the past six years. Market pessimism provides the very basis for market optimism.

In Finney's book, the situation looks desperate for Miles and his girlfriend Becky. But they refuse to give up. "Even prisoners in maximum-security prisons have escaped. We had no right to waste ourselves. We were here—with the pods—and we had no right to waste ourselves. Even though it was hopeless. Even though it made capture an absolute certainty, we had to use ourselves against the pods."

Hope—And Some Time-Tested Principles

Invasion of the Body Snatchers ends on a heroic note. Miles and Becky refused to give up. They put up so much resistance that the pods moved to a more hospitable planet. "Many had lost," the book concludes, "but some of us who had not been caught, trapped without a chance, had fought implacably, and a fragment of a wartime speech moved through my mind: *We shall fight them in the fields, and in the streets, we shall fight in the hills; we shall never surrender.*"

When the bearish meme goes the way of the pod people, the world will start looking normal again, just as it did at the end of the *Body Snatchers*. The people who put all their wealth in money-market accounts paying 1 percent expecting that stocks would go to zero will be hanging around the town plaza, strangely listless and uncommunicative. The death rate will be higher than average for a while, and you'll see empty storefronts where the executives were hauled off in handcuffs and the companies went bankrupt. But all in all, as Jack Finney summed up:

> The empty houses are filling quickly—it's a crowded county and state—and there are new people, most of them young and with children, in town. In five years, maybe two or three, Mill Valley will seem no different to the eye from any other small town. And what once happened here will have faded into final unbelievability.

The empty wallets of those who recently bought stocks for the long term will be filling steadily. The American economy is vigorous and resilient. After periods of disaster, the surviving companies are stronger and healthier, and the returns from buying them are greater. New companies and divisions will be formed that profit from great scientific discoveries. Those who invest prudently can expect to pay for their education, homes, and retirement just the way their parents did in almost all periods in the previous century.

In five years, maybe two or three, the Nasdaq below 1000 and the Dow below 7500 will be bad memories. Those who doubted the fruits of investing and enterprise will have faded into well-deserved obscurity.

Manhattan, NY (Artist: Michael Leu, 1990).

AFTERWORD

Some traders don't take losses personally. For most, however, self-confidence varies with the success of the last trade, as my wife Susan once observed after years of watching traders work for me. I am not immune to this. Since 1997, I have been trying to crawl back up the stairs, not entirely without success. Occasionally, however, I stumble. Then, I think that I'm the world's worst. In this I follow my father, Arthur Niederhoffer. Artie had a beautiful handball and tennis game, but whenever I would ask him to play a money or tournament match, he'd say, "For crying out loud, no. I'm the world's worst. Besides, I can't afford the loss of the quarter."

Artie played football on the Brooklyn College team at the age of 16. The team was paid heavily to play against the best teams in the nation, as they loved to kill the Brooklyn boys. As far as I know, Brooklyn never won a game that Artie played in. What he did get was a broken nose—12 times—and a dislocated shoulder or two. As a result, he could never play any other game, such as tennis or handball, that required a free-flowing swing. So there was some truth to his talk about being the world's worst, even though before he played college football he was a champ at all these.

I often feel the same way. Despite the lessons I learned in 1997, I am invariably too early and too contratrend in my trades. Whatever the big move, it's still likely to get me. I am trying to improve, however, and often when I take a drubbing, like I did in summer 1998 or summer 2002, I step back, kick myself around, and say, like Artie: "I'm the world's worst."

My Uncle Howie is always vigilant not to let me succumb to defeatism, since he always thinks of his little nephew as a winner. After reading a message from me about my latest drubbing in the first weeks of 2003, this is what he had to say:

Your message intimating self-doubt is very upsetting. You have always been supremely confident in your abilities and convictions, and with great justification. As much as we loved your dad, we are not him. His self-deprecation was an expression of modesty, not a true belief in his inferiority. Artie knew what his abilities were, and they were formidable. I know what mine are, and you know what yours are. And, while in many ways we are not the man that Artie was, in others we surpass him. Self-deprecation is not fitting for you or me. Realistic self-assessment is more our style.

Artie, although growing up amid the Depression and never having any excess money, was always very free with a buck. It was never a matter of what he could afford. Unlike most people, he would tip gas station attendants with those quarters that he "couldn't afford to lose." I believe his aversion to gambling (speculation for you—calculated risking for me) had to do with the scarcity of money as well as his not wanting to take advantage of someone else. We regard it differently.

I have no doubt of your ability to overcome any temporary setback you may experience in life. It won't be by chance. It will be by dint of your analysis of all available data and knowledgeable counsel. If, like Ali in "Rumble in the Jungle," you have decided that it is wise to retreat for now and let the enemy punch himself out, like MacArthur you shall return and emerge victorious as you always do. Your positive self-confidence will ensure that result.

I love you,

Howie

NOTES

Introduction

1. Jack Finney, *Invasion of the Body Snatchers* (New York: Simon & Schuster, 1954).
2. Victor Niederhoffer, *The Education of a Speculator* (New York: Wiley, 1997).
3. Geraldine Fabrikant, "Trappings of Faded Richness: Sold!" *New York Times* (December 13, 1998).
4. Mitch Albom, *Tuesdays with Morrie* (New York: Doubleday, 1997).
5. Paul Heyne, *The Economic Way of Thinking* (Upper Saddle River, NJ: Prentice-Hall, 1997).
6. Arthur Niederhoffer, *Behind the Shield: The Police in Urban Society* (Garden City, NY: Doubleday, 1967).
7. Thomas S. Kuhn, *The Structure of Scientific Revolution* (Chicago: University of Chicago Press, 1962).
8. Elroy Dimson, Paul Marsh, and Mike Staunton, *Triumph of the Optimists: 101 Years of Global Investment Returns* (Princeton, NJ: Princeton University Press, 2002).
9. Steve Stigler, *Statistics on the Table* (Cambridge, MA: Harvard University Press, 1999).
10. Robert L. Bacon, *Secrets of Professional Turf Betting* (New York: Amerpub, 1956).

Chapter 1

1. Guy De Maupassant, "The Horla," *Short Stories of the Tragedy and Comedy of Life, Vol. II* (New York: M. Walter Dunne, 1903).
2. Speech by U.S. Federal Reserve Chairman Alan Greenspan, "The Challenge of Central Banking in a Democratic Society," presented December 5, 1996, at an

awards dinner sponsored by the American Enterprise Institute for Public Policy Research, *Bloomberg News* (December 6, 1996).

3. Hal Paul, "U.S. Stock Plunge: Dow's 554-Point Drop Halts Trading," *Bloomberg News* (October 27, 1997).

4. Jeremy J. Siegel, *Stocks for the Long Run: The Definitive Guide to Financial Market Returns and Long-Term Investment Strategies* (New York: McGraw-Hill, 1998).

5. Arthur Levitt, "The Numbers Game," delivered at the New York University Center for Law and Business, New York (September 28, 1998).

6. Carole Loomis, "Lies, Damned Lies, and Managed Earnings," *Fortune* (August 2, 1999).

7. Carole Loomis, "Mr. Buffett on the Stock Market," *Fortune* (November 22, 1999).

8. Mary Buffett and David Clark, *Buffettology* (New York: Fireside, 2001).

9. Monique Wise, "Wall Street Bonuses Could Rise 30 percent to Record as Profits Soar," *Bloomberg News* (December 9, 1999).

10. Brian Rooney, Amy Taxin, and Sara Pepitone, "How Rich Is Bill Gates? The Absurdity of Big Numbers," *Bloomberg News* (December 16, 1999).

11. Albert Jay Nock, *Memoirs of a Superfluous Man* (Delavan, WI: Hallberg Publishing, 1994).

12. Richard Dawkins, *The Selfish Gene* (New York: Oxford University Press, 1989).

13. Robert Shiller, *Irrational Exuberance* (Princeton, NJ: Princeton University Press, 2000).

14. Dan Lonkevich, "Buffett Lukewarm on Stocks, Seeks Acquisitions," *Bloomberg News* (March 9, 2002). Warren Buffett's letter to shareholders, Berkshire Hathaway 2001 annual report.

Chapter 2

1. Mario Puzo, *The Last Don* (New York: Random House, 1996).

2. Steven Sills and Ivan Alexrod, "Profit Participation in the Motion Picture Industry," *Los Angeles Lawyer* (April 1989).

3. *Standard & Poor's Security Price Index Record* (New York: McGraw-Hill, 2001).

4. Kenneth L. Fisher and Meir Statman, "Cognitive Biases in Market Forecasts: The Frailty of Forecasting," *Journal of Portfolio Management* (Fall 2000).

5. Thornton L. O'glove, *Quality of Earnings* (New York: Free Press, 1987).

6. Howard Schilit, *Financial Shenanigans* (New York: McGraw-Hill, 2002).

7. Aswath Damodaran, *The Dark Side of Valuation* (Upper Saddle River, NJ: Prentice Hall, 2001).

8. Bjorn Tuypens, "Stock Market Predictability: A Myth Unveiled," (Unpublished, 2002).

9. Alfred McClung Lee and Elizabeth Briant, *The Fine Art of Propaganda: A Study of Father Coughlin's Speech* (New York: Harcourt, Brace and Company, 1939). Expanded edition published 1971 by Octagon Books. Excerpts available at: http://www.mapinc.org/propaganda/propaganda/fineart.html.

10. Gretchen Morgenson, "As It Beat Profit Forecast, IBM Said Little about Sale of a Unit," *New York Times* (February 15, 2002).

Chapter 3

1. Robert Graves, *Greek Myths* (London: Penguin Books, 1981).
2. Martin S. Schwartz, *Pit Bull: Lessons from Wall Street's Champion Trader* (New York: HarperBusiness, 1999).
3. Joseph Granville, *Granville's Last Stand: Secrets of the Stock Market Revealed* (New York: Hanover House, 1994).
4. Jack Schwager, *Market Wizards: Interviews with Top Traders* (New York: HarperBusiness, 1993); and Jack Schwager, *The New Market Wizards: Interviews with Top Traders* (New York: HarperBusiness, 1994).
5. Philip Jenks and Stephen Eckett, eds., *The Global-Investor Book of Investing Rules: Invaluable Advice from 150 Master Investors* (Hampshire, England: Harriman House, 2001).
6. Thomas Bulkowski, *Trading Classic Chart Patterns* (New York: Wiley, 2002).
7. Venkat R. Eleswarapu and Marc R. Reinganum, "The Predictability of Aggregate Stock Market Returns: Evidence Based on Glamour Stocks" (Dallas, TX: Southern Methodist University, Unpublished paper).
8. Mario Puzo, *Fools Die* (New York: Penguin Books, 1978).
9. Jim Albert and Jay Bennett, *Curve Ball: Baseball, Statistics, and the Role of Chance in the Game* (New York: Copernicus Books, 2001).
10. Barry Nalebuff and Avinash Dixit, *Thinking Strategically: The Competitive Edge in Business, Politics, and Everyday Life* (New York: Norton, 1993).
11. Elroy Dimson, Paul Marsh, and Mike Staunton, "Murphy's Law and Market Anomalies," *Journal of Portfolio Management*, vol. 25–2 (Winter 1999).
12. Daniel Kahneman, Paul Slovic, and Amos Tversky, *Judgment under Uncertainty: Heuristics and Biases* (Cambridge, England: Cambridge University Press, 1982).
13. Steven Nison, *Japanese Candlestick Charting Techniques: A Contemporary Guide to the Ancient Investment Techniques of the Far East* (New York: New York Institute of Finance, 2001).
14. Harro Von Senger, *The Book of Stratagems* (New York: Viking/Penguin, 1991).
15. Sandra Ward, "Barometer Readings: An Interview with Don Hays," *Barron's* (April 2, 2001).
16. Robert Colby and Thomas Meyers, *The Encyclopedia of Technical Market Indicators* (New York: Irwin, 1988).
17. Tushar Chande and Stanley Kroll, *The New Technical Trader* (New York: Wiley, 1994).
18. Daniel Defoe, *A Journal of the Plague Year* (London: Penguin Books, 1986).
19. Carol Osler, "Identifying Noise Traders: The Head-and-Shoulders Pattern in U.S. Equities" (1998). Available from http://www.ny.frb.org/rmaghome/staff_rp/sr42.pdf.
20. Paul Dickson, *Baseball's Greatest Quotations* (New York: Harper, 1991).
21. John E. Cooke, *Life of Stonewall Jackson* (Richmond, VA: Ayres & Wade, 1863).
22. John Sweeney, "Music of the Markets: Victor J. Niederhoffer," *Technical Analysis of Stocks and Commodities* (April, 2000).

23. Bill Williams, *Trading Chaos: Applying Expert Techniques to Maximize Your Profits* (New York: Wiley, 1995).

24. Robert L. Park, *Voodoo Science: From Foolishness to Fraud* (London: Oxford University Press, 2000).

25. Zvi Bodie, *Essentials of Investments* (New York: McGraw-Hill College Division, 2001).

26. David Simon and Roy A. Wiggins, "S&P Futures Returns and Contrary Sentiment Indicators," *Journal of Futures Markets* (May, 2001).

Chapter 4

1. Leon Festinger, H. W. Riecken, and S. Schachter, *When Prophecy Fails* (Minneapolis: University of Minnesota Press, 1956).

2. Peter Bernstein, *Against the Gods: The Remarkable Story of Risk* (New York: Wiley, 1998).

3. Carl I. Hovland and H. C. Kelman, "Reinstatement of the Communicator in Delayed Measurement of Opinion Changes," *Journal of Abnormal Social Psychology*, vol. 48 (1954): 327–335.

4. Flo Conway and Jim Siegelman, *Snapping* (New York: Stillpoint Press, 1995).

5. Ronald W. Rogers and C. Ronald Mewborn, "Fear Appeals and Attitude Change: Effects of a Threat's Noxiousness, Probability of Occurrence, and the Efficacy of the Coping Responses," *Journal of Personality and Social Psychology*, vol. 34 (1976): 56–61.

6. Michael Shermer, *Why People Believe Weird Things: Pseudoscience, Superstition and Other Confusions of Our Time* (New York: Freeman, 1997).

7. William Worthington Fowler, *Ten Years in Wall Street* (Hartford, CT: Worthington, Dustin, 1870).

Chapter 5

1. Mark Leibovich, "A Rain God Confronts a Harsh Climate: CEO's Optimism Tested by Downturn," *Washington Post* (April 6, 2001).

2. John F. Wasik, "Nestegg," *Modern Maturity* (January/February 2002).

3. "Jennifer Lopez Is a Pain in the Butt," *National Enquirer* (April 25, 2001).

4. Robert Sobel, *When Giants Stumble: Classic Business Blunders and How to Avoid Them* (Upper Saddle River, NJ: Prentice Hall Press, 1985).

5. Sir Harold Nicolson, *Diplomacy* (Washington, DC: Georgetown University, School of Foreign Service, Institute for the Study of Diplomacy, 1939 and 1988).

6. "Cisco Head Cautions against Silicon Valley Hubris," *InfoWorld* (February 29, 2000).

7. Kathryn Kranhold, Bryan Lee, and Mitchel Benson, "Enron Rigged Power Market in California, Documents Say," *Wall Street Journal* (May 7, 2002).

8. Peter Burrows, "HP's Carly Fiorina: The Boss," *BusinessWeek* (August 2, 1999).

9. Julie Schmit, "Aggressive Chambers Powers Cisco," *USA Today* (August 13, 1996).

10. Andy Reinhardt, "Meet Cisco's Mr. Internet," *BusinessWeek* (September 13, 1999).

11. Joseph Menn, "Cisco Posts 49% Jump in Profit," *Los Angeles Times* (February 9, 2000).

12. Andy Reinhardt, "The E-Biz 25," *BusinessWeek* (May 2000).

13. Scott Berinato, "What Went Wrong at Cisco," *CIO Magazine* (August 1, 2000).

14. "Cisco Chief Outlines Vision of the Internet of the Future," Confederation of Indian Industry press release (January 17, 2001).

15. Nick Heil, "Eight Great Blunders," *Outside Magazine* (February 2002).

16. Alan Lightman, *Great Ideas in Physics* (New York: McGraw-Hill, 2000).

17. Michael Lewis, "Self-Conscious Emotions," *Gale Encyclopedia of Childhood and Adolescence* (January 1, 1995).

18. Arthur Niederhoffer and Alexander B. Smith, "Power and Personality in the Courtroom: The Trial of the Chicago 7," *Connecticut Law Review* (Winter 1970–1971).

19. James C. Collins, *Good to Great: Why Some Companies Make the Leap and Others Don't* (New York: HarperCollins, 2001).

20. "Web-Exclusive Interview: Good Questions, Great Answers," *Fast Company* (October 2001). Available from http://www.fastcompany.com/online/51/goodtogreat.html.

21. Jose Raul Capablanca, *My Chess Career,* rev. ed. (Mineola, NY: Dover Publications, 1966).

22. William J. Mitchell, "Do We Need Skyscrapers?" *Scientific American* (December 1997).

23. Alcoa executive's *Architectural Forum* interview, cited in Judith Dupre, *Skyscrapers: A History of the World's Most Famous and Important Skyscrapers* (New York: Black Dog & Leventhal, 2001).

24. Ayn Rand, *The Fountainhead* (New York: Penguin Books, 1971).

25. Paul Krugman, "Enron Goes Overboard," *New York Times* (August 17, 2001).

26. Jeffrey Tomich, "Enron to Sell Ballpark Naming Rights for $2.1 Million," *Bloomberg News* (February 27, 2002).

27. "Stadium Jinx: What to Call Enron Field? 'Enron Folds,' Maybe," *Wall Street Journal* (December 4, 2001).

28. James P. Cramer, ed., *Almanac of Architecture and Design* (Norcross, GA: Greenway Consulting, 2002).

29. Richard Roll, "The Hubris Hypothesis of Corporate Takeovers," *Journal of Business,* vol. 59, no. 2 (1986): 197–216.

Chapter 6

1. Sidney Cottle, Roger F. Murray, and Frank E. Block, eds., *Graham and Dodd's Security Analysis,* 5th ed. (New York: McGraw-Hill, 1988).

2. Janet Lowe, *Benjamin Graham on Value Investing: Lessons from the Dean of Wall Street* (Chicago: Dearborn, 1994).

3. Benjamin Graham, *Intelligent Investor* (New York: Harper & Row, 1973).

4. M. Diamond and H. K. Sigmundson, "Sex Reassignment at Birth: Long Term Review and Clinical Implications, *Archives of Pediatric and Adolescent Medicine,* vol. 151 (1997): 298.

Chapter 7

1. Thomas Henry Huxley, "Science and Morals," *Essays Upon Some Controverted Questions* (London: Macmillan, 1886).

Part Two

1. David Bronstein, *The Modern Chess Self-Tutor* (New York: Cadogan, 1995).

Chapter 8

1. Francis Galton, "Kinship and Correlation," *North American Review* 150. Quoted in Stephen M. Stigler, *The History of Statistics: The Measurement of Uncertainty before 1900* (Cambridge, MA: Harvard University Press, 1890).
2. Reed Hastie and Robin M. Dawes, *Rational Choice in an Uncertain World* (London: Sage, 2001).
3. "Purdue University's Spurious Correlations Contest, 2000 Winners" (2001). Available from http://www.mrs.umn.edu.
4. James O'Shaughnessy, *What Works on Wall Street* (New York: McGraw-Hill, 1998).

Chapter 9

1. F. A. Hayek, *The Fatal Conceit: The Errors of Socialism* (Chicago: University of Chicago Press, 1988).

Chapter 10

1. Gerard Piel, *The Age of Science: What Scientists Learned in the Twentieth Century* (New York: Basic Books, 2001).
2. Sanford Jacobs, ed., *The Quotable Investor* (Guilford, CT: Lyons Press, 2001).
3. Fischer Black, "Yes, Virginia There Is Hope: Test of the Value Line Ranking System," *Financial Analysts Journal* (September/October 1973): 10–14.
4. Mark Hulbert, *The Hulbert Financial Digest* (January 2001).
5. James J. Choi, "The Value Line Enigma: The Sum of Known Parts," *Journal of Finance and Quantitative Analysis,* vol. 35, no. 3 (September 2000).
6. Robert S. Kaplan and Roman L. Weil, "Risk and the Value Line Contest," *Financial Analysts Journal* (July/August 1973).
7. Gur Huberman and Shmuel Kandel, "Market Efficiency and Value Line's Record," *Journal of Business* (April 1990).
8. William A. Sherden, *The Fortune Sellers* (New York: Wiley, 1998).
9. Will Durant and Ariel Durant, *The Lessons of History* (New York: Simon & Schuster, 1968).

Chapter 11

1. Paul Dickson, *Baseball's Greatest Quotations* (New York: Harper, 1992).
2. Larry Ritter, *The Story of Baseball* (New York: Beech Tree, 1999).
3. Robert Whiting, *You Gotta Have Wa* (New York: Vintage, 1990).

Chapter 12

1. Henry George, *Progress and Poverty* (San Francisco: W. M. Hinton, 1879).
2. Yoon Dokko, "Real Estate Income and Value Cycles: A Model of Market Dynamics," *Journal of Real Estate Research*, vol. 18, no. 1 (1999): 1–27.
3. Lucy Komisar, "Joseph Stiglitz," *Progressive* (June 2000).
4. Jun Han and Youguo Liang, "The Historical Performance of Real Estate Investment Trusts," *Journal of Real Estate Research*, vol. 10, no. 3 (1995): 235–262.
5. "REITs' Low Correlation to Other Stocks and Bonds Is Key Factor for Portfolio Diversification," *NAREIT* press release (May 29, 2001).
6. Ronald W. Kaiser, "The Long Cycle of Real Estate," *Journal of Real Estate Research*, vol. 14, no. 3 (1997): 233–258.
7. William B. Brueggeman and Jeffrey D. Fisher, *Real Estate Finance & Investments* (New York: McGraw-Hill, 2001).
8. Homer Hoyt, *One Hundred Years of Land Values in Chicago: The Relationship of the Growth of Chicago to the Rise of Its Land Values, 1830–1933* (Washington: Beard Books, 2000).
9. Ray A. Smith, "New Report Questions Strength of REIT Results," *Wall Street Journal* (December 18, 2001).
10. Gary Eldred and Andrew Mclean, *Investing in Real Estate* (New York: Wiley, 2001).
11. Robert Kiyosaki and Sharon Lechter, *Rich Dad, Poor Dad* (New York: Warner Books, 2000).
12. Michael C. Thomsett, *J. K. Lasser's Real Estate Investing* (New York: Wiley, 2002).
13. Jon Markman, "Buy What the S&P Trashes and Get Rich Quick," *CNBC Money* (December 12, 2001). Available from http://www.cnbc.com.
14. Dean Starkman, "Office Buildings Had Sharpest Vacancy Rise in 2001," *Wall Street Journal* (January 31, 2002).
15. Victor Niederhoffer and Laurel Kenner, "Sinking Real Estate Means Rising Stocks" (February 14, 2002); "9 Reasons REITs Are about to Get Rocked" (February 21, 2002); "More Evidence REITs Are on the Brink" (February 28, 2002); and "Small Business or Big, the Rules Are the Same" (March 7, 2002). *CNBC Money*, Available from http://www.cnbc.com.
16. Robert Burgess, "U.S. Office Market Recovery to Be Delayed, Torto Says," *Bloomberg News* (September 19, 2002).
17. Peter Grant, "Commercial Real Estate May Damp the Economy," *Wall Street Journal* (February 25, 2002).

Chapter 13

1. Gordon Kane, *Supersymmetry: Unveiling the Ultimate Laws of Nature* (Oxford, England: Perseus Press, 2000).
2. David Batstone, "Debate: Charles Sanford," *Business 2.0* (October 1998). Available from http://www.business2.com/articles/mag/0,1640,12749%7C2,FF.html.

3. Charbel Tannous and Alain Fessant, "Combustion Models in Finance" (December 12, 2001). Available from http://arxiv.org/PS_cache/physics/pdf/0101/0101042.pdf.

Chapter 15

1. Charles MacKay and Joseph De La Vega, *Extraordinary Popular Delusions and the Madness of Crowds and Confusion de Confusiones* (New York: Wiley, 1995).
2. Theodore C. Bergstrom, "Economics in a Family Way," *Journal of Economic Literature* (forthcoming).
3. Abhinay Muthoo, *Bargaining Theory with Applications* (Cambridge, England: Cambridge University Press, 1999).
4. Thomas C. Scheling, *The Strategy of Conflict* (Cambridge, MA: Harvard University Press, 1980).
5. Norman Lebrecht, *The Book of Musical Anecdotes* (New York: Free Press, 1985).
6. N. Gregory Mankiw, *Principles of Microeconomics* (Fort Worth, TX: Dryden, 1997).
7. George J. Stigler, "The Economics of Information," *Journal of Political Economy*, vol. 69, no. 3 (1961): 213–225.

Chapter 16

1. Juan Enriques and Ray A. Goldberg, "Transforming Life, Transforming Business: the Life-Sciences Revolution." *Harvard Business Review* (March–April 2000).
2. Michael S. Malone, "The Next Bubble: Is Bioinformatics the Next Big Boom . . . and Bust?" *ABCNEWS.com* (March 13, 2001). Available from http://abcnews.go.com/sections/business/SiliconInsider/SiliconInsider_010313.html.

Chapter 17

1. Jacob K. Thomas and Huai Zhang, "Inventory Changes and Future Returns," working paper, December 2001.

Chapter 18

1. Francis Galton, *The Art of Travel* (London: John Murray, 1883).
2. Henry Clews, *Twenty-Eight Years in Wall Street* (New York: J. S. Ogilvie, 1887).
3. "Heretics' Almanac, 1986–96," *Economist* (December 20, 1986).
4. Julian Simon, *The Ultimate Resource 2* (Princeton, NJ: Princeton University Press, 1996).
5. Dean Keith Simonton, *Genius, Creativity, and Leadership: Histriometric Inquiries* (Cambridge, MA: Harvard University Press, 1984).
6. Andrew Orlowski, "Monday Night at the Single's Club? Apple's Real People. *The Register* (June 17, 2002). Available from http://www.theregister.co.uk/content/35/25750.html.
7. Jacques Barzun, *From Dawn to Decadence: 500 Years of Western Cultural Life, 1500 to the Present* (New York: HarperCollins, 2000).
8. Marcia Vickers and Mike McNamee, "The Betrayed Investor," *BusinessWeek* (February 25, 2002).

INDEX